The Scripture Testimony to the Messiah

THE

SCRIPTURE TESTIMONY

TO THE

MESSIAH:

AN

INQUIRY WITH A VIEW TO A SATISFACTORY DETERMINATION

OF THE

DOCTRINE TAUGHT IN THE HOLY SCRIPTURES

CONCERNING

THE PERSON OF CHRIST.

BY

JOHN PYE SMITH, D.D.

IN THREE VOLUMES.

VOL. II.

" A Deo discendum est quid de Deo intelligendum sit: quia nonnisi se
auctore cognoscitur." HILARIUS.

THIRD EDITION,
IMPROVED AND ENLARGED.

LONDON:

JACKSON AND WALFORD,

18, ST. PAUL'S CHURCH-YARD;

HATCHARD AND SON, PICCADILLY; J. H. PARKER, OXFORD; AND
T. STEVENSON, CAMBRIDGE.

1837.

963.

CONTENTS OF VOL. II.

BOOK III.

CONTENTS. vii

ERRATUM.
Page 394, line 4 from bottom, *for* 407 *read* 369.

SCRIPTURE TESTIMONY

TO

THE MESSIAH.

BOOK III.

ON THE INFORMATION TO BE OBTAINED CONCERNING THE PERSON
OF THE CHRIST, FROM THE NARRATIVES OF THE EVANGELICAL
HISTORY, AND FROM OUR LORD'S OWN ASSERTIONS AND INTI-
MATIONS.

Jesus the Messiah.—To him, therefore, all the attributes of the Messiah must
attach.—The testimony of the Christian Scriptures cannot but coincide with
that of the Jewish.—The real humanity of Jesus no objection to the existence
of a superior nature.—Proposed method of the Inquiry.

In the preceding part of this Inquiry we have endeavoured, with caution and scrupulosity, to collect the
characters of the Messiah from the descriptions of
ancient prophecy, and the divinely warranted expectations of those to whom the revelation was afforded.
We have carefully analysed these descriptions, through
the series of the Patriarchal and the Israelitish revelations; and the result is before the reader. *Whomsoever*
we may find to be the Messiah, to him we are assured
that all those characters must belong; and that, in
some way to us unknown and mysterious, he is at
once a man of sorrows, the descendant of Adam and
Abraham and David, and yet possessed of the high

attributes of the Lord God, the Eternal and Unchangeable Jehovah.

All Christians believe that JESUS of Nazareth is the
One and Only Messiah; and that to him, and to no
other, all the characters of the Messiah belong, in their
absolute reality and their broadest extent.   Here,
then, we might not unfairly close our case, and rise
from the search, satisfied that the Author of our Religion is the Root as well as the Offspring of David,
the Mighty God, as well as the Son given to us.

But we have Christian Scriptures, the sequel and
completion of the Jewish; the writings of the personal attendants and disciples of the Messiah, in addition to those of the Prophets, who had before testified
of his sufferings and glories.   If our conclusions are
justly drawn from the Old Testament, they will certainly be confirmed by the declarations of the New.
To the doctrine of the New Testament, therefore, we
direct our attention as a further, but not an independent, branch of evidence.

That Jesus Christ was and is really and properly a
man, is maintained by the orthodox as strenuously as
by the Unitarians.   To bring evidence in proof of
this point is, on either side, unnecessary; unless it
were conceded that proper humanity implies necessarily a mere humanity; or, in other words, that it is
impossible for the Deity to assume the human nature
into an indissoluble union with himself.   Such a
union, let it be carefully remembered, is not a transmutation of either nature into the other; nor a
destruction of the essential properties of either; nor a
confusion of the one with the other.   The question
of such a union is a question of *fact:* and its proper,

its only evidence, is Divine Revelation. Though, for the reason just intimated, it might not be strictly requisite to institute a detailed examination of any other parts of the Christian Scriptures, than those ‹ which are apprehended to contain evidence of the existence of a *superior* nature in the Person of Christ; yet it will conduce to the completeness of the argument and the increase of satisfaction, to examine, with equal care, the leading testimonies to our Lord's humanity, particularly those which are supposed by Unitarians to involve the idea of a sole and exclusive humanity.

We are now arrived at what might be called a position parallel to the commencement of Mr. Belsham's " Calm Inquiry into the Scripture Doctrine concerning the Person of Christ." It would be the easiest plan for me to follow that writer, page by page, in the arrangement of passages which he has adopted ; and, if an exposure of his criticisms and interpretations, and a refutation of his arguments, had been the principal objects of this work, such a method might have been preferred. But I presume to aim at a more independent and permanent order of usefulness, the exhibition of a complete statement of the Scripture Evidence on this great question : and for this purpose, the inductive process, which has been carried on through the former volume, is the most impartial, and appears the most likely to lead us to safe and satisfactory conclusions. We shall, therefore, pursue the lines of evidence, as they are presented to us by the opening and the gradual progress of the New Testament dispensation ; and shall consider the interpretations and reasonings of the *Calm Inquiry*, as they will severally find their places in the course of the work.

CHAP. I.

———

AT the head of his enumeration of supposed arguments in favour of the doctrines which he opposes, the author of the *Calm Inquiry* has placed the weakest that could well be conceived; that " the miraculous birth of Christ is regarded by many as a considerable presumptive evidence of his preexistence."[1]

It is quite sufficient to set aside this alleged argument, to remind those, if such there be, who are disposed to advance it, that Unitarians generally, before Dr. Priestley, accorded with the universal belief of Christians on this head. Dr. Lardner, a professed Socinian, has largely vindicated the authenticity of the disputed portions of the Gospels of Matthew and Luke, against exceptions and difficulties:[2] and, in the days of modern Unitarians, Mr. Gilbert Wakefield, emphatically and designedly, describes the Gospel of Matthew, as " delivering the history of a Covenant between God and the human race, promulgated and ratified *by a man born out of the common course of generation.*[3]

On the other hand, if a much greater force belonged to the arguments by which the Calm Inquirer

[1] Page 12.
[2] *Credibility of the Gosp. Hist.* Part I. Book II.
[3] *Wakefield's New Transl. and Notes on Matthew*, p. 416. 1782.

and others have endeavoured to establish the spuriousness of the initial portions of Matthew and Luke, and if the evidence were satisfactory to the rejection of those portions, I do not see that the doctrine of the Divine Nature in the Person of Christ would be affected by it; any farther than as a few passages, which have furnished some arguments in favour of the doctrine, would be no longer proper to be adduced. Had it pleased God so to. ordain, the sinless purity of our Lord's humanity might have been as certainly provided for *by a miraculous intervention,* on the supposition of its being produced in the ordinary way of nature, as on the generally received, and, in my opinion, true and scriptural view of this subject. But, besides the divine ordination, other reasons are not wanting to show the *superior propriety* and CONDIGNITY of this mode of miraculous formation.[4]

It cannot be denied that the portions of the two Gospels in question are pressed with seeming difficulties, more than any other part of the Evangelical history. These difficulties are alleged to lie in the citations which occur in them from the Old Testament, in the facts related, and in the want of any clear reference to those facts in the subsequent parts of the New Testament. But it is contrary to the principles of sound criticism to reject, as spurious, parts of the works attributed to ancient authors, which stand upon the same ground of external evidence that is found by rigorous examination to be sufficient for the rest;[5] unless there are discrepancies

---

[4] See Note [A], at the end of this Chapter.
[5] See Note [B], at the end of this Chapter.

and contradictions which can be removed by no *fair* methods of interpretation; "such traces and marks of ignorance in language, unskilfulness in history and antiquity, want of accuracy in reasoning, or in short, mistakes of one kind or other, as that we might safely, and without suspicion of prejudice, pronounce it impossible to be the work of"[6]—the author to whom it is attributed.

In the case before us, the internal difficulties are capable of being disposed of, to a candid and reasonable satisfaction. The citations from the Old Testament are rather of the nature of classical passages, capable of a descriptive application to the events, than direct prophecies. Such applications have been always common, not only among the Jews, but with every other nation possessing any literature. So we every day apply to observable events, striking sentences of our own poets.[7] The facts related have been solidly vindicated, and the objections to their credibility answered.[8] We shall see, also, that the chronological difficulties have been obviated; and that some solution may be given to the difficulty which arises from the want of reference to these facts in the succeeding parts of the Christian Scriptures.

The positive evidence for the authenticity of the passages is complete. All manuscript authority that exists is in their favour: and equally so is that of the ancient versions. Christian writers who lived within

[6] *Markland's Remarks on the Epistles ascribed to Cicero and Brutus, &c.* p. 4. 1745. See also *Tunstalli Epist. ad Conyers Middleton,* p. 194. 1741.

[7] See Vol. i. p. 216, and Note [C], at the end of this Chapter.

[8] See Note [D], at the end of this Chapter.

a hundred years of the events, mention the facts as of undoubted certainty, and quote the passages as parts of accredited Scripture.[9]   Celsus, the able and acute adversary of Christianity, who flourished in the second century; and Origen, in his reply to him; both consider the history of the miraculous conception as an unquestionable part of the Christian records.   So also does the Jewish slanderer who wrote the *Toldoth Jesu*.[10]   In modern times, the most distinguished Scripture-critics, who with all the aids of every kind of learning that could bear upon such inquiries, have devoted their time and talents to these researches; and who have been the most remote from any suspicion of what some would call *orthodox predilections;* have given their most decided suffrage in favour of the disputed portions of Matthew and Luke.[11]

[9] See this evidence stated at length in a valuable work, intitled, *A Vindication of the Authenticity of the Narratives contained in the First Two Chapters of the Gospel of St. Matthew and St. Luke: by a Layman.* 1822. pp. 32—60.   Now known to have been written by the late Mr. John Bevans, a justly esteemed member of the Society of Friends, who died in 1835.

[10] Edited by Wagenseil; Altdorf, 1681.

[11] Lardner, Griesbach, Eichhorn, Paulus, Ammon, Kuinœl, &c. I subjoin the concluding paragraph of Griesbach's *Epimetron*, on the authenticity of the portion in Matthew's Gospel which the Editor of the Improved Version has presumed to brand with the note of probable spuriousness, and the Calm Inquirer has, with the same presumption, pronounced to be " of very doubtful authority." Griesbach's opinion was also equally strong with respect to the portion of Luke, chap. i. 5; ii. 52.

" If now the reader will attentively review all that I have advanced, in detailed discussion, or where no more was necessary by brief mention, he will readily, I trust, give his assent to the following positions.

" 1. That it is put beyond all possibility of reasonable doubt, that

Mr. B. lays much stress on the allegation that " the Ebionite Gospel of Matthew and the Marcionite Gospel of Luke, did not contain these accounts :" and in the Notes to the Improved Version, he tells us concerning the chapters in Matthew, that " from the testimonies of Epiphanius and Jerome, we are assured that they were wanting in the copies used by the Nazarenes and Ebionites." On these assertions we offer two or three remarks.

1. All reasoning from these apocryphal gospels must be extremely uncertain. Our knowledge of them is scanty and imperfect ; but it is sufficiently plain that they had no character of authenticity or trustworthiness.

2. Epiphanius says of the Nazarenes : " They possess the Gospel of Matthew in Hebrew, in the fullest form ; for that Gospel is manifestly preserved to the present time among them, as it was at first written in the Hebrew language." He adds, that he knows not whether they retained the genealogies.[12] He, there-

the Greek text of Matthew's Gospel never existed without the two chapters in dispute.

" 2. That there are no solid arguments in support of the hypothesis that there ever existed another Gospel, from whence the present Greek copy was derived, and which was destitute of those chapters.

" 3. That it is very probable that Matthew himself was the author of those chapters, [*i. e.* in distinction from their being one of those documents of the most unquestionable authority, though insulated fragments, which we have reason to believe were often introduced by the first three Evangelists into their respective compositions :] except the genealogy, which having been communicated to him by others, he thought proper to prefix to his work."—*Griesbachii Comment. Critic. in Textum Græcum N. Test.* vol. ii. p. 64. Jena, 1811.

[12] Ἔχουσι δὲ τὸ κατὰ Ματθαῖον Εὐαγγέλιον πληρίστατον Ἑβραϊστὶ

fore, had not seen, or had not examined, the Nazarene Gospel. Bishop Marsh has satisfactorily proved from Jerome, that the Gospel of the Nazarenes contained the matter of at least the second chapter of Matthew, if not that of the first.[13]

3. Whatever information we have, concerning the Gospel of the Ebionites, shows that it was a work extremely corrupted, both by mutilations and by fabulous insertions. Epiphanius calls it "the Gospel in use among them, bearing the name of Matthew, but which is not the whole in the fullest form, but on the contrary is characterised by spurious additions and curtailments."[14] It did, indeed, want the matter of the first and second chapters of Matthew, beginning according to the quotations in Epiphanius, with these words, " It came to pass in the days of Herod the king of Judæa, [that] John came baptizing the baptism of repentance in the river Jordan; who was said to be of the race of Aarons the priest, a son of Zacharias and Elizabeth: and all went out to him."[15] Thus

παρ' αὐτοῖς γὰρ σαφῶς τοῦτο, καθὼς ἐξ ἀρχῆς ἐγράφη, Ἑβραϊκοῖς γράμμασιν, ἔτι σώζεται. Οὐκ οἶδα δὲ εἰ καὶ τὰς γενεαλογίας τὰς ἀπὸ τοῦ Ἀβραὰμ ἄχρι Χριστοῦ περιεῖλον.—Epiphan. Hær. xxix. sect. 9. Op. ed. Petav. tom. i. p. 124.

[13] On Michaelis's Introd. vol. iii. part ii. Note 10 and 11, on chap. iv. sect. 9. " It is thus indubitably clear, from the testimony of Jerome, whether it relates to the Hebrew Gospel of the Nazarenes, or to the sentiments of the Nazarenes, that the account of the Miraculous Conception and Birth of Christ must have been in their Gospel."—The Layman's Vindication, p. 103.

[14] —— Ἐν τῷ γοῦν παρ' αὐτοῖς Εὐαγγελίῳ, κατὰ Ματθαῖον ὀνομα- ζομένῳ, οὐχ ὅλῳ δὲ πληρεστάτῳ, ἀλλὰ νενοθευμένῳ καὶ ἠκρωτηριασμένῳ, Ἑβραϊκὸν δὲ τοῦτο καλοῦσιν.—Epiphan. Hær. xxx. sect. 13, p. 137.

[15] Ἐγένετο ἐν ταῖς ἡμέραις Ἡρώδου τοῦ βασιλέως τῆς Ἰουδαίας, ἦλθεν Ἰωάννης βαπτίζων βάπτισμα μετανοίας ἐν τῷ Ἰορδάνῃ ποταμῷ, ὃς ἐλέγετο εἶναι ἐκ γένους Ἀαρὼν τοῦ ἱερέως, παῖς Ζαχαρίου καὶ Ἐλισά-

clumsy is this forgery; making John's mature age to
coincide with the reign of the first Herod! Yet the
Inquirer and Annotator represents this paltry production of some grossly ignorant person, as a worthy
witness against the accredited text of the Evangelist!
Such pleadings betray either some suspension of sagacity, or a more deplorable want of candour.[16]

4. To· the hasty assertion of the Annotator, a
complete reply had been already furnished by a distinguished author in this department of criticism, and whom
one cannot but be surprised that the writer did not
consult before he committed himself. " The Nazarene
Gospel, which, according to Jerome, was St. Matthew's
original, must have been very different from the
Ebionite Gospel. For it is hardly credible, if the
Nazarene Gospel had differed from the Greek text of

βετ· καὶ ἐξήρχοντο πρὸς αὐτὸν πάντες· *Epiphan. Hær.* xxx. sect. 13,
p. 138. That the reader who may not have Epiphanius at hand, may
have a further specimen of the style and character of this spurious
Gospel, the passages preserved by him will be inserted at length in
the Supplementary Note [E].

[16] A fragment of Hegesippus, a Jewish Christian of the second
century, " contains a reference to the history in the second chapter
of St. Matthew, and shows plainly that this part of St. Matthew's
Gospel was owned by this Hebrew Christian. It is plain—that
Hegesippus received the history in the second chapter of St. Matthew ; so that he used our Greek Gospel : or, if he used only the
Hebrew edition of St. Matthew's Gospel, this history must have
been in it in his time."—*Lardner's Credib.* vol. i. p. 318. The
fragment referred to will be found at length in the following part of
this volume.

" If we were to form our opinion respecting the contents of the
Gospel of the Hebrews, from the general character of the fragments
which are left of it, we should pronounce it equally unallied to any
of our canonical Gospels, and the work of a later age and a different
spirit."—*Mr. Thirlwall's Introd. to his Translation of Schleiermacher's Essay on the Gospel of St. Luke.* 1825. p. xlix.

St. Matthew, as much as the Ebionite Gospel, that Jerome, who transcribed and translated it, could have taken it, even after deducting the interpolations, for the original of St. Matthew's Gospel. It is true that Jerome makes no distinction between the Nazarene and Ebionite Gospel : for he says in his note to Matt. xii. 13, In Evangelio quo utuntur Nazaræni et Ebionitæ——quod vocatur a plerisque Matthæi authenticum. But we must recollect that Jerome never saw the Hebrew Gospel which was used by the Ebionites ; he was acquainted only with that which was used by the Nazarenes, and therefore had no opportunity of comparing the one with the other. Through want of knowledge, then, he might suppose that they were the same, though they were really different." [17]

5. If it be conceded that the Gospel used by Marcion, who lived in the second century, did not contain the first two chapters of Luke ; it must also be considered that neither did it contain the third chapter, nor more than one half of the fourth ; and in the subsequent parts, as we are informed by Dr. Lardner, who had examined this subject with his usual minuteness and accuracy, it was " mutilated and altered, and even interpolated in a great variety of places. He would not allow it to be called the Gospel of St. Luke, erasing the name of that Evangelist from the beginning of his copy." [18] His alterations were

---

[17] *Michaelis's Introd. to N.T. by Marsh*, vol. iii. part i. pp. 180, 181. " The editors of the Improved Version act in defiance of all evidence, when they represent the Ebionite Gospel to be the genuine Gospel of St. Matthew."—*The Layman's Vind.* p. 112.

[18] *Lardner's Hist. of Heretics*, Book X. Sect. 36. *Works, Kippis's ed.* vol. ix. pp. 393—401.

not made on any critical principles, but in an arbitrary manner, in order to suit his own extravagant theology. Many distinguished Biblical scholars of modern times, particularly Semler, Eichhorn, Griesbach, Lœffler, and Marsh, entirely reject the opinion that he used the Gospel of Luke in any considerable degree. Griesbach maintained that Marcion compiled a work of his own, for the service of his system and the use of his followers, from the writings of the Evangelists, and particularly of Luke.[19] "That Marcion used St. Luke's Gospel at all," says Bishop Marsh, " is a position which has been taken for granted without the least proof. Marcion himself never pretended that it was the Gospel of St. Luke ; as Tertullian acknowledges, saying, 'Marcion Evangelio suo nullum adscribit autorem.' (Adv. Marcion. lib. iv. cap. 2.) It is probable, therefore, that he used some apocryphal Gospel, which had much matter in common with that of St. Luke, but yet was not the same."[20]   But,

[19] *Griesbachii Hist. Text. Gr. Epist. Paul,* p. 92.

[20] *Marsh's Michaelis,* vol. iii. part. ii. p 159. Löffler has very fully examined the question, in his Dissertation, entitled, *Marcionem Paulli Epistolas et Lucæ Evangelium adulterasse dubitatur ;* Frankfort on the Oder, 1788. The conclusions of his minute investigations are, that, (1.) The Gospel used by Marcion was anonymous : (2.) Marcion rejected all our four Gospels, and maintained the authenticity of his own in opposition to them : (3.) His followers afterwards maintained that Christ himself and Paul were the authors of it : (4.) Irenæus, Tertullian, and Epiphanius had no reason for regarding Marcion's Gospel as an altered edition of Luke's ; and their assertion is a mere conjecture resting upon none but frivolous and absurd allegations : (5.) The difference of Marcion's Gospel from Luke's is inconsistent with the supposition : (6.) There are no just grounds for believing that Marcion had any pressing motives to induce him to adopt a garbled copy of Luke ; and the motives assigned by the fathers are inconsistent and self-destructive.

whether this was the case or not, the fact that Marcion's compilation was made upon the principle of omitting and altering whatever did not coincide with his own previous opinions, must deprive it of all trustworthiness in any case which interfered with those opinions.[21]

[21] "The Gospel of Luke was probably the basis of Marcion's Evangelium. His variations from the Gospel of Luke were intended, as will appear upon examination, to make it more conformable to his own opinions, that the God of the Jews was not the Father of Christ; that the Jewish prophets did not foretell his advent; that Christ was not born of a woman, and so did not partake of flesh and blood, but was man in appearance only: yet Mr. Belsham gravely asserts that there was nothing in his system, that we know of, which was inconsistent with the history of the miraculous conception!"— *Layman's Vind.* p. 119.

"The question has been discussed in a masterly manner by Prof. Hahn of Königsberg, whose work must, I think, satisfy every impartial inquirer that the ancient opinion has been abandoned without ground. He there states and clears from misrepresentation the evidence of the fathers on this head, gives a full and distinct view of the peculiarities of Marcion's theological system, exhibits the real character of his work, shows, by an elaborate comparison of Tertullian, Epiphanius, and other writers who have quoted or mentioned this Gospel, that it coincided exactly in contents and arrangement with St. Luke's, except where *doctrinal motives naturally led to omission and alteration;* and, finally, he removes the objections which had induced modern critics to reject the old opinion."— *Mr. Connop Thirlwall's Intr. to Schleiermacher on Luke,* p. lii. Dr. Hahn's work was published at Königsberg, in 1823; intitled, *The Gospel of Marcion in its Original Form.* He is now Div. Prof. at Leipzig, and honourably known by other works.

Dr. Hermann Olshausen has devoted 120 pages of his work *On the Genuineness of the Four Canonical Gospels* (Königsb. 1823,) to an examination of this question, and he gives as the result that "the so called Gospel of Marcion was nothing but Luke's Gospel mutilated and otherwise altered to suit his system."—P. 214. In substantially the same opinion concur the Fathers generally; Simon and Mill; and of recent Bible-critics, Hug, Kleuker, Storr, Arneth, Schütz, De Wette, and Schott (lately deceased) in his *Isagoge Hist.*

Mr. B. continues; "From Luke iii. 1, compared with verse 23, it appears that Jesus was born fifteen years before the death of Augustus, that is, at least two years after the death of Herod: a fact which completely falsifies the whole narrative contained in the preliminary chapters of Matthew and Luke." Thus precipitately, not to say profanely, does this writer rush to conclusions, on a topic which has exercised the laborious industry, not only of orthodox critics and commentators, but of writers as unbelieving as himself, yet more learned and more temperate. "It is wonderful," says the judicious and elegant Ernesti, "that more reverence is often paid to the books of men, than to the book of God. In the former, if difficulties and seeming discrepancies occur, correction or conciliation is sought for, as if the writers were incapable of error: but if such are discovered in the latter, the opportunity is seized for cavilling either at the writers or at their matter itself.[22]

Every one, who has attended to the subject of ancient chronology, is aware that there is no point in relation to which so great difficulties occur, as the adjusting of the notes of time which are found in the Greek and Latin historical writers. They had no

Crit. in N. T. Jena, 1830; a work deserving recommendation to students, for its perspicuity, comprehensiveness, impartiality, and moderate price.

[22] "Admirandum est plus reverentiæ tribui libris humanis quàm divinis. Nam in illis, de antiquis loquimur, cum aliquid ejusmodi incidit, correctio aut conciliatio quæritur, velut ἀναμάρτητοι fuerint; in his occasio arripitur carpendi vel scriptores vel doctrinam ipsam." J. A. Ernesti Instit. Interp. N. T. p. 13. Or, in Dr. Henderson's edition of Prof. Stuart's Translation of Ernesti's Elements of Bibl. Crit. p. 45.

conception of that perfect accuracy of dates which the researches and the habits of modern times lead us to require: and, had they perceived the necessity, they had scarcely the means, from the defect of established epochs, and from other impediments, of answering the purpose.   Many difficulties from this cause occur which have appeared to the most patient critics absolutely insuperable, except by cutting the knot.   It requires exquisite caution to construct a positive argument upon such grounds.

Lardner has treated this subject in his usual minute and circumstantial manner, and has shown that it may be maintained on just grounds ; that, by " the fifteenth year of the government[23] of Tiberius Cæsar," Luke might intend the fifteenth from his being associated with Augustus as colleague in the empire;[24] and that the phraseology "Jesus was about thirty years old when beginning [his ministry,]" may be properly applied to an age two or three years over, or under, the round sum mentioned.[25]   Campbell proposes to understand ἀρχόμενος in the sense of ὑποτασσόμενος in chap. ii. 51, but, I apprehend, without any sufficient authority.   " In this passage, however," says a learned and laborious modern critic, "the use of the adverb

---

[23] Ἡγεμονία is a more general term than *reign*, and is applicable to any kind of rule or presidency.

[24] Filius, COLLEGA imperii, consors tribunitiæ potestatis adsumitur. *Taciti Annal.* i. 3.

[25] *Credib.* Part I. Book II. ch. iii.   If the reader should have listened to any insinuations, that Dr. Lardner was not so deeply acquainted with this chronological difficulty as Dr. Priestley and Mr. Belsham were, and that they have brought to light arguments of which he was not aware, and objections to which he has provided no answer; I request his attention to the excellent work of Mr. Bevans before quoted, the *Layman's Vindication*, pp. 169—184.

ὡσεὶ clearly shows that nothing can be with certainty
determined with respect to the year of Christ's age,
at the time of his baptism, and his entrance on his
public ministry." [26]

The Inquirer adds : " If the relation given of the
miraculous conception were true, it is utterly unac-
countable that these extraordinary events should have
been wholly omitted by Mark and John, and that
there should not be a single allusion to them in the
New Testament, and particularly that in John's
history, Jesus should be so frequently spoken of as
the son of Joseph and Mary, without any comment,
or the least hint that this statement was erroneous." [27]

This objection carries a plausible front : but we ask
an impartial attention to the following considerations.

The fact in question was of the most private and
delicate nature possible, and, as to human attestation,
it rested of necessity solely on the word of Mary
herself, the person most deeply interested.   Joseph's
mind was satisfied with regard to her honour and
veracity, by a divine vision ; which, in whatever way
it was evinced to him to be no delusion, was still a
private and personal affair.   But this was not the
kind of facts to which the first teachers of Christianity
were in the habit of appealing.   The miracles, on
which they rested their claims, were such as had mul-
tiplied witnesses to attest them, and generally enemies
not less than friends.   Here then, we see a reason

[26] " Hic verò ipse usus adverbii ὡσεὶ luculenter docet, nihil certi
definiri posse de ætatis Christi anno quo baptizari se siverit, quove
doctoris publici partes agere cœperit."—*Kuinöl* (Prof. Theol. at
Giessen in Hesse Darmstadt.) *Comm. in Libros Histor. N. T.* Lips.
1817 ; vol. ii. p. 357.

[27] *Calm Inq.* p. 13.

why Jesus and his disciples did not refer to this circumstance, so peculiar and necessarily private. At
the same time, let it not be forgotten that our Lord,
in repelling the assaults of his enemies, habitually
insisted upon the spotlessness of his character ; but,
if there had been any ambiguity about his origin,
it is more than probable that their malignant industry
would have brought it forwards to his disparagement,
as they did not hesitate to do in the case of a very
poor man whom they thought they might insult with
impunity.[28]   Surely, also, reason and feeling dictate
that there is a high propriety, a sort of natural congruity, in the idea, that He who was to be the Saviour
of men from sin should receive his bodily frame in a
manner absolutely free from the semblance of any
predisposition to moral infirmity.

The account in Matthew had probably been transmitted through the family of Joseph and Mary, and
that in Luke through the family or intimates of
Zacharias and Elizabeth ; a supposition which furnishes a reason why the two narratives contain so
little matter in common.   The same reason will account for the absence of reference to this miracle in
the epistolary writings of the New Testament, if that
absence be admitted to the fullest extent : for there is
one passage which appears to carry an implication of
the fact.[29]   The writer of the Epistle to the Hebrews,

---

[28] John ix. 34.

[29] Some conceive that it is also implied in the phrase, " *made of a
woman*," (Gal. iv. 14,) γενόμενος, not γεννώμενος, or γεννητὸς, *born*,
as in LXX. of Job xiv. 1 ; xv. 14 ; xxv. 4, and twice in the N. T.,
Matt. xi. 11 ; Luke vii. 28.   But this does not appear a ground
sufficient to support the inference : for γίνομαι is sometimes used in
this sense, both in the LXX. and in common writers ; Gen. iv. 25 ;

in explaining the symbolical representations by which
it pleased the Holy Spirit, under the former dispensation, to prefigure the blessings of Christianity, seems
to put the interior sanctuary, or " holy of holies," as
the sign of the heavenly state ; and the outer tabernacle as that of " the flesh," or human nature of the
Messiah. As the Aaronical high-priest, on the great
anniversary of expiation, was first to officiate in the
tabernacle, offering the sacrifices and sprinkling the
blood of symbolical pardon and purification, and then
was to advance, through that tabernacle, into the
most holy place, the representation of the divine
presence; so Christ, our "Great High-Priest," and
" Minister of the sanctuary and of the true tabernacle,"
—" entered into the sanctuary,—through the greater
and more perfect tabernacle,—his own blood." [30]
Now, of *this* tabernacle it is declared that " the
Lord pitched it, and not man ;" that it was " not
made with hands, that is, not of this creation." [31]
The expression in Scripture, " not made with hands,"
denotes that which is effected by the immediate power
of God, without the intervention of any inferior
agency. It, therefore, in the case before us, intimates
that the fleshly tabernacle of our Lord's humanity was

xxxv. 26. Τινὸς θεοῦ γενέσθαι τοὺς παῖδας· *Josephi Ant. Jud.* XV.
ii. 6. Σωκράτης ἐν ταὺτῃ [ἡμέρᾳ] ἐγένετο· *Æliani Var. Hist.* ii. 25.
Γίνονται μεθ' ὅπλων [they are born armed ;] iii. 18. Γένεσθαι αὐτὸν
ἐκ νύμφης· x. 18. Ἦν ἐξ Ἰλλυρίδος γυναικὸς τῷ Φιλίππῳ γενομένη·
xiii. 36. But, in the last instance, some editions have γεννωμένη.
Bishop Squire, in his *Plutarch on Isis and Osiris*, shows that the
interchange of the two words is frequent in manuscripts ; pp. 79,162.
See also, in Griesbach, the various readings of Luke i. 35.

[30] Heb. iv. 14 ; viii. 2 ; ix. 11, 12. See note [F] at the end of
this Chapter.

[31] Heb. viii. 2 ; ix. 11.

formed, not in the ordinary way of nature, but by the immediate exercise of Omnipotence.

In the passage from the *Calm Inquiry* under consideration, we meet with an observable specimen of the subserviency to hypothesis which marks the Inquirer's principles of interpretation. He never scruples to expatiate on the *fewness* of the texts which (according to him) can with any plausibility be alleged as favouring the doctrines of the preexistence and deity of Christ; and yet, few as he would have us believe them to be, those passages occupy many pages of his own enumeration and rapid criticism. But, when another turn is to be served, it is roundly assumed that there is a remarkable *frequency* of instances in which Jesus is spoken of, " in John's history," as the son of Joseph and Mary. Was the Inquirer aware that his " *so frequently*," differed little from a *so seldom?* The instances of this frequency are only *two!*[31]   The

---

[31] John i. 46.—vi. 42. Dr. Paulus, a patriarch of the Antisupranaturalists, and one of the most daring of them, remarks on the latter passage, that " it cannot be inferred from the silence of the Evangelist, that Jesus admitted himself to be really the son of Joseph; for, to the matter in question, Whether he had come down from heaven? it had no relation to determine in what sense he was called the son of Joseph : neither was it Jesus's object to prove his descent from heaven by the circumstance of his birth having been out of the ordinary course of nature ; *but by* THIS, *that before his birth, he was a celestial being*, enjoying supreme happiness with God."—(*Kuinöl*, vol. iii. p. 339.) Paulus, in his recent work on the Gospels, treats this subject at great length, not to say with a wearisome tediousness. He appears unwilling to admit, yet unable to deny, the miraculous conception of Jesus. He places in a convincing light the *irrefragable* character of the historical narrative, in both Matthew and Luke. He speaks in the most decided terms of the perfect purity and chastity of both Joseph and Mary, and of the strict veracity of their testimony. He, somewhat obscurely, seems

one is the language of a stranger, just now convinced of the divine mission of Jesus; the other, that of virulent enemies; and both would of course speak according to the common opinion. A parallel instance occurs in Luke,[33] and two still stronger:[34] but they are reasonably interpreted as the style of common parlance, on the ground laid by the same Evangelist, of Jesus being, " as was *supposed*, the son of Joseph."[35]

The doctrine of the miraculous conception has no necessary influence on the determination of the great

to be labouring to insinuate an idea, which he appears unable to venture upon putting into plain words; namely, that *the physical effect was produced on Mary* by the power of a most exalted, transporting spiritualism, the sublimely enraptured feelings of holy devotion to God, (signified by the term *holy spirit*,) combined with her firm faith in the prophecies concerning the Messiah! He likewise presumes to assign a very important practical object, in the plan of providence, for permitting or effecting this extraordinary phænomenon; " that this commencement of the earthly life of our Christ must have had the greatest influence upon the manner in which from the very first he was treated as an infant, upon the developement of his powers of mind, upon his training for the holy object for which he was destined, upon the direction which he would voluntarily give to his active energies, (according to Lu. ii. 40,) and upon the relation of all circumstances that affected him. To us all is Jesus the Teacher and Ruler sent by God to bring salvation to man [*der Heilbringende Lehrregent Gottes*], not through the undescribed [mystery] of his corporal origin, but by the operations of his powerful spirit of holiness. Rom. i. 3; Heb. ix. 14; Mark ii. 8; Lu. x. 21."
—*Exegetisches Handbuch uber die drei ersten Evangelien*, vol. i. p. 113. Heidelberg, 1830—1832, 3 vols. but not completed.—This is the man who has brought forward so many wild imaginations (of the conjuncture of favourable circumstances, and the like,) to explain away the miracles of the New Testament!—Do not his suppositions involve more of the miraculous, than any of the facts which he is so anxious to get rid of?

[33] Chap. iv. 22.   [34] Chap. ii. 41—48.   [35] Chap. iii. 23.

point in the controversy concerning the person of Christ.   The preceding observations, therefore, are made principally with a view to show how much it concerns a sincere inquirer after truth to be jealous of the positive assertions and the style of criticism employed by the Calm Inquirer.   The proof, however, of the authenticity of the disputed passages is of the more importance, as they include some texts, which we shall hereafter have occasion to consider.

In this part of the Gospel-history a passage occurs, which has been by many regarded as of importance in the great question before us.   " All this took place, in order that the declaration might be fulfilled which was spoken by the Lord through the prophet : Behold, the Virgin shall become pregnant, and shall bear a son ; and they shall call his name EMMANUEL, which explained, is, *God with us.*"[36]   This passage has been already considered as it stands in the Prophecies of Isaiah.[37]   The friendly censure of a respectable journal[38] has called upon me to reconsider the sentiments which I had expressed : I have carefully done so ; and have examined the authors to whom the reviewer refers, mentioned below ; but am obliged to acknowledge that I can discover no sufficient grounds for changing my opinion.   It still appears to me that the passage can be proved to be a prophecy of the Messiah, in no other than a secondary sense ; and that no argument can be drawn, from the words or context, capable of determining whether EMMANUEL was designed to be a *descriptive title*, and therefore

[36] Matt. i. 23.   [37] Vol. I. pp. 354—370.
[38] *Congregational Magazine*, March 1819. *Spanhemii Dub. Evang.* Par. I. cap. xxxiv. *Vitringæ Obs. Sacr.* Lib. V. cap. i.

declaratory of the union of the Divine Nature with the
human, or a *commemorative name*, to express and
celebrate the fact of the divine interposition for the
salvation of mankind. Of the latter class of names,
there are many in Scripture, such as Joshua, which signifies *Jehovah the Saviour ;* Elijah, *my God Jehovah ;*
Abijah, *my Father Jah;* Eliah, *my God Jah ;* Eliatha,
thou my God. On the position, that the fact of a
Divine nature in the constitution of the person of the
Messiah is already established by other evidence, we
are undoubtedly at liberty to apply the word Emmanuel to our Lord and Redeemer as a title directly
descriptive of himself: but I confess myself unable to
perceive that it can, by any process of fair criticism or
conclusive reasoning, be made an independent argument.[39] In such cases, however, it is to be remembered that the secondary sense is the *principal* one in
the original intention, the *great and ultimate* design
of the Holy Spirit, " who spake by the prophets."[40]

[39] See Note [G], at the end of this Chapter.
[40] " —There are kinds of composition in which an apparent sense
is presented, which every intelligent reader sees is only an envelope
for another meaning ; and it is *this other* meaning which is the
author's actual design, his one and true intention. [*E. g.* proverbs,
hyperboles, allegories, &c.] But there was a *peculiarity* in the
inspired writings of the Hebrews, which *could* belong to *no other*
writings ; because it arose out of the religious and political constitution which the Author of truth had been pleased to confer upon
them. That constitution was formed upon a principle of subserviency to the spiritual reign of which we have before spoken, the
progressive kingdom of the Messiah. Hence, many descriptions
occur in the prophetic parts of the Old Testament which are applicable to the persons who are their immediate subjects, only in a
partial and very imperfect manner ; but which find a complete and
satisfactory correspondence to their *full* meaning in the Messiah, and
the new dispensation of which he is the Head. It is one sense ; it

is one predicate or collection of predicates; but, by original design and construction, formed so as to be applied to two subjects; to the first, by anticipation and partially, and to the second in complete perfection; the former being the temporary representative and introduction to the latter."—*Disc. on the Principles of Interpretation, as applied to the Prophecies,* p. 52.

SUPPLEMENTARY NOTES TO CHAP. I.

Note [A], page 5.

" This is that ' great mystery of godliness, God manifested in the flesh;' the King of glory after a manner divesting himself of his royal robes, and truly putting on the form of a servant, the Holy Ghost framing him a body in the virgin's womb: not that it was impossible to have made his human nature sinless in the ordinary way, though the schools [the scholastic divines of the middle ages] usually give that reason; but that, by that miraculous and peculiar manner of birth, he might be declared more than man; as being a way more congruous, both to the greatness of his person and the purity of his human nature."—*Archbishop Leighton on the Creed,* Art. 3.

" Supposing that Almighty God, by his divine power, had so ordered the matter, and so perfectly sanctified an earthly father and mother from all original spot, that the human nature might have been transmitted immaculate to him, as well as the Holy Ghost did purge that part of the flesh of the virgin of which the body of Christ was made; yet it was not convenient that that person, that was *God blessed for ever,* as well as man, partaking of our nature, should have a conception in the same manner as ours; but different, and in some measure conformable to the infinite dignity of his person; which could not have been, had not a supernatural power and a divine person been concerned as an active principle in it. Besides, such a birth had not been agreeable to the first promise, which calls him *the seed of the woman,* not of the man; and so the veracity of God had suffered some detriment; the *seed of the woman,* Gen. i. 15, only, is set in opposition to the *seed of the serpent.* By this manner of conception, the holiness of his nature is secured, and his fitness for his office is assured to us. It is now a pure and unpolluted humanity that is the temple and tabernacle of the Divinity."—*Charnock, on the Power of God; Works,* 8vo. vol. ii. p. 414.

An author whom Unitarians commonly, and very deservedly, profess to hold in high esteem, glances at an argument in favour of the *propriety* of " the miraculous conception of Christ," which he considers as of great weight ; namely, that the present order of nature for perpetuating the human species is " to be considered as one of the marks of our present fallen, degenerate state. The mortality of the present body, introduced by Adam's sin, would of course require some such method of propagation as now subsists, though nothing of this kind had taken place before the Fall ; and therefore it may be, that nothing did, or something greatly different from the present method."—*Hartley on Man*, 8vo. ed. vol. ii. p. 233.

Note [B], page 5.

If the reader will try the disputed portions of Matthew and Luke, by Le Clerc's diagnostic " Aphorisms" on the characters of genuine and spurious books, he will find the result to be most satisfactorily affirmative. I subjoin these Aphorisms (from the *Ars Critica*, P. III. sect. ii. cap. 2—6,) somewhat abridged.

" 1. If, in the oldest manuscripts, a book is attributed to a different author from the one whose name has been affixed by later editors ; or if, in the oldest copies, it is anonymous ; and if no other reason can be alleged in favour of the more modern and common attribution—in the first case the modern name is *supposititious*, in the latter it is an *interpolation*.

" 2. If citations from any book occur in ancient writers, which are wanting in the present copies professed to be of the same work ; the work, as now existing, is either a *different* work, or is *mutilated*. If the citations materially differ, there is ground to *suspect* the present copy. If the whole be found with no variations, or trivial ones, the book is *genuine*, unless other grounds of suspicion exist.

" 3. Works not mentioned by any writer of the two or three centuries immediately following, are *spurious*, or at least *liable to suspicion*.

" 4. Books which the more ancient writers rejected, or held to be doubtful, can scarcely ever be received on later authority.

" 5. A work containing opinions contrary to what the alleged writer is known to have constantly defended, especially if they are opinions of any importance, is most probably *spurious* ; or, at least, it is *interpolated*.

" 6. A book gravely asserting impossibilities, fables, or absurdities, or containing marks of ignorance on the subject in hand, cannot be received as written by a serious, competent, and upright author.

" 7. A book in which allusions exist to opinions, controversies, facts, or persons, certainly subsequent to the time of the alleged writer; or which has any manifest imitation of a later writer; is *spurious*, or at least *interpolated*.

" 8. If the style be manifestly different from the known style of the age, or of the writer; or if there occur words of a lower age, it is wrongly attributed to him. If it is found, by competent examination, to be the same as the style of another writer, it ought to be attributed to that writer, other considerations being equal.

" —— I trust," subjoins M. le Clerc, " that these Aphorisms will be found to be so true and just, that a diligent observance of them will scarcely ever fail to conduct to a true result. But, clear as they are in themselves, it must be confessed that it will require something more than a mediocrity of learning to make a safe and correct use of them; and that no little time and practice will be needful, to acquire the art of applying them with promptitude and success. In this respect, however, they resemble all preceptive institutes : of which, though the propriety and obligation may be very speedily made intelligible, yet men not inured to their observance can only be brought by time and reflection to an intelligent and cordial submission to them. But here lies the difference; that, while all men are bound to be virtuous and observant of moral precepts, no man is obliged to be a critic. Whoever then does attempt the study of this difficult art, should well understand what a task he undertakes, and by what laws he must be governed: or else he will be a most infelicitous critic : and, instead of reaping that high honour which men of real erudition have obtained from this art, he will become contemptible and ridiculous.

" I think I hear my reader asking me, Whether I myself look for any portion of this honour ?—This is really an invidious question ; and whatever reply I give may be turned against me. I will only venture to say, that I do not PROFESS this arduous and hazardous study, though I highly honour those who profess it, and have long read their writings with great pleasure, from which perhaps some tinge of criticism may have adhered to me."

Note [C], page 6.

" It was a very favourite custom with the Jews to employ terms and phrases taken from the Old Testament ; especially when some striking points of resemblance really existed between the circumstances of the passage and the new fact to which it was adapted. Hence in the Rabbinical writings the verbs מלא and כלה, and in the New Testament πληρωθῆναι, and τελεσθῆναι, occur in different acceptations. The oracles and declarations of the Prophets were thus said to be *fulfilled* and *accomplished*, not only when the very event occurred which was in the design of the prediction, but when any thing took place which was *like the prophetic descriptions* which *brought them to recollection*, or which was in any way a *confirmation* or *illustration* of them."—*Kuinöl*, tom. i. p. 41.

" Many passages of the Old Testament are introduced [in the N. T.] merely on account of some remarkable similarity in the circumstances or in the expression; as citations in the same way are common in all writings, meaning, *that is true in this sense, which occurs elsewhere in another sense.* So Isa. liii. 4, 5, ' He took away our diseases,' which denotes the maladies of the soul, is applied in Matt. viii. 17, to bodily diseases. A similar example is, in John xviii. 9, deduced from the discourse of Christ in chap. xvii. 12." *Knapp's* (des verewigten) *Vorlesungen über die Christliche Glaubenslehre;* vol. ii. p. 136. Halle, 1827. This accomplished divine and excellent man, Dr. George Christian Knapp, Senior Professor of the Theological Faculty in the United University of Halle and Wittenberg, died Oct. 14, 1825, æt. 72.

Note [D], page 6.

The Calm Inquirer speaks in a strain of unwarrantable positiveness when he asserts, that " if the facts related in the account of our Lord's nativity were true—*viz.* the appearances of Angels, the star in the East, the visit of the Magi, the massacre of Bethlehem, &c. they *must* have excited great public attention and expectation, and *could not have failed* to have been noticed by contemporary writers, who nevertheless observe a total silence on the subject." P. 18.

The history of Jesus and his first followers presents many instances of " appearances of angels," as well as other facts out of the course of nature, which were not less remarkable than those recorded of Zacharias and Elizabeth, Mary, Joseph, and a company of probably not more than four or five pious shepherds, obscure and poor men. Yet will even the scepticism of this author deem them unworthy of credit, because they are recorded only by Matthew or Luke, and " contemporary historians have observed a total silence" upon them?

The star was, in all probability, a meteoric flame, visible at no great distance (otherwise it could not have " stood over" a particular house), and becoming extinct when its purpose was answered.

The visit of the Magi, probably Persians, (see *Hyde de Rel. Vet. Pers.* Ox. 1700, cap. 31,) was certainly a most remarkable fact:

but among the numerous bodies of foreign Jews who were frequently visiting Jerusalem, and especially in the perturbed state of the country towards the latter part of Herod's reign, such an occurrence might meet with less attention and be sooner forgotten than it deserved. A fact of much more astonishing magnitude and importance is related by Matthew in the most brief and unimpassioned manner ; a fact which, so far as it was known, not only " could not have failed" to excite great attention, but must have produced impressions the most overpowering and 'alarming ; yet a fact which no " contemporary writer has noticed," and which the Annotator on the Improved Version passes over without any mark of doubt or difficulty, and without explication. " The sepulchres were opened, and many bodies of holy persons who had slept were raised ; and coming out of the sepulchres, after His resurrection, they entered into the holy city, and were made visible to many," Matt. xxvii. 53.

" Josephus makes no mention of the murder of the infants :—— but he also consigns to silence many other facts, the truth of which is indubitable, and which could not be unknown to him.—Reasons may be assigned for this omisson. Bethlehem was a small town, and of little consideration : the population, including the neighbourhood, scarcely reached a thousand ; so that the number of male infants within the prescribed age could scarcely exceed ten or twelve.—— And this was not the only act of extreme cruelty that Herod perpetrated.——Hence it is very properly observed by *Vossius* in his *Chronologia Sacra*, p. 159, that, ' After so many instances of cruelty exercised by Herod in Jerusalem and throughout all Judea ; after his having murdered so many of his own children, of his wives, his nearest relatives, and his friends, it would not appear a very great matter to order the execution of the children of one town or village and its adjacent country ; a massacre which in a very small place could not be extensive, since not all the children, but the males alone, and of them such only as were under two years old, were cut off.' "— *Kuinöl*, vol. i. pp. 62, 63.

It should also be considered that, excepting Josephus, there are no contemporary writers extant, nor do we even know that any ever existed, from whom a reference to these facts could be expected.

Note [E], page 10.

" In the Gospel which is in use among them (bearing the name of Matthew, but which is not the whole in the fullest form, but on the contrary is characterised by spurious additions and curtailments, and they call it *the Hebrew Gospel*,) it is declared ; ' There was a

man whose name was Jesus, and he was about thirty years of age,
who chose us. And he came into Capernaum, and entered into the
house of Simon who was surnamed Peter : and he opened his mouth
and said, As I was coming by the lake of Tiberias, I chose John and
James the sons of Zebedee, and Simon, and Andrew, and Thaddæus,
and Simon Zelotes, and Judas Iscariot ; and thee, Matthew, I called,
sitting at the receipt of custom, and thou followedst me. You therefore, I appoint to be twelve Apostles, for a testimony unto Israel.
And John was baptizing, and the Pharisees and all Jerusalem came
out unto him, and were baptized. And John had his clothing of
camel's hair, and a leathern girdle about his loins ; and his food was
wild honey, of which the taste was that of manna, as a sweet cake
in oil.'"

After the passage cited before as the commencement of the Ebionite
Gospel, and " after much matter besides," Epiphanius says, " it
proceeds thus :

" ' When the people were baptized, Jesus also came and was baptized by John. And as he came up from the water, the heavens
were opened, and he saw the Holy Spirit of God, in the form of a
dove, descending and coming upon him. And a voice came from
heaven, saying, Thou art my beloved Son ; in thee I am well
pleased. And again, This day have I begotten thee. And immediately a great light shone around the place. John, beholding him,
said to him, Who art thou, Lord ? And again a voice came to him
from heaven, This is my beloved Son, in whom I am well pleased.
And then John, falling down before him, said, I beseech thee, Lord,
baptize thou me. But he forbad him, saying, Let alone, for thus it
is proper that all things should be fulfilled.' "—*Epiphanii Op.* tom. i.
pp. 137, 138.

Note [F], page 18.

Many modern interpreters understand " the tabernacle" in these
passages as signifying the heavenly state. Yet these writers make
" the sanctuary" also to signify the same object ; thus confounding
two very distinct images. The propriety of the figures, the argument
of the connexion, and the frequent use of σκῆνος and σκήνωμα to denote
the human body (2 Cor. v. 1—4; 2 Pet. i. 13, 14, and this use of
at least σκῆνος is common in Greek writers ; see *Wetstein* on 2 Cor.
v. 1, and *Schleusneri Lex.*) satisfy me of the justness of the interpretation of Calvin, Grotius, James Cappel, Dr. Owen, &c. It is no
objection that in Heb. x. 20, " the veil" is the symbol of the
Messiah's human nature : for the veil, as one of the boundaries of

the tabernacle, in a natural sense belonged to it ; and the passage relates to our Lord's *death*, so that the *veil* is very fitly introduced, marking the transition out of life into another state. A further argument that our Lord's human body is here meant, arises from the antithesis to " the blood of goats and bullocks," and the position of " his own blood," which may be viewed as exegetical of the subject first mentioned ; each of the three members having διά.

The text was partially quoted above, for the sake of presenting alone the clauses on which the argument rests. It is proper here to insert it at length. The reader will observe the apposition of " the tabernacle" and the " blood."

" But Christ, having presented himself, a High-Priest of the blessings to come, through the greater and more perfect tabernacle, not made with hands, (that is, not of this creation,) and not through the blood of goats and calves, but through his own blood, entered once [*i. e.* once for ever, never to be repeated,] into the sanctuary, having acquired eternal redemption."

Grotius's note is so judicious and satisfactory that it deserves to be inserted.

" The design of the writer is to declare that Christ entered the highest heavens through his sufferings and death. To keep up the comparison with the high-priest under the law, his object is to declare that Christ *entered through his body and blood ;* for the *body* is very properly put by metonymy for *bodily sufferings ;* and it is common in all languages to use the term *blood* to denote *death*, as death follows upon any very copious effusion of blood. Yet he does not express *the body* by its proper word, but uses a symbolical description suitable for carrying on the comparison, as I have observed above. The Hebrews were accustomed to call the body a *tabernacle :* and from them the disciples of Pythagoras deduced the expression, as I have said on the Wisdom of Sol. ix. 15, and 2 Cor. v. 1—4. In particular the body of Christ is called a *temple*, on account of the indwelling divine energy: John ii. 21. Here this body is said to be " not made with hands," and the writer explains his meaning by adding, " that is, not of this creation," understanding by *creation* the usual order of nature ; as the Jews apply the Talmudical term *Beriah* [creation, any thing created]: for the body of Christ was conceived in a supernatural manner. In this sense he properly employs the term *not made with hands*, because in the Hebrew idiom any thing is said to be made with hands which is brought to pass in the ordinary course of nature. See ver. 24, and Mark xiv. 58 ; Acts vii. 48 ; xvii. 24 ; Eph. ii. 11. The Prophets frequently give to idols the appellation *made with hands*, as the opposite to any thing divine."—*Grotii Annot.* in Heb. ix. 11.

Note [G], page 22.

" Matt. i. 22, 23. The following are evidently the words, not of the angel, but of the evangelist, referring his Jewish readers to the O. T. in order to show them, that this new thing [Jer. xxxi. 22,] at the outset of the glad tidings, was already prepared for in their sacred ground of faith. Yet he does not take up any single or detached circumstance, for, in relation to such, discrepancies would present themselves, (*e. g.* the child which Mary bore was called Jesus, not Immanuel,) but the *entire whole* of the transaction ; and this answered to the prophecy. *The Lord* himself is here presented as the *efficient cause* (ὑπὸ, as in ver. 20, ἐκ, denoting the source or first spring of an action ;) and the prophet merely the mediate organ of the action : for διά, in contradistinction from ὑπὸ, signifies the instrument *by means* of which any thing is effected.—With respect to the meaning of the phrase ἵνα or ὅπως πληρωθῇ (*that it might be fulfilled*,) which is used with a characteristic frequency by Matthew, it is, in the first place, very evident that the N. T. writers themselves understood it in the obvious and literal sense : and, in the same plain comprehension of meaning, πληροῦσθαι (*to be fulfilled*) to convey the idea that something, which had at a past time been promised or engaged for as to take place *in future*, is now *brought into a present existence ;* so that πληροῦσθαι always presupposes a promise or prediction as having gone before. The conjunction ἵνα cannot be translated ecbatically, *so that*, as if it merely designated the sequent event ; but it must be taken telically, as expressing the design, *in order that.* In the whole phrase the *designed* character of the effect is clearly prominent ; to which idea the verb itself necessarily leads. Therefore the ellipsis to τοῦτο γέγονεν (*this was done*) may be supplied by ὑπὸ τοῦ Κυρίου (*by the Lord ;*) since that which took place cannot be regarded as a matter of accident. The form of expression is, by some interpreters, allowed to have its simple, proper, grammatical meaning, only where, in their judgment, prophecies strictly so called are adduced from the O.T. ; but where this does not appear to them to be the case, they attach a wider meaning to the phrase, thus ; the occurrence was such, that such or such words of the O. T. might very suitably be applied to it. In support of this method of explaining, it is urged that ἵνα is used ecbatically in the N. T. I admit that this is the case in some passages, as John vii. 23, and ix. 2, though Fritzsche, in his *Commentary on Matthew*, p. 49, and in his *Excursus* I., denies this. Yet, see what he says upon Matt. xiii. 13. But, because ἵνα *may* be so used, it does not follow that it *must* be so in any passage. This peculiar phrase, which is of constant occurrence in the N. T., can have only one and the same meaning in all the places in which it is used. An appeal to the universal custom of applying passages of the O. T. to objects altogether alien from their proper reference as shown in their connexion, cannot be allowed to be available; for we cannot think that the sacred writers would have accommodated to themselves a practice both absurd and pernicious, and which was really a *perverting of the word of God.* Such it really would have been; and had those sacred writers followed that practice, they must also have received the principle on which it rested, namely, that the Scripture has unlimited meanings, and that it may therefore be applied to all possible relations and circumstances. The rabbinical authors made their applications of Scripture, even the most preposterous, upon this principle; and in pursuance of their view of the all-sided relation of the holy writings, they believed every one of the applications which they made, to be an actual fulfilment of the written word. In my opinion, it is only a doctrinal prejudice that has given occasion to the style of explanation which deviates from the plain grammatical meaning of the phrase, "that it might be fulfilled." It was conscientiously believed that, in the N. T. passages out of the O. T. are cited, as prophecies, which in their original connexion are not prophecies at all : therefore, to prevent its appearing as if the N. T. writers had cited out of the O. T. passages as prophecies which really contain no prophecy, recourse was had to the way of explanation which I have mentioned. Only then let the difficulty be taken out of the way, and there will be no occasion for departing from the proximate sense of the words. Now the difficulty is taken away by admitting, in the O. T. prophecies, a *twofold* reference; in the inferior, to an object immediately present; in a superior, to a future object. With this admission, we can always maintain the one reference ; the proximate, simple, grammatical, literal sense ; and, at the same time, comprehending the other, ascribe to the citations in the N. T. their full meaning as prophecies. *It is a part of the peculiar* INTENTION *and* CONSTITUTION of the Scriptures, that the *life* and *being* of the O. T. is a mirror of the N. T. life ; and that all the lines of the religious ideas and institutions of the O. T. unite expressly in the person of Christ, as the chief object presented in the N. T.

" This universal character of the O. T. is expressed in the passage

(Isa. vii. 14,) here cited. The proximate, grammatical and literal
sense necessarily requires a reference to an object actually present,
as the virgin who was to bear the Immanuel, was presented by the
prophet to king Ahaz as a sign. A reference to the Messiah, to be
born of a virgin some centuries after, appears totally inapplicable to
the occasion. Under the word *virgin* (παρθένος, עַלְמָה an unmarried
female, in itself indeed different from בְּתוּלָה whch necessarily signifies
pure virginity ; but עַלְמָה *may*, here it *must*, be understood of a virgin
in the strict and proper sense :) under this word, the mind most
naturally recurs to the *betrothed spouse* of the prophet, designated in
Isa. viii. 3, by the feminine termination to the word signifying
Isaiah's own office, meaning therefore the wife of the prophet.
Thus the passage obtains the plain and natural sense, that Isaiah
presented as a sign to Ahaz, this series of facts, that his now only
betrothed spouse, but who was soon to be his wife, would have a son,
of the name Immanuel; and that, before this child should come to the
usual early developement of faculties (that is, in two or three years,)
the promises now made would be fulfilled. So king Ahaz had given to
him a sign which was *immediate* and *intelligible* ; while yet the birth
of the Immanuel had its *superior* reference to the Messiah, in whom
it acquired its fulfilment in a far higher and deeper sense, he being
born of a virgin as a *sign* to the unbelieving world, represented in
Ahab. This explication well suits the whole plan of the symbolical
names which Isaiah gave to his sons. A complete series of *sentiments* and *facts*, of especial importance to him in the then existing
circumstances, was represented by the names of his children ; Shear-
jashub, Maher-shalal-hashbaz, and Immanuel. Thus, connecting
the names of his children, he formed the circle of ideas in which his
spirit so actively moved.[1] Such a method of conveying instruction
is perfectly in unison with the plan of *speaking by actions* which was
one of the peculiar characters of the prophetic office : and thus also
the evangelist Matthew had the ground of perfect right to apply the
occurrence, the birth of an Immanuel, to the birth of Christ."—
Olshausen's Commentar. ub. d. N. T. vol. i. pp. 51—54. Königsberg, 1830.

[1] Meaning, I presume, that the three names would form a sentence, as a prediction of the deliverance of Ahaz and his people from their great national
dangers; q. d. Fear not, thy country shall not be long oppressed; the prisoners
shall be released, *a remnant shall return :* because *God is with us ;*—and thou shalt
retaliate and be indemnified, therefore *hasten to the spoil, quick to the prey.* Dr. O.
must also have supposed that Shear-jashub was the son of Isaiah by a former
wife, or his scheme falls at once to the ground.

CHAP. II.

ON THE EVIDENCE RELATIVE TO THE PERSON OF THE CHRIST,
WHICH MAY BE DERIVED FROM THE OFFICE AND THE TESTI-
MONY OF JOHN THE BAPTIST.

A forerunner peculiar to the dignity of the Messiah.—Terms in which the office of John was described.—His testimony.—His resemblance to Elijah.

Luke i. 15—17. " For he shall be great in the presence of the Lord ;—and " many of the children of Israel shall he turn unto the Lord their God: and he " shall go before his presence in the spirit and power of Elijah, to turn the hearts " of fathers to children, and the disobedient to the wisdom of the righteous, and to " make ready for the Lord a prepared people."—Ver. 43. " And whence is this to " me, that the mother of my Lord should come unto me?"—Ver. 76. " And, thou, " child, shalt be called, Prophet of the Most High; for thou shalt go before the " presence of the Lord, to prepare his ways."

Matt. iii. 3. " This is he who was spoken of by Isaiah the Prophet, saying, A " voice of one, proclaiming in the wilderness, Prepare ye the way of the Lord! " Make ye straight his paths!"—Vers. 11, 12. " I indeed baptize you with water, " unto repentance: but He who is coming after me is more mighty than I, whose " sandals I am not worthy to carry. He will baptize you with the Holy Spirit " and fire. Whose fan is in his hand, and he will thoroughly cleanse his corn- " floor; and he will gather his wheat into the granary, but the straw he will burn " with unquenchable fire."

John i. 29, 30—34. " Behold the Lamb of God, who beareth away the sin of " the world! This is he concerning whom I said, After me cometh a man who has " become before me; for he was prior to me.[1]——And I have seen, and have testi- " fied that this is the Son of God."

AMONG the peculiarities which distinguish the most perfect dispensation of revealed religion, was the fact that its Author and Finisher was introduced to his work of mercy to man, by a special harbinger. No such preparation had divine wisdom judged necessary to any preceding disclosure of truth or authority.

[1] See Note [A], at the end of this Chapter.

This honour was reserved till God should " bring the First-Begotten into the world."

This is a circumstance eminently fitted to awaken expectation. It marks importance in the event, and dignity in the Person for whose approach such preparation is made. This impression is strengthened when we observe, that this arrangement was a particular topic of prophecy ; and that, not the Sovereign only, but his servant and herald likewise, was expressly predicted.

When a sincere inquirer has duly reflected upon this, let him take up the terms of the declaration ; let him examine the form of the proclamation ; but let him leave out of his mind the designation of *the person announced.* " He shall go before his presence. Thou shalt be called, Prophet of ——. Thou shalt go before the presence of ——. A voice of one proclaiming, Prepare ye the way of ——!" Let it be imagined that these were lacunæ in every existing copy ; and that, in the remediless absence of all critical authority, we were reduced to fill them up by conjecture. Would it not, in such case, be deemed one of the most safe and certain of conjectural readings, to supply " THE MESSIAH," or some equivalent term? Would not all men consent in this supplement? Would not the most scrupulous acquiesce in it, as indisputably justified, and even required, by the sense and the connexion?

But there is no chasm. We have the words complete, and no one disputes their authenticity. The Sovereign thus announced and introduced, is THE LORD GOD of Israel, THE MOST HIGH, THE LORD JEHOVAH of the Prophets. Can honesty of interpre-

tation require any more?[2]   Is not the obedience of
faith, which is the characteristic of every real Christian,
satisfied, that the Christ, whom John proclaimed in
the wilderness, is GOD JEHOVAH, THE MOST HIGH?
The language of Elizabeth implies that she had so
understood the prophecy of her husband; and that
the same spirit of faith was given to her, by which she
saw in the child to be born of Mary, him whom she
owned as her Lord.   Indeed, it is expressly recorded
that, on this occasion, " Elizabeth was filled with the
Holy Spirit."

The faithful herald proclaimed the dignity of his
Lord and Master, not only by declaring that he was
greater and mightier than himself, but by giving
instances of the exertion of his power.   John had
baptized by the symbolical use of water: the Messiah
was actually to confer the blessing thus signified, that
divine influence which would produce and nourish all
piety and religion; "HE will baptize you with the
Holy Spirit."   According to the lowest hypothesis
which at all admits of divine influences upon the
human mind, for the purposes of restoration to holiness
and happiness, the power to confer those influences
can belong to no merely human being.   However, the
generality of Unitarians, denying any such influences,
understand the phrase as denoting only the commu-
nicating of divine knowledge, by outward instruction;
and to them this argument may be of little weight.
But it will not be equally easy to elude the other parts
of the declaration, which attribute to Christ the inward
scrutiny and unerring decision of human character,
the purgation of the church, the protection of the

[2] See Note [B], at the end of this Chapter.

upright, and the infliction of judgments upon the
impenitent. The *baptism with fire*, and other parts
of the description, correspond with one of the usual
scripture metaphors for expressing the infliction of
divine judgments for the sins of men.[3] Both the
right and the power to inflict such punishments, are,
according to the uniform testimony of the sacred
word, among the exclusive prerogatives of the Supreme
Being.[4]

The resemblance between John and Elijah was to
be so great, that he was described as coming " in the
spirit and power" of that great Israelitish prophet,
and was predicted as even another Elijah. The stern
integrity, the independent and occasionally recluse
mode of life, the simple and austere manners, and the
bold reproving of royal criminals, which distinguished
Elijah, were also conspicuous in John. But the capital circumstance in Elijah's character was his testimony
against polytheism, and his recalling his countrymen
to the acknowledgment and worship of the One and
Only God. What shall we find corresponding with
this, in the character and ministry of John? His
great, and strictly speaking his single, object was to
bear testimony that Jesus was the Messiah, and invite
his countrymen to receive him: and this office is
explicitly described thus ; " Many of the children of
Israel shall he turn unto the Lord their God." Now,
if that Messiah were God, the correspondence is made
complete *in the chief particular :* but if not, it fails
where we should *most* expect it to hold. As a colla-

---

[3] See especially Exod. xv. 7 ; Job xxi. 18 ; Ps. i. 4 ; Isa. v. 24 ;
lxvi. 16, 24.

[4] See Note [C], at the end of this Chapter.

teral and indirect evidence, this appears to me to have
great weight.

It may be asked whether John himself understood
that such was the nature of his office, and the amount
of his testimony. I answer, that there does not appear
to be any reason for supposing him to have been, in
that respect, in different circumstances from those of
preceding prophets. Though "the Spirit of Christ
was in them, testifying before" concerning him, it is
evident that they did not, and that by the nature of
the case they could not, entertain other than indistinct apprehensions of the subjects on which they delivered the oracles of God. It was essential to the
scheme of prophecy, that it should not be " of *self-
solution;*"[5] that is, that it could not be explained from
itself, by any scrutiny of its own terms, till light should
be cast upon it by the event. The testimony of John,
clear as it is rendered to us by the subsequent developements of the gospel, might to himself be clouded
with much obscurity; for he, like the other prophets,
uttered not the dictates of his own judgment, genius,
or conjecture; but spake what he had in charge from
God to deliver. Neither can the subsequent hesitation of John[6] be admitted as any bar to our interpretation of the testimony which he was inspired to bear.
We have no reason to think that he was raised above
the current opinion of his countrymen, that the reign
of the Messiah would be established with temporal
authority and power, exercised for the vindication of
the injured and the deliverance of the oppressed; and
that his righteous dominion would greatly consist in

---

[5] 2 Pet. i. 20.   [6] See Matt. xi. 3.

such deeds of honour. That John should have been
so long the victim of unprincipled cruelty ; and apparently neglected, and even abandoned, by the very
person to whom he had borne witness; and his fidelity
to whom had been the occasion of his present sufferings ; were circumstances to put the strongest faith to
the severest trial. Those must know little of human
nature who think it impossible for doubts to arise
under such pressing difficulties. But his message to
Jesus may be justly regarded as the utterance of com-
plaint and remonstrance, rather than of serious doubt:
" If thou art indeed the Hope and Deliverer of Israel,
why dost thou permit thine enemies to triumph? Why
dost thou forsake thy faithful messenger, and leave him
to pine in chains and misery ?"[7]

But, in this very message of embarrassment and de-
spondency, we find an important circumstance of reference to prophecy : " Art thou He that should come,"
—ὁ ἐρχόμενος, *the coming one* ? Now this was a part
of the descriptions of the Messiah occurring in the Old
Testament: the Shiloh that should come,——God,
who would come and save,——the Adonai Jehovah,
who would come to feed his flock,——the Lord, who
would suddenly come to his temple, the Angel of the
covenant.[8]—The Messiah, in the estimation of John,
was distinctively *the coming one ;* but the prophetic

---

[7] " Σὺ εἶ ὁ ἐρχόμενος, ἤ ἕτερον προσδοκῶμεν ; *i. e.* Tu ita agis quasi
non sis Messias, quasi alius exspectandus sit !"—*Borger de Constanti Jesu Christi Indole,* p. 137. Leyden, 1816.

[8] " Facta nimirum cum veteribus de Christo oraculis apertissime
congruentia.——Ille de quo verbum illud veniendi usurpavit Jacobus,
Gen. xlix. 10, et Esais, xxxv. 4." *Grotius* in loc.—Isa. xl. 10.
Mal. iii. 1.

passages which speak of the great expected advent, connect it with plain attributions of the names of Deity to that Coming One.

SUPPLEMENTARY NOTES TO CHAP. II.

Note [A], page 33.

Great difficulty hangs upon the translation and interpretation of this sentence, repeated from verse 15 and 27. The common version and some other high authorities, among whom are Chrysostom and Theophylact (among the ancients, and, probably, the generality of modern interpreters) give an easy sense: "he is before me in dignity, for he was before me in time." But I apprehend that it cannot be sustained with sufficient evidence, because ἔμπροσθεν never, in the LXX., the Apocrypha or the New Testament, or in classical usage, is applied to *rank*, but only to *local situation* and to *time*. Newcome renders ὃς ἔμπροσθέν μου γέγονεν, "who goeth before me:" but this construction cannot be put upon the words. The Calm Inquirer adopts "has got before me, for he was my principal:" and he approves the interpretation of the late Rev. Newcome Cappe, of York, "He who set out after me, whose harbinger I was, ἔμπροσθέν μου γέγονεν, has overtaken and passed me in the career. The idea is taken from the relation of the harbinger to the prince whom he precedes."—*Calm Inq.* p. 39. The precise meaning of γέγονα is, *I have become*, *i. e.* I have come into a state in which I was not before; which certainly may be well rendered by the colloquial phrase, *I have got into* the state or relation in question. A single instance occurs in the LXX. 2 Chron. xiii. 13. "Jeroboam turned the ambuscade to come upon him from behind, and he got before Judah, (ἐγένετο ἔμπροσθεν Ἰούδα.)" On the other hand, the phrase usually refers to time. It is the ordinary expression when the kings of Judah and Israel are characterised as better or worse than those who had "been before them, (οἱ γενόμενοι ἔμπροσθεν αὐτοῦ,") 3 Kings xvi. 25, &c. See also Ecclesiastes i. 10, 16 ; ii. 7 ; iv. 16. But the phrase more exactly occurs in 3 Kings iii. 12. "No one like thee has been before thee, (ὡς σὺ οὐ γέγονεν ἔμπροσθέν σου·)" and in ver. 13, "A man like thee has not been, (οὐ γέγονεν ἀνὴρ ὅμοιός σοι.)" Thus it would appear, that the general current of example and analogy obliges us to understand the phrase, in the passage under consideration, as referring to *time past.*

Undoubtedly πρῶτος is of common occurrence in the sense of *chief* or *principal;* but that is always when eminence in a class or specified denomination is intended. So it is twice used in the LXX. to signify the *chief priest,* (4 Kings xxv. 18 ; 2 Chron. xxvi. 20,) and so we have, the *chief of the captains,* (1 Chron. xi. 11,) the *king's principal friend,* (ib. xxvii. 33,) the *chief commandment,* (Matt. xxii. 38,) the *best robe,* (Luke xv. 22,) the *chief city* of a district, (Acts xvi. 12,) the *chief person* of the island, (ib. xxviii. 7,) and a *chief of sinners,* (1 Tim. i. 15, 16.)——But our instance is not on a par with any of these : and indeed examples of the same construction are extremely rare in Greek writers. There are, so far as I can discover, none in the LXX. or the Apocrypha; and the only one in the New Testament is in this same book, John xv. 18, " If the world hate you, know that it hath hated me *before you,* (ἐμὲ πρῶτον ὑμῶν.)" Another instance occurs in Athenæus, (ed. *Schweighæuser,* vol. v. p. 284,) ΠΡΩΤΗ δὲ εὕρηται ἡ περὶ τοὺς πόδας κίνησις ΤΗΣ διὰ τῶν χειρῶν. " The movement with the feet was invented *before that* with the hands." Another is in Chariton, (ed. *d'Orville,* Amst. 1750, p. 85,) Δεῖ δὲ ΠΡΩΤΟΝ ΤΩΝ ΛΟΓΩΝ ἅπαντας παρεῖναι τοὺς ἀναγκαίους ἐν τῇ δίκῃ. " It is requisite that, *before the pleadings,* all the relations should be present at the trial." The learned editor, in his note on this passage, refers to John i. 15, as an instance of the same construction : and he cites a passage from the Fragments of Manetho (lib. i. 330, collected by James Gronovius, Leyden,1698,) in which occurs γεννήτορα πρῶτον μητέρος, " the father before the mother."——Hoogeveen refers John i. 15, and xv. 18, to the use of the superlative for a comparative, in which case it also governs a genitive. (Not in *Viger. de Idiotism.* Cap. III. Sect. ii. Reg. 11.) Bos and Schwebelius maintain that in these constructions there is an ellipsis of the preposition πρὸ to govern the genitive : " Πρῶτός μου pro πρῶτος vel πρότερος πρό μου. (*Ellipses Græcæ,* sub præp. πρό.)

Another objection to this interpretation of πρῶτος lies in the tense of the verb, which, upon this hypothesis, could not have been ἦν, but must have been in the present, " he is my principal."

The very learned and judicious Morus, however, does not shrink from this embarrassment ; for he renders the two clauses, " me anteit, quia erat reverâ præstantior me :" and the Genevese version of 1805 boldly attaches to each of the expressions the idea of dignity ;

"un homme qui m'a été préféré, parce qu'il était plus excellent que moi." But the impartiality of philological evidence will not allow us, in either of the cases, to turn the words from the idea of time. Kuinöl takes ὅτι in the sense of *certainly, truly, assuredly*, as it is occasionally used by the LXX. to render the Hebrew particles אַךְ and אָכֵן. "Simplicior," he says, "omnino, et orationis seriei convenientior, hæc est: *Qui post me munus suum auspicaturus est, ante me fuit, certè prior me fuit:* repetitur aliis verbis eadem sententia quæ præcessit, quo fortius inculcetur:" "By far the more simple interpretation, and the more agreeable to the connexion, is this, *He who shall enter on his office after me, existed before me; assuredly he was before me.* The sentiment is repeated in other words, to produce a stronger impression." (*Comment. in Libros Hist. N. T.* vol. iii. p. 120.) Wetstein's opinion is not dissimilar. He considers the final clause as a clearer and explanatory declaration of the preceding. Le Clerc, Rosenmüller sen., Tittmann, Lücke, Tholuck, and Olshausen support the interpretation.

A difficulty, however, of another kind exists in this interpretation. The assertion of priority of *time* cannot be understood as if Jesus were older than John; for he was younger, and had it been otherwise, the thing was altogether trivial. It must then be referred, as is observed by Tittmann, Kuinöl, and other critics just mentioned, to the *preexistence* of the Messiah. But the text is expressly, "After me cometh a MAN." We are then in a dilemma. Either we must understand the predicate in a sense contrary to the rules of language: or we must suppose that the Christ is called *a man* (though the reference is to his superior and preexistent nature), by a natural and easy *catachresis*, a figure extremely frequent in the flow of speech; so that the sentiments may be thus expressed; 'A man is following me, as if he were my disciple and inferior; but, notwithstanding his circumstances of humiliation, he really existed before his human birth.' Or the expression may be referred to another kind of tropical diction, the *enallage*; and this would undoubtedly have been Dr. Owen's method of solution, according to the principle which he thus lays down: "Sometimes" the person of Christ "being denominated from one nature, the properties and acts of the other are assigned to it. So, 'They crucified the Lord of glory.' He is the Lord of glory, on account of his divine nature only; and thence is his person *denominated*, when he is said to be crucified, which was in the human nature only. So, on the other side, 'The Son of man who is in heaven.' The *denomination* of the person is from the human nature only; 'the Son of man:' that [property] ascribed to it was with respect unto the divine nature only: 'who is in heaven.'"—*On the Person of Christ*, chap. xviii.

Thus, on both sides difficulties press; and for this reason no conclusion is drawn from this part of John's testimony, in the observations above submitted to the reader's judgment.

Note [B], page 35.

Luke i. 17. Αὐτὸς προελεύσεται ἐνώπιον αὐτοῦ. It is difficult to believe that any principle but a dishonest subserviency to hypothesis, could have dictated the following translations of this most plain and unambiguous clause; "'He will lead the way in the sight of God.' Wakefield, with whom Archbishop Newcome agrees." *Calm. Inq.* p. 218. "He shall go before [Christ] in the sight [of the Lord God.]"—*Impr. Vers.*——Upon men who can thus set at defiance all critical integrity, reasoning and remonstrating would be thrown away.

To evade the argument from this passage, the writer adopts two measures.

1. He flies to his assumption of "the doubtful authenticity of this story." To refute this opinion, we have adduced evidence in the preceding chapter.

2. He adds, "Though strictness of construction warrants the application of the pronoun *him* to the antecedent *God*, yet as the phrase 'Lord our God,' is never applied to Christ in the New Testament, no Jew would ever think of such an application of the words. John was the forerunner of the Lord their God by being the forerunner of Jesus, the great messenger of God to mankind." Pp. 217, 218. To these gratuitous assertions we reply:

(1.) That strictness and even fairness of construction not only "warrants," as he is forced to allow, but *necessitates*, the reference of the pronoun to the antecedent, GOD.

(2.) That the assumption which follows, is a gross begging of the question. The sequel of this inquiry will perhaps enable us to determine whether, if not verbally the same, yet equivalent phrases are not applied to Christ in the New Testament. For the moment, however, let the reader compare two clauses in the solemn and beautiful passage which concludes the book of Revelation, chap. xxii. 6—20. "The Lord, the God of the spirits of the Prophets, hath sent his angel to show unto his servants the things which must come to pass shortly." "I, Jesus, have sent mine angel to testify unto you these things." vers. 6, 16.

(3.) That no Jew, if he knew how to construe grammatically the words before him, could avoid perceiving, that such an application of them was the intention of the writer, whether it might comport or not with his own previous opinions. But we have before found sufficient evidence, that the application of these and other designations of Deity, to the Messiah, was not unknown or unauthorized among the Jews contemporary with the Apostles.

(4.) That the Inquirer's closing sentence, meant as an interpretation, is a gratuitous assertion, destitute of proof, and contrary to the fair and legitimate use of language.

Note [C], page 36.

" He will commence his religion with a more powerful baptism than I. I have only water, but he hath a twofold baptism.——He will baptize with the Holy Spirit; *i. e.* he will pour out, in the richest abundance, the supernatural gifts of.the Holy Spirit, namely prophecy and miracles, (which took place on the remarkable pentecost ;) and those who reject him he will plunge into a sea of fire. The temple, Jerusalem, and almost the whole land of Judæa, became literally the prey of the flames : though the term *fire*, in this place, may equally comprehend. all the righteous punishments which the Messiah should inflict."—*Michaelis Anmerk. z. Matt.* iii. 11.

" If we compare the expressions in vers. 10 and 12, we can scarcely have a doubt that the *baptism with fire* signifies the awful punishments which the Messiah will inflict upon the wicked. John shows why he describes the Messiah as much greater than himself. He (says the Baptist) who will enter upon his office after me, will not only bestow excellent gifts on men, but, as their Lord, will chastise the disobedient; while I, his unworthy subject and servant, can only bind men to reformation by the solemn rite of baptism, and thus prepare the way for him as the Messiah.——Ver. 12. The sense is, He accurately discriminates the good and the wicked, for he sees through the inmost recesses of the mind."—*Rosenmüller in Matt.* iii. 11, 12.

CHAP. III.

IT entered into the scheme of divine wisdom that, while the Messiah was actually sojourning among men, and was pursuing the preliminary objects of his mission, the truth concerning his person and offices, and other characteristics of his dispensations, should be gradually and slowly unfolded. He himself lay in deep obscurity, during all but a very short period of his life. After he had begun his public labours, it was long before he unreservedly and openly declared himself to be the Messiah. Till towards the end of his course, he rarely made this avowal but in private, and to those who were his friends and tried adherents; and, on several occasions, he prohibited them from publishing the fact to the world. Such a plan of studied reserve and slow developement would not have been chosen or approved by human wisdom: but, whether we can penetrate the reasons for it or not, the fact itself is indisputable, that such was the course adopted by the Founder of our faith. He seems to have deemed this the proper course to be taken;—to awaken the attention of men, to stimulate their expectations, to present them with circumstances, hints, and implications, and thus to furnish a growing body of *data*, from which they for themselves might, in due time, draw the most important conclusions with increasing light and certainty.

Besides this, it is to be observed, that the Lord Jesus professedly withheld the full manifestation of his doctrines, till the period subsequent to his death and resurrection ; when the instruments of communication were to be his inspired messengers. The evangelists repeatedly observe, that our Lord's most intimate disciples " understood not those things, and the word " was hidden from them, and they knew not the things " spoken," by him.[1] But he assured them that, though they were not then competent to receive many important things *concerning* HIMSELF, they should subsequently become so, and should be led by an unerring Guide into a perfect knowledge of those truths.[2]

If we duly consider these features of the early Christian economy, we shall not expect to find a full declaration of the doctrine respecting our Lord's person, in the narratives of the Evangelists, or in his own discourses ; but we shall rather look for *intimations*, for *principles implied* in facts and assertions, and for *conclusions* from such facts and assertions deduced by minute attention and close examination on our own part. Such attention and examination are a part of that " obedience of faith," which is the indispensable duty of every man who has, or can obtain, a knowledge of the inspired volume.

[1] See Luke ix. 45 ; xviii. 34. John xii. 16, &c.
[2] See John xvi. 12—15.

CAPITULE I.

DECLARATIONS MADE OR ACQUIESCED IN, BY JESUS CHRIST, ELU-
CIDATING THE IMPORT OF THE APPELLATION, SON OF GOD.

ALL mankind, and, on the same principle, all other
intelligent creatures, are justly called *children* or *sons
of God*, as they are the offspring of his power and
beneficence.[1] In a more restricted and of course a
higher sense, the Scriptures give this title to persons
who are dignified with any special kind of resemblance,
or any constituted relation to God. Thus kings and
other magistrates, who bear some shadow of supremacy and government,[2] the worshippers of the true
God, in distinction from debased idolaters,[3] and especially the faithful and obedient servants of the Most

[1] " Have we not all one Father? Hath not one God created us?"
Mal. ii. 10. " We are the offspring of God." Acts xvii. 29. " When
the morning stars sang together, and all the sons of God shouted for
joy." Job xxxviii. 7, and i. 6.

[2] Psalm lxxxii. 6. " I said, gods are ye! And sons of the Most
High, all of you!" The Psalmist appears to use the language of an
ironical concession, in order to give the greater force to the humiliating contrast which instantly follows.—So the heathen called their
heroes διογενεῖς, διοτρεφεῖς and *diis geniti*. In the earlier ages, it was
believed that those persons were the physical offspring of the gods;
and afterwards the style was kept up by the ignorance of the people
and the audacity of political flatterers.

[3] Gen. vi. 4. Deut. xxxii. 19. Psa. ii. 7. The application of
Dan. iii. 25, is disputable.

High,[4] who are " conformed to the image" of his moral excellency, are, on these respective accounts, styled *sons of God*.

The MESSIAH is called THE SON OF GOD, once at least in the Old Testament : in the New, as all know, the epithet is of frequent occurrence.   It is evident, however, that the application of this name to Christ will prove no superiority of nature, nor any dignity but such as we have just mentioned ; unless it should be accompanied with other circumstances of description, pointing out a different *ground* of application. This ground and reason, therefore, requires our principal attention.

[4] In numerous passages.

Section I.

SON OF THE MOST HIGH.

" He shall be great, and he shall be called THE SON OF THE MOST HIGH; and
" the Lord God shall give unto him the throne of David his father; and he shall
" reign over the house of Jacob for ever, and of his kingdom there shall be no end."
—Luke i. 32.

THIS is the first instance of the occurrence of this
term in the history of Jesus Christ; and a reason of
the appellation is assigned, plainly referring it to his
dignity as a Sovereign. If he had literally occupied
the throne of Israel, if his reign had been of this
world, we should have been authorized to understand
the title as merely falling under the description just
before mentioned, in which magistrates and chieftains
are called *sons of the Most High.* But this was not
the fact. The case turns out immensely different.
The dominion of the Messiah, in its nature, purposes,
subjects, authority, power, extent, and duration, is
infinitely above comparison with the empires of men:
and it will be remembered that, in the various imagery
of this representation, the Messiah is preeminently
exhibited in the Old Testament.[1] Therefore, before
we can, on safe principles of interpretation, determine
the sense of the title as here applied to him, we must
obtain a satisfactory knowledge of the *peculiar* nature
of his regal office and dominion. We must ponder

[1] See Vol. I. pp. 256, 264, 291—293.

well, that it is an empire over mind and conscience, requiring not only outward acknowledgments but an inward and spiritual homage, an allegiance of faith and the most radical affections of the soul; in short, the whole course of duty involved in religious responsibility, that which is the *peculiar* domain of God, and of God only. But further light will accrue to this subject, from future parts of our inquiry.

SECTION II.

" The Holy Spirit shall come upon thee; and the power of the Most High
" shall overshadow thee: on which account the Holy Offspring shall be called THE
" SON OF GOD."—Luke i. 35.[1]

HERE it is manifest, that the production of the
Messiah's human nature, by the immediate operation
of God, is assigned as the reason of the appellation.
The words of the passage are evidently selected with
a view to convey, in the most emphatical manner, the
idea of such a miraculous production. Whatever
may be our opinion on the general meaning of the
term HOLY SPIRIT, it cannot be doubted that, in this
instance, the design of the whole expression is to
represent a peculiar exercise of almighty power, for
the production of an extraordinary effect. This act
of the Holy Spirit is put in parallelism with "the
power of the Most High." It is said to "come upon"
her, and to "overshadow" her: expressions which,
agreeably to the scriptural usage, mark the exercise
of a peculiar, extraordinary, and divine energy.[2] The

[1] In this and the last cited passage, though there is no article
before Υἱός, it must be translated with the definite article, since the
noun is the predicate of a verb of designation or appellation. See
Middleton on the Greek Article, p. 62, where also is quoted the
decisive authority of the ancient Greek grammarian Apollonius.

[2] See in the LXX. Psalm xc. (xci.) 4; cxxxix. (cxl.) 7. "The
verb ἐπισκιάζειν answers to ἐνδύεσθαι, which the writers of the Old
Testament use in passages when the Spirit of God is said *to take*

uncommon expression also, " the holy offspring," seems
to be especially adapted to denote that the child
would be produced in a way different from the generation of the rest of mankind. On the appellation,
Son of the Most High, Kuinöl observes " that it
seems to be used to signify that Christ was procreated
by an immediate divine intervention : in which sense
Adam also is called " the Son of God."[3] The Messiah was to be a new Head of the human race, a
" second Adam," to retrieve the apostasy and remedy
the ruin of the first.[4] It was, therefore, proper that
he should be produced, as the first Adam was, by the
immediate power of the Creator. Not only was it
proper, on the ground of a becoming distinction and
superior dignity; but it was absolutely *necessary*,
unless some other equivalent miracle had been
wrought, of which however we can form no rational
idea, in order that the Deliverer from moral corruption might not himself be the subject of it. The
experience of all mankind has demonstrated that depraved moral propensities, both in their general
nature and in their numerous specific varieties, are
propagated, however mysterious is the mode of this
humiliating fact, by the physical descent of human
beings from their progenitors.[5] But, by an obvious

men, to *come upon* them, or to *rest upon* them; and thus to exert
his power upon them. The expression therefore intimates that
Mary should bear a son, by the interposition of divine power."—
Rosenm. in loc.

[3] *Comment. in Libros. Hist. N. T.* vol. ii. p. 271, and see Luke
iii. 38.

[4] Passages in the Rabbinical writings are adduced by Schöttgen,
from which it appears that the Jews applied to the Messiah the terms
Last Adam and *Heavenly Adam.*—*Horæ Hebr. et Talmud.* i. 670.

[5] " In order to account for a sinful corruption of nature, yea, a

necessity of reason, he who was to be the Saviour from sin, was not to be subjected to this connate predisposition to sin. The supposition involves a contradiction ; for, had it been so, he would have needed a Saviour for himself. But it was not so. He was " [TO γεννώμενον 'ΑΓΙΟΝ] the Holy thing produced," or " the Holy Offspring."—Such a High Priest was necessary for us ; holy, guiltless, spotless, separated from sinners."[6]

total native depravity of the heart of man, there is not the least need of supposing any evil quality, infused, implanted, or wrought into the nature of man, by any positive cause or influence whatsoever, either from God or the creature ; or of supposing that man is conceived and born with a fountain of evil in his heart, such as is any thing properly positive. I think, a little attention to the nature of things will be sufficient to satisfy any impartial, considerate, inquirer, that the *absence of positive good principles*, and so the withholding of a special divine influence to impart and maintain those good principles, (leaving the common, natural principles of self-love, natural appetite, &c. to themselves, without the government of superior divine principles,)—will certainly be followed with the corruption, yea, the total corruption, of the heart, without occasion for any positive influence at all."—*Edwards on Orig. Sin.* Part IV. ch. ii. sect. 2.

   [6] Heb. vii. 26.

SECTION III.

SON OF GOD, IN A HIGHER SENSE.

The title, SON OF GOD, a known designation of the Messiah.—Not a synonym.—
Understood to imply a superior and even Divine nature.

" The beginning of the glad tidings concerning Jesus the Christ the SON OF
" GOD." Mark i. 1.   " This is my BELOVED SON, in whom I am well pleased."
Matt. iii. 17.   " I have seen and borne witness, that this is the SON OF GOD."
John i. 34.   " Thou art the Christ, the SON OF THE LIVING GOD." Matt. xvi. 16,
" Art thou the Christ the SON OF GOD?" Ib. xxvi. 63.   " —— the SON OF THE
" BLESSED?" Mark xiv. 61.

THESE passages, and some others parallel or similar
in the four Gospels, furnish the following results.

1. The title, *Son of God*, was recognised by Jesus
himself, by his friends and followers, by his enemies,
and by the Jewish nation at large, as a designation of
the Messiah. This acceptation seems to have been
universally known and indisputably held. It must,
therefore, have had a satisfactory and authoritative
origin; or it could not have been so received and
established. Such an origin is most naturally to be
sought in the Prophetic Scriptures. Nowhere else
could an authority be found to which the whole
Jewish nation would bow, and to which it would, at
the same time, be congruous for the Divine Majesty
itself to conform. This title we have already found
among the prophetic descriptions of the Messiah, and
we have seen that it was recognised in the Jewish
theology of the period intermediate between the Old
and the New Testament.[1]

[1] Vol. I. pp. 290, 567, 589.

2. Though it be undoubtedly an appropriated appellation of the Messiah, it is not a mere synonym of that word. Some respectable writers [2] have fallen into this inaccuracy. Two or more terms may be generally, or even with an exclusive uniformity, applied to the same object, and yet be respectively of very different import. Christ is called Lord, Mediator, Saviour, Prince of Life, Captain of Salvation, King of kings: but it would betray great ignorance or rashness to say, that these were *synonymous* expressions. The term *Messiah* designates a person divinely appointed and consecrated to one or more of the offices of a king, a priest, or a prophet. The other term, unless it be taken in a sense wholly figurative, is manifestly expressive of the *nature* of the being to whom it is applied, and of a *natural relationship* to another person. The frequent instances in which these two designations are put in apposition, strongly imply that each presents the same object, but under a different view or with a different relation. [3]

3. It becomes, therefore, important for us to ascer-

[2] *Calm Inquiry*, p. 261. Also J. D. Michaelis, Rosenmüller, sen. &c. Grotius says with more discrimination, "Apparet hoc cognomen vulgò Messiæ datum."—*Annot. in Matt.* xiv. 33.

[3] Besides the instances quoted at the head of this section, see John vi. 69, "Thou art the Christ, the Son of God:" ib. xi. 27.—xx. 31, "These things are written, that ye may believe that Jesus is the Christ, the Son of God." Acts ix. 20, "He preached the Christ, that he is the Son of God." Rom. i. 1—4, "—Jesus Christ —the powerfully demonstrated Son of God." The reply of Nathanael may be properly added to these passages, as the style *King of Israel* is acknowledged to be equivalent to *Messiah*: John i. 49, "Teacher, thou art the Son of God; thou art the King of Israel!" We do not suppose that Nathanael understood, at that time, the full import of the expression; but that he was merely using a term which was, in the usual speech of his countrymen, a designation of

tain, whether this epithet be given to Christ in one of its figurative meanings stated above, or in a strict and proper sense. Now, if the former were the fact, if the Messiah were styled *the Son of God* merely as an expression of his royal dignity, or preeminent sanctity, or prophetic mission, how could we conceive that his claiming this appellation, or his admitting, on the interrogation of an enemy, that it belonged to him, could be made the ground of a charge of *blas-phemy?* A proof so broad and palpable in the opinion of the Jewish lawyers, as to render further inquiry needless, and to be decisive of the alleged guilt.[4] The law of Israel against blasphemy was expressed with the utmost precision. "Whosoever "curseth his God shall bear his sin : and he who blas-"phemeth the name of Jehovah shall surely be put to "death ; all the congregation shall surely stone him : "as well the foreigner as the native ; for his blasphem-"ing THE NAME he shall be put to death."[5] The cases of real or imputed blasphemy which occur in the Old Testament, and in the Apocrypha, all wear this distinctive character ;[6] they are a *reproaching,* a *contempt,*

the eagerly expected Messiah, and to which they attached ideas of an obscure and mysterious grandeur.

[4] "The high-priest said to him, I adjure thee by the living God, "that thou tell us whether thou art the Christ the Son of the living "God ! Jesus saith to him, Thou hast said," [in the Hebrew idiom equivalent to *I am; as* it is given in Mark xiv. 62.] "Then the "high-priest rent his garments, saying, He has blasphemed ! What "further need have we of witnesses ? Behold, you have now heard "his blasphemy !" Matt. xxvi. 63, 65. "We have a law ; and accord-"ing to that law he ought to die, because he hath made himself the "Son of God." John xix. 7.

[5] Lev. xxiv. 15, 16.

[6] In the instances of Naboth, Rabshakeh, Sennacherib, Antiochus,

a *designed insult*, upon the name and attributes of the living God, or of some supposed deity. He would be guilty of "blaspheming the NAME," who should apply " that fearful and glorious name" to an idol, inanimate or animate : and, most evidently, he would not be less chargeable with the same crime, who could have the boldness to apply it unwarrantably to *himself!* Of this latter form of blasphemy Sennacherib was guilty, in ascribing to himself powers and a command over success and victory, such as can belong to none but an omnipotent being.' The Mishna enumerates blasphemy among the crimes to be punished with the highest kind of capital punishment, that of being stoned to death ; and adds, " No one is to be esteemed a blasphemer unless he has expressly uttered THE NAME ;"' that is, the revered word JEHOVAH. Blasphemy, therefore, in the Jewish sense, is justly defined by Schleusner to be, " the saying or doing any thing by which the majesty of God is insulted, uttering curses or reproaches against God, speaking impiously, arrogating and taking to one's self that which belongs

Nicanor, &c. See 1 Kings xxi. 10 ; 2 Kings xix. 22 ; Isaiah lii. 5 ; Dan. iii. 29 in LXX.; Bel and the Dragon, ver. 9 ; 2 Maccab. ix. 28 ; xv. 3, 5, 24.

' See 2 Kings xix. 22—24.

' *Tract. de Sanhedrim, in Mischna Surenhusii,* vol. iv. pp. 238—242. The Mishna is a body of Rabbinical interpretations of the written law, pretended to have been revealed to Moses on Mount Sinai, and to have been handed down by tradition to the Prophets, the Great Sanhedrim, &c. and finally to have been committed to writing by Rabbi Judah the holy. Dr. Lardner assigns A. D. 180 or 190 as the probable period of its compilation.—*Jewish Testim.* chap. v. The work contains internal evidence of being a collection of traditions really very ancient, far beyond the time of the compiler. —See *Prideaux's Connexion,* i. 326, &c.

to God."[9] In this latter sense the Jews manifestly understood it, when they said, "We stone thee for blasphemy, and that thou, being a man, makest thyself God."[10]

This was the crime which Caiaphas and the Sanhedrim affirmed that Jesus had in very fact committed in their presence, and for which they instantly passed judgment of death. Let it be observed, that, according to the hypothesis of the Unitarians, Jesus, in admitting that he was the Messiah, claimed nothing above the rank and functions of a human being, nothing beyond an office, august indeed and venerable, but which every Jew believed would be executed by a mere man. To those who rejected his claim, he might have appeared chargeable with fanaticism, imposture, or even constructive treason: but where was the colourable pretext for the charge of *blasphemy*, a crime so closely defined by the original law, and the limits of which were so anxiously fixed by the tradition which had all the force of law? Let it also be observed, that the apparent reason of the charge was so clear as to admit of no demur or hesitation. Had the High-priest and the Sanhedrim been proceeding upon grounds which they were conscious were notoriously false; had they applied the law of blasphemy to a case in which it was manifest that not the semblance of that offence had been committed; it is credible that they would have adopted some circuitous course for the accom-

---

[9] " Dicere et facere quibus majestas Dei violatur, maledicum in Deum esse, impiè loqui, arrogare sibi et sumere quæ sunt Dei."— *Schleusn. Lex.* voce βλασφημέω.

[10] John x. 33.

plishment of their purpose. But they did no such thing : they found their way plain before them. If, however, we were to concede to Dr. Campbell,[11] that the Sanhedrim imputed this crime to Jesus dishonestly upon their own principles, it would only follow that they gave a wrong name to their charge. The allegation was, that he had, by claiming to be the Son of God, arrogated to himself *divine honours ;* and this, as a fact, remains the same, whether it was designated rightly or not by the term *blasphemy.*

It is not unworthy of remark, that Josephus mentions various instances of impostors, who rose up about the time of the siege of Jerusalem, calling themselves prophets, announcing to their adherents a speedy deliverance by divine interposition from their calamities, and " promising to show signs and præternatural appearances" for that purpose.[12] From comparing our Lord's prediction[13] with the facts which he relates, it appears probable that several of those persons gave out themselves to be the Messiah. But, though the historian paints in strong colours their falsehood and their other atrocities, he never, so far as I can discover, charges them with *blasphemy.*

It seems, therefore, impossible for us to escape the conclusion, that the avowal of Jesus that he was THE SON OF GOD was understood, by the highest legal and ecclesiastical authorities of his country, to be more than declaring himself to be the Messiah, and to involve the assertion of something belonging to his person that was superhuman and DIVINE ; or to be a

[11] *On the Four Gospels,* Dissert. ix. part ii.
[12] *De Bello Jud.* lib. vi. cap. v. sect. 3 ; lib. vii. cap. xi. sect. 1.
[13] Mark xiii. 6.

constructive assumption of such dignity as belongs only to God.

That such ideas of dignity and powers, above what belong to the rank of man, were attached to this epithet by the Jewish people at large, is at least a probable inference from the taunting language which they held to our Lord in his last sufferings: "If thou art the Son of God, come down from the cross."[14]

This conclusion is corroborated by another of the passages cited at the beginning of this Section. "Who, do men say, that I, the Son of Man, am?—Who say ye that I am?—Thou art the Christ, the Son of the living God."[15] The position of the terms plainly intimates, that the appellation, *Son of the living God,* was conceived by Peter to be of higher dignity than the other, *Son of Man,* which was the designation most commonly assumed by our Lord himself, evidently as the least offensive profession of being the Messiah. Neither is it probable that the two terms, *the Christ* and *the Son of God,* would have been used, if they were tautological. Our Lord further declares that the fact affirmed by Peter was not properly apprehended but by divine instruction; "Happy "art thou, Simon son of Jonas, for flesh and blood" (a well known Jewish idiom, denoting the unassisted principles and powers of human nature) "hath not "revealed [it] unto thee; but my Father who is in the "heavens." But surely it required no such divine influence to enable a man, who had so copiously witnessed the evidences of the claims advanced by Jesus, to perceive the rational conclusion from those evidences. Peter needed but the common understanding

[14] Matt. xxvii. 40.   [15] Matt. xvi. 13—19.

of men, to receive the proof of the Messiahship of Jesus. The fact thus asserted by the Saviour, of a special divine influence enabling Peter to make this good confession, suggests to us also the strong probability that the apostle did not at present comprehend the full import of the declaration which he made. The subsequent teachings of the Holy Spirit would bring it to his remembrance, with a much higher measure of knowledge and understanding. It is further worthy of being observed, that Christ immediately connects his being the Son of God with the exercise of sovereign authority and power, in relation to the salvation of men and to matters of moral obligation: yet *this* is the sole province of Deity. " I will build " my church: the gates of hell shall not prevail against " it: I will give unto thee the keys of the kingdom of " heaven." Let a man seriously reflect on the magnitude of this work, the power requisite to accomplish it, and the nature of the ground of certainty here assumed that it should be accomplished; and can he refuse to exclaim, " From Jehovah is this: It is marvellous in our eyes!"[16]

[16] Ps. cxviii. 23.

SECTION IV.

HIS PERSON, EQUALLY WITH THAT OF THE FATHER, SURPASSING
HUMAN KNOWLEDGE.

Intimate and accurate knowledge expressed in the terms.—Such knowledge communicated by divine influence.—This communication the province of Christ.—
The inherent knowledge of the Father, and of Christ, reciprocal.—Both expressed in convertible terms.

" All things have been committed to me by my Father; and no one knoweth
" perfectly the Son, except the Father; neither doth any one know perfectly the
" Father, except the Son, and he to whom the Son may be pleased to unveil [this
" knowledge]."   Matt. xi. 27.   " As the Father knoweth me, even so I know the
" Father."—John x..15.

THE passage in the Gospel of Luke parallel to the
preceding one in that of Matthew, has this difference:
" No one knoweth who the Son is, except the Father:
and who the Father is, except the Son." In such
cases it appears a reasonable maxim to consider the
actual phraseology of the speaker, as it was uttered in
the vernacular language of Judæa, to have been susceptible of both the modes of the Greek expression;
so that the one may be taken as an assistance of the
highest authority, for the explication of the other.
On this principle, the seeming discrepancy in the present instance vanishes; for ἐπιγινώσκειν, used by
Matthew, signifying such *knowledge* as is peculiarly
intimate and *accurate*, *full* and *perfect*,[1] will well

---

[1] The force of ἐπι, in composition, appears to be *closeness*, in
situation or in succession.   See *Dunbar on the Greek Prepositions.*
If the reader will examine the diversities of meaning laid down by

comport with Luke's phrase γινώσκειν τίς ἐστιν. If
this observation be just, it nullifies Mr. Belsham's
interpretation of the words,[2] and shows that the
knowledge refers primarily to the *nature* and *person*
of the Father and of the Son ; " WHO he is." This
writer triumphs in what he regards to be a key to the
passage ; that what a man may learn of God, by the
revelation of the Son, is nothing but his revealed will.
But it is not the *will* of God, strictly speaking, either
decretive or preceptive, that is the sole object of
revelation. A manifestation of the peculiar excellencies and glorious *perfections* of God, as the Supreme
and Infinite Possessor of all natural and moral good,
is no small part of the design of revealed truth : and
this is a species of knowledge in the highest degree
necessary to piety and happiness. It is such knowledge as is not merely intellectual, but is associated
with a sense of beauty, sweetness, and worth, exciting
the affections of love and delight, and every grateful
sensation of the mind. This mental sense of moral
loveliness, in our conceptions of the Divine Being,

Schleusner, and study all his and many more examples, he will find
them in general, if not universally, reducible to this as their circumstance of distinction from γινώσκειν. Among other renderings he
has, " *sensu cognosco, satis cognitum habeo, idoneâ scientiâ imbuor ;
passivè accipio pleniorem et perfectiorem cognitionem.*" Under
Ἐπίγνωσις he says, " speciatim, *major, perfectior, et exactior cognitio
et scientia ;* nam ἐπὶ in compositis haud rarò auget significationem."

[1] " It is plain that he to whom the Son reveals the Father
knows the Father. But what can a man thus learn of God?
Nothing surely but his revealed will. In the same sense, precisely,
the Son knows the Father, *i. e.* he knows his will, his thoughts, and
purposes of mercy to mankind. And the Father alone knows the
Son, knows the nature, the object, and the extent of his mission."—
Calm Inq. p. 187.

forms the great distinction between the true and the nominal believer. I am aware that this doctrine will meet only the scorn of those who hold the system on which I feel myself bound to animadvert; but I must not, for that reason, shrink from avowing it. To this momentous and interesting truth, I conceive, our blessed Lord refers in the instance of Peter, which may be taken as a special case under the general fact stated in the passage before us: " Happy art thou; " for flesh and blood hath not revealed this to thee, but " MY FATHER who is in heaven." This is a glory to which they are blind who " will not behold the majesty of the Lord:" but of all genuine Christians it is declared, that " God, who commanded the light " to shine out of darkness, hath shined in their hearts, " to their illumination with the knowledge of the glory " of God, in the face of Jesus Christ."¹

The passages under consideration, on due examination, are found to include these statements of truth:

¹ 2 Cor. iv. 6. Some good authorities translate ἐν προσώπῳ, " in the person of Jesus Christ." But, as there is probably an allusion to " the face of Moses" concealed by a veil, (ch. iii. 7, 13,) the other term appears preferable. The subject intended, however, is manifestly Christ, personally, as representing the grandeur and amiableness of the divine character towards men, in the constitution of the gospel and its practical effect. The elder Rosenmüller says, on this passage; " The *glory of God in the face of Christ* consisted in this, —that those who beheld Christ on earth, as the Teacher of divine truth, perceived God representing himself in the doctrine and miracles of Christ." But that might be only a "knowing Christ according to the flesh," which alone had no beneficial effect. (ch. v. 16.) The knowledge here spoken of is of a spiritual and far more excellent kind: it belongs to all true Christians, and it is the basis of their pure and active faith. In Christ, " though now they see him not, they rejoice with joy unspeakable and full of glory."

1. That the communication to mankind of the doctrines which refer to their highest interest in knowledge, holiness, and happiness, is by a constitution of
Divine wisdom, made the province of the Messiah, as
the Mediator between God and man. The " all things
committed[4] to him by the Father," are evidently the
important and humbling truths of the gospel, which he
had just before mentioned as " hidden from the wise
and prudent." Now, the KNOWLEDGE OF GOD, in all
the ways which have appeared good to infinite wisdom
and rectitude, forms, as we have before observed, an
essential part of the blessings communicated by the
Christian revelation, when known and received according to its proper design.

2. That this knowledge of the Father and knowledge of Christ, are expressed in the way of a perfect
reciprocity. The description and properties of the
one, are the description and properties of the other ;
without limitation on the one side, or extension on the
other. Is it conceivable that a wise and good teacher,
conscious of no dignity above that which was strictly
and merely human, or arising only from his office and
delegated powers, would select, for the purpose of
conveying what might have been expressed in plain
words, language which unquestionably describes himself and the Eternal Being by *equivalent* and *convertible*
terms ?[5]

[4] Παρεδόθη, so used in Luke i. 3 ; 1 Cor. xv. 3 ; and therefore
doctrines are called παραδόσεις in 2 Thess. ii. 15 ; 1 Cor. xi. 2, &c.
[5] The *Monthly Repos.* Reviewer considers the phraseology of
these passages as of similar import to that in Matt. v. 48 ; and, he
might have added, Pet. i. 15. He says, " Precisely in the same
manner as when the disciples were exhorted to *be perfect as their
Father in heaven is perfect*, they and the Eternal are described in

3. That, in relation to both the Father and the Son, this knowledge is not attainable by the ordinary means of human investigation. Now, this cannot be said of the gracious will and purpose of God in showing mercy to mankind; nor of the nature, object, and extent of the mission of Jesus, as the instructor and reformer of the world. On both these topics, a considerable degree of information was not only accessible, but was actually possessed by many persons. But such a knowledge of the unspeakable glory of the Divine perfections as appears to be here intended, is

equivalent and convertible terms." (P. 66.) I am astonished at this assertion of the acute and ingenious writer. Is it possible that he cannot see the wide discrepance between the cases? On the one side, are *commands* to that which is the indispensable duty of every rational creature, a conformity, to the highest reach of his powers and capacities, to the moral perfection of God, his holiness and beneficence: on the other, *declarations*, in plain narrative terms, of an existing twofold fact, each of whose parts corresponds to the other. Alas! It is the case in this, as in other instances of religious controversies upon subjects which lie at the very base of the fabric, that we seem to have no ultimate community of judgment, no perception of the ground of evidence, lower than which we cannot go; for the next step could only be to the axiom, that the same thing cannot both be and not be, all the relations being the same.—Thus: it is shown, in regard to the first principles of theology, which MUST BE the foundation of personal religion, that our intellectual determinations, and the state of our affections towards God (in scripture language, the *eye* and the *heart*,) have the strongest influence upon each other; but that the governing power lies in the latter. Would to God that myself and all my readers felt this great fact as we ought!—Then should we better understand the spirit of those models for our prayers; " Open mine eyes; let my heart be sound in thy " statutes; lead me in thy truth!—That the God of our Lord Jesus " Christ, the Father of glory, may give unto you the Spirit of wisdom " and revelation, in the acknowledgment of HIM; the eyes of your " heart being enlightened!" (Eph. i. 17, 18; *heart* is the reading of the best editions, supported by ample authority).

a far more sublime attainment : it is fundamental to a saving and practical knowledge of true religion; it has its seat in the affections as well as in the intellect ; and it is here affirmed to be a special communication of Divine influence.

4. That this knowledge, as existing in the state of communication from Christ to any of mankind ."to whom the Son may be pleased to unveil" it, though the same in kind, cannot be imagined to be the same in *degree* or *extent;* unless it be assumed that the capacity and attainment of the instructed, must, as a matter of course, be equal to those of the INSTRUCTOR.

5. Had the member of the sentence which introduces the Son as the object of knowledge been wanting, I think that the obvious, and probably the generally admitted, interpretation of the remaining part of the passage, would have been, that it referred to the *peculiar glories* of the Divine Being, or THAT which distinctively constitutes him God. Had it stood thus ; " No one knoweth God, or WHO God is, except Jesus of Nazareth, and those to whom Jesus may communicate the knowledge ;"—would it not have unquestionably conveyed this position, that the Infinite Majesty and Perfection of the Adorable Supreme, as distinguished from the imaginary deities of the heathen world, were revealed and demonstrated by the christian religion alone ? Would any one have controverted the propriety of this paraphrase ?—Restore, then, the clause which has been withdrawn ; and will not fairness of interpretation require us to accept it, as *equally* attributing to the Son *the same* Infinite Majesty and Perfection ?

Section V.

SON OF GOD, CLAIMING A PARITY IN POWER AND HONOUR WITH
THE FATHER.

State of the question between Jesus and his opponents.—Characters of subordination belonging to Christ:—Mission,—Reception of a function,—Accurate
knowledge,—Judicial commission.—Characters of supremacy:—Parity of
power,—Ability to confer physical life,—Determining the final state of men,—
Claim of supreme homage.—Observations on Mr. Lindsey's and Mr. Belsham's
interpretation.

" Jesus answered them, My Father worketh until now: I also work. On this
" account, therefore, the Jews were the more eager to put him to death, that he not
" only broke the Sabbath, but even called God his own Father; making himself
" equal to God.
" Then Jesus answered and said to them, Verily, verily, I say to you; the Son
" can do nothing from himself; [he doeth] only what he seeth the Father doing :
" for whatever things he doeth, those things the Son also doeth in like manner.
" For the Father loveth the Son, and sheweth to him all things which he himself
" doeth : and he will shew to him greater works than these, that ye may admire.
" Because, as the Father raiseth and giveth life to the dead, so the Son also giveth
" life to whom he willeth.　And neither doth the Father pass judgment upon any
" one : but the whole [exercise of] judgment he hath given to the Son, that all may
" honour the Son as they honour the Father.　He who honoureth not the Son,
" honoureth not the Father who hath sent him. Verily, verily, I say to you; that
" he who attendeth to my word and confideth in him that hath sent me, hath eternal
" life, and into [condemnatory] judgment he cometh not, but is passed over from
" death to life.　Verily, verily, I say to you; that the hour is coming, and now it
" is, when the dead shall hear the voice of the Son of God, and hearing they shall
" live.　For, as the Father hath life in himself, so he hath given to the Son also to
" have life in himself: and he hath given to him authority also to exercise judg-
" ment, because he is the Son of man.　Be not astonished at this : for the hour is
" coming, in which all who are in the tombs shall hear his voice and shall come
" forth ; those who have done good actions to the resurrection of life, but those who
" have done base actions to the resurrection of [condemnatory] judgment.　Not
" that I can do any thing from myself.　As I hear, [i. e. am instructed,] I judge ;
" and my judgment is righteous, for I seek not mine own will, but the will of him
" who sent me."——" The works, which the Father assigned to me in order that
" I might finish them, those very works which I do, testify concerning me that
" the Father sent me."—John v. 17—30, 36.[1]

[1] Ver. 17.　" Mon Père agit continuellement, et je le fais aussi."
New Genevese Version.　Ver. 19.　" —— aus eigenem triebe,"

To collect satisfactorily the information contained
in this important passage, it is, in the first place,
necessary to have a clear view of the STATE OF THE
CAUSE between the Lord Jesus and the Jews who
opposed him. The question turned upon the RIGHT
*to perform works on the day appropriated, by the
divine command, to cessation from labour.* For an
act performed on the Sabbath, Jesus was charged
with the immorality of breaking the fourth commandment. This charge he had to repel. The most
obvious course, and which on other occasions of
the like kind he took,[2] was to plead the *character of the work*, that it was an act of mercy and
beneficence; and that the performing of such acts,
however laborious and troublesome, was known to be
strictly consistent with the law. But he took a course
entirely different. He advanced a claim of *superiority
to the law.* He adduced the example of God his
Father, who carries on the operations of nature and
providence without a sabbatic rest or any intermission
whatsoever; and he asserted his own right to do the
same: " My Father worketh until now; I ALSO
work."[3] Let the serious reader impartially reflect

' of his own impulse.' *J. D. Michaelis.* The different rendering of
γὰρ in. vers. 20, 21, 22, appears necessary to convey the sense in our
own language, as it is not only a causal particle, but frequently its
only force is connexive and continuative. Vers. 25, 28. Michaelis,
Tittmann, the New Genevese, and Van Ess, render ὥρα very properly
by the more general term, *time.* The sense given to ἀκούω in ver. 30,
is supported by chap. iii. 32: viii. 26; xv. 15.

[2] See Matt. xii. 12. Luke xiii. 14; xiv. 3.

[3] Thus paraphrased by Semler. "Deus, Pater meus, nullâ sabbati
religione impeditus, nunquam non digna ipso opera per omnem
mundum corporeum efficit; itaque similia licet et me pari jure
efficere."—" God, my Father, under no restriction from the law of

upon the fair meaning and the implications of these words. The subject is works of *power*. The speaker puts *his own* work of power, in the miraculous cure which he had effected, on the *same footing* of consideration, as the works of the Deity in the conservation and government of the universe : and *upon this parity*, he grounds his right thus to work on the sabbath-day. If we suppose that Jesus was conscious of no relation to the Deity except such as belonged to a mere human being, or to any other mere creature, can we free his assertion and his argument from extreme absurdity and arrogant impiety ?

His opponents understood him as adhering to his crime, and aggravating it. They conceived him to be " making himself equal to God." He did not deny their inference. He did not protest against their construction of his words. Yea, he proceeded to use language plainly *confirmatory* of what he had before said, and which was understood to be so by those who heard him.[4] In this second speech we find that remarkable mixture of *characters of subordination* with *characters of supremacy*, which we have before found in the descriptions of the Messiah, when he was the object of inspired expectation.[5]

The following characters of *subordination* are clearly to be collected from this passage :

1. A *mission* from the Divine Father : ver. 36. This is among the most usual declarations both of

the Sabbath, never desists from the performance of works worthy of himself, throughout the whole material world; and I therefore claim an equal right to do the like."—*Semleri Paraphr. Evang. Joann.* vol. i. p. 166.

[4] See Note [A], at the end of this Section.
[5] See Vol. I. pp. 291, 293, 502.

Jesus himself and of his apostles. For instance;
"God so loved the world, that he gave his Only-
" begotten Son ;—he sent his Son into the world."
" Jesus, the Christ whom thou hast sent." " The
" Father sent the Son to be the Saviour of the world."
" The Apostle [*i. e.* messenger, person sent,] of our
" profession."⁶ We have seen also, that under the
same character, the prophecies of the Old Testament
represented the Messiah, and the ancient Jews looked
for him as such.⁷

2. A *giving, appointing,* or *assigning* of special
functions to be discharged: ver. 36. This also is the
frequent language of Jesus Christ concerning himself.
" My food is, that I may do the will of him that sent
" me, and may complete his work." " I must work
" the works of him that sent me."⁸

The same declaration of a mission and a specific
purpose is made in the negative form :—" I can do
" nothing from myself :—I seek not mine own will :"
vers. 19, 30. This also is in our Lord's accustomed
style ;⁹ and it denotes that he had no disposition, or
inclination, in the slightest degree, discordant with
the purposes of that infinite wisdom which formed
and directed his mediatorial mission. To " act from
one's self," in the scriptural sense of the expression,
is to act from one's own mind, assumption, or authority ; and is opposed to the acting from a divine
commission.¹⁰ The form of expression is that of the

⁶ John iii. 16, 17 ; xvii. 3. 1 John iv. 14. Heb. iii. 1.
⁷ See Vol. I. pp. 442, 454, 497, 567, 589, 594.
⁸ John iv. 34 ; ix. 4.
⁹ See John vi. 38, 40 ; vii. 16.
¹⁰ This use of the phrase is confirmed by the LXX. version of
Numbers xvi. 28. " By this ye shall know, that the Lord hath sent

known Hebraizing idiom, which conveys a comparative idea by an absolute term,[11] but which it would
be absurd to understand in literal strictness. The
inability of the Blessed Jesus to "do any thing from
himself," was not physical incapacity, but was a necessary part of his moral perfection. In this sense, it is
declared to be a part of his glory that "he *cannot*
deny himself :"[12] and, in the same sense, the Great
Promiser of eternal life is called "God who cannot
lie."[13]

3. An *exact knowledge* of the will and purposes of
the Father. "The Son doeth—only what he seeth
the Father doing.—As I hear, I judge," vers. 19, 30.
By a well-known scriptural idiom, common indeed to
the early state of all languages, the organic senses are
put for mental actions.[14] Christ declares, that he has
a most intimate and perfect knowledge of all the
powers and operations of the Almighty and Eternal
God ; such a knowledge as may be justly compared
to the most acute vision,—an *intuitive* knowledge :
and that, in the exercise of judgment, he is susceptible
of no bias ; he is incapable of imperfect information,
deceptive impressions, or partial decisions ; he judges
according to a *perfect perception* of the dictates of the
Divine Mind.

---

me to do all these works, that [I have done them] not from myself."
See also John xvi. 13.

[11] Thus our Lord says, "Whosoever receiveth me, receiveth not
"me, but him who sent me." Mark ix. 37. "My doctrine is not
"mine, but his who sent me." John vii. 16. "He who believeth
"on me, believeth not on me, but on him who sent me." Ib. xii. 44.

[12] 2 Tim. ii. 13.   [13] Ὁ ἀψευδὴς Θεός.   Tit. i. 2.

[14] See Ps. xxxiv. 8. 1 Pet. ii. 3. Heb. vi. 4. Matt. v. 8. Rom.
vii. 23. Acts xvii. 27.

. 4. The possession, by communication from the Father, of that very LIFE which is *peculiar* to the Divine Nature, which depends upon nothing extrinsic, which is essential and self-active, and which is the cause of all dependent existence : ver. 26.   The terms are plain, that *the same* spontaneous and independent life, which belongs to the Living God, the Father of spirits, belongs also to the Messiah.   But the circumstance of this being "*given* to the Son," and the connexion with the succeeding particular, lead to the belief that the reference is to our Lord's official prerogative, as Mediator and Saviour, of bestowing those spiritual blessings which constitute "everlasting life." The appointing of the Son of God to be the Messiah, is repeatedly expressed by the term *giving*.[15] As, however, according to the scholastic maxim, whatsoever is given must be given according to the capacity of the receiver, it is manifest that the Being who is *competent* to such a function as "the giving of ever-lasting life" to the "multitude which no man can number," must have original powers of the highest kind.   It is the Father's will to constitute him the Fountain of divine life to mankind, *because* he is, IN HIMSELF, adequate to such a function.   It betrays a gross want of argumentative equity, to say of this doctrine, " It appears, after all, that nothing was given to Christ which he did not already possess."[16] Surely no sagacity is required, beyond what a child of ordinary intellect possesses, to observe the distinction, between an *original ground* of suitableness, in the capacity and qualifications of an agent for a given purpose, and a

[15] For example, Isaiah lv. 4. John iii. 16.
[16] *Calm Inq.* p. 316.

consequent investment of that agent with a particular function appropriated to that purpose.

5. A commission to execute a supreme *judicial authority* in deciding upon the moral character and the future condition of mankind: ver. 27. This authority is given to him " BECAUSE he is *the Son of man ;*" the distinctive appellation of the Messiah which our Lord chose to employ more than any other, and which has a marked and evident reference to his state of humiliation. The Calm Inquirer observes, and very truly, that " it is even implied, John v. 27, that the proper humanity of Christ is an essential qualifi-. cation for the office." [17] Certainly it is ; as, without a participation of a real and proper humanity, the Son of God could not have been the Messiah. But is it necessary to be perpetually repeating to the Unitarians, that their opponents believe " the proper humanity of Christ" no less than themselves ?—It is, moreover, peculiarly congruous with the nature and requisites of the case, in the estimation of Divine Wisdom, that the Judge of men should be himself a real, but spotless and perfect man; who experimentally knows the cir- cumstances of human nature, and can be touched with the fellow-feeling of its infirmities and sorrows. [18] Some understand, by this authority to execute judg- ment, our Lord's presiding, as the Founder of Chris- tianity, over the moral resurrection, or the reformation of mankind by the efficacy of his doctrine. But it is manifest that, without the most unreasonable violence of construction, the terms of vers. 28 and 29 cannot be applied to any other than the literal and universal

[17] *Calm Inq.* p. 341.
[18] See Note [B], at the end of this Section.

resurrection of the dead, and to the final judgment which will be connected with it.

Now, all these circumstances of delegation, instruction, commission, and a perfect union of will, motive, and purpose with the Divine Father, were the necessary attributives of a Mediator and Saviour; who, by the nature and conditions of his office, was to be the "servant of God, his chosen, the delight of his soul," whom "the Father set apart and sent into the world," and who was "faithful to him that constituted him,— "as a Son over his [the Father's] house." [19] They are all characters of *official* subordination.

The other parts of the description present characters of *supremacy.*

1. A *parity* of *operative power :* ver. 17. It may be objected that the words do not necessarily imply more than a *resemblance*, and that only in some respects.   But this construction is resisted by two circumstances.

(1.) The turn of the argument. Upon the principle of the objection, Jesus is made to say, "Because the divine agency is incessantly exerted in the machinery of the universe, therefore I may do any thing, though it violate the sabbatic law." If such reasoning could be admitted, it would be equally allowable to argue that, as God in his infinite dominion deprives men of their enjoyments, health, and lives, so a creature might rightfully take away the property or the life of his fellow. The implication in our Lord's words evidently is a *right* to work on the Sabbath, *because* providential agency is not intermitted on that day:

---

[19] Isa. xlii. 1 ; John x. 36 ; Heb. iii. 2, 6, reading, with the best authorities, αὐτοῦ, not αὑτοῦ.

thus putting both his will and his power on a par with those of his Father.

(2.) The nature of the work from which the discussion originated. It was a miracle. Now, on the supposition of the mere humanity of the Christ, the work was wrought by God; Jesus was but the organ, or rather the declarer, of the divine agency. His reply to his adversaries would then have been, "This work was wrought by the immediate interposition of God himself, to whom the law of the sabbatic rest cannot be applied." On the other hand, as Jesus so manifestly makes himself, in distinction from the Father, the agent of the miracle, he asserts for himself a power *to control* the laws of nature, a power undeniably the same with that which fixed them, and which actuates the universe according to them. Thus, on this ground also, we are inevitably led to understand the words as denoting an equality both of power and of right : "My Father worketh until now ; I also work."

This interpretation is strengthened by another assertion, with which our Lord follows up the former : " Whatsoever things the Father doeth, those things the " Son also doeth, in like manner." There is nothing in the connexion to restrict the universal terms to any specific objects. They plainly affirm a proper universality of operations, and an identity in the mode of performing those operations : that is, that the works of the Father, as to both their nature and manner, are equally the works of the Son.

2. The sovereign power to confer *animal life:* ver. 21. "The Son also giveth life to whom he will."

The occasion of the discourse was the restoration of
vital action to paralytic limbs, which, in a popular
sense, might be called dead. This shows that physical
life was the object intended: and the same thing is
proved by the connexion of the topic with the great
future fact of revelation, the resurrection of all the
dead.[20]

3. The effecting of that mysterious and astonishing
work, the future *restoration to life* of the whole human
race: ver. 25. It is not "incredible that GOD should
" raise the dead;" but it is absolutely so that any other
being should. To *hear the voice* of any one is, in
scriptural phraseology, to acknowledge and obey the
authority of the person.[21]   When it is declared that
"the dead shall hear the voice of the Son of God,"
the evident implication is, that such power is possessed
by him, as can and will effect that most stupendous
work, the universal resurrection.

4. The exercise of *judicial authority* in determining
the final condition of all the individuals of mankind:
vers. 27, 29. Such a work as this could no more be
delegated to an inferior intelligence, than could the

---

[20] " Thus the meaning is, ' he raiseth to eternal life whom he will.'
No man surely can imagine that this is an irrational will, without
motive, a party-inclination which has no respect to the actions and
character of those who shall be raised. In what follows, Jesus explains himself by saying, that it is ' those who have done good,' who
believe in him, whom he will raise to eternal life. The expression
' whom he will,' is likewise equivalent to saying, the Father hath
subjected all things to *the will* of Christ; the same idea that is
expressed, in the next verse, by giving *all judgment* to him."—*J. D.
Michaelis Anmerk. z. d. o.*

[21] Exod. xxiv. 7. Deut. iv. 30; viii. 20. Ps. xcv. 7. Nehem.
xiii. 27, and many other instances.

government of the universe. It requires the highest attributes of Deity for its performance.[22]

5. A claim of *homage* to the Son, the same in kind and equal in degree, with the homage which is due to the Almighty Father: ver. 23. " That all may " honour the Son as they honour the Father." It has been pleaded that not an identity or an equality of honour is here intended, but only such a *resemblance* as would still reserve the infinite distance between the objects : as, because it was the eastern custom to pay respect to kings with the same bodily gestures that were used in divine worship, the convention of Israel " bowed " down their heads, and prostrated themselves to Jeho- " vah and to the king."[23] But there is a total want of similarity in the cases. The circumstances of the occasion put the expression used by Jesus quite out of the range of comparison with the Hebrew phrase. The thing in question was, not civil homage, but *religious supremacy and honour*. The point of the case lay in his having used language, which the Jews construed into an assumption of equality with God. Upon Unitarian principles, our Lord must have been

---

[22] See the further examination of this subject in Capitule VI. of this Chapter.

[23] 1 Chron. xxix. 20. Three words, of which the first and last are used in this passage, " have this difference of meaning : (1.) קֹדַד is *to incline the head and shoulders*, which sometimes preceded a more profound gesture of respect. (2.) כָּרַע signifies *the bowing of the upper parts of the body down to the knees*, as in 2 Chron. vii. 3. (3.) הִשְׁתַּחֲוָה denotes *to fall down on the knees, and put the forehead on the ground or floor ; to prostrate one's-self*; which was practised in the civil homage of the oriental nations, not only to superiors, but to equals also."—*Simonis et Eichhorn, Lex.* p. 1617. The same distinctions are stated by Gesenius, under the respective words, in his *Handwörterbuch*, and *Lex. Man.*

among the most unfortunate of apologists: for he
ought to have said, " It is true that I claim an honour,
but I arrogate not that which belongs to God: it is,
indeed, his will that all should honour the Son ; but,
be not mistaken, this honour is essentially different
from that which is due to the Father, and is altogether
inferior to it." Yet, so far from this, the Lord Jesus
reasserts his claim in language more striking, and less
capable of being misunderstood ; language which, if it
were indeed not meant to affirm an identity of nature
and dignity, cannot be freed from the charge of
being the most ill-timed, offensive, and dangerous
that can be imagined ; not to say, absolutely impious.
Whenever in Scripture the phrase *to honour God* occurs,
or any equivalent expression, it always denotes *religious* homage ; the making God our end and object
in all our actions, the celebration of his praises, obe-
dience to him, and confidence in him: and this " his
glory, he will not give to another."[24] To honour,
then, the Son AS we honour the Father, must be to
have our thoughts, affections, and actions, directed to
him, and our hope and confidence reposed on him, in
the same manner. It is a paltry evasion to say, with
Mr. Lindsey, that this text " does not relate to worship at all ;"[25] for, though the formal act of prayer or
any other explicit mode of adoration be not mentioned,
all and every act or mode of worship is *included*, as
the species under a genus. A very liberal divine, and
a scholar and critic incomparably superior to Mr.
Lindsey, the celebrated Döderlein, says of this pas-

[24] See 1 Sam. ii. 30. Ps. xxix. 2. Prov. iii. 9. Isa. xlii. 8 ;
xxix. 13 ; lviii. 13. 1 Tim. i. 17. Rev. xix. 7.
[25] *Lindsey's Sequel to his Apol.* p. 110.

sage, " These words of Jesus possess such perspicuity, that nothing can be desired more decisive."[26]

Mr. Belsham disposes of this argument by a summary assertion.[27] According to his interpretation, Moses, John, or Paul, might have used the same language; for each of them was the bearer of a message from God, a message to which " the very same regard is due as to an oracle delivered by God himself;" and each might, with the greatest propriety, have said, as one of them actually did say, " He that " despiseth, despiseth not man, but God, who hath also " given unto us his Holy Spirit." But can any person think it compatible with their character and spirit, to have declared, " In consequence of the message with which we are charged, it is the will of the Eternal God that all men should honour us, as they honour HIM : he that honoureth not us, honoureth not the Great Being who commissioned us ?"——Is any sentiment analogous to this to be found in their speeches or writings ? Is not every turn of thought and expression invariably of the contrary description, and marked with the most scrupulous jealousy, to " give " unto the Lord the glory due unto his name ?" Can the implication be imagined, without shocking every pious feeling?—And can we suppose that Jesus, the pure and lowly in heart, " the wisest and best of teachers," had less delicacy of soul, less sensibility to

[26] *Institutio Theologi Christiani, nostris Temporibus accommodata ;* Norimb. 1784. vol. i. p. 333. The author died in 1792.
[27] " The obvious meaning is, that, Christ being the messenger of God, the very same regard is due to his message which would be due to an oracle delivered by God himself; and that to disregard Christ under this character is the same affront to the Supreme Being, as it would be to disregard the voice of God himself."—*Calm Inq.* p. 362.

the approaches of pride, or less horror at the semblance of blasphemy, than his far inferior followers ?

The Inquirer is also mistaken in that which he assumes as the ground of our Lord's claim. That ground is not his quality as a messenger from God, but it is expressly declared to be his exercise of universal judgment; a work which the Father hath, indeed, committed to him, it being a part of his official functions as the Messiah, but which plainly implies *prerequisites* not lower than divine perfections.[26]

It is, to say the least, not improbable that the offence taken by the opponents of Jesus had respect also to the language which he had used to the object of his miraculous beneficence: for it is the same leading sentiment (the controverted question concerning the dignity and the claims of the admired and reviled Teacher) which runs through the dialogues and narrative of chapters ix. and x. The first part (ch. ix. 1 ; x. 21,) appears to have occurred a very short time, perhaps only one day, before the second, (x. 22—38,) in which we find resumed both the subject and the imagery of the former. Our Lord had graciously sought out the poor man who had made so good a use of his imperfect knowledge; " and said " to him, Thou believest on the Son of God ! The " man answered, Who is he, Lord, that I may believe " on him ? Jesus said to him, Even thou hast seen " him, and he that is speaking with thee is he. And " he said, I believe, Lord ! and worshipped him." The man had confessed his belief that Jesus was a prophet, evidently meaning a person commissioned and

[26] See Note [C], at the end of this Section.

authorized by God : but the sentence (put in the form of an assertion, to denote that, though it required an answer of assent, our Lord knew his state of mind, and the answer which would correspond to it), " Thou " believest on the Son of God!" seems intended to conduct the mind to an order of thought superior to the miracle or the authority which had been already acknowledged; to the quality of the person, rather than to the dignity of the office. The *worship* which the grateful beneficiary paid to his Lord appears, from the very mode in which it is introduced, to have been something more deep and solemn than any act of civil homage. We cannot doubt that it corresponded to his views of his Benefactor, though they could as yet be only obscure and defective; and that therefore it rose to a strong religious veneration. Jesus evidently accepted it with approbation : but it may well be doubted, whether to have accepted any mere civil homage would have been congruous with his spirit and character. It is further worthy of observation, that the apostle John never uses this verb but to express a religious act; either the adoration of the True God, or, in several instances in the Book of Revelation, the idolatrous homage paid to the antichristian power, which is certainly to be understood as an impious rivalship to lawful worship. Of course I except ch. xx. 28 ; which, with other passages upon the homage accepted by Christ, will be considered in a following part of this Inquiry.

SUPPLEMENTARY NOTES TO SECT. V.

Note [A], page 69.

" From the established doctrine of the Jews [on the lawfulness of works of mercy on the sabbath] Jesus might have made a vindication, easy and offensive to no one, of what he had done and commanded : but he was pleased, on occasion of this irrefragable and public miracle, to speak of his own superhuman dignity.—When Jesus says, not ' the Father worketh still,' but ' MY Father,' &c. he gives us to understand, as every one must perceive, that God is his Father in a manner altogether peculiar. The least that could be deduced from it would have been, that he avowed himself to be the Messiah, whom it was the practice of the Jews to call *the Son of God*. But when we read forwards, we find it clear that he declares himself to be the Son of God, in a much higher sense than that in which the Jews conceived of the Messiah.—' And I also work.' In this expression, Jesus ascribes this miracle to himself, as a partaker with God in a common operation. No prophet, no mere man, can say this of himself: such a one has no part in the production of a miracle ; it is the reverse ; God is the sole author of the whole. But still greater is the case, when the miracle is described as a breach of the great sabbath of the world, and Jesus is represented as ' working still' with God ; for thus he declares himself to be He who, on the seventh day of the creation ' rested from all his works ;' and who is that Being, but the Creator of the world ? But can we understand these words of Christ, as referring to a subject so very great as a Divine Nature dwelling in him ? I scarcely see how they can possibly be understood otherwise : and at least the apostle John, who recites this discourse, must have so understood it.   In the positions which he lays down against certain erroneous teachers, he maintains that ' all things were made by the Word,' and that, ' without him, nothing was made that has been made.' In his Gospel, he selects the particular discourses of Jesus which were adapted to confirm those positions ; and thus—the man Jesus is described as united with the Eternal Word, who created the world.   Even the Jews find in these words, something exceedingly great : ' He maketh himself equal to God.' This he certainly does, when he represents himself as resting with God from the creation of the world ; but as, from time to time, interrupting this rest, this sabbath of the world, by miracles ; and as working those very miracles in conjunction with God. In his answer to the Jews, he does not tell them that they had misunderstood him, and that he by no means intended to make himself equal to God; but he repeats the matter, and expresses it in terms which may even be regarded as stronger than the former; since he maintains that he performs all divine works, in a community of operation with the Father, not excepting the resurrection of the dead itself" [that most stupendous work of omnipotence]. *J. D. Michaelis, Anmerkung z. d. o.*

Note [B], page 73.

" It can scarcely be deemed a difficulty that Jesus is declared to be the judge of men ' BECAUSE he is a son of man,' that is *a man*, and so far like the rest of mankind. For, in this very debate with the Jews, he also declared himself to be the Son of God, entitled to the same honours as the Father, and possessed of those divine perfections by which he is competent to this work of judgment, as being possessed of infinite knowledge, holiness, and righteousness: and, through the whole of his discourse, he so urges this point that the reader cannot lose sight of it. But, in this paragraph, he assigns as the reason why God had given to his Son the authority of judgment over mankind, that he was *a man*, a partaker of the human nature. In this we admire the arrangement of divine benignity, that God has given to mankind a Saviour and Sovereign, who possesses our own nature united with his Divine Majesty, and is, in all respects, sin excepted, like unto us. (—The same sentiment is advanced in 1 Tim. ii. 5; Phil. ii. 7, 9; Heb. ii. 6, 17—iv. 15, 16—v. 1, 2.) On this account, the apostle, preaching to the Athenians that Christ was ordained by God to be the Judge of the world, with express purpose denominates him, *a man*, ἀνήρ. But what appears to me as perhaps the most remarkable circumstance in our Lord's design, is his intending a reference to the sublime vision of Daniel, in which the Messiah is described as ' like to a son of man;' to convey the idea that his character and government would not be like those of the worldly monarchies which are represented by savage animals, but that his conduct would be gentle and humane, as that of a man with men." *Specimen Hermeneutico-Theologicum de Appellatione* τοῦ Υἱοῦ τοῦ Ἀνθρώπου, *auctore Wesselio Scholten;* pp. 18, 19. Utrecht, 1809.

These remarks are just and important; but Mr. Scholten is mistaken in his supposition that the absence of the article in this passage distinguishes the phrase from ὁ Υἱὸς τοῦ ἀνθρώπου, and brings it under the anarthrous form which signifies, in the Hebrew and Syriac idiom, merely *a human being*. The form of the clause here, ὅτι Υἱὸς ἀνθρώπου ἐστί, is in consequence of a rule of the Greek idiom, established by the most satisfactory evidence, that the predicate of a proposition, whether the substantive verb be expressed or not, should be without the article. See *Bishop Middleton's* long and satisfactory Note, in his *Doctrine of the Greek Article*, pp. 71,—76.

Note [C], page 80.

If we possessed any unexceptionable method of ascertaining in what manner the terms and phrases of ancient writers, which have become matter of controversy in later times, were understood by those who lived in or near the age of the authors, and who spoke the same language, we might be apt to think that we enjoyed a signal assistance for interpretation. In some respects this circumstance, could it be realized, would be found advantageous; yet by no means to a great extent. If passions and prepossessing opinions could be laid aside, the difficulty of interpreting the writings of antiquity would not be so great as it is often represented to be. This difficulty is little complained of with regard to the didactic Greek and Roman writers; and, with respect to the historians and poets, still less. The great stream of that traditional communication of grammar and interpretation, which has been transmitted, by a living and *really uninterrupted* succession, in schools and colleges, from the purest classic times to the present day; the ancient scholia, glossaries, lexicons, and grammatical treatises, which are extant;—the study of the context;—the comparison of passages:—and an acquired familiarity with the language, style, and manner of authors;—have been found sufficient to establish in the minds of rational men a prevailing acquiescence in the generally received understanding of the Greek and Latin languages. The chief toil of criticism has been the emendation of corrupt passages, and the explanation of technical terms and uncommon phrases.

It might be thought that an advantage of this kind is to be derived to the study of the New Testament, from the writings of the earliest Greek fathers. But such an expectation would be disappointed. Those authors had little knowledge of rational and impartial principles of interpretation; and they appear to have adopted, with unsuspecting acquiescence, any arbitrary and fanciful gloss on the words of scripture, which promised to answer a present purpose. Though a better judgment is manifested in the comments of Basil, Chrysostom, and some others of the fourth century, yet the controversies which had been so warmly agitated, and the active part taken by those eminent men, prevent our adducing them as witnesses, except when a reasonable ground can be assigned for regarding their judgment, in any particular case, as unbiassed.

If, however, we had a writer who was merely a man of letters, and who had transfused into any kind of explicatory composition those passages of the New Testament which affect our inquiry, upon other principles and with other views than what might be presumed to actuate a professed theologian; such a writer would, in all men's estimation, be entitled to considerable regard.

An author approaching to this idea is Nonnus of Panopolis in Egypt. Unfortunately his age is rather late, he having flourished at the end of the fourth, or the beginning of the fifth century; yet this was many centuries before the ancient Greek ceased to be a living language. Nothing is known of the life or character of Nonnus. Two poems of his are extant; the *Dionysiaca*, a long epic composition on the life and actions of Bacchus, but so loaded with digressions and episodes as to include a chaos of heathen fables, lavish in mythological learning, and, with much extravagance, exhibiting marks of genius; and a *Paraphrase of the Gospel of John*, in Homeric versification. The style and manner of this latter composition shows that the author's design was to display his poetical talent, rather than to produce a theological work. All things considered, I think it may be taken as a fair specimen of the manner in which a man, whose vernacular language was Greek, understood the phraseology of the evangelist, at the distance of three hundred years from the publication of his gospel. It is adduced as an illustration rather than as an evidence; and the judicious reader will form his own opinion upon the degree of regard to which it is entitled. I shall copy this metaphrase on the principal passages which are quoted in Sections V. and VI.

Εἰσέτι νῦν γενέτης ἐργάζεται ἠθάδι κόσμῳ
Ἤθεσιν ἀντιτύποις, καὶ ἐγὼ ταῖς ἔργων ὑφαίνω.

" The Father worketh until now in modes corresponding with the constant order of the universe, and I the Son skilfully execute the work." John v. 17.

Καὶ Θεὸν αὐτογένεθλον ἑὸν κίκλησκε τοκῆα,
Ἰσάζων ἑὸν εὖχος ἐπουρανίῳ Βασιλῆϊ.

" ———— and called the self-existent God his own Father, equalling his own glory to the celestial king." ver. 18.

Οὐδὲν ἐῇ ἱότητι δυνήσεται υἱὸς ἀνύσσαι,
Εἰ μὴ ἐσαθρήσειεν ἐὸν τελέοντα τοκῆα·
Ἔργα γὰρ εἰν ἑνὶ παντὰ Πατὴρ ἐμὸς ὁππόσα ῥέζει,
Ταῦτα Θεὸν γενέτην μιμούμενος υἱὸς ἀνύσσει.

" The Son can never perform any thing by his own determination,
only what he beholds his own Father accomplishing : for all the
works whatsoever my Father doeth, those in one [i. e. in unison or
together,] the Son performeth, imitating God the Father." ver. 19.

'Ανδρομέην δὲ
Ὄψιμον υἱεῖ δῶκεν ὅλην κρίσιν, ὄφρά κε πάντες
Ὗεα τιμήσωσιν ἰσόζυγον ᾧ γενετῆρι,
Οἷά τε κυδαίνουσι καὶ ὑψιμέδοντα τοκῆα.
Εἰ δὲ τις ἀλλοπρόσαλλον ἔχει νόον, οὐ δὲ τοκῆος
Κυδαίνει Λόγον υἷα, καὶ οὐ γενετῆρα γεραίρει.

" The whole final judgment of mankind he hath given to the Son,
in order that all may honour the Son as equal in rank to his Father,
and in the manner in which they glorify the Father who reigns on
high.   But if any one has a versatile mind, and does not glorify the
Word the Son of the Father, he does not pay homage to the Father."
ver. 23.

Οὔποτε ποίμνης
Οὔποτε πώεα ταῦτα διόλλυται, εἰσόκε μίμνῃ
Αὐτομάταις δψῖσιν ἕλιξι κυκλούμενος αἰών.
Οὐδέ τις ἀρπάξειεν ἐμὴν μινυτόφρονα ποίμνην
Χειρὸς ἀφ' ἡμετέρης, γενέτης ἐμὸς ὅττι, νομεύειν
Ὅς μοι πώεα δῶκεν, ὑπέρτερος ἔπλετο πάντων.
Αὐτὸς ἐγώ, μεδέων τε Πατὴρ ἐμὸς, ἓν γένος ἐσμὲν,
Ἔμφυτον, αὐτόπερεμνον, ὅθεν φυτὰ μύρια κόσμου.

" Never, never shall these sheep ·of my flock perish, while the
world remains revolving in spirals on its self-moving arches.   Nor
can any snatch my timid flock from our hand ; for my Father who
gave me the sheep to feed, is superior to all.   I myself and my
sovereign Father, are one genus, of mutual nature, self-originated,
and from which are derived the innumerable offspring of the
universe." chap. x. ver. 28, 29.

Λόγον αὐτοὶ ὃν ὑψιμέδων πύρε κοσμῷ
Καὶ καθαρῆς παλάμης ἁγίῳ σφρηγίσσατο θεσμῷ,
Ὑμεῖς ἄφρονα μῦθον ἐπεφθέγξασθε μανέντες,
Ὅττι Θεοῦ ζώοντος ἐγὼ παῖς ;——

" The Word whom the Sovereign Ruler sent into the world, and
sealed by the holy decree of his pure hand, do you in your fury
charge with a foolish speech [for saying] that, I am the Son of the
living God ?" ver. 36.

Εἰ βιοδώτερι μύθῳ
Ἡμετέρου γενετῆρος ἀτέρμονος ἄξια ῥέζω,
Ἔργοις ἡμετέροις τάπερ ἔδρακε μάρτυς ὀπωπή,
Ὄφρά κε γινώσκοιτε θεοπνεύστῳ τινὶ μύθῳ
Ὡς ἐν ἐμοὶ τελέθει γενέτης ἐμος, ὅττι καὶ αὐτὸς
Ἀγχιφανὴς, ἀμέριστος, ὁμόζυγός εἰμι τοκῆος.

" If, by my life-giving word, I do things worthy of my infinite Father, by my works which your eyes have witnessed, that ye may know, by a divinely-inspired declaration, that my Father exists in me, that I also am manifested as near to my Father, indivisible from him, equal to him." ver. 38.

SECTION VI.

SON OF GOD, ONE WITH THE FATHER.

Sum of the assertions here made by Jesus Christ.—Investigation of the scriptural phrase, *to be one.*—A characteristic of our Lord's manner of teaching.—Peculiarity of the oneness of Christ with the Father.

"The Jews surrounded him and said to him, How long dost thou hold us in
"suspense? If thou art the Christ, tell us plainly.

"Jesus answered them; I did tell you, and ye do not believe. The works
"which I do in the name of my Father, these testify concerning me. But ye
"believe not, for ye are not of my sheep. As I said unto you, my sheep hear
"my voice, and I know them, and they follow me; and I give unto them eternal
"life, and they shall never perish, and no one shall snatch them out of my hand.
"My Father, who gave [them] to me, is greater than all; and no one is able to
"snatch [them] out of the hand of my Father. I and the Father are one.

"Then again the Jews took up stones, with a view to stone him. Jesus an-
"swered them; Many good works I have shewn to you from my Father; for which
"of those works do ye stone me?

"The Jews answered him; For a good work we stone thee not, but for
"blasphemy; and because thou, who art a man, makest thyself God.

"Jesus answered them; Is it not written in your law, 'I said, ye are gods?'
"If he called gods, those to whom the word of God was [addressed], (and the
"Scripture cannot be annulled,) do ye say to him whom the Father hath set apart
"and sent into the world, Thou blasphemest, because I said, I am the Son of
"God? If I do not the works of my Father, give me not credit: but, if I
"do [them], though ye give not credit to me, give credit to the works; that ye
"may know and be assured that in me is the Father, and I in him."—John x.
24—38.¹

In this portion of the doctrine of Jesus, we find the
following particulars:

1. The avowal, so often made on other occasions,

¹ The clause, " as I said unto you," (ver. 27,) is joined to the
following words, not only in conformity with the best editions and
translations, but because this position appears more closely accordant
with the instances of clauses beginning with καθὼς, in the writings
of John. Many authorities omit it.

of his *official subordination* to the Father; in having been designated, commissioned, sent, and endowed with a peculiar property in his people; and in exercising miraculous powers by the authority of the Father.

2. The assertion of *his own power to confer* the blessings of salvation; namely, holy character, immortal happiness, deliverance from moral danger, and security against all possible hostility. Let it be observed that, in the evident nature of the case, and according to the uniform tenor of Scripture, the bestowment of SUCH gifts implies the attribute of All-sufficiency in the Donor.

3. This assurance of security is repeated, with a confirmatory declaration that the *Omnipotence* of the Almighty Father is pledged to the same object.

4. These two assurances are consolidated into the proposition, "I and my Father ARE ONE."

To obtain a satisfactory conclusion as to the meaning of the expression, "to be one," (ἐν εἶναι) it is necessary to review the few passages of the New Testament in which it occurs.

In John xvii. 11, 21—23,[*] the connexion shows that the *being reciprocally one* which is predicated of Christ, his Divine Father, and his disciples, is the union of cordial and generous *love* in the present life, and of celestial *happiness* in the future state.

1 Cor. iii. 8, "He that planteth, and he that watereth, are one." Here the union of *design* and *cooperation* is plainly intended.

There are no other instances, except the one now under consideration. The phrase occurs, indeed, in

---

[*] Cited at length in p. 93.

a passage which is regarded, upon strong evidence, as spurious, 1 John v. 7, and, if we were to argue from that passage, we should say that the connexion shows the reference to be to *consent*, or the union of *testimony*. The Septuagint furnishes only two or three examples : and their manifest signification is the closest union, either of *resemblance*, or of *conjunction*.[3]

It is, therefore, manifest, that the grammatical sense of the phrase will not, of itself, determine its exact import ; and that the meaning must be ascertained, in every instance, by an attention to the *nature* and *circumstances* of the given case.

What, then, is the kind of union which the nature and circumstances of the case before us point out ? It is a union for the bestowment of the most important blessings, for the averting of the greatest evils, for a sovereign and effectual preservation from spiritual danger and eternal ruin. *These* are the plain facts of the case. It is, therefore, a *union* of POWER.—" No " one shall snatch them out of MY hand ;—no one can " snatch them out of MY FATHER's hand :—I and the " Father are ONE."

The argumentative connexion of the clause requires also to be attended to. Jesus had affirmed the adequacy of *his own* power for the certain salvation of his sincere followers ; as well as that of God his Father. Therefore, to show that he had not exceeded the bounds of truth in the assertion, and to furnish a sufficient ground of reason for it, he adds, "I and the Father are one." The union of power is thus shown to be a real *identity* of power:[4]

[3] They are Gen. xli. 25, 26. Exod. xxvi. 11.

[4] " Not εἷς (*unus*) one and the same *person*, but ἕν (*unum*) one

The hearers of Jesus instantly accused him of assuming DIVINE honours, and were proceeding to a summary execution of their capital law against blasphemy. Whether their alarm was sincere or affected, it is clear that there must have been an *apparent* ground for it.

The Lord Jesus might have answered; " I accept your construction, but I deny your charge. I have uttered no impiety, for I have claimed no more than I have a right to claim. I am the Messiah, whose goings forth have been from of old, even from the days of eternity. I am not only a man like yourselves, but I existed and acted before my taking flesh, as the Shepherd of Israel, the Lord of David, the King whose throne is for ever and ever."

And if this were true, why did he not so answer? We reply, that, admitting the truth of the assertion supposed, there are good reasons to account for his having declined to make it. It would have been inconsistent with the present stage of the advancement of his dispensation; it would have been a departure from that rule of reserve which we have ample evidence that he most carefully adhered to; and he had

and the same *thing*. The Father has communicated his power to the Son." *Calm Inq.* p. 235. But what is this to the purpose? No Trinitarian interpreter ever contended for the former representation, which would be as inconsistent with his doctrine as it is with the words of the passage. The neuter form is necessary to the idiomatical expression : and it has been often insisted on by divines, from Tertullian downwards, as indicating the unity, not of *person*, but of *essence*. As for the writer's assertion of the " communicated power," he seems to have little reflected on the kind, degree, and extent of the *power* which the case requires ; a power which could be neither communicated to, nor exercised by, any being merely a creature.

before him another mode of proceeding, which we shall presently see was in accordance with his usual practice as a teacher.

But, upon the Unitarian hypothesis, no motive can be imagined why he should not have met the accusation with the clearest and most pointed denial. Though he saw it not to be proper, as yet, to avow himself publicly to be the Messiah, there could be no reason why he should omit to protest that he was merely a man, such as other men; and every consideration of piety and veracity, and all other good principles, demanded the most prompt and unambiguous declaration against the blasphemy with which he was charged. This course, however, he did not take. It has, indeed, been said that " he peremptorily denies the conclusion which the Jews drew from his language."[5] Such denial I acknowledge myself unable to discover, either in a " peremptory" or in an implied form. The serious and attentive reader must decide for himself, on a careful scrutiny of the language held by Jesus in his reply.

It was so frequently practised, that we may pronounce it to have been one of the characteristics of our Lord's style of teaching, to reason with men *upon their own* real, or pretended *principles ;* and to conduct them to a point in which *their own minds could not escape* from drawing *the very conclusion* which they had been, at the outset, anxious to avoid.[6]

In this way, therefore, he proceeds. He reminds his accusers that, in the phrase of their own scrip-

---

[5] *Calm Inq.* p. 218.

[6] For example, Matt. xii. 1—12; xix. 3—9, 16—22; xxi. 23—27; xxii. 16—22.

tures, even wicked rulers were denominated gods.
He infers that no prejudice could be justly entertained
against him, for having used language implying that
God was his Father in a special and unique sense;
while he had not called himself God, but only, by
the shewing of his opponents, had claimed to be the
Son of God. At the same time, he evidently assumes
that his own title to the disputed honour was greater
than that of the Jewish magistrates. He then appeals
to his unquestionable miracles, as the attestation of
his truth, in again affirming *the very thing* which had
created the offence; in terms different, indeed, but
clearly of the same import, and most strongly expressive, *not of a union of power merely*, though that
involved a claim of omnipotence, but of a union in
the very *nature* and *manner* of existence:—" IN ME
is the Father, and I IN HIM."

But this interpretation is contested, because the
"phrase is applicable to believers in general."[1] The
passages in which such application occurs are these:—

" In that day ye shall know that I am in my Father,
" and ye in me, and I in you:" John xiv. 20. "Holy
" Father, keep in thine own name those whom thou
" hast given me, that they may be one, as we.—That
" they all may be one, as thou, Father, in me and I in
" thee, that also they in us may be one; that the world
" may believe that thou hast sent me: and the glory
" which thou hast given to me, I have given to them,
" that they may be one as we are one. I in them, and
" thou in me: that they may be completed into one,
" and that the world may know that thou hast sent

---

[1] *Calm Inq.* p. 235. The same line of argument is followed by
Arian, Socinian, and Unitarian writers in general.

" me, and hast loved them as thou hast loved me.
" That the love with which thou hast loved me may be
" in them, and I in them." chap. xvii. 11, 21—23, 26.
" If we love one another, God abideth in us, and his
" love is completed in us. By this we know that we
" abide in him, and he in us, that he hath given us of
" his Spirit.—Whosoever confesseth that Jesus is the
" Son of God, God abideth in him and he in God:
" and we know and are confident of the love which
" God hath towards us. God is love; and he who
" abideth in love abideth in God, and God in him."
1 John iv. 12, 13, 15, 16.

From these passages, no one can doubt that the
phrase of a reciprocal in-dwelling, or *in-being*, is scrip-
turally predicable of the relations which subsist between
God and sincere Christians in general. The passages
evidently express an intimate union of *holy mental
affections* between the Father of spirits and his faithful
servants, in the present state; the communion of
gracious influences on his part, and of *devotional feelings and actions* on theirs; and that *perfection of both*
which will subsist in the heavenly state. This use of
the expression may be rationally accounted for, by
referring it to the principle, which is more or less
conspicuous in the structure of all languages, that
terms and phrases are occasionally used in senses
greatly below their native strength and significancy;
the nature of the subject and the circumstances of its
association pointing out, in all such cases, the re-
strictions which are understood.[*] So Christians are
directed to aim at being " partakers of a divine disposition," to be " perfect as God is perfect," to be

---

[*] See *Lord Kaims's Elements of Criticism*, chap. xx. sect. 3.

" holy as he is holy ;"[9] and so, by a different direction
of the same figure, Christ is represented as "being
" made sin for us," and disbelievers of the divine testimony are said to "make God a liar."[10]

Why, then, may not this phrase, when applied to
Christ and the Father, be regarded as conveying no
more than a metaphorical in-dwelling, a union of
affection and moral principles? We reply that the
rule just mentioned, *a regard to the nature and circumstances of the application,* will not permit us so to
regard it. The case in question refers not to any
moral quality, but to a oneness of *power* for the performance of works which imply omnipotence. Our
Lord adduces the in-dwelling of the Father and himself as a synonymous expression of that identity of
power; or, more exactly speaking, as a superior and
more extensive declaration, confirming, and including
the other. The peculiarity of the case, therefore,
lying in its relation to the exertion of omnipotence,
excludes a metaphorical or merely moral signification,
and obliges us to understand it in a strict, proper, and
physical sense : it is an *identity of* POWER, such power
as can belong to Deity alone, implying and resting
upon an *identity of* NATURE. It clearly follows that
the title *Son of God,* as belonging to Christ, and as
vindicated by him in this passage, denotes one who

[9] 2 Pet. i. 4, Φύσις, " origo,—ipsa rei natura et essentia, *pro-
prietas insita, indoles, mores.*" *Schleusner.* Matt. v. 48 ; 1 Pet.
i. 16.

[10] 2 Cor. v. 21, taking ἁμαρτία in its primary and obvious sense,
with which a rhetorician would first be concerned ; for the interpretation of *sin-offering,* derived from a more narrowed inquiry into
the peculiarities of Bible-idiom, is a matter of ulterior consideration.
1 John v. 10.

has the same *essential nature* as that of the Father:
or, in the words which our Lord, so far from refusing,
fixed upon himself, one who " maketh," or repre-
senteth "himself to be GOD."

This conclusion is strengthened by observing the
ground which our Lord lays to confirm his declaration: " If I do not the works of my Father, give
" me not credit; but, if I do, though ye give not
" credit to me, give credit to the works." The term,
" works of my Father," may denote either actions
done by the command and authority of God,[11] or
such as are wrought by the immediate power of God.
To take it here in the former sense, is evidently
inapplicable to the occasion, and would make the
reasoning nugatory. In the other sense, it suits the
argument. " By the miracles, and wonders, and
signs, which God wrought through him,—Jesus of
Nazareth was a man demonstrated by God"[12] to be all
that he himself claimed, whether by assertion or implication. So far he differs not from other inspired
messengers. God confirmed the mission of prophets
and apostles by exhibiting miraculous powers through
them.[13] Jesus had all this honour as a man and a
prophet. But the divine testimony does not permit
us to rest at this point. Jesus Christ constantly
speaks of himself as being, not an instrument only,
but the AGENT, in works of miraculous power : and it
is remarkable that, while the apostles manifested a
studious anxiety to avoid using language that could

---

[11] As in John vi. 28, and Rev. ii. 26.

[12] Acts ii. 22.

[13] " God wrought very extraordinary [οὐ τὰς τυχούσας] miracles
" through the hands of Paul." Acts xix. 11.

be construed into any representation of themselves above that of a powerless instrumentality, they ascribed the final agency to Christ as readily as to God the Father. The " signs and wonders" which sanctioned the ministry of Paul, and of which the number and variety was so great, that his modesty refused to speak of them, beyond a slight and necessary allusion, he definitely attributes to CHRIST as their AUTHOR: " Christ wrought them through me."[14] Here, therefore, are reasons for understanding our Lord's words as asserting *for himself* a power of divine agency, and consequently the possession of divine perfections, " I " do the works of my Father,—that ye may know and " be assured that in me is the Father, and I in him."

Let the experiment, in imagination, be made of putting these words into the mouth of an apostle. Let Peter, John, or Paul say, " I and God are one: I do the works of God: God is in me, and I in him." Every one feels that the supposition is, not monstrous only, but intolerable. Yet, on Unitarian principles, (which affirm that these phrases are " applicable to believers in general," without any investigation of the grounds and the diversity of application,) we ought to feel no difficulty in making the supposition. The assumption of such language by any inspired man, must be, not barely allowable, not merely capable of being palliated, but strictly and unequivocally in character with piety, humility, meekness, and lowliness of heart,—Unitarianism requires me to believe this!

[14] Rom. xv. 18.

Capitule II.

IN the discourses of our Lord, whether private or public, whether in the bosom of his friends or under the jealous observation of his enemies, the style which he was pleased most frequently to use, for describing himself, was that of *the Son of man*, ὁ υἱὸς τοῦ ἀνθρώπου,[1] with the article to denote particularity. On an examination of all the passages in which it occurs, it appears that, when this appellation is used, it is always with a reference to some acknowledged character, function, or work of the Messiah: so that, in nearly every instance, the sentence is an apophthegm of the doctrine concerning the Messiah, and might stand as such, quite independently of any particular

[1] Some have affirmed that we ought to translate the phrase, *the son of the man*, and that the allusion is to David as the ancestor of Jesus. But this assertion proceeds on ignorance of the Greek idiom, or inattention to it. A noun governed by another noun which has the article, must itself also take the article; and *vice versâ*. See *Middleton on the Greek Article*, pp. 69—71. On this particular phrase, that distinguished scholar observes, " He [Christ] was to be designated as ὁ υἱὸς, for otherwise he would not have been distinguished from any other individual of the human race; and if ὁ υἱὸς then ΤΟΥ ἀνθρώπου, for ὁ υἱὸς ἀνθρώπου would offend against *Regimen*. Hence it is plain that the article before ἀνθρώπου is not, if I may say so, *naturally* and *essentially* necessary, but is so only *accidentally;* and consequently it will not be admitted unless where *Regimen* requires it, *i. e.* where ὁ υἱὸς precedes."—P. 354.

individual who claimed to be that Messiah.   While it was the title which Jesus evidently preferred to every other, and which he was most in the habit of employing, it is observable that it was never applied to him by any other person, except in the single instance of the martyr Stephen; that Jesus himself never returned to the use of it after his resurrection; and that the apostles on no occasion employed it, either in their preaching or in their writings.[2]

To rehearse the numerous and different opinions which have been given of this appellation, and the reason on which it has been supposed to rest, would be tedious and of little profit.   That which appears to me the best supported by evidence, has been mentioned in a former part of this work.[3]   It is the interpretation which has been advanced by scholars and divines of the first erudition, and of very different theological sentiments: Beza, Episcopius, the Dutch Annotators of the Synod of Dort, Leigh, Venema, Wetstein, Bengelius, Abresch, Semler, Eichhorn, and many others, for the enumeration of whose names I am indebted to the ample and exact dissertation of

---

[2] Rev. i. 13, and xiv. 14, are not exceptions to this remark, for in them the phrase is $\nu i\tilde{\varphi}\ \mathring{a}\nu\theta\rho\acute{\omega}\pi ov$ without the articles, corresponding with the Hebrew and Syriac idiom, which occurs very frequently in the Old Testament (e. g. Num. xxiii. 19.   Job xvi. 21; xxv. 6. Psa. viii. 4.   Isa. lii. 14; lvi. 2,) and is universally known to be merely a periphrasis for *a human being*.   In both those passages this is evidently the sense; so that they are improperly rendered in the common version, *the*, instead of *a son of man*.   In the Peshito Syriac the phrase, *barnosh* and *bar-nosho*, is used in many places for $\mathring{a}\nu\theta\rho\omega\pi o\varsigma$, especially, though not only, when the word is a general term, as in Matt. xii. 12. John ii. 25. Rom. i. 23.   It is even used in Rom. vii. 22, and in the two instances in 1 Cor. xv. 47.

[3] See Vol. I. pp. 412—414.

Mr. Scholten,[4] a divine of the University of Utrecht,
whose learning, diligence, and acuteness have anticipated almost every thing that could be advanced on
the question.   This opinion is, that the term was used
with a designed allusion to the prophecy of Daniel:
" I looked in visions of the night, and, behold! with
" the clouds of heaven, came one like a SON OF
" MAN."[5]   This is among the clearest prophetic descriptions of the Messiah: and, though in its original
connexion it is combined with lofty characters of
majesty and honour, the expression in itself is such
that nothing can be conceived more simple and unas-
suming.   It was, therefore, admirably calculated to
answer the purposes of our Lord's habitual testimony
concerning himself, during that period in which his
wisdom saw it right to suspend the universal declara-

---

[4] Cited above, p. 91.   Kuinöl accedes to this idea of the origin of
the phrase.   See his *Comment. in Lib. N. T. Hist.* vol. i. p. 259.
Gesenius, citing Dan. vii. 13, adds, " In the *Book of Enoch*, which
was written about the time of the birth of Christ, partly as an imitation of the Book of Daniel, this expression [*Son of Man*] is in constant use for the Messiah, and is employed synonymously with *Son
of God, Anointed*, &c. as in the New Testament."   *Handwörterbuch*,
art. אֱנָשׁ.   See the former volume, Book II. ch. vii. § 3.

[5] Dan. vii. 13.   Mr. B. remarks that " the expression may possibly signify nothing more than a person in human form; and ——
this symbol of a human figure is explained, not of an individual, but
of the kingdom of the saints of the Most High." P. 392.   But these
objections are, I think, removed by the considerations, that, (1.) In
other instances of prophetic description the Messiah is exhibited in
his own person, though associated with allegorical personages and
scenery.   See Rev. i. 13—20; xix. 11—16.   (2.) The expressions
of " the saints possessing the kingdom," &c. vers. 18, 22, 27, are
fairly interpreted, in conformity with the elucidations supplied by the
New Testament, of the deliverance from sin, persecution, and all
evil, and of the final triumph and perfect happiness, which the
servants of Christ shall receive from him as their Head and Saviour.

tion of his claim to be the Messiah. It could hurt no
feelings, rouse no prejudices, offend no pride. It
could minister no fuel to the rage of the violent, nor
furnish any occasion to the captiousness of the artful,
nor be wrested into a pretext for exciting civil dis-
cord, nor awaken the jealous fears of the Roman
government. But, while thus humble and inoffensive,
it was intelligible, clear, and definite, to those who
" searched the Scriptures ;" and it went the full
length of a claim to the Messiahship.

   This view of the origin and design of the phrase
leads to the conclusion, that, though it literally expresses only a human nature, it is applied, on the
generalizing principle of language, to designate the
MESSIAH, *in the whole comprehension* of his person
and character, yet with an especial view to his state
of humiliation.[6] The circumstances of glory, power,
and relation to the Divine Father, which in the original passage are attributed to him who bore the likeness of a Son of man, excite and seem to warrant this
notion ; especially if the interpretation be admitted,

   [6] " The very title ' Son of man' has every where a reference to
the *Incarnation of Christ*, and is therefore significant of his acquaintance with human weakness. I have, indeed, observed that, in a
majority of the places in which our Saviour calls himself the Son of
man (and he is never in the N. T. so called, by others, before his
ascension) the allusion is either to his present humiliation, or to his
future glory : and, if this remark be true, we have, though an
indirect, yet a strong and perpetual declaration, that the human
nature did not originally belong to him, and was not properly his
own. He who shall examine the passages throughout, with a view
to this observation, will be able duly to estimate its value. For
myself, I scruple not to aver, that I consider this single phrase so
employed, as an irrefragable proof of the Pre-existence and Divinity
of Christ." *Bishop Middleton on the Greek Article*, p. 354.

which was proposed in the former volume, of a
clause in that passage as declaring a close and intimate
conjunction, by the greatest of all miracles, of the
frail and lowly nature of a child of man with that
of the Ancient of days, so as to form *one person*.
Thus we are also furnished with a guide to the interpretation of several passages of the New Testament,
which, on any other hypothesis, Trinitarian or Unitarian, present great difficulties.[7] The principal of
these passages are now before us to be examined.

---

[7] " When we want to open a lock, and after having tried, to no
purpose, a number of keys, we hit upon one which opens it with
facility, we conclude that we have met with the right key. In like
manner, when any phænomenon in nature is to be explained, such,
for instance, as the aberration of the fixed stars ; and we find that
the hypothesis of the progressive motion of light, combined with that
of the annual motion of the earth in its orbit, will completely solve
that wonderful appearance, we rightly conclude that light is progressive : or, when we find that the colours, figure, position, and all the
other appearances of the primary and secondary rainbows, can be
solved from the different refrangibility of the rays of light passing
through globular drops of rain, we rightly conclude that the rays of
light are differently refrangible, and the drops of rain globular ; why
may we not argue in the same manner on other subjects ?" *Bishop
Watson's Anecdotes of his own Life.* 8vo. ed. vol. ii. p. 222.

SECTION I.

ON CHRIST'S DESCENDING FROM HEAVEN.

Unitarian Interpretation stated and examined.—Idea of a local heaven.—Hebrew phrase, to ascend into heaven.—Its Rabbinical use.—Its true meaning.—The correlate phrase, to descend from heaven.—Applied to the Divine Being,—and to signal blessings from him.—Applied to persons only, when a real presence is signified.—The leading idea.—Its application to the passage under consideration.

" No one hath ascended into heaven, except he who descended from heaven, " the Son of man, who is in heaven." John iii. 13.

THOSE believers in the Deity of the Messiah who understand the phrase under consideration as denoting him in his human nature restrictively, have no plausible method, as appears to me, of interpreting this passage, unless they coincide with the usual gloss of the Unitarians.

Socinus and some of his immediate followers, believed in an actual translation of Jesus to some celestial region, in the interval between his baptism and his entrance on his public ministry; and that he there received instructions and qualifications for his mission.[1]

The opinion preferred by the Calm Inquirer, and by the generality of modern Unitarians, may be thus represented :

[1] *Socini Opera*, tom. ii. pp. 511, 610. *Enjedini Explic. Locorum*, p. 217. *Calm Inq.* p. 40.

The Jewish notion of a local heaven is an absurd
and puerile hypothesis. God is at all times equally
and every where present ; and heaven is a state, not a
place. To be perfectly virtuous, and to be perfectly
happy, is to be in heaven. But *to ascend into heaven*
is a Hebrew form of expression, to denote the acquisition of such knowledge as lies remote from common
apprehension, or is unattainable by the ordinary
faculties of men: for example, Deut. xxx. 12. Prov.
xxx. 4. Baruch iii. 29. Rom. x. 26. The phrase,
therefore, here denotes, "No one is instructed in the
divine counsels." The next clause is to be understood in the same figurative manner, and is perfectly
correlative with the first ; signifying, "Excepting the
Son of man, who had a commission from God to
reveal his will to mankind." This form of expression
also is used in Scripture, to signify what is of divine
origin or authority ; as when our Lord asks, "the
"baptism of John was it *from heaven* or of men?"
Matt. xxi. 25. The last clause in John iii. 13 is a
continuation of the same figure, so that the true sense
of the whole text may be expressed thus: No one
has ever been admitted to a participation of the divine
counsels, except the Son of man, Jesus of Nazareth,
who has been commissioned to reveal the will of God
to men, and who is perfectly instructed and qualified
for this office.[2]

Upon this scheme I submit some remarks :—

1. The idea of a local heaven runs through the
whole tenor of the Old and New Testament, and may
be held without involving any absurd or puerile conceptions, without at all derogating from the most

[2] Abridged from the *Calm Inq.* pp. 45—55.

exalted belief of the Divine immensity, and without
any inconsistency with the facts of just science. That
there are orders of intelligent creatures distinct from
man, and inhabiting other parts of the universe than
our planet, is rendered to the highest degree probable
by " modern discoveries in astronomy,"[*] and is, in a
variety of ways, asserted and implied in the volume of
revelation. There is nothing incongruous with the
most rigid philosophy in the supposition, that the very
locality of perfectly holy and happy beings should be
distinguished by peculiar, and even external, manifestations of that favour of the Deity, which is rich
and diversified in its resources above all human conception. All known analogies countenance such a
supposition. Neither is there improbability in the
idea, that some part of the inconceivably extended
universe may have been prepared by the wisdom of
God, as a region above all others proper for the most
sublime manifestations of that glorious favour. To
such an idea, the language of the Scriptures is not
merely favourable, but decidedly and constantly proceeds on its admission. To affirm that the Omnipresence of the Divine Nature renders impossible any
such peculiar manifestation, is a gratuitous assertion,
and could not be maintained without virtually denying
the attribute of Omnipotence. The question does not
refer to the essential presence of the Deity, but to
special manifestations of his attributes, and communications of the highest blessings from him.

2. The statement is not correct, that " *to ascend to
heaven* is a Hebrew form of expression, to denote the

[*] Mr. Belsham asserts that " modern discoveries in astronomy
amply refute this puerile hypothesis." P. 55.

knowledge of things mysterious and remote from common apprehension." The four passages referred to by Mr. B. and other writers, evidently signify a real and local ascent, with a view to obtain the knowledge, or other blessing, adverted to in the connexion of each. Let the reader impartially examine them. That the sacred writers believed in the possibility of such a corporal ascent, no more derogates from their inspiration, than does their being ignorant of the true construction of the solar system. It was no part of the design of revelation to teach men natural philosophy. In their using the phrase, *ascending into heaven*, the writers evidently conceived of a real penetration into the regions of celestial light and happiness, *in order to the acquisition of the knowledge which is peculiar to the Divine Being.* When Jesus, in the case before us, employs the expression, he neither affirms nor denies the hypothetical possibility of such ascending into heaven; but he states the fact to be that no human being ever had actually so ascended.

Other examples which occur in Scripture of this phrase, clearly refer to a real ascent. The following are all that I have been able to discover, which can affect the present inquiry.

" It is not in the heavens, that [ye should have] to " say, Who will ascend for us into the heavens, and " bring it to us, and cause us to hear it? And [then] " we will do it." Deut. xxx. 12. That is, as Le Clerc paraphrases it, " God hath not expressed in an obscure and perplexing manner the rites of worship and practice of religion, by which ye may obtain his favour; so that it should be in your power to say that it is concealed from you, as if it were known only in

heaven." The succeeding sentence, which in the
same manner affirms that the Israelites needed not to
make long journeys or perilous voyages, to acquire the
knowledge of the Divine will, proves that the words of
the former question intend an actual ascent to some
celestial region.

"Who hath ascended into the heavens, and hath
" descended? Who hath gathered the wind in his
" fists? Who hath established all the ends of the
" earth? Who hath tied up the waters in a garment?
" What is his name? And what the name of his Son?
" For knowest thou?" Prov. xxx. 4.   That the
ascending and descending are here assumed to be the
undoubted properties of the Most High, is manifest
from the succeeding questions: and, as they respect
his supreme power as the Lord of nature, this clause
may probably refer to his universal presence and
agency. I would here, in passing, observe that the
concluding clauses of this energetic passage are rationally and easily interpreted, if we admit that the
ancient Jews had some obscure ideas of a plurality
in the Divine nature.[4] This was the opinion of the
late J. D. Michaelis.[5] Döderlein and Dathe conceive
the expression to be merely the Hebraism for *a pupil*,
as Elijah was a father to Elisha and other *sons* of the
prophets.[6] But this seems far-fetched, and foreign to
the design of the passage.

[4] See Vol. I. pp. 12, 484.
[5] " I will not anticipate the judgment of my reader, by presuming
to determine whether an Only-Begotten Son is here ascribed to
God; though I must candidly acknowledge that, without this doctrine of the New Testament, I cannot explain the words, especially
considering their connexion." *Anmerkung in loc.*
[6] *Dathe Vers. et Not. in Prov.* p. 346.

"If I mount the heavens, there art Thou." Psa.
cxxxix. 8. "Thou hast said in thy heart, Into the
"heavens I will ascend, above the stars of God I will
"exalt my throne;—I will be like the Most High."
Isaiah xiv. 13, 14. "David hath not ascended into
"the heavens." Acts ii. 34. These instances need
no comment. They plainly show that the expression
was commonly understood among the Jews to signify
a real translation to heaven as to a place. This is not
contradicted but confirmed, by the hyperboles and
metaphors, which are derived from this phrase, and
applied to lofty towers, the waves in a storm, splendid
prosperity, exalted privileges, and prodigious sins.[7]

Mr. Belsham, on the authority of Dr. Whitby,
affirms that "the Jews in the Targum say, in honour
of Moses, that 'he ascended into the high heavens,'
by which they could mean no more than his admission to the divine counsels."[8] Whitby, perhaps copying from some author, has not understood the passage,
nor even referred to it rightly. It is evident that
neither he nor Mr. B., who borrows it from him, took
the pains to consult the Targum. The place is in
the paraphrase on Canticles iii. 3, and it very plainly
refers to Moses going up to the top of Mount Sinai,
to intercede for the people on their having made the
golden calf. Some antecedent passages will give light
to it. "The righteous of that generation said, Lord
of the whole world,—bring us near to the acclivity of

[7] See Deut. ix. 1. Ps. cvii. 26. Job xx. 6. Matt. xi. 23. Rev.
xviii. 5.

[8] P. 47. Whitby's words are, "The Jews say, for the honour of
their prophet Moses, that he ascended לשמי מרומה into the high
heavens: Targ. in Cant. i. 5, 11, 12." Paraph. and Notes, John
iii. 13.

Mount Sinai, and give us thy law from the house of thy treasury, which is in the firmament.—Moses their leader ascended to the firmament, and made peace between them and their king.—Then was it said to Moses, Ascend to the firmament, and I will give to thee the two tables of stone carved from the sapphire of the throne of my preciousness.—And, while Moses their leader was in the firmament, to receive the two tables of stone and the law and the commandments, the wicked of that generation arose and made a golden calf.   Then Moses came down, and the two tables of stone in his hands: and on account of the offences of Israel his hands became heavy; and they fell, and were broken.———And he ascended the second time to the firmament and prayed before Jah, and propitiated for the children of Israel.———Moses the chief scribe of Israel answered and spoke thus, *I will ascend to the heavens on high,* and I will pray before Jah, if perhaps he may be propitiated on account of your offences.[9]   According to the frequent acceptation of the Hebrew word for *heaven* or *the heavens,* to denote a moderate elevation in the atmosphere,[10] it is easy to conceive that the summits of lofty mountains might be said to be *on high* and *in the heavens.*   The expression would appear still more appropriate in application to Sinai at the giving of the law, on account of the awful darkness, the thick clouds, the lightnings, and the miraculous phænomena.   But all doubt is set at rest by the occurrence of the very phrase in the writings of Moses.   "Jehovah said to Moses, thus

⁹ *Targum in Cant. Salom.* i. 4, 5, 11, 12; iii. 3. ap. *Waltoni Polygl.* tom. iii. pp. 428, 430, 434.

¹⁰ See Gen. i. 20 ; Ps. civ. 12, and many other places.

" thou shalt say to the children of Israel, Ye are be-
" holders that from the heavens I have spoken with
" you."[11]

However, better authorities[12] than Whitby have
maintained that *to ascend into heaven* is a Hebrew
metaphorical idiom to denote *the diligent application
of the mind to the investigation and attainment of
abstruse knowledge, especially that of God and sacred
things.*[13] Of these critics Schöttgen may be, without
injustice, reckoned the chief, for the extent of his
acquaintance with the Hebraized idioms and the Talmudical writings.   His annotation on John iii. 13, is
as follows : " *No mortal knows the will of my heavenly
Father*, so as to be able to advance any thing from
his own knowledge on this doctrine of regeneration.
That this is the sense of our Lord's words, appears
from Deut. xxx. 12, and Rom. x. 6.   It is a Jewish
expression : for the Rabbinical writers often say of
Moses that he ascended into heaven, and there received a'revelation on the institutions of divine worship.
' At the time when Moses ascended into heaven, he
heard the voice of the holy and blessed God.' (*Bam-
midbar Rabba*, sect. 19, fol. 238, 1. and *Tanchuma*,
fol. 70, 1.) ' It is not in heaven, that thou shouldst
say, O that we had one like Moses the servant of the
Lord, to ascend into heaven and bring it down to us !'
(*Jerusalem Targum* on Deut. xxx. 12.) So also the

[11] Exod. xx. 22.

[12] Vatablus, Cameron, Grotius, &c. as cited by the younger
Raphelius in his Preface to his father's *Annotationes* in SS. ed. 1747.
tom. i.   Mr. B. refers to this Preface, and has made considerable
use of it.

[13] " Μεταφορικῶς verò et impropriè denotat *scrutationem atque
pervestigationem rerum absconditarum.*"   *Raphel. præf.* p. 5.

Commentators on Psalm lxviii. 18, generally explain the words *Thou hast ascended on high*, as referring to Moses, when he received the revelation of the divine law." [14]

The passages before cited from the Targum on Canticles render it highly probable, at least, that these Rabbinical writers intended nothing more than the ascent to the top of Sinai. But, whatever was their meaning, as to the nature and manner of this ascent to heaven, it is very evident from their phraseology that they understood it to have been a literal fact.

It is still more remarkable that Schöttgen and the other learned persons should not have perceived that they were putting the result for the operation, the consequent for the antecedent, the end for the means to which that end was attributed. This seems to me to have been the point of their error. The Jews used a phrase, not improbably derived from the history of Moses, to express what they considered as a *way* or *means* of obtaining the highest divine knowledge; and these authors have transferred it to signify the *acquisition* itself.

3. The correlate expression, *to descend from heaven*, is repeatedly used in Scripture in reference to the Divine Being. [15] Yet it cannot be supposed that a local motion of the Infinite Spirit is intended. The design of such passages undoubtedly is to describe any remarkable *manifestation* to men of the power, intel-

[14] *Schöttgen. Horæ Hebr.* tom. i. p. 330.

[15] For instance, Gen. xlvi. 4. Exod. iii. 8. Ps. xviii. 9 ; cxliv. 5. Isa. lxiv. 1. Nehem. ix. 13. Micah i. 2, 3. " Ex sensu omnino humano, maximeque poetico, sæpissime Deus in libris V. T. dicitur descendisse de cœlo." *Koppe in Eph.* iv. 8.

ligence, mercy, or other attributes of Him, "who inhabiteth eternity."

4. By a natural and easy figure, arising from the phraseology just mentioned, any revealed doctrine, precept, or prediction, or any signal interposition of the divine government, is in Scripture said *to be*, or *to come, from heaven*. So it was predicted that, in the constitution of the Gospel, ": righteousness should "look down from heaven:" "the baptism of John "was from heaven:" "every good and perfect gift is "from above:" "the wrath of God is revealed from "heaven against all ungodliness and unrighteousness "of men:"[16] and, in the Apocalyptic visions, special acts of the divine dispensations, respecting either the present state or the retributions of the future, are described as "coming down from heaven;" and, in these passages, it is evident that the imagery requires the idea to be maintained of a real and local descent.[17] It is also observable that, in every instance in which a *person* is said to be, or to come, from heaven, a *real and literal presence* of the person is manifestly in the design of the sacred writer; and that the improper or figurative use is applied to *things*, such as doctrines and messages, promises, threatenings, and providential dispensations.[18]

5. Though this figurative use of the expression, in application to signal benefits conferred by God, is of frequent occurrence in Scripture, and it would have been scarcely less natural to have employed the same in relation to eminent persons raised up by providence

[16] Ps. lxxxv. 11. Matt. xxi. 25. James i. 17. Rom. i. 18.
[17] Rev. iii. 12 ; xviii. 1 ; xxi. 2.
[18] The reader can judge of this by the use of a Concordance.

for peculiar services to mankind; yet no instance of such application exists, excepting to the Saviour of the world. Upon the notion of the Unitarians, that the expression is synonymous with bearing a divine commission, we might well have expected to find it often used in such a sense. Yet we find not this phrase, or any one like it, ever applied to any illustrious *deliverer* of the Hebrew nation, though commissioned and miraculously supported by God, such as Moses the greatest of political benefactors, or any of the Israelitish judges, or David, or Cyrus, or Zerubbabel; nor to any *prophet*, though divinely inspired to bring glad tidings from the Fountain of mercy, as Elijah, Isaiah, or Malachi; nor to any of the inspired *teachers*, who "received not their doctrine from man, " nor were taught it"[19] by any human means, as Peter, John, or Paul.[20] On the contrary, in the sequel of the passage before us, this is made the very ground of distinction between John the Baptist and Christ. " He who cometh from above is over all: he who is " from the earth, is from the earth, and from the " earth he speaketh : he who cometh from heaven is " over all."[21]

[19] Gal. i. 12.

[20] Yet, even without any suggestion from an established phraseology, such a figure was very likely to occur, in drawing the character of a singularly beneficent person in some high station of authority. Cicero uses it to his brother. "Græci quidem sic te ita viventem intuebuntur, ut quendam ex annalium memoriâ, aut etiam de cœlo divinum hominem esse in provinciam delapsum, putent." "Thus the Greeks will see you acting in such a manner as to fancy that one of their ancient heroes, or even a son of some deity, has descended from heaven to govern the province." *Ep. ad Quint. fratr.* lib. i. ep. i. sect. 2.

[21] Ver. 31.

6. From a careful examination of the scriptural use of the expressions, *from heaven,* and *being, coming,* or *descending from heaven,* it appears to me that the idea intended is A DIVINE ORIGIN, which is, of course, applied variously according to the nature of the subject. Now, if we compare the passages in which such language is employed, in relation to Christ, with those which are acknowledged to refer simply to the peculiar manifestation or energy of God, we shall find that the former are fully as express and definite as the latter, for denoting an ACTUAL and PERSONAL PRESENCE in distinction from any merely figurative idea.

Of the one class we have such passages as these. " I am God, the God of thy father ; I will *go down* " with thee.—I know their sorrows, and I am *come* " *down* to deliver them.—I will *come* to thee, and I " will bless thee.—I will *come down,* and speak with " thee there.—Upon mount Sinai thou didst *descend,* " and speak with them from heaven !——Arouse thy " strength and *come* for our salvation !—O that thou " wouldest bow the heavens, that thou wouldest *come* " *down !*—The Lord Jehovah will be a witness against " you, the Lord from the temple of his holiness : for, " behold ! Jehovah will *come forth* from his own place " and will *descend,* and tread upon the lofty places of " the earth."[23]

On the other hand we have the passage under consideration, and similar declarations concerning the Messiah made by himself or by his inspired servants. We shall proceed to the examination of these in detail. In the mean time, the weight of philological and scrip-

[23] Gen. xlvi. 4. Exod. iii. 7, 8 ; xx. 24. Numb. xi. 17. Nehem. ix. 13. Ps. lxxx. 2. Is. lxiv. 1. Micah i. 2, 3.

tural evidence appears to me to determine the passage
at present before us to this signification :—

" If ye are so averse from apprehending and em-
bracing my testimony with respect to those subjects of
religion which refer to your own reason and conscience
in the present state, how will ye be capable of understanding those more sublime truths, the knowledge of
which is entirely dependent on a revelation from the
Deity himself?   Yet doubt not my ability to give you
correct information, even on those exalted themes.
No human being, indeed, has ever been, or could be,
admitted to that most immediate and perfect manifestation of the Divine Presence which would communicate to him that knowledge.   But the Messiah,
whose superior nature is Eternal, Omniscient, and in
every respect Divine, has assumed the nature of man
for the express purpose of bringing this knowledge
and all other divine blessings to your enjoyment.[23]

[23] Καὶ, the first word in this passage, may be rendered *for, because*.
See *Schleusner* in voc. signif. 8.   *Borger de Constanti Jesu Christi
Indole*, p. 179.   Semler paraphrases vers. 12 and 13, thus :—" But
if ye refuse to give me credit, though I have as yet spoken only of
things which are beginning to be transacted now upon earth among
men ; how will ye believe if I set before you those greater and more
divine subjects on which ye have formed the most erroneous prejudices.   For example, no one before me hath ascended into heaven,
and taught you heavenly things ; however ye are wont to boast of
Moses and others.   He alone knows heavenly things, who hath come
down from heaven, that Son of man who was in heaven before, with
God.   My abode on this earth will not be permanent, nor will any
place be found in my kingdom for those sensual pleasures of which
the Jews are forming their imaginations."   In his Annotations he
says, " this passage intimates that Jesus was that Only-begotten, the
Existing One (ὁ ὢν) who was before with God, and who knows all
things.   He *descended*, when he lived a man among men ; and only
he could teach us *heavenly things*.   'Ο ὢν is put for ὃς ἦν, both here

I 2

Perhaps it will be objected that Nicodemus was not likely to understand our Lord's words as including all this. I reply, that it is not so supposed. It is sufficient if we have evidence, from the subsequent lights of the New Testament doctrine, to assist *our* understanding the comprehensive meaning of the Divine Teacher. The general purport, however, Nicodemus might easily comprehend, notwithstanding his prejudices; and subsequent events and information would gradually enlighten his mind.[24] It is also to be observed, and it is of great importance to be always kept in mind, that it was an essential feature in the plan of our Lord's personal ministry, to deliver some of the

and in chap. i. 18." *Paraph. et Notæ in Johann.* vol. i. p. 97—100. The last remark cannot be absolutely disproved, as the participle is of both tenses; but I see no evidence to *determine* it to the imperfect, and without some such evidence the proper construction must be in the present.

[24] " He here explicitly declares himself to Nicodemus, as more than a mere man; as one descended from heaven, yea, as in heaven when Nicodemus beheld him present before his own eyes. I know not how to understand this but of a superior nature, which is united with the visible human nature: the same that is declared in chap. i. 14." *J. D. Michaelis Anmerk.* "It is not the Saviour's object to show whence heavenly mysteries may and must be learned. Nicodemus knew that already, as he acknowledged Jesus to be a special Divine Teacher sent from heaven. But it was our Lord's design to lead Nicodemus to the knowledge of two heavenly doctrines, as examples" [for the further direction of his mind in divine things:] " his coming forth from God and his divine birth; and his intimate communion with God, in both his natures. The conjunction *and*, introducing the sentence, may be taken as explanatory of the immediately preceding declaration. So καί is used by the best Greek writers; see *Devarius de Particulis* L. Gr. p. 177." *Brucker*, in the Leipzig Variorum Bible. This exegetical use of καί is confirmed and well illustrated by Schleusner, Wahl, and Bretschneider, in their Lexicons.

chief truths of his dispensation in terms of designed
obscurity and reserve. This method of procedure
was necessary till after his death and resurrection.
Then "he opened the understandings of his dis-
" ciples ;" he " showed them plainly of the Father ;"
and he gave to them his Holy Spirit, " to lead them
" into all truth." A great part of our Lord's personal
teachings was the sowing of seed which, though to all
appearance buried in the earth, was destined to spring
up at a future day, and bear an abundant harvest of
knowledge and holiness.

Section II.

ON CHRIST'S COMING FROM ABOVE, AND FROM HEAVEN.

The Calm Inquirer's interpretations stated and examined.—Signification of the
terms.—Connexion and design.

" He who COMETH FROM ABOVE IS OVER ALL: he who is from the earth, is from
" the earth, and from the earth he speaketh: he who COMETH FROM HEAVEN IS
" OVER ALL." John iii. 31.

In these words, the forerunner of Christ draws an
express contrast between his own origin, as merely
human, and the entrance of his Lord among men.
Bengelius, Wetstein, Kuinöl, and others, suppose that
this sentence and those following to the end of ver. 36,
are the reflections of the Evangelist. But, the absence
of any intimation, even the slightest, of a change of
speaker; the violence of such a transition; the want
of any apparent reason for interposing a comment of
the historian; the incongruity of such interpositions
with the ordinary manner of the evangelical historians;
and the suitableness of the whole passage to the obvious
design of John the Baptist, which was to repress the
exaggerated sentiments of his own adherents; are
strong reasons against such an opinion.

Mr. Belsham proposes two interpretations. The
first, and which he seems to prefer, is also that of
Semler. It supposes that the contrast is not between
Christ and John, but between Christ and the pre-

tenders to religious knowledge and authority, "the priests and Levites, who instructed the people and expounded the law." This appears to me to be not only a forced construction, and altogether destitute of any countenance from any terms or allusions in the context, but to be at manifest variance with the continuity of the argument and the design of the whole passage.

His other comment, agreeing with those of Grotius[1] and Mr. Lindsey, is, that the Baptist "may mean to speak modestly and disparagingly of his own authority and commission from God, in comparison with that of Jesus, which was indeed far more illustrious and divine."[2]

This interpretation is not destitute of plausibility: for it suits the design of the connexion, and it is not unusual with the sacred writers to express in absolute terms what is to be understood comparatively. But it is at variance with the undeniable use of scripture phraseology: as we have before observed that no deliverer, benefactor, or prophet, however attended by the most striking evidences of a divine mission, is ever said to have come *from heaven*, or *from above*. To no *person* are these attributes given, except to the Messiah. It is also to be observed, that the passage

---

[1] Grotius, though his predilections lay that way, cannot be adduced as consistently supporting this interpretation: for he explains the *being from the earth*, as referring to the human origin of John, in opposition to that of which he speaks indeed ambiguously, as his words may apply either to the miraculous conception of Jesus, or to a union with the divine indwelling energy. "Ὁ ὢν ἐκ τῆς γῆς natus secundùm Adami legem; in quo non est illa verè divina potestas."

[2] Page 57. So also the Impr. Vers. on the passage.

before us treats the *persons* and the *doctrine* of the parties compared as distinct objects of consideration. With regard to the doctrine, it says that the one teacher "speaketh from the earth," but the other "witnesseth what he had seen and heard." The remaining clauses, therefore, rationally fall under the former head of consideration, with which the fair and literal meaning of the terms more justly agrees. John was "a man sent from God"[3] as well as Jesus: and the simple fact of a divine mission admits not of degrees: it must either be or be not. One divine mission may from its circumstances be "more illustrious" than another; but it cannot, without absurdity, be called "more divine." It is, further, a circumstance of some weight in the determining of this question, that the expressions, *being from above, being from heaven,* and *being over all,* coincide with other instances of phraseology in the Gospel of John: as, when the Messiah is declared to have been "with God, and "upon the bosom of the Father;" and in other passages which will be particularly considered in the following pages. The first of these phrases is also illustrated by Col. iii. 1. "Seek the things above "(τὰ ἄνω) where Christ is, seated at the right hand "of God;" clearly denoting a region, or, which is for the present purpose equivalent, a state of supreme blessedness and dignity. The Messiah, in parallel with Adam, and considered as a new head of mercy and happiness to mankind, is called "the Second "Man, from heaven,"[4] in opposition to the origin of "the first man," who was "of the earth, earthly."

---

[3] John i. 6.
[4] See Note [A], at the end of this Section.

So, likewise, the apostle says that Christ " descended " into the lower parts of the earth," and afterwards " ascended above all the heavens."[5]

From the whole, it appears to me clearly established that, in this passage, the forerunner of Christ expressly puts his own personal origin in contrast with that of his Lord; the one earthly and human, the other heavenly and divine.[6]

[5] Eph. iv. 9. The phrase, " the lower parts of the earth," is probably put for *the earth* merely, by a Hebraism, as opposed to *the skies,* " the height of heaven." Job xxii. 12. See Prov. xxv. 3. Isa. xliv. 23. Joshua ii. 11. " The expression *to descend into the lower parts of the earth,* applied to Christ, signifies that *he came down to this world,* i. e. that he became man, lived on earth, died, was buried, and rose from the dead. John xii. 46; xvi. 28. Κατώτερα has the sense of the positive, not of the superlative." *Rosenmüller in Eph.* iv. 9.

[6] See Note [B] at the end of this Section.

SUPPLEMENTARY NOTES TO SECT. II.

Note [A], page 120.

1 Cor. xv. 47. The words ὁ Κύριος, *the Lord,* are wanting in many of the best authorities. Knapp, Tittman, and Scholz retain them; Dr. Bloomfield is in doubt. The Calm Inquirer says, " The Vulgate renders the text, ' The first man was of the earth, earthy: the second man will be from heaven, heavenly.'—This is not improbably the true reading; and the sense is, ' The first man, taken from the earth, was frail and mortal; the second man will descend from heaven in a heavenly form, and with immortal radiance and vigour.'" p. 121. Upon this I submit these remarks:

1. The addition, *cœlestis,* ὁ οὐράνιος, *the heavenly One,* is found in other good authorities besides the Vulgate (see Wetstein and Griesbach), but I doubt whether the evidence in its favour is sufficient to warrant its reception. It is wanting in the *most* ancient and the best manuscripts, and in all the ancient versions except the Vulgate and the Æthiopic, and the margin of some copies of the Armenian, which is known to have been retouched after the Vulgate.

The addition was probably made from an idea that it was necessary to complete the antithesis. It is, however, of no importance to the sense, either way. Scholz (though a Roman catholic) rejects it.

2. It is unfaithful in the Inquirer to insert *was* and *will be*, without notice to his unlearned readers that those words are not in the Vulgate. The Latin idiom, and the structure of vers. 46 and 48, plainly show that *is* is the proper supplement in both clauses : " Primus homo de terrâ, terrenus : secundus homo de cœlo, cœlestis." These unwarrantable insertions give a turn to the passage in favour of the writer's doctrines.

3. Is not his paraphrase of the second clause, " the second man will descend from heaven," exposed to his own contemptuous censure " of the Jewish notion of a local heaven ?"

Note [B] page 121.

The paraphrase of Nonnus shows, in a striking manner, how ancient and native Greeks understood the words :

Οὔποτε δὲ βροτὸς ἄλλος, ὑπηνέμιον πόδα πάλλων,
Οὐρανίων ἐπάτησεν ἀνέμβατον ἄντυγα κύκλων,
Εἰ μὴ Θέσκελος οὗτος, ὃς ἀθανάτην ἑο μορφὴν
Οὐρανόθεν κατέβαινεν ἀήθεα σαρκὶ συνάπτων·
Ἀνθρώπου μόνος υἱὸς, ὃς, ἀστερόεντι μελάθρῳ
Πάτριον οὖδας ἔχων, αἰώνιος, αἰθέρα ναίει.

" Never did mortal, walking swifter than the winds, tread the inaccessible summit of the heavenly orbs, except that Divine Person who descended from heaven, to unite, in unwonted manner, his own immortal form to flesh ; that only Son of man who, possessing his paternal dwelling in the starry palace, immortal inhabits the sky."

" *He who cometh from above, i. e.* the Son of God ; chap. i. 34. This expression of the Baptist, and the declaration of Christ himself, ver. 13, that the Son of man, before his coming into the world as actually a man, was *in heaven*, i. e. *with God*, is parallel to the expressions in chap. i, 18. *Semler in loc.*

" In this passage, Jesus is placed in contradistinction from other prophets, who received the Spirit in a limited measure ; and even the greatest of them all, John the Baptist. Therefore the clause, ' He who cometh from heaven,' does not signify, ' He who is sent from God,' for the other prophets were that ; but its meaning is ' He who preexisted in heaven, and has really come down from heaven :' the same truth which Jesus affirms of himself in ver. 13. Thus John not only proclaims him to be the Messiah, but also ascribes to him a superior nature." *J. D. Michaelis in loc.*

SECTION III.

ON CHRIST'S DESCENDING FROM HEAVEN, AS THE BREAD OF LIFE.

Occasion of this discourse.—Its design.—Manner of pursuing that design.—Involving a prediction of our Lord's expiatory death.—The reference not to the doctrine of Christ, but to his Person.—Meaning and application of the discourse.

"My Father giveth you the real bread, that from heaven. The bread of God "is that which descendeth from heaven, and giveth life to the world.—I am that "bread of life.—I have descended from heaven, that I might perform, not mine "own will, but the will of him who sent me.—The Jews then murmured concern- "ing him, because he had said, I am the bread which descended from heaven. "And they said, Is not this Jesus the son of Joseph, whose father and mother we "know? How then doth he say, I descended from heaven? Jesus answered, "Murmur not among each other.—Every one who hath heard from the Father, "and hath learned, cometh to me. Not that any one hath beheld the Father; "excepting he who is from God: he hath beheld the Father.—This is the bread "which descendeth from heaven.—I am that living bread which descendeth from "heaven. If any one eat of this bread, he shall live for ever; and this bread "which I will give is my flesh, which I will give for the life of the world.—As "the Father who liveth hath sent me, and I live by means of the Father; so he "who feedeth on me, he also shall live by means of me. This is the bread which "hath descended from heaven.—Jesus, knowing in himself that his disciples "murmured about this, said to them, Is this revolting to you? If, then, ye "should see the Son of Man ascending where he was at the first! The spirit is "that which giveth life; the flesh availeth nothing. The words which I speak "unto you are spirit, and are life." John vi. 32, 35, 38, 41—43, 45, 46, 50, 51, 57, 58, 61—63.

IT must be allowed by all, that the discourse of our Lord, from which the preceding extracts are taken, presents great difficulties to any one who desires to be an unbiassed and faithful interpreter. I cannot, however, persuade myself that it was intended for the single and temporary purpose, as the Calm Inquirer represents, of getting rid of some pretended disciples of Jesus, "who had followed him from mercenary and political motives only." Had this been the object, it was a very transient one, it was immediately answered, and the discourse was not necessary or even proper to be preserved. I trust it is not irreverent to say this: for upon the hypothesis of the discourse having been contrived to be obscure, incomprehensible, and repulsive, only to answer a purpose of momentary exigency; it cannot but appear unfit for general use, more likely to perplex than to instruct future generations, who would have neither the prejudices nor the vices of our Lord's immediate hearers, and upon the whole calculated to lead into serious error. Yet it is recorded at great length, and with extraordinary minuteness. Surely, then, it is but reasonable to assume that, besides whatever immediate effect it was intended to produce, it contains instructions interesting and momentous to men of all times and countries.

The *Occasion*, indeed, of the discourse was furnished by the mercenary professions and pertinacious adherence of a multitude, who were moved by the hope of his gratifying their national ambition, and still more by the expectation of being fed, without their own care or toil, by his miraculous power. They sought Jesus, only "because they had eaten of the loaves and " were filled :" and they showed what was principal in their hearts, by artfully insinuating that the most eligible kind of miracle would be one to give them plenty of food: vers. 31, 34. The more politic of them probably extended their designs much farther; and contemplated his being able to support armies, for the establishment of their expected dominion over

all other nations. From the appetite of hunger, therefore, Jesus, who could with dignity employ any object
or any circumstance as a vehicle of divine instruction,
derived the occasion of this address; and taught them
that they were labouring under a much deeper necessity, and that God had graciously provided a suitable
relief : " Work not [only] for the food which perisheth,
" but for the food which endureth to eternal life,
" which the Son of man will give to you : for him
" hath the Father, even God, sealed;" that is, hath
sanctioned and set him apart for this great purpose of
heavenly mercy.

Hence arose the discourse which, notwithstanding
repeated interruptions, our Divine Teacher continued
to a clear and perfect close, so as to afford the idea of
having embraced all the parts of his design. That
Design, as a careful attention will perceive, was to
break the charm of destructive ambition, to wean his
hearers from their low voluptuousness, to produce
a conviction in their minds of that all-important,
but neglected, spiritual necessity under which they
laboured, and to excite them to seek the supplies
of divine grace by humble and earnest supplication : " I am the bread of life; he who cometh
" to me shall not hunger : him who cometh to me I
" will in no wise cast out : I will give my flesh for
" the life of the world." Vers. 35, 37, 51. Such a
design of kindness to the most unworthy was in
harmony with the whole conduct of the meek and
patient Saviour, who " bore the contradiction of sinners against himself," and always showed the tenderest compassion for his most malignant enemies.
The Calm Inquirer appears to have paid but a super-

ficial attention to the spirit of this discourse and the
affections which it indicates, when he says that its
" design was to shock their prejudices, to disgust their
feelings, and to alienate them from his society." [1]

The *Manner* of pursuing this design is by declaring,
that *his own death* [2] must intervene as the means of
procuring for men those blessings which they so
needed ; that a *participation* of those benefits, analogous in its effects on the mind to the use of nutriment
for corporal sustenance, was necessary to the desired
deliverance from evil and possession of immortal hap-

---

[1] Page 57.

[2] Mr. Belsham admits it to be " not improbable that our Lord
here has an allusion to his own death." *Impr. V. in loc.*   But
critics of the greatest name, and those who were far from being
favourable to the doctrines usually called evangelical, have thought
the allusion to be certain. " Not only my doctrine is food unto
eternal life, but also my death will so be.—He uses the separate
terms, *flesh* and *blood*, to intimate, not death in any way, but a violent
and bloody death."   *Grot. in vers.* 51, 53.   " Unless I die for you
(meaning a violent death, by which the blood is separated from the
body), and unless ye believe my words, and consequently in me : for
by faith we derive to ourselves the power and efficacy of the death of
Christ." *Schlicting. in ver.* 53.   " The blood is mentioned in distinction from the flesh, to denote the suffering by a violent death.
My death is equally useful and necessary to the obtaining of eternal
life, as food and drink are to the sustenance of the present." *Wetst.
in ver.* 53.   " My death, which I shall suffer for the salvation of
mankind, is bread : *i. e.* it will furnish your minds with motives to
virtue, and with the glad hope and consolation of eternal life.   It is
evident that Christ speaks of his body, in reference to his intention
of yielding it to be slain.   Any one is said to *give his body*, who
yields it to be tortured and put to death : see 1 Cor. xiii. 3.   To *eat
the flesh and drink the blood* of Christ, denotes to receive and appropriate the blessings resulting from his bloody death ; pardon of sin,
and peace of mind."—*Rosenmüller in vers.* 51, 53.   In the Hebrew
idiom, *blood* is applied to denote death by violence.   See *Vorstius de
Hebraismis N. T.* ed. Fischeri, p. 413. Leipz. 1778.

piness; and that a *preparatory discipline,* by a gracious and divine influence, was requisite for the understanding of his doctrine and the enjoyment of his benefits. " Verily, verily, I say unto you, except ye eat the " flesh of the Son of Man, and drink his blood, ye " have not life in yourselves.—For my flesh is truly " food, and my blood is truly drink. He who feedeth " on me shall live by means of me : he abideth in me, " and I in him.—No one can come to me, except the " Father, who hath sent me, draw him.—Every one " who hath heard from the Father, and learneth, " cometh unto me." Vers. 53, 55, 57 ; and 44, 45.

The declaration which is the basis of the discourse, is, therefore, a *Prediction ;* and may be expected to partake of the essential characters of scripture-prophecy. Now we find these two characters, in particular, actually belonging to it.

(1.) The mixture of literal and figurative diction, which every studious reader must have noticed to be so observable a feature in the style of the Old Testament Prophets. Thus, when Christ says that he came down from heaven, that he was from God, that he performed the will of God, that he would give himself to a violent and bloody death for the salvation of mankind, that he would then return to his previous state of dignity (ver. 62), and that divine teaching was necessary to a right and efficient compliance with his will, I conceive that he uses language in its plain and ordinary sense, and in which his hearers would readily understand him : but, when he calls himself the bread of life, and his flesh and blood food and drink, and declares that men must accordingly feed upon them, he uses figurative, but not unintelligible or very

obscure language, to express that the fact of his dying
for the salvation of men was necessary to be cordially
believed, and to be acted upon as a principle of religious obedience, in order to the acquisition of true
happiness.

(2.) The envelope of obscurity, which was necessary to guard the *public* prediction of any future
event, and which was to continue till it should be
taken off by the event itself.   That event, in this case,
was the extreme sufferings and cruel death of the
Saviour.   Of this catastrophe it was his manner to
speak "obscurely and darkly," as Archbishop Newcome observes,[3] to his public and promiscuous audi-
tories;[4] and it was only to his disciples in private
that he, greatly to their surprise, foretold it in plain
terms.[5]

From thus considering the Occasion, the Design,
the Tenor, and the Manner, of this important discourse,
we may obtain some light for the satisfactory interpreting of its terms and clauses.   But that which
alone concerns our present investigation, is to determine WHAT that is which is repeatedly said "to have
" descended from heaven."

Dr. Priestley, and others before him, conceive that
our Lord " means, by his flesh and blood, his *doctrine*,
which may be called the food of the soul:"[6] and the
Calm Inquirer adopts the same hypothesis.

Of the doctrine of Christ it may, indeed, be truly
said, that it "came down from heaven," as being the

---

[3] *On our Lord's Conduct as a Divine Instructor,* p. 179.

[4] For example, John ii. 20, 21 ; iii. 14 ; viii. 28.   Matt. xxi.
33—40.

[5] Matt. xvii. 12, 22.   Mark viii. 31, &c.

[6] *Notes on Script.* vol. iii. p. 232.

revelation of God, and that, as the instrument, "it
" giveth life to the world."

But the subject described by our Lord is something
which could "*give itself for*[1] the life of the world,"
and which, in so doing, was to suffer a violent and
cruel death, as the text expresses in the Hebraized
idiom. Could this be said of a doctrine, or a system
of doctrines?

It was something which had *intelligence*, capacity of
design, and *voluntary action*. " I have descended
" from heaven, that I might perform, not mine own
" will, but the will of him who sent me." Can this
be a doctrine?

It was something which "the Father who liveth
" had sent, and which lived by means of the Father ;"
evidently signifying the same kind of real and active
(not figurative) life which belongs to the Parent and
Fountain of existence. Was this a doctrine?

Further: if we maintain that, in all these explicit
declarations of personal acts performed by the speaker
himself, nothing was intended but to describe a doctrine given by revelation to Jesus, and by him communicated to the rest of mankind, I do not see that
we can avoid to deem our Lord's discourse, not merely
(as Mr. B. admits) "extravagant, offensive, and dis-
gusting," and calculated to " confound and perplex
the understanding ;"[2] but absolutely irreconcilable

---

[1] 'Υπὲρ with the genitive, denoting *substitution*, or acting *on the
behalf* of another. So we read, " Christ died *for* the ungodly.":
Rom. v. 6. " My body, given *for* you ;—my blood, poured out *for*
" you." Luke xxii. 19, 20. " Christ Jesus gave himself a ransom *for*
" all." 1 Tim. ii. 6. " Who gave himself *for* us." Titus ii. 14. " If
" God be *for* us." Rom. viii. 31. " The Spirit maketh intercession
" *for* us." Ib. ver. 26, &c.

[2] Pages 59, 62, &c.

with any just ideas of wisdom, benevolence, and integrity in the Teacher himself.

These appear to me solid and decisive reasons for concluding that it was, not of his doctrine, but of HIS PERSON, that our Lord, in this memorable passage, says that " it *came down from heaven*," and was given to a violent and cruel death " for the life of the world."

But it may be said, that this argument overthrows itself by proving too much. If the conclusion be that " the flesh and blood," which suffered on the cross, had a preexistent and celestial dignity, and " de-" scended from heaven;" it is palpably erroneous: on no hypothesis is this supposed; therefore the premises must be false, or the illation incorrect, and the argument is reduced to an absurdity.

I reply, that this conclusion is neither asserted nor implied; that the description *Son of man* is a *formula* equivalent to the term *Messiah*, and is to be construed according to its conventional, not its etymological, signification; and that the premises do not contain what the objection imputes to them, but only this, that the Preexistent and Divine Nature which " de-" scended from heaven," and, when its object was accomplished, "ascended where it was before" (in the sense of those phrases as they occur in the Old Testament), united itself to human flesh and blood for the most wise and gracious purposes; among which purposes it was, that suffering and death should be endured for the redemption of sinful mankind. This method of conceiving the case is both authorized and exemplified by the declaration, "The WORD became " flesh:" chap. i. 14.[9]

---

[9] " The Jews were peculiarly indignant at Jesus's representing

The pretended admirers of Jesus were now convinced, that he would never countenance their views, nor promote their ambitious and worldly objects; and were especially displeased at the prediction of his sufferings and death, so repugnant to their preposessions on the nature and enjoyments of the Messiah's reign, and their expectations of grandeur and voluptuous pleasures from his conquests. They, therefore, manifested strong feelings of disappointment and irritation. But "Jesus said to them, Is this revolting "to you? If, then, ye should see the Son of Man "ascending where he was at the first! The spirit is "that which giveth life; the flesh availeth nothing. "The words which I speak unto you are spirit and "are life."

The last sentence is regarded by Mr. B. as a "key to the whole preceding discourse."[10] I have no objection to accept it as such; and it seems to me to substantiate the view above given of the design and meaning of the whole. I therefore propose the following as a fair paraphrase of our Lord's words:

himself as coming down from heaven; by which expression he ascribes to himself a nature superior to the human which they beheld. The design of the Evangelist in the introduction of this discourse, is easily perceived by comparing it with chap. i. 1—14. The doctrines there delivered, John here designs to confirm by Jesus's own declarations." *J. D. Mich.* on v. 40, 41.

[10] He thus paraphrases ver. 63. " It is the hidden meaning of my enigmatical discourse which alone is useful. If you could actually eat my flesh, it would do you no good. The doctrine which I teach is that heavenly bread, that flesh and blood, which if received, digested, and reduced to a living principle of action, will lead to everlasting life." P. 69.——" What would my flesh avail you to eternal life, even if ye were carnally to eat it ?" *Schlicting.* " Eating my flesh, in the gross and literal sense, would be of no manner of advantage to the life of souls." *Guyse.*

K 2

" If your prejudices are so shocked by my assurance that the Messiah must pass through the lowest degradation and an excruciating death, how will your disappointment be increased when you find that, on his reassuming his pristine dignity, and ascending to the throne of his glory, in the exercise of all power in heaven and on earth, he will confer on his disciples no such happiness as you desire! He will give no provinces nor estates ; no titles, nor riches, nor carnal gratifications. The blessings of his reign are not those of sense, but are of an intellectual and holy kind. The divine energy, which accompanies the truth taught by me, is the only cause of the enjoyment of those immortal blessings : while every profession, observance, or privilege, that is merely external, can be of no avail to your real and eternal happiness ; nor could even the actual feeding on my flesh and blood, if so horrid an attempt were made. My doctrine teaches, and when sincerely believed communicates, that divine energy and that real happiness."

SECTION IV.

ON CHRIST'S COMING FROM ABOVE, AND FROM GOD.

Scope and terms of the passage.—Preexistence implied.—Our Lord's argument
resting on the fact of his superior nature.

" I know whence I came and whither I go ; but ye know not whence I come,
" or whither I go.—Ye are of the things below, I am of those above : ye are of
" this world, I am not of this world.—If ye believe not that I am [that which I
" have now been declaring], ye shall die in your sins.—I proceeded forth from
" God, and I am come : for I have not come of myself, but he hath sent me."—
John viii. 14, 23, 24, 42.

THIS passage is attended with considerable difficulty.
On the one hand, the address of our Lord to the
Jews, " Ye are of the things below, ye are of this
" world," undoubtedly describes moral qualities : *q. d.*
" Your principles and motives are selfish, base and
worldly." Of course, the opposed clauses must be
understood of moral qualities also ; and are an avowal
of the pure, holy, and elevated character of the Blessed
Jesus, in contradiction to the calumnies of his adversaries.

But, on the other hand, philological justice is not
done to the expressions of Christ, unless we take them
in a more extended sense. The phrases ἄνω and τὰ
ἄνω, in the New Testament and in the Septuagint, are
scarcely, if ever, used in relation to sacred things,
except when there is a manifest reference to the heavenly state : and in their common use they always

relate to local elevation.[1] I am, therefore, disposed
to think that an impartial regard to the fair meaning
of the words would lead to some such paraphrase as
the following :

" As ye are earthly in your origin, so are ye low,
mean, and carnal in your sentiments and desires.
This lower world gave you birth, and ye accordingly
show yourselves to have no taste for any enjoyments
but the pleasures and pursuits of this transitory and
degenerate state. But I am of a higher nature and
character. I have come into this humbled condition
from the immediate manifestation of the presence and
glory of God. My principles, doctrines, and objects
are, therefore, pure and holy, spiritual and heavenly."

But the other parts of the passage are less capable
of being bent from their plain and obvious meaning.
" I know whence I came ; ye know not whence I
" come : I proceeded forth from God, and I am come,"
or, as would be perhaps a more exact rendering,
" I am arrived." Let the reader examine, by the
help of Trommius's and Schmidt's Concordances, the
very numerous instances, in which these common
words occur : and he will not, I think, find an instance in which a real transition of place or of state is
not manifestly intended. These " expressions," says
Mr. B., " very naturally indicate that Jesus was the
chosen messenger of God to the human race :"[2] Of
this there is no question : but do they not as naturally,
and even necessarily, bear the indication of a *pre-*

---

[1] See Gal. iv. 26. Col. iii. 1, 2. Phil. iii. 14. and in the LXX,
Exod. xx. 4. 3 Kings viii. 23. Ps. l. (LXX. xlix.) 4. and other
places.

[2] Page 70.

existent state, in relation to a change from which the Divine Messiah could say, "Behold I *am come* to do " thy will, O God! I proceeded forth from the Father, " and I have come into the world?"[3] A similar objection lies against the Inquirer's gloss on the 14th verse,[4] and on the third verse of chap. xiii. as in each case not answering to the grammatical and honest construction of the words.

From the very remarkable kind of argument contained in this verse, another important consideration arises. The words which have been cited contain the premises of our Lord's conclusion, that his own testimony in his own favour had a claim of right to be admitted as valid. The Mosaic law required two witnesses, at the least, for the establishment of a litigated matter.[5] To this law Jesus refers in ver. 17 ; and, in allusion to it, he had said, on a previous occasion, that his own testimony could not be admitted on his own behalf : " If I were to bear witness concern-

---

[3] Heb. x. 7, ἥκω, the last of the verbs used in our text. John xvi. 28 : this passage Mr. Belsham considers to denote only that Jesus " appeared in public as a messenger from God." (P. 104.) But this interpretation is plainly inconsistent with the meaning of the words, and can be sustained only on the principle of *quidlibet ex quolibet.* The reply of the disciples, ver. 30, " By this we believe that thou " hast proceeded forth from God ;"—is connected with a declaration of the omniscience of Christ : and we have seen evidence (Vol. I. pp. 525, 572, 578, 590,) that the ancient Jews had notions, however obscure and imperfect, of the superior nature and preexistence of the Messiah. As for the mere construction of the words, on all the principles of grammar and usage, it is incapable of being questioned. We have the phrase in John iv. 30, " They came out from the city, " and came to him."

[4] " I know from whom I received my authority, and to whom I am accountable ; but you are wilfully ignorant of both." P. 153.

[5] Deut. xix. 15, and other places.

" ing myself, my testimony would not be worthy of
" credit."⁶ But now he declares what is apparently
a contradiction in terms. " If I even bear witness
" concerning myself, my testimony is worthy of credit.
" In your law it is written, that the testimony of two
" persons is worthy of credit. I am he that beareth
" witness concerning myself; and the Father who
" hath sent me beareth witness concerning me."⁷ Was
it ever known, under any system of law, in any court
of judicature, that when the written law had prescribed
two witnesses as the lowest number admissible, a party
in a cause⁸ should step forward and demand, upon
the footing of that very law, to be accepted as himself
the second witness in his own favour? Would such
a composition of "two witnesses" be for a moment
listened to? It is useless to say, as commentators
have generally done, to solve the difficulty, that the
blamelessness of our Lord's life and manners entitled
him to have his veracity unquestioned: for it is of the
very essence of juridical testimony that it should be
from other persons than the parties to a suit, and the
very design of admitting witnesses is to take the facts
of a case out of the hands of parties.

⁶ Chap. v. 31. "'Αληθής' vim juris habens;—quod in dubium
vocari non potest;—fidem habens publicam." *Schleusn.* " Certæ
fidei ;—fide dignissimum." *Kuinöl.*

⁷ Vers. 14, 17, 18.

⁸ The Jewish Rabbinical law says, " A person is not a credible
witness on his own account." *Mischna, Surenhusii,* tom. iii. p. 63.
" More majorum comparatum est, ut in minimis rebus homines
amplissimi testimonium de suâ re non dicerent. It has been established by the practice of our ancestors, that men, even of the
highest respectability, should never be witnesses in their own cause,
even on the most trivial occasions." *Cicer. Or. pro Roscio Am.*
sect. 36.

"I must confess that I can discover no mode of freeing the Blessed Jesus from the charge of employing a low and disingenuous sophistry, (*horresco reputans !*) —except the supposition that his mind referred to THAT HEAVENLY AND DIVINE NATURE which, upon our hypothesis, *he was conscious dwelt within him.* If this be admitted, we have a ground on which to rest the truth and honour of our Lord's assertions, and the justness of his argument : we have the distinct testimony of the Father, at the baptism and transfiguration of Jesus and on other occasions; and we have that of the Son, the Eternal Word, in the miracles which he performed : two witnesses above all exception, bearing distinct yet united testimony to the words of the man of Nazareth. Thus, also, the *argument* of our Lord is put in an intelligible position. "If I even bear witness concerning myself, my testi-" mony is worthy of credit :"—Why ?—"*Because* I " know whence I came and whither I go ;" *q. d.* "My consciousness of that Superior and Divine Nature, which has manifested itself in this real and proper human existence, and which will shine forth in that glorified state to which this humanity will shortly be advanced, is the ground of my alleging that this second testimony, additional to that of my Father, is independent and certain."

SECTION V.

ON CHRIST'S POSSESSING GLORY WITH THE FATHER, BEFORE THE
WORLD.

Import of the Glory belonging to Christ.—Reciprocal to the Father and the Son.
—Its progression.—How conferred upon the Apostles and other Christians.—
How possessed by the Messiah before the existence of the created universe.—
How given in his mediatorial exaltation.—Unitarian interpretation stated and
examined.—Classification of passages appealed to, and investigation of their
sense.—The Calm Inquirer's criticism examined.—Rabbinical phraseology
not applicable to this case.

" And now, Thou, O Father, glorify me, with thyself, by the glory which I had
" before the world was, with thee !"—John xvii. 5.

MR. BELSHAM concludes, from his investigation of
this passage, "that the true interpretation of this
celebrated clause in our Lord's valedictory prayer,—
that which best suits the connexion, and which is
most consistent with the dignity and disinterestedness
of his character,—contains no proof of his preexistence, but is perfectly compatible with his proper
humanity; *viz.* ' And now, O Father, glorify thou
' me with thy own self ;' *q. d.* allow me to participate
in that which is thy own greatest glory, 'with the
' glory which I had with thee before the world was ;'
the glory of recovering lost mankind to virtue and
happiness, a glory which was intended and reserved
for me in the eternal immutable counsels of infinite
wisdom and benevolence."[1]

[1] Page 114.

The principal grounds on which he rests this interpretation are, the position which, he says, few, if any,
before Mr. Lindsey, had perceived, that the *glory* of
Christ consisted in the success of his doctrine as the
means of recovering mankind from sin and death to
virtue and happiness; and that this glory, "having
been the object of the divine, eternal, and immutable
purpose, and the subject of the divine promise, is
represented by our Lord as what he possessed with
the Father before the world was."

We must, therefore, endeavour to ascertain the real
import of the *glory* spoken of by our Lord, and to
determine whether his language can be rationally
understood as merely anticipative.

(1.) I agree with Mr. Lindsey and the Inquirer,
that the GLORY desired by Jesus Christ was not any
"personal benefit," or "high distinction," or any
other "selfish" object; and that the "fulfilling the
purposes of his divine mission" was associated with
that object, or, more properly speaking, included in
it : but I do not think that they have discovered the
just idea of the term.

The words in question are in continuity with others
which clearly refer to the same object. "I have
"glorified Thee on the earth : I have completed the
"work which thou hast given me to perform :—I
"have manifested Thy Name to the men whom thou
"hast given me." Thus the MANIFESTATION of the
DIVINE NAME, to the selected objects of divine grace,
is that "glorifying the Father" which the Lord Jesus
has perfectly accomplished.

The Scripture uses THE NAME OF GOD as a com-
pendious formula to denote His Infinite and Absolute

Perfection, His Fulness of all possible Excellencies, the Total of Jehovah's Awful and Lovely Attributes, so far as they can be known by finite intelligences. The presenting of this great object to the accountable universe, in order to excite and direct the love and admiration, homage and obedience, of every rational creature to HIM whom this name represents, is declared to be the supreme purpose of the Most High in the creation and government of the world : and this *display*, or *emanation* of the Divine Excellency, is called in Scripture *the* GLORY *of God.* Passages to this effect, of which the following is a selection, are extremely numerous.—" And what wilt thou do for " thy great name? Jehovah, our Lord, how excellent " is thy name in all the earth ! He led them by the " right hand of Moses,—to make to himself an ever- " lasting name. And in very deed for this purpose I " have raised thee up, to display in thee my power, " and to declare my name in all the earth. I wrought " for the sake of my name, that it might not be pro- " faned in the eyes of the nations. For the sake of " my name,—for mine own sake, for mine own sake, " I will work ; for how shall it be profaned? And " my glory to another I will not give. As truly as I " live, the whole earth shall be filled with the glory of " Jehovah."[1]

To make known this NAME and GLORY to mortals, in all the efficacious methods which eternal wisdom has deemed fit, was a chief object of our Lord's labours and instructions. We have "the illumination of the " knowledge of the glory of God in the face of Jesus

[1] Josh. vii. 9.   Ps. viii. 1.   Isa. lxiii. 12.   Exod. ix. 16.   Ezek. xx. 9.   Isa. xlviii. 9, 11.   Numb. xiv. 21.

" Christ: No one hath beheld God at any time: the
" Only-begotten Son, who is on the bosom of the
" Father; he hath declared him." Hence the Lord
Jesus Christ is " the Image of the Invisible God," and
" the Effulgence of his glory."[1] This is the display
of *moral* and *spiritual* Excellency, " the manifestation
" of the Name of God, the glorifying of the Father,"
which the Lord Jesus declares himself to have accomplished.

Now, it is evident that our Lord represents the
glorifying of himself by the Father, as *reciprocal* to
that which he had rendered to the Father. This idea
of reciprocity is clearly and strongly expressed in his
words; " Glorify thy Son, that thy Son also may
" glorify thee :—I have glorified thee ;—and now do
" thou, O Father, glorify me !"

It therefore follows that the " glorifying of Christ,"
or the " giving to him of glory," by the Divine
Father, is the MANIFESTATION OF HIS NAME, the unveiling of THE SAME moral and spiritual Excellence,
THE SAME Absolute and Infinite Perfection, in the
person and character of the Son of God. This was
to be effected, so far as the present imperfect state will
admit, by the extension and success of the Christian
religion, according to the suggestion of Mr. Lindsey,
but with a purity and power to which I fear his ideas
did not extend. Of this interpretation, however, he
was not the discoverer. Greater and better divines
maintained it before him. President Edwards has
considered the subject at length, and places it in a
clear and strong light.[4]—Yet this is not all, " The

---

[1] 2 Cor. iv. 6.   John i. 18.   Col. i. 15.   Heb. i. 3.
[4] *Dissertation on the Chief End of God in the Creation of the*

" whole earth must indeed be filled with the glory"
of the Messiah; and " all people, nations, and lan-
" guages, shall serve him." His GLORY, by the eventual triumphs of knowledge, holiness, and happiness
in the present state of mankind, will be divinely great :
but every blessing which earth can enjoy, will be no
more than the dawn of a celestial and immortal day.
The communication of all that constitutes supreme
felicity, will for ever flow to the occupants of the
heavenly state, from the unspeakable fulness of the
Redeemer. They, partakers of his holiness and his
joy, " shall be with him where he is, and shall BEHOLD
" HIS GLORY," his unrivalled and infinite perfection of
all natural and moral excellence. They " shall see
" Him AS HE IS."——" They sing a new song, saying,
" Thou art worthy to take the book and to open its
" seals, for thou wast slain and hast redeemed us to
" God by thy blood, from every tribe and tongue and
" people and nation : and hast made us unto our God
" kings and priests, and we shall reign upon the earth.
" And I beheld, and I heard the voice of many angels
" round about the throne, and the living beings, and
" the elders : and their number was ten thousand
" times ten thousand and thousands of thousands,
" saying with a loud voice, Worthy is the Lamb who
" was slain, to receive power and riches and wisdom
" and strength and honour and glory and blessing !

World; in his Works, vol. i. p. 515, &c. " It appears," says that
penetrating writer, " that the expressions of divine grace, in the
sanctification and happiness of the redeemed, are especially that
GLORY of Christ, and of his Father, which was ' the joy that was set
before him,' for which he ' endured the cross and despised the
shame ;' and, that this glory was especially the end of ' the travail of
his soul,' in obtaining which end he was ' satisfied.'" P. 522.

" And every creature which is in the heaven and upon
" the earth, and under the earth and in the sea, and
" all things in them, I heard saying, To HIM who
" sitteth upon the throne, and to THE LAMB, be bless-
" ing and honour and glory and power, for ever and
" ever !"[5]

It is in accordance with this truth that the New
Testament attributes THE SAME *importance* and *dignity*
to the Name of Christ, which the current style of the
Old Testament does to the Name of Jehovah.   To
" bear the Name" of Christ was the great honour of
the Apostolic ministry.[6]   " In his Name" the miracles
were wrought.[7]   " Believing in his Name" is uniformly represented as of absolute necessity to salvation.[8]   " In his Name the nations shall hope."[9]   ¶ In
" his Name," religious instruction, baptism, ecclesiastical discipline, and other divine institutions were to
be administered.[10]   Christian obedience to moral precepts is to be rendered " all in his Name."[11]   It was
the very designation of his primitive disciples, that
" they called upon his Name."[12]   Pardon of sin, and
all the blessings of salvation and eternal life, are conferred upon mankind " in his Name" alone, and
" on account of his Name."[13]   In fine, his Name is

[4] 1 John iii. 2.   Rev. v. 9—12.

[6] Acts ix. 15.   [7] Ib. iii. 16.

[8] John iii. 18.   [9] Matt. xii. 21.

[10] Acts ix. 27 ; xix. 5.   1 Cor. v. 4.   3 John 7.

[11] Col. iii. 17.

[12] Acts ix. 13, 14.   1 Cor. i. 2.   This branch of our subject will
be more fully considered in a following chapter.   It may be sufficient, here to observe that the just construction of ἐπικαλεῖσθαι with
the accusative case, is *active*, and denotes address, entreaty, or
invocation.

[13] Acts x. 43 ; iv. 12.   1 John v. 13 ; ii. 12.

INSCRUTABLE: "no one knoweth it, except HIM-
"SELF."[14]

Under the Old Testament, God had declared,
" I am Jehovah, that is my Name, and my Glory I
" will not give to another."[15]. But in this exalted
and diversified manner does the New Testament give
GLORY *to the* NAME of our Lord Jesus Christ. Thus
" is the Son of man glorified, and God is glorified in
" him." The sublime subject is, therefore, but one,
though viewed under different aspects. As the glory,
the manifestation of the name, of the Eternal Father,
is the unveiling to created minds of His All-Perfect
Majesty; so is the glory of the Son the manifestation
of HIS Name, his Divine Nature and Perfections, to
all holy and happy beings, for ever and ever.

The consummation of this manifested glory will be
in the blessed discoveries of the heavenly state: but
its commencement and progress are by the efficacy of
the gospel now. It is the doctrine of Christ, as
" revealed to his holy apostles and prophets by the
" Spirit," that makes known to men His Name, his
true character and glory, in relation to his person, his
holy obedience, his sufferings and death, his exaltation
and dominion, his benevolence, and the blessings
which he confers, his final exercise of judgment and
its everlasting consequences. This doctrine presents
to our view " the unsearchable riches of Christ, the
" love of Christ which passeth knowledge, the fulness
" of Christ whence all true believers receive grace for
" grace, the great mystery of godliness, the mystery of
" Christ;—that the NAME of our Lord Jesus Christ

---

[14] Rev. xix. 12.   [15] Isa. xlii. 8.

may be glorified, upon whose head are many crowns, and whose name is above every name."

Thus is apparent the propriety of our Lord's further declaration : " The glory, which thou hast given to me, " I have given to them." The apostles were his instruments and agents in making known " the riches of his " glory." They published his inspired truth, and conveyed through the earth the declaration of his Name : he manifested to them his glory, and, by their faithful and unerring promulgation of it, " he was glorified in " them :" and they, with all who have believed their testimony, and trod in the steps of their obedience, shall be sharers in the glory of their Saviour's divine happiness. " They shall be with HIM, where He is, " and shall behold His glory."[16]

This then appears to have been the precise object of our Lord's prayer ; that, as he had, by his mediation and doctrine, manifested the Name and Glory of his Divine Father, so his own Name and Glory might be manifested, by his word and his Spirit, in the ministry of his servants, in the knowledge, faith, and holiness of his people universally, in the triumphs of his truth on earth, and in the unclouded brightness of that state in which his faithful followers " shall see " him AS HE IS."[17] Now this is no other than, that his Original and Divine Excellency, which by his assumption of the human nature had been obscured, as the sun behind a dense cloud, might be unveiled, and might shine forth in its proper and unchangeable character.

(2.) If this view be correct, on the real import of the peculiar glory predicated of Christ, it shows at

[16] Ver. 24.   [17] 1 John iii. 2.

once 'the propriety of the remaining clauses—" the
" glory which I had, with Thee, before the world was."
It is the *primeval perfection* of the Messiah, the Son of
God, to whom, as we have before found satisfactory
evidence, names, characters, and attributes were assigned in the prophetic writings, declaring him to be
the Eternal and Immutable Being, the Creator, God;
the Mighty God, Adonai, Elohim, Jehovah; and
whose comings forth are from eternity, from the days
of the everlasting period:[18] a perfection which had
not been lost or diminished, but which was now to
shine forth with a lustre never before beheld by
created beings.[19]

This interpretation, also, shows the irrelevancy of
Dr. Priestley's question : " What propriety could
there be in Christ's praying, as the reward of his
sufferings, for the same state of glory which he had
enjoyed before them ? This would be to make it no
reward at all."[20] The answer to this query is that,
though the glory, in itself considered, is the same, yet
the object sought was a new and more advantageous
manner of its manifestation. Exactly upon the same
principle, the essential glory of Jehovah, which is
infinite and immutable, and therefore can admit of no
accession, is spoken of in Scripture as receiving great
additions with respect to the modes of its various and
higher display. " It shall be unto me for a name of
" joy, for praise, and for honour, to all nations of the
" earth. By those that approach unto me I will be
" sanctified, and in the presence of all the people I

[18] Vol. I. pp. 420, 499, &c.
[19] See Note [A], at the end of this Section.
[20] *Notes on SS.* vol. iii. p. 476.

"will be glorified: Jehovah hath redeemed Jacob,
"and in Israel he will honour himself. Unto the
"praise of the glory of his grace. The branch of my
"planting, the work of my hands, that I may be
"honoured."[21]

Dr. Priestley, Mr. Lindsey, Mr. Belsham, and Unitarian writers in general, from Socinus downwards,
understand the words of Christ, ("the glory which I
"had, before the world was, with thee,") as referring
only to "the counsels and decrees" of God. Grotius,
Le Clare, and Wetstein adopted this interpretation.
Their reasons are the following:—

1. Admitting the doctrine of the divine and preexistent nature in Christ, the glory of that nature
could not be recovered, because it could never have
been lost.

2. The same glory is said to be given to the disciples of Christ.—To both these arguments we have
already replied.

3. "In the language of the sacred writers, a being,
or a state of things is said to exist, when it is the
eternal immutable purpose of God *that it shall exist,*
at the time and in the circumstances which his infinite
wisdom hath chosen and ordained."[22]

That this anticipation of future events, by describing them in words of past or present time, is often
found in Scripture, I readily allow: but it appears to
me that a careful examination of the instances of this
figure will show that it does not admit of an application to the present purpose. The passages which
Faustus Socinus, and those who follow him in this

[21] Jer. xxxiii. 9. Lev. x. 3. Isa. xliv. 23. Eph. i. 6. Isa. lx. 21.
[22] *Calm Inq.* p. 88.

opinion, have adduced in its support, are, so far as I have been able to collect them, reducible to the following classes.

Class 1. Passages describing actions of which the very nature consists in a purpose or intention.

Matt. xxv. 34. " The kingdom prepared for you " from the foundation of the world." Eph. i. 4. " He " hath chosen us in him before the foundation of the " world." 2 Tim. i. 9. " His own purpose and grace, " given to us in Christ Jesus before the ancient times." Titus i. 2. " Eternal life, which God, who cannot lie, " hath promised before the ancient times."

These are manifestly irrelevant to the occasion. The actions which they designate are perfectly intelligible without any prolepsis. The very terms denote a mere design, or a preparatory arrangement, or an assurance of the design. Nothing is more common among men than gifts and devises to future posterity.

Class 2. Passages which point out an action begun, and in continuance, but not completed.

Ver. 4. " I have finished the work which thou hast " given me to do." Our Lord's labours and sufferings were arrived nearly at their close : the objects of his teaching, his humiliation, and his example, were on the very point of being attained. Ver. 11. " I am no " more in the world :—I am coming to thee." His departure out of life might be considered as already begun : he had set out on the journey of death. Ver. 22. " The glory which thou hast given to me, " I have given to them." Christ had already begun to instruct and qualify his apostles. Ver. 12. " Not " one of them has perished except the son of perdi- " tion." Judas was lost, or had perished, already, as

to his religious profession... Wicked men in general,
those who reject the gospel, are described by the
same word, evidently signifying their actually present
state, in 1 Cor. i. 18, and 2 Cor. iv. 3.   1 Sam. xv. 28.
" Jehovah hath cut off the kingdom of Israel from
" thee this day; and he hath given it to thy com-
" panion, who is better than thou."   The act of
excision was past, and it was beginning to be put in
execution; for the very next step in the history
is the anointing of David by Samuel.   The same
solution applies to chap. xxviii. 17, 18.   Gen. xvii. 5.
" I have given thee to be a father of a crowd of
" nations :" or, as it is expressed by the apostle,
Rom. iv. 17, " I have constituted [or appointed,
" τέθεικα,] thee a father of many nations."   Rom. viii.
30, 31., " Whom he foreordained, them he also
" called, and whom he called, them he also justified,
" and whom he justified, them he also glorified :"
that is in purpose glorified, say Archbishop Newcome
and others.   But there is no reason to have recourse
to this solution.   The verbs are all aoristic; which
form, says Fischer, denotes uncertain, indefinite, and
continuous time, and ought to be translated in Latin
by either the present indicative, or by an infinitive
with soleo prefixed.[23]   Thus the text denotes that this

[23] Animadv. ad Welleri Gramm. Gr. vol. ii. p. 260.   " As a philosophical and practical grammarian, Professor Buttmann, of the University of Berlin, is allowed by his countrymen to hold the first
rank.'—Preface of the Cambridge Translator, to Buttmann's Greek
Grammar, 1824.   He takes a considerably different view of the
aorists.   His leading idea is that both the first and the second (which
he considers as not differing in meaning) express an action that
ceases immediately, in contrast with some other more continued
action.   But he adds, " that this distinction is often very slight, con-

is the *plan* and *established order* of divine grace; "whom
God forecordains he calls, whom he calls he justifies,
and whom he justifies he glorifies:" (εν τουτ) such is his
constant course of proceeding. 2 Cor. v. 1. "When
[which is sometimes the sense of εαν,] our earthly
" house of this tabernacle is dissolved, we have a
" building from God, a house not made with hands,
" eternal, in the heavens." There is no prolepsis
here, any more than in the case of a person's being
called the proprietor of an estate, who is embarking
for a foreign country to take possession of it: he is
not the less the actual owner, though he has not yet
seen his domain. The same obvious remark applies
to passages in which believers are said to have eternal
life, to have treasure in heaven, to have for themselves in heaven a better and enduring substance.[24]
In all these cases, persons are said *to have* that which
is *destined* for them to possess, and of which they
actually have the assurance, evidence, or commencement: but where is an instance to be found of a
person being said *to have* a thing, when neither the
person nor the possession are in existence?

All passages of this kind, therefore, make nothing
to the purpose for which they are adduced.

Class 3. Passages in the descriptive style of prophecy. Mr. B. justly observes, that " in the Old
Testament nothing is more common than to express

veying only a trifling modification of idea; and that, therefore, there
is often no choice between the present and the aorist." Page 237.
It is obvious that the " momentaneous" signification would ill suit
the passage, (Rom. viii. 30,) but to render it as is proposed above is
justified by Buttman's doctrine, equally as by Fischer's or Hermann's.

[24] John iii. 16. Matt. xix. 21. Heb. x. 34.

prophecy in the language of history, and to state future events as present or even past." But, it is remarkable that those who apply this principle to the passage under consideration have overlooked a material point. They may find instances without end of events *future*, and even *remotely future*, described as being, at the time of the speaker's utterance, in *actual existence*: but they bring forwards no instance of an event which is *present*, or so *near* that, in the ordinary use of language, it may be fairly spoken of as present, being described as having taken place *ages before*." Yet, till this is satisfactorily done, it appears to me that they have not brought the passage before us within the range of that peculiarity in the prophetic style to which they would refer it.

One instance, indeed, they have adduced which seems to promise them the aid desired. Christ's ", violent death constituting an essential part of the divine plan, he is represented, Rev. xiii. 8, as " the ", Lamb slain from the foundation of the world."[27] How seducing a thing is an hypothesis! Do these acute critics need to be reminded that the clause, " from the foundation of the world," ought to be construed with the preceding, " whose names were not " written?" It was remarkable that the Editor of

* Page 88.—The examples which he adduces, (and every student knows that they might be increased indefinitely,) are Is. xlv. 1; ix. 6; xlii. 1; xlix. 5—10; liii. lxi. 1—3. Exod. xiv. 14—17. (1 Sam. xv. 28; xxviii. 17, 18, noticed under Class 2.),

" Excepting Rev. xiii. 8, which will be immediately considered. Such passages as Matt. xxv. 34; John xvii. 24; 1 Pet. i. 20; Acts ii. 23; iv. 28; 1 John v. 11, need no observation. That the greatest Unitarian writers have adduced them, seems to be a symptom of anxiety and weakness.

[27] *Calm Inq.* p. 94.

the Improved Version could forget the just translation published under his own hand,—"whose name was "not written from the foundation of the world, in the "book of life of the Lamb that was slain?"[28]

4. The Inquirer further labours to strengthen his scheme from the clauses, *with thyself,—with thee* (παρὰ σεαυτῷ, παρὰ σοί). "That is, in thy immutable purpose and decree.—It is not true that the preposition παρά with a dative case always has a local signification. When applied personally it sometimes signifies 'in that person's estimation or account;' vid. 2 Pet. iii. 8, 'One day is with the Lord (παρὰ Κυρίῳ, in the account or estimation of the Lord,') as a thousand years."[29]

If we were to grant the justness of this criticism, I doubt whether it would greatly serve the purpose of its patronizer. "The glory which I had *in thy account* or *estimation*," would rather comport with the idea of a *supposition, conjecture,* or *opinion,* than with that of an "immutable purpose and decree." But the writer overlooks the distinction between a paraphrase of a clause derived from the context, and the genuine and inherent meaning of a single word. If his explication of 2 Pet. iii. 8, be admitted; it is as a gloss upon the phrase, and not as the proper sense of the preposition. He is also mistaken in his grammatical assertion. The radical meaning of παρά is *contiguity,* and all its applications retain the idea: they all refer to some mode of closeness, intimate connexion,

[28] *Impr. Vers.* following ὧν τὸ ὄνομα, the reading preferred by Griesbach.

[29] *Calm Inq.* pp. 109, 113.

or union.[20] With the dative case applied to a person, it signifies, in the presence, society, or abode, of that person. In the passage under consideration, it is manifestly put in opposition to the state of being *on the earth*. "I have glorified thee on the earth;—now "glorify me with thyself."

In studying the speeches of Jesus Christ it is often an assistance to a correct apprehension of their import, if we can represent them to ourselves in the language of Judæa, in which he undoubtedly delivered his divine discourses. Our best aid, in making such attempts, is the Peshito Syriac version of the New Testament;

---

[20] " Παρὰ *beside*, may justly be set down as a noun signifying, *side* or *flank ;* and from the different aspects under which an object may be viewed, as occupying the *side* of another, the different applications of παρὰ take their rise.—Παρὰ then commonly signifies, (1.) With the genitive, *from beside ;*—(2.) With the dative, *close beside ;*—(3.) With the accusative, motion *to beside*." *Dunbar on the Greek Prepositions,* 2d ed. p. 266. " Παρά, with a dative, denotes commutation." *Hermann de Emend. Ratione Græcæ Gramm. Lips. 1801,* p. 162. " Præpositionem παρὰ cum dativo personæ Græci fere ita conjunxerunt, ut indicaretur locus in quo versaretur is cujus nomen additum esset.—The Greeks usually used παρὰ joined to a dative of the person, to signify the place of abode of the person whose name is so governed : as *Æschin. Dial. 3, 7, παρὰ Καλλίᾳ, in the house of Callias ; Eurip. Alc. 542, παρὰ κλαίουσι, in the habitation of mourners ; Lysias, p. 34 of Taylor's 8vo. ed. παρ' ἐμοι, at home with me ; Acts x. 6, παρά τινι Σίμωνι, with one Simon*." *Welleri Gramm. Græca, cum Animadv: Fischeri et Kuinœl,* vol. v. p. 267. Lips. 1781—1791. Many examples might be added, as 1 Cor. xvi. 2, *παρ' ἑαυτῷ, at his own home,* John xiv. 23, *we will make our abode (παρ' αὐτῷ) with him.* 2 Pet. ii. 11, *they bring not a railing accusation (παρὰ Κυρίῳ) in the presence of the Lord.* Matt. xix. 26, *παρ' ἀνθρώποις,—παρὰ Θεῷ, with men, with God,* i. e. in their presence ; in close contact, so to speak, with their power to effect the object... 2 Pet. iii. 8, *one day is (παρὰ Κυρίῳ) in the presence of the Lord as a thousand years,* &c. 2 Tim. iv. 13, *παρὰ Κάρπῳ, in the house, or under the care of Carpus.*

whose language differs but little from that which was
the vernacular tongue of our Lord and his disciples,
and whose antiquity approaches, if it does not actually
belong to, the apostolic age. Now the preposition in
question, is rendered, in that venerable translation, by
one whose radical idea is, *conjunction* or *close and
intimate association.*[31]

Some of the advocates for the interpretation contended for by Unitarian writers endeavour further to
sustain it, by affirming that, in the Rabbinical phraseology, certain things of great importance are said to
have existed before the creation, meaning of course in
the divine purpose. Thus the Bereshith Rabba, an
ancient commentary on the book of Genesis, says:
"Six things preceded the creation of the world. The
Law, the Throne of glory, the Fathers, Israel, the
House of holiness, and the Name of the Messiah, came
up into the thought of God before the creation of the
world." On this I remark :

1. There is no evidence without begging the question, that a phraseology of this character was made
use of by Jesus Christ. His style, excepting when he
borrows the proverbial hyperboles which were current
among his countrymen,[32] is always most simple and
modest, and at the greatest distance from any semblance of exaggeration: and he would be the least
likely to use any such expressions in a prayer to his

[31] The verse is given in an almost literal translation from the
Greek. As closely as I can represent it in English, it stands thus:
"And now, glorify-me, thou Father, with-thee ; by-that glory
which-was-itself to-me with-thee, from before the-being of-the-
world." Thus no distinction is made between παρὰ σεαυτῷ and
παρὰ σοί.

[32] As in Matt. v. 29, 30, 39, 40 ; vi. 34.

heavenly Father. When Unitarian paraphrasts subjoin the clause, *in thy purpose and decree,* they are
not only making their own arbitrary addition to our
Lord's words, but they are imposing upon him a style
of speaking altogether different from his characteristic
manner.

2. The Rabbinical example does not apply to the
case. It is universally admitted that the glory of the
Messiah, in the present and in the future state, and all
other beings and events that have existed, or that shall
exist, were "in the thought" of the First Cause, from
eternity: so that, upon the hypothesis, Christ was
praying for that which, in this respect, was no distinction to him above others. But what the case requires
is proof, that the plain, unadorned, definite, expression, "*which I had with thee,*" was likely or proper to
be used, by such a speaker and on such an occasion,
when he meant nothing more than "that which was
destined for me to have."[33] The happy state of every

[33] "Παρὰ σεαυτῷ, *with thyself,* is opposed to *the earth,* on which
there was no more need of Christ's being present: he was, therefore, to return to heaven, as to his former residence. Τῇ δόξῃ ᾗ
εἶχον, *with the glory which I had,* &c. This glory, his peculiar property, was now beginning to be manifested, and to be more clearly
laid open to mankind. Those who explain this clause by, *I had in
purpose or destination,* put force, not upon this passage only, but
upon others which are neither few nor obscure, both in this book
and the other Scriptures. The verb εἶχον cannot, without violence,
be explained in any other way than as in the frequent declarations
of Chap. i. ' he was with God : he was God; we beheld his glory,'
which he had as ' the Only-begotten,' before he took a human life.
If it be understood of *destination,* that is equally true of all men.—
Christ clearly intimates, *that this his glory had been hitherto unknown
to men;* and therefore he prays that it may now break forth into
manifestation. This is very clear from what follows : *I have manifested thy glory, therefore do thou now manifest my glory to men.* All

good man, is equally that which the divine purpose has destined that he should have.

"I have thus endeavoured to examine, I trust with a candid disposition, all the pleadings of the Calm Inquirer, and of other writers on the same side, with respect to this important text. It appears to me that their criticisms are destitute of grammatical truth, and their arguments of logical conclusiveness. The impartial and serious reader will form his own judgment.

this is very evident, unless a man have surrendered himself to other opinions." *Semler in loc.* Even *De Wette*, with all his unhappy unbelief, yet feeling as an honourable translator, seems to have been anxious to convey the strength and definiteness of the original, too. "the glory which I, before the world was, with thee [bey dir] had."

SUPPLEMENTARY NOTE TO SECT. V.

Note [A], page 146.

"'Christ declare qu'il ne désire rien de nouveau, mais seulement qu'il apparoisse tel en chair qu'il étoit devant la création du monde ; ou, pour parler plus clairement, que la Majesté Divine qu'il avoit toujours eue, réluise en la personne du Médiateur, et en la chair humaine qu'il avoit vêtue."—' Christ declares that he desires nothing new, but only that he may appear in the flesh such as he was before the creation of the world ; or, to speak more clearly, that the Divine Majesty which he had always possessed, might shine forth in the person of the Mediator and in the human flesh which he had assumed.'—*Calvin in loc.*

"Having quoted this from the illustrious author's own French edition of his *Commentary*, an extremely rare book, rather than from the Latin copy, it will not be unwelcome to the candid reader to see a testimony to the literary character of JOHN CALVIN, from a quarter which was far indeed from being prejudiced in his favour.—" Calvin, qui jouissait avec justice d'une grande réputation, homme de lettres du premier ordre, écrivant en Latin aussi bien qu'on le peut faire dans une langue morte, et en Français avec une pureté singulière pour son tems ; cette pureté, que nos habiles grammairiens admirent encore aujourd'hui, rend ses écrits bien supérieurs à presque tous ceux du même siècle ; comme les ouvrages de MM. de Port-Royal se distinguent encore aujourd'hui, par la même raison, des rhapsodies barbares de leurs adversaires et de leurs contemporains. Calvin, jurisconsulte habile, et théologien aussi éclairé qu'un hérétique le peut être, dressa de concert avec les magistrats un récueil des lois, &c. 'Calvin, who with justice enjoyed a high reputation, was a scholar of the first order. He wrote in Latin, as well as 'is possible in a dead language, and in French with a purity which was extraordinary for his time. This purity, which is to the present day admired by our skilful critics, renders his writings greatly superior to almost all of the same age ; as the works of Messieurs de Port Royal are still distinguished on the same account, from the barbarous rhapsodies of their opponents and contemporaries. Calvin, being a skilful lawyer, and as enlightened a divine as a heretic can be, drew up in concert with the magistrates a code of laws,' &c.—*Encyclopédie de Diderot et d'Alembert; Art.* GENÈVE. The author of this article was d'Alembert.

Apart from the dire and indelible stain on Calvin's memory, the persecution to death of Servetus, (with respect to which, however, it is but just to recollect the almost universal ignorance, and the deep yet criminal prejudices, of that age, on the religious rights of mankind,[1] and in which not only Calvin and Beza, but Melanchthon, Cranmer, and Socinus were partakers,) history scarcely furnishes a more illustrious character for piety, integrity, and labours almost incredible. Such was the man, that to traduce his name has been found by many a short road to celebrity; according to the epigram, which I read I know not where many years ago:

"........... mis nebulo, sycophanta, et turpis adulter;"
"........ Calvinum ferias fulmine, magnus eris."

"I know no man," says the acute and holy RICHARD BAXTER, "since the apostles' days, whom I value and honour more than CALVIN ; and whose judgment in all things, one with another, I more esteem and come nearer to." *Saints' Everlasting Rest,* Part III, chap. xiv. sect. 10.

[1] A very pleasing exception occurs in the name and writings of an amiable but very unfortunate scholar, Sebastian Castellio, once the protégé of Calvin, but afterwards cast off and unkindly treated by him.

CAPITULE III.

ON OUR LORD'S DECLARATION OF AN EXISTENCE BEFORE ABRAHAM.

The occasion of the assertion made by Jesus Christ.—The question directly refers to coexistence.—The signification of the terms.—Their just construction will admit no other sense than that of preexistence.—Objections of Mr. Lindsey and the Calm Inquirer examined and answered.—The Unitarian interpretation examined:—and shown to be destitute of satisfactory proof;—contrary to the reason of the occasion,—to the circumstances of the narrative,—and to our Lord's ordinary course of proceeding;—attended with other difficulties;—inconsistent with the scripture idiom;—inefficient for its purpose;—not supported, but contradicted, by the phraseology of the prophets;—productive of a nugatory sense.—Observations on other assertions of the Calm Inquirer.—The interpretation invented by Lælius Socinus, and represented by his nephew as probably given by a special revelation.—Reasons against it.

"Jesus said to them, Verily, verily, I say unto you, Before Abraham existed, I am." John viii. 58.

THE general body of Christians have understood this passage as plainly declaring the preexistence of Christ, in a nature of course superior to the human, two thousand years before he was born of Mary.

Unitarians interpret it as affirming that Jesus might be said to have existed, as the Messiah, in the purpose and decree of God; that is, "that he was designated to his office, before Abraham was born."[1]

---

[1] *Impr. Ver.* Note on the place. More fully expressed in the Inquirer's paraphrase: " Before that eminent patriarch was brought into being, my existence and appearance under the character of the Messiah at this period, and in these circumstances, was so com-

To judge between these opposite interpretations we must attend to the *occasion* of our Lord's assertion, and to the proper meaning of the *terms* in which he expresses it.

The opponents of Jesus, in their virulent cavils against him, had mentioned Abraham their national ancestor; a man so signally favoured of God that his name served as a proverbial example of dignity and honour. They understood our Lord's declarations as involving such assumptions of superiority, that they demanded, " Art thou greater than our " father Abraham?—Whom makest thou thyself?" With his characteristic calmness, he assured them that Abraham had indeed regarded him as a superior; that, guided by supernatural revelation, the patriarch had really enjoyed such a mental prospect of the time when the Messiah should appear, and of the blessings of his reign, as filled him with pleasure and exultation! " Your father Abraham earnestly desired that he might " see my day; and he did see it, and rejoiced." This turned the conversation. The Jews, not understanding, or affecting not to understand, that Jesus spoke of an anticipative vision, exclaimed, " Thou art not yet " fifty years old, and hast thou seen Abraham?" Now, therefore, the question was brought to the *single point of examination*. It was necessary for Jesus either to deny the assumption, or to admit and confirm it. He did not do the former: but he gave an answer which his opponents viewed as being either directly or constructively impious and blasphemous, that is, as

pletely arranged, and so irrevocably fixed in the immutable counsels and purposes of God, that in this sense I may be said even then to have existed." P. 85.

admitting their imputation.[1] He "said to them,
" Verily, verily, I say unto you, before Abraham
" existed, I was."—Is it not manifest that he did not
take the former part of the alternative, but that he
did take the latter ; that he admitted himself to have
been actually *contemporary with* Abraham ; also that
he went farther, and affirmed that he had possessed
existence even *before* Abraham ?

Such is the bearing of the argument, as deduced
from the occasion. Let us see whether the honest
construction of the words will permit us to draw any
different conclusion. The precise meaning of γίνεσθαι
and its synonymous form γενέσθαι is *to be brought into
existence.* Whether, therefore, we prefer the received
translation, " before Abraham was ;" or that here proposed, " before Abraham existed ;" or, that of many
translators, both ancient and modern,[2] " before Abraham was born ;" the effect is the same.

The remaining clause is however attended with
some difficulty.

---

[1] " Hoc enim postulat series orationis. In objectione Judæorum
sermo erat de existentiâ ; ergo etiam in responsione de existentiâ
sermo esse debet. Objectio erat, ' Non potes vidisse Abrahamum,
quia nondum es quinquagenarius, nec tum natus eras.' Respondet
Jesus, ' Ego fui, antequam ille fuit.' Sic sensu pari respondetur
objectioni."—" This interpretation is required by the tenor of the
discussion. The objection turned upon existence : therefore the
reply must refer to existence also. The objection was, ' Thou canst
not have seen Abraham, for thou art not yet fifty years old ; thou
wast not then born.' Jesus answered, ' I was before he was.' Thus
the reply corresponds to the objection." *Rosenmüller in loc.*

[2] Erasmus, Vatablus, Diodati, Doddridge, Campbell, Michaelis,
Rosenmüller, the Improved Version, Stolz, Van Ess. De Wette
retains Luther's *Ehe denn Abraham war, bin ich;* thus showing that,
in his judgment, that was the just version. Scholz gives essentially
the same.

1. Some suppose that, in using the expression, " I am," our Lord intended a reference to the divine appellation announced to Moses, " I am that which I " am." But it is to be remarked that the words of that passage are in the future tense, " I will be that " which I will be;"⁴ and most probably it was not intended as a name, but as a declaration of the certain fulfilment of all the promises of God, especially those which related to the deliverance of the Israelites. There does not appear, therefore, sufficient ground to sustain the idea of an allusion to this.

2. It may be thought that, in this instance, as in several others of the same form, our Lord purposely suppressed the predicate of his proposition; leaving it to be supplied by the minds of his hearers, under the impression of that evidence by which they might all have been convinced of the justness of his claims, had their dispositions been candid and upright. So, in this very discussion with his opponents, Jesus says, " Except ye believe that I AM;—Ye shall know that " I AM;"—and to his disciples, " that ye may believe

⁴ Exod. iii. 14. אֶהְיֶה אֲשֶׁר אֶהְיֶה " By which words God signifies that what he from eternity had been, he for ever would be; the same, in deed and effect, as in his promises." *Rosenm.* The LXX. renders it Ἐγώ εἰμι ὁ ὤν, *I am the existing one.* I do not see why the suppressed predicate might not be supplied from this passage, and the tacit allusion rationally maintained, if all other reasons concurred : but they do not. To show, however, the fallaciousness of arguing from the mere identity of words, let us observe that, in both the Greek and the Latin idiom, the answer to such a question as, *Who has done that?* *Who is there?* (which we make in our language by the third person, *'tis I, c'est moi;*) is by this very phrase, *I am,* ἐγώ εἰμι, *ego sum.* For examples in the N. T. see Matt. xiv. 27 ; xxvi. 22, 25. Mark vi. 50 ; xiv. 62. Luke xxiv. 39. John iv. 26 ; ix. 9.

" that I AM." In his prediction of false Messiahs, as given by the Evangelist Mark, the same use of the phrase occurs: " Many will come in my name, say-" ing, I AM ;" the parallel place to which, in Matthew, supplies the omitted predicate, " the Christ."[5]

According to this interpretation, the passage is read, " Before Abraham existed, I am [the Messiah."] But every one must perceive that, if the notion of the present tense be rigorously insisted on, a solœcism is involved: a *present* event cannot be prior to one *past*.

3. The present, *I am*, may be taken in the sense of the past, *I was*. This is not unusual in the Greek idiom, especially when the action or state of the verb is understood as *continued to the present time*.[6] This

---

[5] John viii. 24, 28 ; xiii. 19.   Mark xiii. 6.   Matt. xxiv. 5.

[6] " This tense is often put for the preterperfect: especially when it is signified that the action is continued." *Joh. Frid. Fischeri Animadv. ad Welleri Gramm. Græc.* vol. ii. p. 256. Lips. 1798 ; who has adduced many examples from Xenophon and other authors. " The present tense is very often put so as to have the force of the imperfect : especially when the thing which is said to have been at any past time, continues still to be.—*E. g.* Luke xv. 31.   John i. 9, and in the LXX.   Ps. lxxxix. (xc.) 2.   Prov. viii. 25.   Jerem. i. 5." *Kuinöl in Libros N. T. Hist.* vol. iii. p. 437.   Tittmann adds these rather feeble instances from the Gospel of John ; i. 19 ; ix. 8 ; xiv. 9 ; xv. 27. *Meletemata Sacra*, p. 353.   " The use of the verb in the present tense denotes *continuation*, as chap. xiv. 9, ' Am I so ' long with you,' *i. e. have been and still am*, which could not have been both expressed by a past tense.   Thus in Latin we say, jam quatuor dies ægrotat." *Castellio in loc.*   " Ἐγὼ εἰμὶ may indeed be rendered, *I was*.   The present for the imperfect, or even for the preterperfect, is no unusual figure with this writer.   However, as an uninterrupted duration from the time spoken of to the time then present, seems to have been suggested, I thought it better to follow the common method [I am]." *Campbell.*   The excellent French Version of De Sacy, and the Genevese of 1805, have *I was.*

renders the construction plain and the sense evident:
" Verily, verily, I say unto you, before Abraham was
" brought into existence, I was."[7]

But there seems to be little reason for debate about
the tense of the verb, when it is considered that Jesus,
speaking in the dialect of his country, most probably
used no verb at all. The idiom of the Hebraic languages would have required, I HE, as it occurs in
several passages of the Old Testament, which contain
a peculiar and most solemn declaration of the supremacy and eternity of Jehovah;[8] or as the clause
before us is translated in the venerable Syriac version,
whose antiquity is nearly apostolic, and whose lan-

---

[7] " Præter hanc corpoream naturam, est mihi φύσις antiquior."
' Besides this material nature, I have another of higher dignity and
origin.' *Semler in loc.* " Etenim verbum utrumque, et γενέσθαι
et είναι, in promptu est denotare *esse, existere.*—Jam Judæi, quando
quærunt quomodo Abrahamum videre potuerit nondum quinquagenarius, intelligere aliud quid non poterant, nisi hoc, quomodo esse
potuerit tempore Abrahami. Ut verò objiciunt illi, ita respondet
Dominus. Illi negant eum esse potuisse Abrahami tempore : Dominus affirmat ; neque tantum affirmat, sed addit etiam aliquid
amplius, scilicet, se fuisse non tantùm tempore Abrahami, sed adeò
etiam ante Abrahamum." ' Each of these verbs, γενέσθαι and
είναι, manifestly denotes *being, existence.* When the Jews inquired
how it was possible for a person, who was not yet fifty years old, to
have seen Abraham ; their meaning could be no other than this,
How could he have been in the time of Abraham ? To their objection, our Lord's answer corresponds. That he could have been in
the time of Abraham, they deny, and he affirms ; nor does he merely
affirm it, but he adds something more, namely, that he had existed
not only in the time of Abraham, but even before Abraham.'
Tittmanni Melet. Sacra, p. 352.

[8] אֲנִי הוּא Deut. xxxii. 39 ; Isa. xli. 4 ; xliii. 10, 13 ; xlvi. 4 ;
xlviii. 12. In these passages the translation of the LXX. is the very
phrase under consideration, ἐγώ εἰμί, *I am.* See also the instance of
Elijah, 1 Kings xviii. 18.

guage differs by very slight shades from that which
was spoken by Jesus and his countrymen, "I, I
MYSELF."[9]

From these considerations, it plainly follows that an
unexceptionable translation of the clause would be
this, "Before Abraham existed, I myself existed."

Thus we are led, both by the facts of the case and
by the phraseology, to the conclusion that our Lord
certainly affirmed himself to have a superior and PRE-
EXISTENT *nature.*

To this interpretation Mr. Belsham makes the following objections:[10]—

(1.) " That the word εἰμὶ, even when used abso-

---

[9] אִל exactly the same as the Chaldee אִיתַי יֵשׁ The
indeclinable word joined to the suffixed pronoun is the same, differing only in dialect, with the Hebrew יֵשׁ. " It is a noun, whose root
remains in the Arabic *aasa* (for *ayasa*)—and its radical meaning is
strength, ability, firmness, efficiency, existence." *Körberi Lexicon
Nominum et Verborum Hebr. vulgò pro Particulis Habitorum,* p. 21,
subjoined to Tympe's ed. of *Noldii Partic. Hebr.* Jenæ, 1734.
" Solidum et reale quid; res consistens et subsistens. Propriè
nomen est, sed pro verbo substantivo adhiberi solet." *Simonis et
Eichhorn. Lex.* p. 755.   The same is maintained in *Schröderi
Instit. Ling. Hebr.* Ulm. 1792, p. 272.   The work on Hebrew
Grammar which, with very probable reason, may be considered as
the most perfect that the world has ever seen, says; " The frequently
occurring particle יֵשׁ is a peculiar adverb, or it may be considered
as an impersonal verb.   It is in Aramæan אִית, and in Arabic *aysh*.
The radical idea is, that an object is *present, close at hand;* and
thus it serves to express the idea of *being* or *existing,* in all the
relations of time and person." GESENIUS *Ausführliches Gramm.
Krit. Lehrgebäude, &c.* i. e. *A Full and Minute System of the
Grammar and Criticism of the Hebrew Language, compared with its
Cognate Dialects;* p. 829.   Leipzig, 1817.

Yet the Inquirer complacently quotes Grotius for the affirmation
that the Syriac Version uses a verb in the imperfect tense. p. 96.

[10] *Calm. Inq.* p. 79.

lutely, very rarely, if ever, expresses simple ex
istence."

Reply. Mr. B. and his guide, the late Mr. Simp-
son of Bath, are greatly mistaken. In a note on the
preceding page several passages are referred to, in
which the Septuagint uses the phrase in question
to denote the " simple existence" of the Deity : " I,
even I, am :" and other instances are not wanting.
Ὁ ὤν, " the Existing One." Exod. iii. 14. Ὁ ὤν, Κύριε,
" O Lord, the Existing One," where it stands as
the translation of JEHOVAH. Jerem. xiv. 13. Ἰδοὺ
οὐκ ἦν, " Behold, he was not." Ps. xxxvi. (xxxvii.)
36. Οὐκ ἔτι εἰμί, " I am no more in being." Job vii. 8.
Also in the New Testament : " He that cometh unto
" God must believe that he existeth," ὅτι ἐστί. Heb.
xi. 6. And the very memorable description of the
Deity, which is repeated five times in the Apocalypse ;
ὁ ὤν, καὶ ὁ ἦν, καὶ ὁ ἐρχόμενος, " He who is, and
" who was, and who is to come."

Examples of the same use of the verb might be
collected from Plato, Philo, Plutarch, and other Greek
writers : but the foregoing passages are more to our
purpose; and I conceive they are sufficient to show
that the application to simple existence is not very
unusual in the New Testament and the Hellenistic
Version of the Old.

(2.) " That it is not probable that our Lord would
have been so very open and explicit upon this high
and mysterious subject to his enemies, when he was
so reserved to his friends, and does not appear to have
hinted it even to his disciples."

Reply. Whatever might have been the meaning of
our Lord's declarations on this and other occasions,

it is altogether an unwarrantable assumption that
Jesus communicated any information to his enemies
which he withheld from his friends. It is, to say the
least, highly probable that some of his disciples were
present at all the public discourses and conversations
which he held. If this, in any rare instance, were not
the case, we cannot reasonably doubt that he would
say similar things to his intimate followers, on suitable
occasions. It is recorded that " he expounded all
" things to his disciples when they were alone :"[11] and
with respect to the doctrine which he taught, or the
intimations which he gave, with any supposed reference to a superior and preexistent nature, we have
already examined other passages which it cannot be
pretended were unknown to our Lord's familiar attendants. But every one must perceive how extremely
fallacious are objections of this kind, who considers
how small a portion of the discourses of Jesus Christ
are preserved to us in the evangelical records. Had
Mr. Lindsey possessed the moderation and candour
for which it has been the fashion to laud him, he
would have spared his scornful surprise " that any
could ever suppose our Lord to be so very open
and familiar with—his most bitter enemies, as to tell
them such a wonderful secret concerning himself—
at the same time that he kept his disciples quite in the
dark about things so prodigious and extraordinary."[12]
This attempt at wit, on a question so serious, is not the
offspring of either reason or piety.

(3.) " That if he had intended in this instance to
announce his own preexistence so very explicitly as
many believe, he would have taught this extraordinary

---

[11] Mark iv. 34.   [12] Quoted in the *Calm Inq.* p. 79.

doctrine more frequently, in a greater variety of phrase, and would have laid greater stress upon it.

Reply. [1.] This objection is, in a great measure, begging the question; for we conceive, and the grounds of our opinion are before the reader, that Christ did teach this doctrine, not infrequently, and in a considerable " variety of phrase."

[2.] As to the *explicitness* of the declaration, let a candid Unitarian say whether he would have discerned any want of explicitness, had the same phraseology occurred with respect to any point now undisputed. Let it be imagined, for instance, that a question had been raised, and that some results of consequence depended upon it, whether Jesus or the son of Germanicus were the elder person; and that the former had said, " I most assuredly declare to you, before Caligula existed, I was." Let the terms have been the very same as in the case before us:[13] and would any one have said that the assertion was not " explicit?" Or will he find any want of explicitness in the language of Moses, " Before the mountains were brought into existence—thou art?"[14]

---

[13] The useful industry of Wetstein has furnished us with several instances of this expression, from which I select the following: Ἐις τὸ ὁμοίως εἶναι τὴν τε ψυχὴν ἡμῶν πρὶν γενέσθαι ἡμᾶς, " Even to this point, that our souls likewise existed before we were born." *Plato, Phæd.* sect. 22, ed. *Forster*, Ox. 1745, p. 206, and repeatedly in that dialogue. Τὸ γὰρ χωρίον τοῦτο περιφκοδόμησεν ὁ πατήρ μοῦ, μικροῦ δεῖν, πρὶν ἐμὲ γενέσθαι. " My father walled this field round within a little, before I was born." *Demosth. Or. adv. Callic.* ed. *Wolf.* Francof. 1604, p. 1116. Ἔλεγεν ὑγιεινόν τι καὶ νοσερὸν, πρὶν Ἱπποκράτη γενέσθαι. " He described the symptoms of health and disease, before Hippocrates was born." *Arrian in Epict.* lib. ii. cap. 17.

[14] Psalm lxxxix. (xc.) 2. LXX. Πρὸ τοῦ ὄρη γενηθῆναι—σὺ εἶ.

[3.] To demand that this doctrine, supposing it to be true, should have been taught by our Lord himself in the most clear and decisive manner, is not reasonable; for it was of the very genius and character of his ministry, that by it the *peculiar* doctrines of the Christian dispensation should not be fully unfolded. That complete manifestation was reserved for the ministration of the Spirit, who was to take of the things of Christ, and show them to the apostles, and to *glorify Him* by leading them into *all the truth*. Jesus himself appears to have plainly insisted, in his own teachings, upon no doctrines but those which were generally admitted by his countrymen as resting on the authority of Moses and the prophets. Other truths, though deducible from the Old Testament by consequences less obvious or less generally recognised, he taught by allusions, assumptions, parables, and implications; or sometimes by a direct, but abrupt and insulated assertion, the import of which would become the more apparent by being afterwards reflected upon, with the advantage of the subsequent developments by the Holy Spirit, according to our Lord's promises. Of the last kind the instance before us seems to have been.

(4.) "And finally that this fact, so solemnly declared, would have been more attended to, and would have made a more permanent and vivid impression. It would have been a subject of general conversation and scrutiny, of admiration or offence. Whereas the idea of such a claim on the part of our Lord vanished immediately. The disciples did not notice it. The Jews did not repeat it. And it is not alleged as a charge against our Saviour that he arrogated this extraordinary attribute.

Reply. I acknowledge that this is a great difficulty; but that it is not of the decisive nature which the Inquirer apprehends; and that, on a close examination, it is considerably diminished, if not entirely removed, I submit these reasons:

[1.] It is contrary to sound principles of reasoning, to make hypothetical objections outweigh positive evidence. Every studious person knows, often to his disappointment and pain, that, in relation to many objects of human knowledge, the most perplexing difficulties occur on a theoretical view of the case, but which the commanding evidence of facts obliges us to subdue: and we do not charge ourselves with acting an irrational part in so disposing of those difficulties; because we are aware of the imperfection of all human knowledge; and because we are assured that indubitable experiments, or facts clearly ascertained, are entitled to a decisive weight, as affirmative evidence, in opposition to a thousand objections invented by reasoning on our own suppositions, suppositions which we have probably made too soon, and in which some material error is latent. In the present case, we have direct evidence, from the plain meaning and construction of the words, and from the tenor of the occasion, that an actual preexistence is affirmed: we are bound, then, to regard abstract difficulties as superseded.

[2.] We are, in fact, but incompetent judges of the manner in which such a declaration would have operated on the minds of our Lord's countrymen and contemporaries; but we may be assured that it would

have made an impression very different from that
which we should receive, under our circumstances of
education and life.   Their habits of thinking and feeling were of a character extremely remote from ours.
They generally believed (whether rightly or wrongly,
is immaterial to our argument,) in the existence and
frequent occurrence among themselves of supernatural influence, both from the Divine Being and
from inferior, but spiritual and powerful, agents.[15]
The doctrines and history of their scriptures were
understood by them so as to keep alive the constant
expectation of miraculous intercourse with the Deity :
and there is reason to suppose, that a belief in the
preexistence of souls had been derived by them from
the Persian or from the Judæo-Alexandrian theology,
and prevailed among them to a considerable extent.[16]
The influence of such opinions could not but operate
powerfully to prevent those strong impressions of surprise, " admiration or offence," which the Inquirer too
readily assumes to have been necessary.

[3.] I venture to think that some evidence has been
adduced that, amidst the perplexity and discordance
of opinions which existed among the Jews in this
degenerate period, there were many persons who did
hold the superior nature and preexistence of the
Messiah.   Consequently, this declaration of our Lord
might be received as simply equivalent to an avowal
of his being the Messiah.   As to the allegation that

[15] On this subject, so deeply interesting to every one who cul-
tivates accuracy of acquaintance with scripture-theology, I beg
permission to recommend the *Considerations on Miracles* of a most
judicious, elegant, and pious author, Professor *Le Bas.*
[16] See *Lightfoot's Horæ Hebr. et Talm.* on John ix. 2.

"the disciples did not notice it, and the Jews did not repeat it;" we have already observed how extremely uncertain and fallacious such negative assertions must be.

[4.] "It is not alleged as a charge against our Saviour that he arrogated this extraordinary attribute." I conceive that it was included in the general charge of having claimed to be the Messiah: and it is remarkable that this accusation itself, of claiming to be the Messiah, though it was the most obvious and the most subservient to the purpose of our Lord's prosecutors, was not brought forwards by them at all. They seem to have been afraid to touch it, and to have contented themselves with vamping up frivolous defamations, till the high-priest proposed the interrogatory which Jesus met by a direct declaration; a declaration which was instantly seized as the ground of a charge of *blasphemy*, the same charge, be it observed, which the conduct of the Jews shows that they attached to the words of Christ, now under consideration: "they took up stones to cast at " him."

The impartial and judicious reader will now review what has been advanced; and will consider whether our interpretation be sufficiently supported by *proper* and *direct* evidence, and whether the objections to it are candidly met and satisfactorily answered.

We proceed to consider the arguments in support of the usual Unitarian interpretation, that of applying to the words the meaning, " not of real existence, but of existence in the divine *purpose*."

(1.) " This interpretation well accords with the connexion and context. Our Lord declares, ver. 56,

'Your father Abraham longed to see my day; and he did see it.' The Jews, foolishly or perversely misrepresenting his language, ask, 'Hast thou seen Abraham?' Our Lord never pretended that he had seen him: and, not deigning to rectify this silly mistake, he goes on to establish the reasonableness of his assertion; *q. d.* Abraham did foresee my appearance, and the blessings of my kingdom. And this was possible; because though I was not then born, yet my appearance under the character of the Messiah, and all the happy consequences which flow from it, had been determined in the divine counsels long before that eminent patriarch was in existence."

Reply. [1.] The whole of this allegation rests upon the assumption that our Lord's words were merely a continuation of his discourse, "not deigning" to notice the question or "silly mistake" of the Jews, but going on with his subject as if he had not been at all interrupted. But to this assumption we demur, as destitute of proof; and as also contrary to the reason of the case, to the order of the narrative, and to our Lord's ordinary practice.

It is *destitute of proof.* None is even attempted to be shown. The recommendation of it can be only that of its suiting the hypothesis which it is brought to help.

It is *contrary to the reason of the case.* If the interjected query of the Jews were of that "silly" and irrelevant kind which the Inquirer pronounces it, there seems no rational motive for its having been preserved in the recital; unless the writer had gone upon the principle of introducing every thing that was said on the occasions narrated, pertinent or impertinent.

But it is certain that neither John nor any other of the Evangelical historians, adopted such a principle: their plan is professedly that of selection. Besides, upon the assumption, the interlocution is not only impertinent and useless, but it is pernicious: it perplexes and misleads the reader, without answering any good purpose to compensate for the disadvantage.

It is contrary to the order of the narrative. The objection of the Jews is introduced by the usual formula, "Then said the Jews unto him:" and our Lord's rejoinder is also brought in with the correspondent phrase, "Jesus said to them." It is impossible, without doing violence to the common use of language and the common sense of mankind, not to regard the latter as a designed and direct answer to the former.

It is contrary to our Lord's ordinary practice. We never find him, except on one occasion when his very silence was eloquent,[17] refusing to answer with the meekness of wisdom, the questions, objections, and even cavils of his enemies. Neither was it his manner to evade the point of difficult and severe remarks made against himself. Often indeed, he spoke to the motives and concealed intentions of those who accosted him, as well as to their outward professions; but his replies and defences were always sincere and pertinent.

[2.] If we were to grant the assumption, we should not be relieved from difficulty. Let it be supposed that the Inquirer's paraphrase truly represents the meaning of our Lord: and we are compelled to ask, Why did he convey it in so strange a style? Why

---

[17] Matt. xxvi. 63; xxvii. 14.

did he not speak intelligibly? Why did he use language, of which the genuine and direct signification was calculated to convey, *not the thing* which he *intended* to say, but *another thing*, widely and dangerously different from it?—There was no want of words and phrases, proper for his purpose, and in current use among his countrymen and by himself. He could have employed one of the expressions which he has used on other occasions, or which afterwards his followers used.   He could have said, for example, " Before Abraham existed, I was foreordained'; my day was appointed : my kingdom was prepared, in the determinate counsel and foreknowledge of God : and God showed it, by his Spirit, unto Abraham." Such as this is the language of the New Testament; and I cannot but think it most reasonable to believe that our Lord would have used one of these phrases; or some other analogous to them, had his meaning been what is imputed to him.

(2.) " The words *I am* ($\dot{\epsilon}\gamma\grave{\omega}$ $\epsilon\dot{\iota}\mu\grave{\iota}$) must be understood to mean, and should be translated, *I was.*"

(3.) " The ellipsis must be supplied by the word *he,* i. e. ' he who cometh,' or ' the Christ.'—(See vers. 24 and 28.)—The same phrase in this instance also ought to have been translated in the same form : ' Before Abraham was born, I was *he,*' i. e. the prophet who was to come, the Messiah."

We have before observed that arguments about the tense of the verb are nugatory, for we have reason to believe that our Lord used no verb at all, but said in his native language, I HE, the emphatic formula which most usually denotes simple existence, in *whatever relation to time* the nature of the case may suggest.

For example: " Behold now, that I, I HE, and no god
" with me!—I Jehovah, the beginning, and with the
" last things, I HE.—That ye may know, and believe
" me, and understand that I HE;—before me no god
" is formed, nor after me shall be.—Even before the
" day, I HE!—Even to old age, I HE.—I HE, I the
" beginning, also I the ending!"[18] Whether therefore we supply the verb or not, the proper and emphatic meaning of the formula is *actual existence* at
the time spoken of, whenever that might be.

But if, neglecting the proper point of attention, the
Hebraic idiom, an opponent were to insist on the
Greek usage, he would be met by another difficulty.
The examples in which *I am* is to be supplied by the
predicate, *the Christ*, are all of the present tense.
Such examples will not warrant the supposition of the
same ellipsis when the present tense is put for the past:
because the very ground and reason of the enallage
of time lies in the *action* or *state expressed by the verb*,
which precludes any other predicate from being understood, than the concrete idea derived from that
action or state. This rule will, I think, bear the
closest examination. But, if we decline to press it,
we have still a right to demand clear instances of the
enallage of the time combined with the ellipsis of the
predicate: but they have not been given to us.

Yet should we, in the face of these reasons, consent
to his rendering, "Before Abraham was born, I was
the Messiah:" what does the opponent gain? Could
any reader or hearer, not preoccupied by hypothesis,
imagine otherwise than that the person speaking thus
certainly existed when Abraham was born? And do

[18] Referred to in a note on page 163.

not the words, as thus amplified, plainly express that
he had such existence?—We arrive at the last and
palmary argument.

(4.) " In the language of the sacred writers, a being,
or a state of things, is said to EXIST, when it is the
ETERNAL IMMUTABLE PURPOSE OF GOD THAT IT SHALL
EXIST, at the time and in the circumstances which his
infinite wisdom hath chosen and ordained."

This notion, therefore, is the sheet-anchor of the
Unitarian interpretation. We have, in a preceding
Section,[19] examined it and the pleadings in its favour;
and, I trust, have satisfactorily shown that it is weak
and incompetent, proceeding upon a mistaken view of
scripture-language, and quite inapplicable to the purpose of those who use it. By an egregious kind of
blunder, they gravely bring forward the *prolepsis* of
the prophetic style, as if it made for their case:
whereas that which they want is a figure of the *opposite*
effect, a *metalepsis*. Because, in the language of
prophecy, *future* persons and events are described as
if they were present, or had already taken place; it is
sagaciously inferred that a present person or event
may, by the same figure, be said to have existed in
long *past* time !

Mr. B. proceeds to argue : " If the prophets describe the Messiah as contemporary with them, Christ
might with propriety speak of himself under that
character, as their contemporary. If Isaiah writes as
having seen the Messiah, having heard his complaints,
and having been witness to his labours, his miracles,
and his sufferings; our Lord might with equal propriety represent himself under his official character, as

[19] Of this volume, pp. 147—152.

having existed in the days of Isaiah. If Abraham saw his day; "he, as the Messiah, must have coexisted with the patriarch, and by parity of reason, before Abraham's birth. But all allow that the prophetic representations of the Messiah's existence are figurative; they only express what existed in the divine purpose, and imply nothing more than certainty of event. Let it then be granted, that when our Lord speaks of himself as the Messiah before Abraham was born, he means the same thing: that his language only implies that he was the Messiah in the divine purpose. No reasoning, I think, can be more conclusive."

Reply [1.] The prophets did not " describe the Messiah as contemporary with" themselves. In their most vivid descriptions, though, to increase the poetic force and beauty of the representation, the present tense, or rather the Hebrew perfect, be frequently employed, enough exists of marked circumstances to have prevented any from imagining that the prophets designed to exhibit any mortal contemporary as the Sovereign and Saviour to whom they bore testimony. There is no evidence that any of the Jews ever understood their prophets as representing the Messiah to be their own contemporary: but there is all the proof which the nature of the case admits of, that both the prophets themselves, and their countrymen through successive generations, looked forwards to ONE who was yet to COME, as the ultimate object of those sublime representations. Let the reader examine the instances selected by the Inquirer as the basis of his theory, or any other prophetic descriptions of the Messiah; and

---

" Recited in a note at p. 151, of this volume.

he will find, either in the very phraseology of the context, or in the association of the parts of the description, sufficient to designate that the persons introduced and the events depicted were as yet in the womb of futurity.

[2.] The frequent use of the picturesque mode of representation, in the works of the ancient prophets, was not the result of a sacred or theological principle, but of the character of their composition. It was not as prophets, but as poets, that they employed this figure of speech, so suitable to their energetic conceptions, and which is indeed all but essential to the very soul of poetry. But the style which was eminently proper for poetry, or for sublime description in oratory, would have been out of place, ridiculous, and even pernicious, in a plain, calm, grave conversation. Cyrus, John the Baptist, and probably other individuals, were graphically pointed out in the prophecies of Isaiah, long before they were born; and that by expressions in the past or present tense. Would it, then, have been proper for either of them, to have said, " I was contemporary with the prophet: I co-existed with him, for he in prophetic vision saw my day, and described me, my actions, my character, my office, as if I were then actually existing and executing my commission: yea, by parity of reason, I may say that I existed before the prophet's birth: *before Isaiah was, I was:* I was the deliverer of the captives, I was the messenger of heaven."—Yet such low trifling, such absolute folly, is, by these interpreters, to help their theory out of a fatal difficulty, attributed without misgivings of taste or conscience, to the Lowly, Wise, and Holy JESUS!

[3.] If it were conceded, that the existence, which our Lord attributes to himself, was an existence only in the divine purpose, justness of criticism would require us likewise to take the existence ascribed to Abraham in the same acceptation : " Before Abraham " existed in the purpose of God, I was the Messiah in " the same purpose and decree." The use of the two verbs γενέσθαι and εἶναι does not destroy the ground of this observation : for the difference between them is, that the one denotes *to be brought into exist-ence,* and the other *to be in existence ;* a difference not at all affecting the argument. Thus it appears that, to concede the principle of the Unitarian interpre-tation, would convert the passage into a puerile absurdity.

On Mr. B.'s closing remark, " No reasoning, I think, can be more conclusive ;" I hope it will not be deemed a want of courtesy in me, to ask the candid and attentive reader, whether we may not justly reverse the declaration, and say, No reasoning can be more *inconclusive.*

He evidently bestowed great labour upon his disqui-sition on this text, " because," he observes, " it is in a great measure decisive of the whole controversy : for, if this declaration does not establish the preexistence of Christ, no other passage can."[21] It may, then, be taken as admitted that, if the interpretation for which he so earnestly pleads cannot be maintained on grounds of fair and sound criticism, the preexistence of Christ is established, and the Unitarian scheme is exploded. The serious and candid reader will bring to the examination his closest attention, his critical

[21] Page 102.

N 2

attainments, his strict impartiality, and his solemn devotion. Thus let him judge for himself, in the sight
of God: and may that Gracious Being direct his
decision!

But if the assertion be taken conversely, to intimate
that, if this text were given up to the Unitarian interpretation, the controversy would be decided, I must
protest against it, as uncandid and untrue; as one of
those bold, but gratuitous and unfounded, dogmatical
assertions, which too frequently appear in the pages of
the Calm Inquiry. Admit the supposition, and what
would be the effect? This particular passage would
be taken out of the field; it would make nothing in
favour of the preexistence of Christ: but it would
make nothing against it. The principle of the interpretation might also go to the neutralizing of some
other declarations of our Lord; but this would be all.
The general body of argument, from many particular
passages, and from the universal tenor of revelation,
in favour of the preexistence and the Deity of Christ
would remain untouched, and standing in its full independence. Yet unfair, both logically and morally, as
the Inquirer's observation is, it will not be without its
effect. Such dogmatical assertions often pass without
examination, and are apt to sink deeply into hasty
and half-thinking minds.

In one sense, however, I will not contest that there
may be truth in the assertion: " If this declaration
does not establish the preexistence of Christ, no other
passage can." If the assertor thereby mean that, *upon
the principles of interpretation which he adopts*, no
language, within the compass of the characteristic
style and manner of the New Testament, could de-

clare that doctrine so as not to be set aside by some
of those manœuvrings; let him keep possession of his
opinion. It is, I fear, too well founded. But let us
consider whether, on the admission of those principles,
we should not be obliged to abandon ourselves to a
hopeless incapacity of ever acquiring satisfaction, upon
any controverted point whatever of revealed theology,
or of any other knowledge depending on the use of
words.[22]

There is another interpretation of this celebrated
passage, which it will not be improper to notice; for
not only was it enthusiastically admired by Faustus
Socinus and some of his immediate followers, but it is
preferred by some Unitarians of the present day.

---

[22] With Mr. B.'s assertions, let the reader contrast the observations of Michaelis. " Jesus had not said that *he had seen Abraham*.
This was another perverse construction, by which the Jews endeavoured to hold up his discourse to ridicule. Jesus might very properly have replied accordingly : but he allows the inference which
they had drawn from his words ; and he accepts it, in order to say
of himself something still greater.—*Before Abraham was born,
I AM.* Thus he proclaims himself to be more than a mere man,
even one in whom dwells a superior and celestial nature. I AM,
sounds somewhat harsh in our language : but I have retained it, as
Luther did ; for in the Greek itself this is not the usual form of expression, but it intimates something emphatical, something resembling
the style in which the unchangeable God speaks of himself. The
Jews well understood what Jesus meant : they regarded it as a blasphemy, and they wished to stone him. They considered the guilt
of blasphemy as so indubitable, that they were desirous of putting
him instantly to death, in an extra-judicial manner. Yet I do not
maintain that these words are of themselves a complete proof of the
eternal deity of Christ ; for he might have been before Abraham, yea,
before the creation of the world, without being IN THE BEGINNING,
as is said of the WORD in chap. i. 1, 2. Nevertheless, considering
that passage with this, I believe that Christ here speaks of his eternal
Divine Nature." *Anmerkung.*

This interpretation rests upon the supposition, that our Lord did not intend to answer the question proposed to him, or to speak in a way that could at the time be understood by the Jews; but that his object was to denounce the divine displeasure against them, and to foretel their rejection, and the admission of the gentile world to the blessings of the gospel state; and that he clothed this meaning in a species of ænigma, derived from the signification of the name *Abraham*, denoting *father of a numerous multitude*, which was given to Abram as a prediction of the calling of the Gentiles. Upon this foundation, the passage is paraphrased to the following purport:—

" Ye boast of being the posterity of Abraham: but ye know neither what Abraham is, nor what are his posterity. Ye are not Abraham's seed: for by your deeds ye prove that ye are of your father the devil, and God is able from these stones (the Gentiles) to raise up a posterity to Abraham. Neither do ye know who is Abraham. He who can truly claim that prophetic title, must be the father, not of one nation only, but of many. But your great ancestor is as yet only your father; and not the father of many nations, as his name imports. He is not yet, in this eminent and final sense, *Abraham;* though he will soon become so, · if ye continue to act as ye have hitherto done, proving yourselves unworthy of the kingdom of God. For your privilege shall be taken from you, and given to nations who will act more worthily of it. Of them Abraham will be truly the father: then will he answer to his name, and be in reality what he has been hitherto only in promise. But I now am, the promised Messiah, plainly before your eyes. Therefore, *verily, verily, I say unto you,* at this very moment, *before Abraham becomes* what his name imports, and what he is on the point of becoming, that *I am* the Messiah whom Abraham desired to see, and in whom all nations shall be blessed."[23]

With this view of the passage Faustus Socinus was so delighted that he goes near to declare his persuasion of its having been communicated to his uncle Lælius by a special revelation, and in answer to many prayers offered to Christ himself.[24]

This interpretation may claim the praise of ingenuity : and it would not be a sufficient refutation of

---

[23] Abridged from *Enjedini Explic. Loc.* p. 227.

[24] " *Erasm. Joh.* Fateor me per omnem vitam meam non magis contortam scripturæ interpretationem audivisse ; ideoque eam penitus improbo. *Faust. Socin.* Cùm primùm fatendi verbum in tuis verbis animadverti, sperabam te potius fassurum nullam in vitâ tuâ scripturæ interpretationem te audivisse, quæ hâc sit aut acutior aut verior, quæve magis divinum quid sapiat, et à Deo ipso patefactam fuisse præ se ferat. Ego quidem certè non leves conjecturas habeo, illum, qui primus ætate nostrâ eam in lucem protulit (hic autem is fuit qui primus quoque sententiam de Christi origine quam ego constanter defendo, hâc ætate renovavit), precibus multis ab IPSO CHRISTO impetravit." *F. Socini Opera*, vol. ii. p. 505.

" *Erasmus Johannis.* I confess that in all my life I never heard a more forced interpretation of Scripture. I absolutely disapprove it. *Faustus Socinus.* When I heard you begin to talk of confessing, I hoped that you were about to confess that you had never in your life heard an interpretation of Scripture more signalized by acumen and truth, or which has more of a kind of divine savour, and actually carries the marks of having been communicated by God himself. Indeed I have no slight grounds for thinking that the person who first in our time advanced it, (the same who first in the present age revived the doctrine which I constantly maintain on the person of Christ,) obtained it by many prayers from CHRIST HIMSELF."

it to say that such a meaning could never be penetrated by those to whom it was addressed, and that it
was quite foreign to the purpose of the immediate
conversation between them and our Lord: for its
supporters readily acknowledge both these circumstances.   But our objections to it are, that it represents Jesus Christ as condescending to a kind of
childish punning, totally unworthy of his serious and
elevated character; that on no other occasion do we
find him making use of such a method of expression;
that (borrowing Mr. Belsham's words, in his rejection
of this gloss,) " if the proposed interpretation is just,
the text ought to have stood thus; ' before Abram
shall become Abraham :' the present ellipsis is too
harsh, and the mode of supplying it quite arbitrary ;"
that " the word *Abraham* always in the New Testament occurs as a proper name, and is never used in a
mystical sense ;" and that " it is a trifling proposition,
and unworthy of the solemnity with which it is introduced, that Christ existed as the Messiah before an
event which it was known was not to happen till
many years or ages afterwards."[25]

[25] *Calm Inq.* pp. 83, 84.

Capitule IV.

THE PERPETUAL PRESENCE OF CHRIST PROMISED TO HIS DISCIPLES.

The kind of power here spoken of.—How *given* to Christ.—The phrase, *End of the World.*—Instances of its occurrence.—Examination of Bishop Pearce's interpretation, and Mr. Wakefield's arguments in defence of it.—Matt. xiii. 37—43, 47—50.—Those learned writers mistaken in their application of the terms.—Hebrew and Rabbinical acceptations of *Olam.*—Mr. Wakefield's hasty, inaccurate, and inconsistent assertions.—Interpretations of the most eminent critics adverse to the hypothesis.—Sense of the parable.—Dr. Priestley's testimony.—Matt. xxiv. 3.—Evidence against Mr. Belsham's assertions.—Scope of the passage under consideration.—*The age,* in Jewish usage, would be synonymous with the period of the Messiah's reign.—It cannot be shown that our Lord did not intend the material universe.—Ruhnkenius's opinion of Bishop Pearce's critical talents;—Dr. Parr's and Dr. Burney's, of Mr. Wakefield.—The purpose of our Lord's declaration, and the necessary direction and extent which it gives to the terms.—Mr. Wakefield's gratuitous assertions.—Mr. Lindsey's observations, and replies to them.—Daring language of Mr. Belsham, and remarks upon it.—Mr. Wakefield's candid, but incorrect, acknowledgment.—Testimonies of Origen and Hegesippus.

"Jesus came forward and spake to them, saying, Go, make disciples of all "nations, baptizing them into the name of the Father and of the Son and of the "Holy Spirit; teaching them to observe all things, whatsoever I have com- "manded you: and behold! I am with you always, till the end of the world."— Matt. xxviii. 19, 20.

IT is the last clause only of this passage which at present is the object of consideration.

1. *Heaven and earth* was an ordinary Jewish phrase to denote the universe in its proper extent. " All " power[1] in heaven and upon earth" is an expression

[1] 'Εξουσία, not *authority* merely, but *efficient energy.* Schleusner's first signification is, " Vis et potestas efficiendi aliquid, facultas." But he understands the word, in this passage, of *dominion :* " omnia sunt imperio meo subjecta." So also Michaelis translates it. Kuinöl interprets it, " summa potestas," *supreme power.*

evidently of the largest meaning : but, if we regard it only in relation to the object with which it stands immediately connected, the removal of obstructions to the progress of the gospel, and its eventual diffusion among mankind, we see a field of operation opening before us which evidently requires divine qualifications to occupy it.

That this power must be possessed necessarily and unchangeably by the Divine Nature of the Messiah, admitting such a nature, is evident: how then is it " given" to him?   And that it is so *given*, he repeatedly declares.[2]

The reply is obvious. The mediatorial function, and the assuming of human nature in order to discharge that function, constitute a new office, a new character, new manifestations of the uncreated glory to intelligent beings, a new kind and course of relations to those beings. In the contemplation of these, nothing can be more proper than to say that the dominion and glory of Christ are the GIFT to him of his Divine Father, " of whom are all things :" while the essential excellencies of his superior nature remain necessarily unchangeable, because they are infinite. Unquestionably it is difficult for us to form precise conceptions on the harmonizing of these distinct doctrines: and, as we have repeatedly had occasion to observe, the nature of the subject requires us to expect that it should be so. Philosophy and piety equally dictate the expectation, as eminently befitting our nature, state, and circumstances. Our business is to ascertain the *facts* of the case, by the examination

---

[2] Matt. xi. 27.   John xiii. 3; xvii. 2.

of their proper evidence.   If we find it to be the voice
of revelation that those separate facts really are as
has been here stated, our incompetency to discover
the links of the chain which connects them, ought
indeed to teach us some humbling lessons, but ought
not to give us any anxiety.

> " Heaven is, for thee, too high
> To know what passes there.   Be lowly wise :
> Contented that thus far hath been reveal'd."

2. Unitarian writers object to the common interpretation of the phrase, ἡ συντέλεια τοῦ αἰῶνος, and
contend that it denotes only " the conclusion of this
age,"[3] that is, " the termination of the Jewish dispensation by the destruction of Jerusalem and the
temple."[4]

The phrase is found nowhere in the New Testament,[5] but in the Gospel of Matthew, and, exclusively
of the present passage, in that Gospel only four
times.

The first two instances are in our Lord's impressive
exposition of his parable of the tares.   " He who
" soweth the good seed is the Son of man : the field
" is the world : the sons of the kingdom, they are the
" good seed : but the tares are the sons of the wicked
" one : the enemy who sowed them is the devil : the
" harvest is (συντέλεια τοῦ αἰῶνος) the *end of the*

---

[3] *Calm Inq.* p. 323.   [4] Ib. p. 179.

[5] 'Επὶ συντελείᾳ τῶν αἰώνων, Heb. ix. 26, is not the same phrase,
though it has been added to the enumeration by Mr. Wakefield (on
Matthew, pp. 198, 414), and the Calm Inquirer.   There can be
no question that it signifies, " at the completion of the ages,"
the various dispensations of religion which preceded that of the
Messiah.

" *world :* and the reapers are the angels. As then
" the tares are gathered together and burned with
" fire, so it will be (ἐν τῇ συντελείᾳ τοῦ αἰῶνος τούτου),
" in *the end of this world.* The Son of man will send
" forth his angels, and they will gather together out of
" his kingdom all seducers to sin and those who work
" wickedness, and will cast them into the furnace of
" fire ; there will be weeping and gnashing of teeth.
" Then the righteous will shine forth as the sun, in
" the kingdom of their Father. He that hath ears to
" hear, let him hear." [6]

The phrase occurs again in a parable delivered on
the same occasion, and evidently with the same design.
" Again, the kingdom of heaven is like to a net cast
" into the sea, and gathering of every kind ; which,
" when it is filled, they draw up to the shore, and sit
" down and choose out the good to put into their
" vessels, but the worthless they throw away. So it
" will·be (ἐν τῇ συντελείᾳ τοῦ αἰῶνος) *in the end of the*
" *world.* The angels will come, and will separate the
" wicked out of the midst of the righteous, and cast
" them into the furnace of fire : there will be weeping
" and gnashing of teeth." [7]

The Calm Inquirer inclines not obscurely to the
opinion of Bishop Pearce and Mr. Wakefield, who
" interpret the parables of the tares and of the fish, of
the events which took place at the destruction of Jerusalem, when the Christians, warned by divine admo-

---

[6] Matt. xiii. 37—43. Σκάνδαλα· " Omnes impii, qui aliis errandi
et peccandi occasionem praebent." *Schleusn.* " Abstractum pro
concreto ; exitii auctores, seductores, doctrinâ et exemplo alios in
errorem inducentes." *Kuinöl.* " Verführer und Uebelthäter,"
seducers and evil doers. J. D. Michaelis..

[7] Matt. xiii. 47—50.

nition, retired from Judæa before the desolation of the country by the Romans." [8]

In support of this interpretation, Mr. Wakefield refers to Heb. ix. 26, and adds, "They, therefore, who will determine to interpret συντέλεια τοῦ αἰῶνος, by *the end of the world*, or *the consummation of all things*, at the day of final judgment, will do so without any authority, and in direct opposition to the idiom of the Hebrew language, and the sense of a plain text of Scripture; to subserve some favourite hypothesis, or commonly received doctrine." [9]

The arguments to be examined, therefore, are the following:

1. The allegation that the prediction in ver. 41 was fulfilled in the providential deliverance of the Jewish Christians by their timely withdrawment from their country and chief city. But let the unbiassed reader turn to the verse. He will find that it expresses, *definitively* and *solely*, a selection of the wicked from among the righteous, for the purpose of exemplary punishment! The *impious* are the persons picked out and taken away: the *good* are the mass which remains behind. Did the learned bishop and his followers fail to perceive this most obvious circumstance? Or could they have omitted to give it due effect, had they not been labouring " to subserve some favourite hypothesis ?"

2. " The idiom of the Hebrew language." The word עוֹלָם, which the writers of the New Testament commonly represent by αἰών, is certainly of various signification. It properly denotes any *period of very long duration;* and it is applied to different, but

always great and observable portions of finite time, to
a future immortality, and to a proper eternity.   By
the Rabbinical Jews it is also put occasionally to signify that which exists in time, or the whole system of
dependent nature:[10] in which sense, according to
some distinguished philologists, it is found in the New
Testament.[11]   The ancient Jews denominated the
period before the Messiah, *this age* or *world;* and that
which commences at his advent, *the age* or *world to
come.*   The latter period they considered in a threefold aspect, the reign of the Messiah in the present
life, the state of souls after death, and the state which
will take place immediately upon the resurrection of
the dead: and to each of these they applied the
appellation, *the world to come.*[12]

[10] " In the Jewish Liturgy God is frequently called רַב הָעוֹלָמִים
Lord of the worlds: for they make a threefold עוֹלָם or world. The
first is *the lower world,* this elementary region: the second is *the
middle world,* the heavenly bodies, which they also call גַּלְגַּלִים
wheels, or *orbs:* the third is *the upper world;* what the apostle calls
the third heaven, 2 Cor. xii. 2." *Camero in Heb.* i. 2. " The Jews
used their עוֹלָם in both senses; for though it literally denotes *seculum,* yet they frequently applied it in the sense of *mundus.*" *Michaelis's Introd. N. T. by Marsh,* vol. iv. p. 235.

[11] See *Schleusn. Lex.* in αἰὼν, *signif.* 7. who enumerates Heb.
i. 2; xi. 3. 1 Tim. i. 17. 1 Cor. ii. 7. Matt. xxiv. 3. 1 Cor. i. 20.
1 Tim. vi. 17.   " This word also in the New Testament has the
peculiar signification of *the world,* the great system of created things,
which is otherwise denominated in Greek, κόσμος.—So the Rabbins
use עוֹלָם——and the Latin Fathers *seculum.*" *Vorstius de Hebraismis N. Test. ed. Fischeri.* 1778. pp. 39—43.

[12] See *Buxtorfi Lex. Chald. Rabbin. et Talm.* col. 1620. *Drusius*
on Matt. xii. 32. *Witsii Dissert. de Seculo hoc et fut.* in *Miscell,
Sacr.* vol. i. *Schöttgen. Hor. Hebr.* vol. ii. pp. 23—27. By these
indefatigable scholars a multitude of Rabbinical authorities are
adduced. *Koppe* has an *Excursus* on this topic, annexed to his

It is, therefore, evident that, from the mere use of αἰών, no certain conclusion can be drawn. In every case its acceptation can be determined only by the scope and connexion, or by a combination with some other word producing a known idiomatical phrase. To the former of these modes we shall presently attend. With respect to the latter, it would be a very welcome assistance to us, if a Hebrew or Chaldee or Rabbinical phrase could be found, answering to this in the Greek of the Evangelist, "the end of the "world," or "the completion of the age." Neither Bishop Pearce nor Mr. Wakefield has done us this service: and from all the research that I have been able to make, I have reaped only disappointment. But Mr. Wakefield was not a man to be deterred by what some would have deemed insuperable difficulties. He could not find a precedent, and therefore, maugre all the canons of criticism, *he has made one!*[13]—

Annot. Perpet. in Ep. ad Ephes. Gotting. 1791, but which does not add much information to what is furnished by the preceding authors.

[13] " It appears to me a Jewish phrase, corresponding to קֵץ עוֹלָם." *Wakef.* p. 198. This ingeniously invented clause either might signify *an end of an age*, conceived indefinitely; of which construction we have examples in Mic. v. 1. *days of eternity;* and (יְמוֹת the poetical plural) Deut. xxxii. 7. *days of antiquity:* for, though the proper signification of עוֹלָם is *eternity*, the "expression, as with us in common life, was very frequently used without a regard to strict accuracy, when only a very long period of time was intended:" (*Gesenius Wörterb.*) or, the more certain sense of Mr. Wakefield's construction would have been, *an everlasting end*, as we find בְּרִית עוֹלָם *an everlasting covenant*, Gen. ix. 16. and Is. lv. 3. *everlasting mercy*, liv. 8. *an everlasting name*, lxiii. 12. *an everlasting possession*, Gen. xvii. 8. *an everlasting foundation*, Prov. x. 25. *everlasting desolations*, Jer. li. 26. and other instances, all confirming the observation above made, while not a single example occurs to support Mr. Wakefield's proposal. The proper form would have been

Unfortunately, his Hebrew composition has failed.
Though it consisted of only two words, it is such as a
person moderately skilled in the language will see to
be inadmissible.

3. Mr. Wakefield further urges Heb. ix. 26. as "a
plain text of Scripture," for determining the sense of
the examples in Matthew. "There," he says, "the
author observes that Christ was *manifested once for
all, for the purpose of putting away sin,* ἐπὶ συντελείᾳ
τῶν αἰώνων, *at,* or *upon the* COMPLETION *of the* AGES,
or *age,* for the LXX. use ἀπ᾽ αἰῶνος and ἀπ᾽ αἰώνων,
indiscriminately." On this passage I remark:

(1.) It is *not true* that the authors of the Septuagint
Version "use ἀπ᾽ αἰῶνος and ἀπ᾽ αἰώνων indiscriminately." The former of these phrases, and the form
ἀπὸ τοῦ αἰῶνος, occur often, denoting *from a remote
finite period* and *from eternity;* but neither in the
Septuagint nor in the Apocrypha can, I believe, a single
instance be found of ἀπ᾽ αἰώνων or ἀπὸ τῶν αἰώνων.

(2) In the New Testament, the phrase ἀπ᾽ αἰῶνος
occurs only three times,[14] and those in the writings of
the same person: twice in the sense of *from the*

קַץ הָעוֹלָם; or (as given by Hutter, and in the Hebrew Version of
the New Testament published in London, 1813,) תַּפְלִית הָעוֹלָם;
or in the Chaldaic idiom, שׁוֹלְמָהּ דְּעַלְמָא. For illustrations, see
Numb. xvii. 12. (Engl. Version, xvi. 48.) Exod. viii. 18, (22.)
Ezek. xl. 43. 2 Chron. xxxii. 17. On the Hebrew prefix ה, Gesenius says, "The rules for the position and the absence of the definite
article almost universally coincide with those which obtain in the
German and Greek languages. It is prefixed, when the discourse
refers to a *defined* subject, particularly when it has been *mentioned
before,* or is to be recognised as *already known,* or is a *single* subject
in its kind: but, when it is *indefinite* and *general,* the article is not
put." *Lehrgebäude,* p. 651.

[14] Luke i. 70. Acts iii. 21; xv. 18.

beginning of time, or *from the remotest antiquity;* and once to denote *from eternity.*

Mr. Wakefield must have written without examination, and perhaps from the floating recollection of the two parallel places in the New Testament, in which ἀπὸ τῶν αἰώνων is found.[15] In both those places it gives no sense that will support his hypothesis. Granting that two forms of one expression may signify the same thing, it by no means follows that two forms of another expression are synonymous likewise. In one combination of ideas, the use of the plural number varies not, or scarcely at all, the effect produced: "from eternity," or "from eternal ages." But, with another modification of thought, and a difference both in the related terms and in the purpose intended, the change of the number may be of the greatest consequence. "The completion of the age," and "the completion of the ages," cannot be the same thing. The one describes the closing of a certain great period; the other that of a series of such periods, or, according to a peculiar use of συντέλεια, the boundary which closes one period and begins another.[16]

[15] Eph. iii. 9, and Col. i. 26. Comparing these with Eph. iii. 11, Luke i. 50, Rom. xvi. 25, and 2 Tim. i. 9, it will probably appear to the studious inquirer that these varieties of phrase all denote the same thing, מֵעוֹלָמִים *from eternity.* See *Koppe* and *Rosenmüller.* Or if they be rendered, *from before the ancient dispensations,* the sense will be the same; as that, which was before any of the divisions of time, must have been from eternity.

[16] See Job xxvi. 10. LXX.—μέχρι συντελείας φωτὸς μετὰ σκότους: "unto the *boundary* which divides the light from darkness."

The observations of the distinguished Biblical Hebraist, Schöttgenius, are deserving of attention: "Here is to be observed, 1 Cor. x. 11, *upon whom the ends of the ages are come.* Paul describes the

(3.) The construction which Mr. Wakefield and the Calm Inquirer would put upon the phrase, in the one passage, is inconsistent with their application of it to the other : for the period which *terminated* with the sufferings and death of Christ, could not be the same period to the end of which he, after he had risen from the dead, promised his presence to his disciples ; the one was past and completed, the other future and then only commencing.

4. If any respect be due to the opinions of the most eminent Biblical Critics, it must be remarked that all, so far as I have been able to discover, from Tertullian, Origen, and Jerome downwards, till Bishop Pearce proposed his new interpretation, · have agreed to understand the parables of the tares and the net cast into the sea, of the infinitely solemn events which will take place " at the day of final judgment." The venerable and almost apostolic Syriac Version not obscurely intimates the sense of $a\grave{i}\grave{\omega}\nu$ and the scope of the former of the two parables, by its rendering $\kappa\acute{o}\sigma\mu o\varsigma$, " the world," in ver. 38, by *Olmo ;* the same, differing only in dialect, as the Hebrew word so often cited in the preceding paragraphs, and which is represented by $a\grave{i}\grave{\omega}\nu$ in the scriptural Greek. Of modern

men of his time as those on whom the *boundaries, τὰ τέλη,* of two worlds or ages, had met ; of this world and that to come, of the old covenant and the new. So, in Heb. ix. 26, Christ is said to have been revealed *at the confines of the ages;* where the end of *this age or world,* and the beginning of *that to come,* as it were, touch each other.—A phrase which most exactly describes the time of the coming of the Messiah.—The apostle uses the plural, *ages,* and not the singular, to express these two periods ; and συντέλεια, and not τέλος, to mark the *junction* of the two τέλη, the *extremities* of the periods." *Schöttgen. Lex. N.T.* αἰὼν et συντέλεια. *Ejusd. Hor. Hebr.* tom. ii. p. 27.

commentators I shall instance only those, whose systems and characteristic habits of interpretation might, not unreasonably, be supposed to give them a propensity to glosses resembling that to which we have here objected. Grotius,[17] Hammond, Whitby, Father Simon, Dr. Samuel Clarke, Macknight, Wetstein, Rosenmüller, and Dr. Priestley, accord with the common and obvious acceptation; and to these I must add a name which will, in the present instance, command some attention, as an example of the power of reason and evidence forcing itself through an unguarded avenue. This is no other than the name of Mr. Wakefield himself, who, in his Notes on this very parable of the tares, says, "Our Saviour here points out to the future day of universal judgment, as the season for a complete rectification of these disorders: and [see vers. 29, 30,] alludes to the many inconveniences that would inevitably attend the extirpation and punishment of the wicked in this present life."[18]

The interpretation of language, especially on topics not of a common and palpable kind, is a matter of only moral evidence, and can scarcely ever be freed from the possibility of objection and cavil: but, in most cases, an attentive and unbiassed understanding will find no great difficulty in determining the plain and reasonable construction. To any man who will

[17] Grotius has suggested a minor argument, which appears of no inconsiderable weight in determining the design of the first parable; observing on ver. 38, " *the field is* THE WORLD," that the reference of the discourse cannot be to the Jewish nation only. " The church is not to be confined to a particular country; not to be limited to the people of Israel; but is to spread through the whole world." *J. D. Michaelis, in loc.*

[18] *On Matt.* p. 196.

read, these parables, with such an unprepossessed understanding, with a competent acquaintance with scripture language, and with a due attention to our Lord's characteristic manner as a teacher, may the appeal be made, whether the next to unanimous interpretation of critics and commentators, of all times, sects, and sentiments, be not the just one. The answer to this appeal may be given in the words of Dr. Priestley: " According to this parable, we are not to expect a complete separation of good and bad men, till *the end of the world*, the day of judgment, or the last resurrection.—We are here told that *the harvest is the* END OF THE WORLD, and that the Son of Man at his second coming *will send forth his angels to gather out of his kingdom all things that offend, and them that do iniquity;* and that *then*, and not before, he will order them to be *cast into the furnace of fire;* and that *then*, and not before, *the righteous will shine forth as the sun in the kingdom of their Father*. All our hopes and fears, therefore, should respect that GREAT DAY, emphatically called THAT DAY."[19]

We now proceed to the consideration of the fourth instance, in which the phrase, whose import is to be determined, occurs in the New Testament. " The " disciples came to him apart, saying, Tell us, when " will these things be, and what the sign of thy coming " and (τῆς συντελείας τοῦ αἰῶνος) of the *end of the* " *world?*"[20] This example Mr. Belsham considers as decisive of the question.[21] But he appears to overlook

[19] *Notes on Scripture,* vol. iii. pp. 179, 180.

[20] Matt. xxiv. 3.

[21] " What will be the sign of thy coming, and of the *end of this*

a very obvious circumstance, namely, that this is the
language of the four disciples, and not of Jesus ; and
that it must, therefore, be interpreted in consonance
with what we have reason to believe was the then
present state of their knowledge. The disciples viewed
the *coming* of Christ and the *end of the world* or *age*,
as events nearly related, and which would indisputably
take place together : but no one can suppose that they
had any idea of the dissolution of the Jewish polity,
with the attendant miseries, as really signified, or
included in, either of those events. They conceived
of the event concerning which they inquired, as something inexpressibly great and awful, a total change,
perhaps, in the physical constitution of the universe ;
and they probably expected its occurrence within the
term of their own lives : but they could have no conception of what was really meant by the expression
which they employed, the COMING of Christ. The
occasion, upon which they proposed their question,
was our Lord's assuring them of the ruin of the
magnificent building which they were admiring, one
of their principal subjects of national pride and boast-
ing. "From their very childhood," says a judicious
and penetrating commentator, "they imagined that
the temple would stand to the end of time : and

world, or *age*? Here the phrase unquestionably means the Jewish
dispensation, or rather polity. For, in reply to the question proposed by his disciples, our Lord immediately proceeds to foretel the
calamities which should precede the destruction of Jerusalem. And
ver. 34, he declares, ' This generation shall not pass till all these
things are fulfilled.' " *Calm Inq.* p. 323. The error in the Inquirer's
citation of the passage, *this* for *the*, was undoubtedly unintentional :
but it requires to be noticed, as to cursory readers it appears to
carry some weight in favour of the writer's hypothesis.

this notion was so deeply fixed in their minds,
that they regarded it as impossible for the temple
to be overthrown, while the structure of the universe remained. As soon, therefore, as Christ told
them that the temple would be destroyed, their
thoughts instantly ran to the consummation of all
things. Thus they connect with the destruction of
the temple, as things inseparable, the coming of Christ
and the end of the world.—A fond hope, which they
had conceived without any authority, that the final
perfection of the reign of Christ was very near, and
actually present, led them to indulge the extravagant
expectation of springing all at once to perfect happiness."[22]—A modern scripture-critic, who was a man

[22] CALVIN, *Commentaire sur la Concordance, ou Harmonie, com-
posée des III. Evangelistes*; Gen. 1563, p. 457.   That the illustrious Reformer had a foundation of facts for his observations, and
was not drawing a picture from his own conceptions of probability, is
evinced by the Rabbinical citations adduced in *Lightfoot's Horæ
Hebr. et Talm.* in loc. *Works*, vol. ii. pp. 240, 241, and *Wetstein*,
N. T. in loc.

" Since the Hebrews, by the formula *this world* or *age*, denoted
the time before the coming of the Messiah ; and, by *the world* or
age to come, the time under the Messiah's reign : and since the Jews
believed that, with the destruction of their city and temple, would be
joined the coming of the Messiah to judgment, and the dissolution
of the world : (see *Koppe's Excurs.* i. *in Ep. ad. Eph.* and *Lightfoot's Hor. Hebr.* in loc.)   I assent to those interpreters who understand the formula [ἡ συντέλ. &c.] of the end of the present system of
things, and the coming of Christ as universal Judge." *Kuinöl* in loc.

A high-rated Hebrew and Rabbinical scholar, but deplorable
Neologist, brings much evidence to prove that the phrase signifies
the conclusion of the period assigned to the former part of the reign
of the Messiah ; when the resurrection of the dead and the universal
judgment shall have taken place ; and when the latter part only shall
remain, the infinite duration of eternity. *Bertholdt* (who died Prof.
Theol. at Erlangen, in 1822,) *Christologia Judæorum, Jesu Apostolorumque Ætate.* Erl. 1811, pp. 38—43.

of no weak judgment, likewise observes on this passage; " it is certain that the phrase, ἡ συντέλεια τοῦ αἰῶνος, is understood in the New Testament (Matt. xiii. 39, 40, 49 ; xxviii. 20,) of the end of the world. The disciples spoke according to the opinions of their countrymen. They believed that the end of this world, and the beginning of a new one, would follow immediately upon the destruction of the temple."[22]

Thus, I conceive, we have as satisfactory evidence as the nature of the case admits, that Mr. B. was mistaken when he wrote, " Here the phrase unquestionably means the Jewish dispensation, or rather polity ;" and that, on the other hand, the present instance does not differ from the preceding ones, and is most rationally to be understood as denoting no other than that signal termination of the existing order of the divine government which the Scriptures teach us to expect, the great epoch of the universe.

This discussion of the examples upon which the interpretation of Bishop Pearce and others is attempted to be supported, has, I trust, shown that they render it no aid ; and that they abundantly confirm the old and common interpretation of the phrase in question. We, therefore, return to the passage under consideration, " Behold, I am with you always, even " to *the end of the world*," or " *of the age*" which will extend to the awful scenes of expiring time.

3. If we were to lay out of our minds all respect to the other examples of this phrase, our only means of ascertaining its import, in addition to the grammatical

[22] *Rosenmüller*, the father, in loc. So *Schleusner* also understands the phrase, in all the passages: " finis hujus mundi,—interitus mundi." *Lex.* vol. ii. p. 1019: and so likewise Michaelis.

construction,[24] would be the apparent scope and design of the whole passage. To this we shall now attend.

The use of the term *αἰὼν, age* or *world,* will not of itself, as was before observed, determine what particular system, dispensation, or period is designed; we must search for some characters of specification.

1. Our Lord does not say, *to the end of* THIS *age.;* as the Calm Inquirer has twice cited the clause.[25] It is true that this is not a very material difference, but it has some effect; and that effect, so far as it can go, is not of the nature of just argument. Jesus Christ

[24] The evidence of the Ancient Versions, if it does not put the question out of controversy, inclines strongly in favour of the usual interpretation.

To the Syriac, the remarks before made on the Hebrew term are applicable. But it is an important fact that *Olam,* or in the emphatic state *Olmo,* by which αἰὼν is rendered here (and in every other instance in the N. T. so far as I have discovered, and I have examined many passages), is also the word uniformly employed when κόσμος occurs in the original. At least I have compared every instance in the Gospels and Acts, and many in the Epistles, without finding a single deviation, except in John xviii. 20, where, instead of τῷ κόσμῳ, the Syriac translator evidently had τῷ λαῷ, a reading which is not noticed by Walton, Mill, Wetstein, Griesbach, or Scholz.

The Arabic of Rome, 1591, has *to the dissolution of the age, Alam,* the same word as in the Hebrew and Syriac.

The Arabic in Walton's Polyglott, has *to the completion of ages.* The latter word *daharon,* of which the version uses the plural, is thus explained by Golius: " Tempus, peculiariter longum; seculum; mille anni; quin perpetuitas; finis; extremum." *Lex. Arab.* col. 874.

The Vulgate has *ad consummationem seculi;* and of the Latin versions before Jerome, some read *mundi* and others *seculi;* but the comments and reasonings of the Latin fathers show that they understood by *seculum* the period to the end of time.

With regard to the following, I am obliged to trust to the Latin translations. For the Æthiopic, the editors give *ad finem mundi:* the Persic, *in æternitatem æternitatis:* the Coptic, by Wilkins, *ad finem seculorum.*

[25] Pages 323, 325.

said, " I am with you—to the end of THE age :" for here the use and intent of the Greek and of the English article are the same. What must THE *period of time* have been, which would naturally and necessarily present itself to the minds of our Lord's hearers?— Ignorant though they, even now, remained of the nature and extent of his kingdom, but convinced as they most surely were of his being the True Messiah, could they entertain any other notion of THE *age* by him so emphatically designated, than that it was the destined period of the Messiah's reign, the duration, in the present state, of his official preemi- nence and dominion as the Redeemer of Israel? Their idea of *the age* could not, we conceive, be any other than coincident with those *Days of the Messiah,* with the expectation of which their Rabbinical doc- trines and their popular opinions were so strongly imbued. They could not think of the small and languishing remains of *the Levitical age,* for at this time they knew nothing of the divine plan for its abolition. They could not think of *the end of the Jewish polity,* as an event detached from the conclu- sion of all temporal things, for their deeply rooted opinions would infallibly prevent such an expectation; and, had it been presented to them, they would have shrunk from it with alarm and horror. They could not think of the period commonly called *the apostolic. age,* for both the term and the idea are comparatively modern. It is morally impossible that they could associate with our Lord's words any other conception than that of the long desired period, on which their minds had been previously so accustomed to dwell, and in which they had the strongest feelings of interest

and hope,—" the world to come, the exaltation of
Israel, in the days of the Messiah." [26]

It should also be recollected, that we have not
incontrovertible proof of our Lord's words being
intended or understood to denote *duration* only.
The Hebrew word which, in the dialect then vernacular, our Lord probably, or we almost might say
certainly, employed, was used also, as we have before
observed, to signify *the visible system of the universe*
as associated with the flow of time. That acceptation
is equally pertinent to the connexion and design of
the present passage, and of the four other instances :
nor is it possible, I conceive, to show by any certain
argument that it was not the sense designed by Jesus
Christ, and understood by his apostles. Such was the
opinion of the authors of some of the most esteemed
modern versions,[27] and of critics,[28] whose erudition
and skill will, by all, be admitted to have been at
least not inferior to those qualifications in the worthy
and learned Dr. Pearce,[29] or in that eminent but often
precipitate scholar, Mr. Wakefield.[30]

[26] *Lightfoot, Works,* vol. ii. p. 240.

[27] To our established translation, and the excellent one by the British
refugees at Geneva, may be added the German of Luther, Michaelis,
Seiler, Stolz, Van Ess, Scholz, and De Wette ; the Dutch, whose
reputation among modern versions is very great ; the Protestant
French of different revisions, from the Reformation to the celebrated
revision, or rather new version, by the Pastors and Professors of
Geneva, 1805 ; the French of De Sacy, and other Roman Catholic
versions ; and the Italian of Diodati. Le Cène, indeed, has *à la
fin du siècle.*

[28] *Schleusner,* voce Συντέλεια. " —Ad mundi finem,—ad finem
usque rerum humanarum."—*Mori Comm. Exeg. Histor. in Theol.
Christ.* vol. ii. p. 189. Halæ, 1798.

[29] See Note [A], at the end of this Capitule.

[30] See Note [B], at the end of this Capitule.

2. It is evidently reasonable to consider the extent of our Lord's promise, as commensurate with the purpose for the advancement and success of which it was given. That purpose was " to make ALL NATIONS " disciples" to the doctrine and authority of the Lord Jesus Christ : " preaching repentance and remission " of sins in his name," and " teaching them to observe " all things whatsoever he had commanded." To encourage his servants in their efforts for the effectuating of this design, the Saviour assures them of HIS OWN PRESENCE, as the King possessed of " all power " in heaven and upon earth ;" for their aid and protection, their deliverance from all dangers, their surmounting all difficulties, and their eventual triumph in the full accomplishment of the great and benevolent purpose. But that purpose is not yet accomplished. If any should pretend that it was actually carried into effect, to such an extent as might be construed into a completion of our Lord's intention, by the apostles and their coadjutors ; as the apostle Paul says, that " the gospel was come into all the world :"[31] I beseech them to consider what is involved in their hypothesis. They have, first, to construe the words of the apostle in a sense manifestly repugnant to reason and truth, and to the common use of language.[32] To affirm that the " touching and glancing" of the gospel on the various regions of the earth in

[31] Col. i. 6.

[32] This and similar phrases are common in both ancient and modern languages, to denote a considerable extent of magnitude or number. We say *every where, every body, tout le monde.* The evident meaning of Paul is, that Christianity was now made known in all the principal provinces and cities of the empire, and in some places probably beyond its boundaries. So he had written, some years before, that the faith and piety of the Roman church was " published in the whole world :" Rom. i. 8.

the apostolic age, even joining to it all the subsequent
diffusion of Christianity to the present hour, has
amounted to an equivalent to the "making all nations
" DISCIPLES," sincerely and practically such (for Christ
would so call no other); is not idle and absurd only;
it is profane, contemptuous, and wicked. They have,
further, to admit that the preaching and propagation
of Christian truth ceased to be a duty, when the last
of the primitive disciples expired: for to them only,
according to the hypothesis, was the command given;
to them only was the promise made.

To me, I confess, it appears as manifest as the
reason of the case can make it, that the promise of
our Gracious Redeemer's presence is correlative with
the obligation and work of teaching the Christian
religion, and practising its duties. Hence the promise
is not to be restricted to the apostles, or to the primitive evangelists, but is to be extended, by the reason
of an equal, or even a stronger, necessity, through all
subsequent time, till all nations shall become true
disciples of the Messiah, " shall serve him, and shall
" call him blessed."[33]   I have said, by a *stronger*
necessity, and this rests upon two reasons: first, the
cessation of miracles; and secondly, the undeniable
fact that, after all the glorious success of the apostles
and their fellow-labourers, *by far the larger proportion*
of the work to be done remained undone when the
last of that generation were gathered to their fathers;
—yea, with sorrow and shame should the christian
church acknowledge, that larger proportion of the
most solemn and interesting of public duties remains
to this hour not performed!—"Arise, O God! Judge
" the earth; for thou shalt inherit all nations.   Take

[33] See Psalm lxxii. 11, 17.   Dan. vii. 14.

" to thyself thy great power and reign! Take the
" heathen for thine inheritance, and the uttermost
" parts of the earth for thy possession!"[34]

Attention is also due to the import and implications of the terms in which the promise is couched.
"Behold" (ἰδαὺ) is not merely a note of attention and
of solemn asseveration, but it generally introduces
something new and unexampled, and of high importance.—"I am with you." This is a form of speech
of known and very expressive use in the style of
Scripture. "It is observable," says Grotius, (whose
antievangelical predilections render such a remark
peculiarly important, as what we may well believe
that nothing but mighty evidence would have drawn
from him,) "that *to be with* any one, is peculiarly
spoken of God."[35] The expression standing thus free
from any adjunct, usually, and perhaps constantly,
denotes a manifestation of the wisdom, power, and
grace of God, in an especial manner, for the protection of his servants, their guidance in the ways of
obedience, and the communication to them of all
blessings. Here are some examples of this sacred
phrase. "Behold, I am with thee, and I will keep
" thee in all places whither thou goest.—As I was
" with Moses, I will be with thee; I will not leave
" thee, nor forsake thee.—O my Lord, if Jehovah be
" with us, why have we met with all this?—And
" Jehovah said to him, Surely I will be with thee.—
" Fear not, for I am with thee: be not dismayed, for
" I am thy God."[36] Passages of this kind might be
accumulated. If the reader chooses to search out a

[34] Psalm lxxxii. 8 ; ii. 8.   Rev. xi. 17.   [35] *Annot.* in loc.
[36] Gen. xxviii. 15.   Josh i. 5.   Judg. vi. 13, 16.   Isaiah xli. 10.

greater number of them, I think he will be convinced
that I do not lay an extravagant stress upon the use
of this expression, as what was to Jesus and his countrymen a well-known idiom, designating the exercise
of divine perfections.—Πάσας τὰς ἡμέρας (literally, *all
the days,*) we can render in English only by *always*
or *perpetually.* The French language has the very
idiom, *tous les jours.*[37] The phrase put thus absolutely, without a following noun in the genitive, is of
rare occurrence. It is found in the New Testament
nowhere but here, and in the Septuagint a few times :[38]
and it always signifies an *uninterrupted perpetuity,* as
complete as the nature of the subject will admit.

Mr. Wakefield, however, asserted that the sense of
the promise, that " Christ would be with them to the
end of the age, and how long that period was, will be
best understood from the parallel passage of St. Mark:
—chap. xvi. 17—19. So then our Lord would continue with them in *working miracles* to the end of the
age." [39]

I reply, that it is altogether a gratuitous assumption that the passage in the Gospel of Mark is " the
parallel " to that in Matthew. It is not proved to be
so, either by the series of events in the narration, or
by the correspondence of the terms. But, if we were

[37] De Sacy, and the Protestant Versions including the last Genevese, have *toujours ;* but Le Cène, *tous les jours.* Van Ess and
De Wette follow Luther, in retaining the literal phrase ; *alle Tage,
all days ;* Michaelis has *alle Zeiten, all times ;* Seiler prefers the
adverb *allezeit, always.* Stolz renders the concluding clause, (—*alle
Tage, bis dieser Zeitlauf ein ende nimmt,*) " all days, till this course
of time comes to an end."

[38] See LXX. Gen. xliii. 9. 3 Kings xii. 7. 4 Kings viii. 19 ;
xiii. 3 ; xvii. 37. Tobit xii. 19.

[39] *On Matthew,* p. 415.

to admit that the two passages occurred in the same
address of Jesus to his disciples, they must have been
distinct parts of the discourse, and ought by no means
to be confounded with each other. The narration in
Matthew stands alone, having no *immediate* connexion
with any previous circumstance ; for the facts, the
statement of which is closed in the antecedent sentence, are completely detached, and had taken place
at some distance of time before those now introduced :
and the scene of this narration is a mountain in Galilee,
whither the eleven apostles (and, as many harmonists
suppose, the great body of our Lord's followers, in
number more than five hundred,[40]) had repaired, in
consequence of a direction given by our Lord on the
evening before his death. On the other hand, the
passage of Mark is apparently so connected with its
preceding matter as to render it highly probable, at
least, that the occurrence took place in a private
house, in or near Jerusalem, on the very evening of
our Lord's resurrection, and was that of which we
have other relations in John xx. 19—23, and Luke
xxiv. 36—49.

How far a correspondence can be traced in the
terms of the passages, will the more conveniently be
shown by placing them together :

MATTHEW xxviii. 16—20.

" But the eleven disciples went
into Galilee, to a mountain where
Jesus had appointed them : and
when they saw him, they worshipped him ; but some were in

MARK xvi. 14—18.

" Afterwards, he was manifested to the eleven disciples as
they were sitting at table : and
he reproved them for their dis-
belief and obstinacy, that they

---

[40] See 1 Cor. xv. 6.

MATTHEW xxviii. 16—20.
suspense. And Jesus came forwards and spoke to them, saying,
 "All power is given unto me
in heaven and upon earth. Go,
make disciples of all nations, baptizing them to the name of the
Father, and of the Son, and of
the Holy Spirit; teaching them
to observe all things, whatsoever
I have commanded you; and,
behold! I am with you always,
till the end of the world."

MARK xvi. 14—18.
had not credited those who saw
him risen: and he said to them,
 "Go into the whole world, and
procloim the glad tidings to all
the [human] race. He who believeth and is baptized shall be
saved; but he who disbelieveth
shall be condemned. And miracles shall follow those who believe. In my name they shall
cast out dæmons; they shall
speak in new tongues; they shall
take up serpents: and, if they
drink any deadly poison, it shall
not hurt them; and they shall
lay hands on diseased [persons]
and they shall become well."

The candid reader will now judge whether Mr.
Wakefield's argument deserves any better name than
that of an empty assertion, destitute of any rational
proof.

Mr. B. cites a passage from Mr. Lindsey, as "highly
judicious and important."

"Our Lord says, 'I am with *you*,' that is, as Mr.
Lindsey observes, Seq. p. 75, 'with *you* who are now
present with me, — *you* may be assured of extraordinary assistance and support. But he does not
promise the same to succeeding Christians: the miraculous aid and gifts of which he obviously speaks were
confined to the age of the apostles.'" [41]

On this paragraph I submit two observations.

1. It is *not* "obvious" that our Lord is speaking
of "miraculous aid and gifts:" but it is, on the contrary, *abundantly manifest* that he is speaking of no

[41] *Calm Inq.* p. 325.

such thing, but altogether on subjects which are the common duty and privilege of the Christian church in all ages; his own supremacy, the diffusion of his truth, and the universal obligation of mankind to yield him full obedience.

2. We have already shown, by evidence to which a truly serious inquirer will give its just weight, that the *nature, ground,* and *reason* of the promise, so far from " confining it to the age of the apostles," oblige us, by all the rules of fair interpretation, to regard it as intended by its Blessed Author to reach through every period of time, till " all the ends of the earth " shall see the salvation of our God."

" It may nevertheless be conceded that our Lord is, or may be personally present in this world, and actively engaged at all times in some unknown manner for the benefit of his church.——The truth is, that the Scriptures have left us totally in the dark with regard to the present condition, employment, and attributes of Christ, and therefore it is in vain to speculate upon the subject."[42]

So wrote this author:—and, alas! there is ignorance, and carelessness, and credulity enough in the world to receive such assertions with easy faith.

" It *may be conceded*" that Christ is doing something for the good of his cause among men : but no one can tell what!——Certainly we know little of the state and operations of the invisible world; and, above all, of the Great God himself our best conceptions are feeble and low : but does it follow from thence that we are "totally in the dark" on such subjects?—Concerning the circumstances and the proceedings of our

[42] *Calm Inq.* p. 324.

Lord Jesus Christ, in his glorified state, undoubtedly
we are incompetent to form precise ideas with relation
to specific objects; and we must rest in general notions, derived from our purest and most exalted conceptions of dignity, merit, power, activity, usefulness,
and happiness: but the Scriptures have not left us
in the state of total ignorance so daringly affirmed,
with regard to the Saviour's "present condition,
employment, and attributes." And, though a considerable part of the scriptural declarations on this
head is veiled in the language of figure and allusion
to human affairs and to the services of the Hebrew
sanctuary; still enough of knowledge is permitted us
to elevate our hopes, and excite our love, gratitude,
and confidence. We read that " God hath highly
" exalted him, and hath granted to him a name above
" every name," to which homage is to be done by all
created beings, " heavenly, earthly, and infernal;"
and that. " he sitteth at the right hand of God the
" Father," " all his enemies," and " all things" besides,
being " put beneath his feet:"[43] and, thus using the
figurative representations as the indices of spiritual
and sublime conceptions, we believe that Jesus Christ
possesses a station of GREATNESS, HAPPINESS and
ACTIVE ENERGY, infinitely superior to the state of any
created being, so as to produce in us the idea, which
is inculcated in the Scriptures by a great variety of
phrase, of UNIVERSAL DOMINION. We read that "he
" fills all things;" that believers are " filled by him,
" receiving out of his fulness grace for grace:"[44] and
therefore we believe that he exercises an ACTUAL

[43] Phil. ii. 9, 10. 1 Cor. xv. 25. Eph. i. 20, 22.
[44] Eph. iv. 10. Col. ii. 10.

INFLUENCE, both physical and moral, upon the whole conduct of mundane affairs, and all the motives and actions of men. We read that "he searcheth the "hearts and trieth the reins, and will give to every "man according to his works :"[45] and we therefore conclude that he possesses the most PERFECT, ACCURATE, and UNIVERSAL KNOWLEDGE, and that he is constantly applying that knowledge to purposes of the greatest importance, purposes in which we ourselves have the most solemn concern. We read that "he "appeareth in the presence of God, acting for us :"[46] and we derive from this often-repeated assurance, the belief that he exercises, for the benefit of his obedient servants, all the powers and prerogatives of his supremely blessed state, EFFECTING OUR GOOD IN EVERY POSSIBLE FORM AND MODE, and of which we frame some humble conception by combining the ideas of a Friend ever constant and faithful, a Patron, an Intercessor, an Advocate : in fine, that his state of transcendent happiness has not removed him to an inaccessible distance from us, and has neither dissolved nor impaired his gracious connexion with us : but that he maintains, without any detraction from his own perfect bliss, the most generous SYMPATHY in our sorrows, afflictions, and difficulties;[47] that he is the GIVER OF OUR CONSOLATION, hope, and stability;[48] and that he is the AUTHOR OF ETERNAL SALVATION to all that obey him.[49]

Such is a brief sketch of the information which the Scriptures afford concerning the " present condition, employment, and attributes of Christ." Yet the

---

[45] Rev. ii. 23.   [46] See Note [C] at the end of this Capitule.
[47] Heb. iv. 15.   [48] 2 Thess. ii. 16, 17.   [49] Heb. v. 9.

author of a professed Inquiry into the Scripture Doctrine concerning Him, deliberately tells us, that " upon this subject they leave us *totally in the dark !*" —May the mercy of that Blessed One, whose name is thus dishonoured, forgive the bold impiety or ignorant unbelief!

Before we quit this topic, a few words more are due to Mr. Wakefield.

That gentleman candidly acknowledged " that early Christian writers used this phrase in a more extensive signification, for *the consummation of all things* at *the end of the world ;* and the word αἰὼν for *world.* But their authority is of little weight, as they seem to have been in general very slender proficients in the Hebrew language. See Ignat. Epist. interp. ad Smyrn. sect. 3. Polycarp. Ep. ad. Phil. sect. 5. Orig. cont. Cels. lib. ii. pp. 85 and 140, &c. Ed. Cant. Euseb. Ec. Hist. III. 20. Lactant. lib. vii. sect. 9, and others." [50]

I am no advocate for submission to the authority of the Fathers, either as divines or as interpreters of Scripture. With some honourable exceptions, they were, in the one capacity, injudicious and inconsistent; in the other, arbitrary and irrational. But one of the most useful purposes to which we can put them, is to get their testimony in questions of fact : and the meaning of a word or phrase in their vernacular language, or some other with they were acquainted, is a matter of fact. It is also true that they were, in general, ignorant of the Hebrew and its cognate languages. But, in relation to the passage which we have had so long under consideration, there appear to

[50] *On Matthew,* p. 414.

me to be very fair grounds for making an exception in favour of the first three Fathers referred to by Mr. Wakefield. Though Ignatius and Polycarp were not Jews, and perhaps had little acquaintance with the Hebrew or the Syriac languages, they possessed advantages for knowing the meaning of apostolic phraseology which were more than an equivalent. It is a matter of very credible history, that both of them had been acquainted with some of the apostles, and those the principal writers of the New Testament;[51] and, in their respective churches at Antioch and Smyrna, it is undoubted that they spent a very large part of their lives in the intimacy of many who had been the hearers and friends of Peter, John, Paul, and their contemporaries and colleagues. Ignatius declares that he saw the Lord Jesus in the flesh, after his resurrection:[52] most probably, therefore, he lived in Judæa at that time, and was a child or inmate in some family of our Lord's own disciples.

[51] See *Lardner's Credibility*, vol. i. pp. 145, 189. An epistle of Irenæus to Florinus is preserved by Eusebius (*Eccl. Hist.* lib. v. cap. 20), in which he speaks of his perfect recollection of Polycarp, and the recitals which that venerable man was in the habit of giving, " concerning his intercourse with John and with others who had seen the Lord." This and other testimonies from Christian antiquity are investigated by Dr. Olshausen (in his *Versuch über die Echtheit der IV. Evangelien; Essay on the Genuineness of the Four Gospels;* Königsberg, 1823, p. 221), and are considered by him as satisfactory evidence that Polycarp had enjoyed the personal instruction of several of the apostles. Mr. Thirlwall calls this book of Prof. Olshausen an " elaborate and instructive work;" and adds, " The industry, accuracy, and soundness of judgment, displayed in this work, render it a most valuable companion in all researches connected with the early history of the Gospels and the Canon." *Introduction to Schleiermacher on Luke*, p. li.

[52] *Ep. ad Smyrn.* sect. 3.

But Mr. Wakefield has, I fear, shown more candour than exactness in making this remark : for not only is there no reference to Matt. xxviii. 20, in the places of Ignatius and Polycarp to which he has referred, but, after a diligent inspection, I can find no citation of the passage, or the remotest allusion to it, in either the genuine or the interpolated Epistles of the former, or in the single Epistle of the latter, or in the Epistle of the Church at Smyrna, giving an account of his martyrdom.

Of Origen we have good reason to believe that he was well acquainted with the scriptural Hebrew ; and his long residence in Palestine was likely to excite his active and indefatigable mind to a familiarity with the idioms which had not yet ceased to be vernacular in that country : so that, where only verbal learning was concerned, probably not one of the Greek or Latin Fathers was more competent than he to interpret the phraseology of the New Testament. Besides the instances incorrectly referred to by Mr. Wakefield, there are many of the clearest and strongest kind.[53] They all take αἰὼν, not in the sense of *the physical world* as Mr. Wakefield hastily affirmed, but in the sense of *duration ;* and they most expressly understand that duration as extending to the consummation of all things. In several of those passages, Origen combines the text under consideration with Matt. xviii. 20 ; " Where two or three are " gathered together unto my name, there I am in the

---

[53]. More than twenty instances of this description may readily be found, by the help of the Tables of Scripture passages at the end of each volume of the Paris edition of Origen's Works, by C. and C. V. Delarue, 4 vols. folio, 1733—1759.

midst of them." And in an animated strain of piety and eloquence, he frequently expatiates on the security and happiness of the church, and of individual believers, in the assurance of an ever-present Saviour in all their conflicts and distresses, and through all the periods of time. Nothing indeed can be more decisive than Origen's testimony to the meaning of the phrase, as *the conclusion of the present state.*

The reference to Eusebius is worthy of particular attention. Mr. Wakefield ought to have informed his readers that the passage is not of Eusebius himself, but is a direct citation from Hegesippus, a Jewish Christian who flourished in the second century, and probably used the Hebrew or Syro-Chaldaic Gospel. This fragment is so interesting that I subjoin it.[54] It furnishes the most complete information, and from a very satisfactory quarter, how Jewish Christians, in the very apostolic age itself, understood the words of Jesus.

It would be easy to carry on this argument, by bringing instances of similar interpretation from others of the early christian writers, but it is unnecessary: for, if the evidence adduced from Hegesippus and Origen be not sufficient to determine the question, no accumulation of passages from other, which must be inferior, authorities could be of the smallest weight.

An apology may seem due for the extension to so great a length, of these remarks on a single passage. But, I trust, the impartial reader will see that it has been rendered necessary by the erroneous though confident assertions, the incorrect philology, and the inconclusive reasonings of the writers on whom we have been compelled to animadvert.

[54] See Note [D] at the end of this Capitule.

SUPPLEMENTARY NOTES TO CAPITULE IV.

Note [A], page 203.

The critical reputation of Bishop Pearce is not high.   In relation to his edition of Longinus, which was his literary *chef d'œuvre*, and a fair field for the trial of his talents, David Ruhnkenius (whom none will dispute to have been qualified to pronounce with authority on questions of Geeek criticism,[1]) intersperses such remarks as these : " Pearcius, pro suâ Græcæ linguæ intelligentiâ, ῥοπικὸν exponit *humile* ;—Græcè doctis novum et inauditum.—Male quæ recta et plana sunt pervertit Pearcius.—Pearcius, cum quid λόγοι significarent non videret, sententiam interpungendo corrupit.—Quid sit ἐκκαθαίρειν rectius quam Pearcius intellexerunt.—Errorem errore defendit."—" Pearce, such was his knowledge of Greek, translates ῥοπικὸς by *low* ;—a thing new and strange to every Greek scholar.— Passages which are right and easy he lamentably perverts.—Not perceiving the sense of λόγοι, he has spoiled the sentence by improper punctuation.—They understood the meaning of ἐκκαθαίρει better

---

[1] " The temper or at least the language of verbal critics has been in our days much improved by the examples of Markland, Wesseling, Hemsterhusius, Valckenaer, *Ruhnken*, Heyne, and other illustrious scholars."—" The warmest of Mr. Wakefield's admirers must acknowledge that in taste, erudition, and ingenuity, the celebrated Ruhnken was superior to him.   But they will recollect, with satisfaction, that one praise which Wyttenbach has bestowed upon Ruhnken, may be justly claimed by Wakefield : ' He always spoke as he thought, and he could not · endure those who did otherwise.' "   Dr. PARR, in the *Life of Gilbert Wakefield by Messrs. Rutt and Wainewright* ; vol. ii. pp. 438, 440.

" The intelligence of his [Ruhnkenius's] death reached us very lately :—This melancholy event has carried off the last of the school of Hemsterhusius.   The limits of a Review are by no means calculated to admit a description of his virtues as a man, nor of his learning as a scholar.   Half a century has nearly elapsed since the publication of his first *Epistola Critica* on Homer's Hymns and on Hesiod, addressed to his eminent friend, Ludovic Caspar Valckenaer.   This long period has scarcely produced any critic who has equalled him in elegance of taste, in depth of research, or in soundness of erudition ; and, during all future ages, if the writers of observations and the editors of ancient authors be desirous of arriving at the style of a genuine commentator, pure in his Latinity, clear in his expressions, concise in his phraseology, temperate in his censures, calm in his decisions, sound in his judgment, acute in his conjectures, secure in his quotations, disdainful of imaginary witticisms, and superior to petty cavils, they will ' devote their days and nights' to those perfect models of critical composition, the works of DAVID RUHNKENIUS."   Dr. CHARLES BURNEY, in the *Monthly Review*, N. S. vol. xxviii. p. 98.

than Bishop Pearce.—He defends one blunder by making another."
Ruhnkenii Emendationes in Longinum, passim.

Mr. Toup, who was too much inclined to asperity in his remarks
upon others, takes frequent occasion to speak as respectfully as possible of Bishop Pearce, perhaps from the influence of an affinity in
theological predilections. But even he lays his rebukes upon the
learned prelate. " Viri doctissimi κρίσις minus satisfacit.—Non
recte accepit.—Non animadvertit.—Non intellexit.—Non scopum
tetigit.—Frustra defendit.—Nihil minus.—Perperam sollicitavit.—
Quæ miror viro doctissimo placere potuisse."—" The learned
writer's criticism is unsatisfactory.—He has misunderstood.—He
has not perceived.—He has not comprehended.—He has totally
failed.—In vain has he attempted to defend.—Nothing could be
farther from the truth.—He has wretchedly bungled.—I am surprised that the learned doctor could satisfy himself with such things."
Toupii Notæ et Animadv. in Longinum, passim.

Note [B], page 203.

" I suspect that his [Mr. Wakefield's] mind was embarrassed and
confused by the multiplicity of his reading : that it was not sufficiently stored with those principles which a man of his industry and
sagacity might have easily collected ——; that he had read much,
observed much, and remembered much : that he was eager to produce the multifarious matter which he had accumulated ; and that he
wanted time or patience for that discrimination which would have
made his conjectures fewer, indeed, but more probable ; and his
principles in forming or illustrating them more exact." DR. PARR,
in *Mr. Rutt's Life of Gilbert Wakefield*, vol. ii. p. 445.

Another of the three celebrated men, (Porson, Parr, and Burney,)
who in our times have adorned ancient learning, inflicted on Mr.
Wakefield his powerful castigation, in the following exquisite passage :—

" The genuine CRITIC, when he undertakes the examination of
any work, deliberates with coolness, and investigates with caution.
His objections are stated with civility, unalloyed by sarcasm ; and
his opinions are delivered with firmness, unmixed with petulance.
His judgment is not obscured by an overweening confidence in his
own acquirements. His taste is not vitiated by a perpetual search
after novelty. His ardour in the cause of learning is superior to
petty considerations ; and the sportive obtrusions of a playful fancy
never diminish the force of his arguments. He proposes his own
emendations with diffidence ; while he does not rashly infer that the

silence of his contemporaries has its source in malevolence; nor does he attribute their objections to a desire of degrading him from that post, to which he is entitled in the ranks of literature." Dr. CHARLES BURNEY, in the *Monthly Review*, January, 1799, N. S. vol. xxviii. page 86.

Note [C] page 211.

Rom. viii. 27, 34. Heb. vii. 25. The true meaning of ἐντυγχάνειν seems to be more closely expressed by this term than by the word usually employed, *interceding*, which in its English acceptation has too restricted a signification. The proper meaning of ἐντυγχάνω is, *I apply to a person upon the concerns of a third party,* whether favourably or the reverse. We have an example of the unfavourable application in Acts xxv. 24. " All the multitude of the Jews *have "been applying* to me, both at Jerusalem and here, exclaiming that he " ought no longer to live." In the favourable and more usual sense, it denotes *the using one's interest with a person* on behalf of *another,* whether by recommendation, supplication, entering into an engagement, adjusting an account, or in any other way.

" The phrase ἐντυγχάνειν ὑπὲρ τινὸς signifies either, in a legal sense *to be the agent, atorney, or advocate in a cause for any one;* or in any transaction of common life, *to interpose on another's behalf, to do any thing for another's benefit, to assist, to aid.*—Rom. viii. 27. The Holy Spirit helps Christians in their prayers, and teaches them how to pray agreeably to the will of God. In the same chap. ver. 34, and Heb. vii. 25, Christ is said ἐντυγχάνειν ὑπὲρ ἀνθρώπων, which expression, I have not a doubt, signifies *the perpetual and eternal efficacy of the merits of Christ, maintained by him on our behalf in his glorified state.* The expression seems to have been derived from the Jewish high-priest, on the great annual day of atonement, offering to God an expiatory sacrifice in the name of the whole nation, and thus interceding with God for the people. In the former of these two passages, therefore, the meaning is, ' Who now sitteth -at the right hand of God, and maintains for us the efficacy of his death :' in the latter place, ' He ever liveth to be, and always to remain, the cause of their salvation.' " *Schleusner in vocem.*

I cannot but remark on the extreme unfairness of the author of the Calm Inquiry, in quoting a detached clause out of the preceding passage, in such a manner as to lead the unwary reader to suppose that Schleusner supports the sentiments of the Inquirer. It stands thus in page 327, " ἐντυγχάνειν ὑπὲρ τινὸς, pro commodo alicujus facere aliquid. *Schleusner. i. e.* to do any thing for another's benefit."

The learned, moderate, and judicious Morus of Leipzig, after a minute examination, concludes that the word denotes any sort of interposing or acting on the behalf of another ; and that, in its New-Testament application, the proper signification is, that Christ is the constant and only Author and Bestower of eternal salvation, so that those who seek it may be assured that they shall obtain it, for his sake and by his gift. *Dissert. de Notionibus Universis in Theologiâ;* ap. *Dissert. Theol. et Philol.* Lips. 1798. vol. i. pp. 298—306.

Note [D], page 215.

" There were still surviving some of the family of the Lord, two grandsons of Jude, who is called his brother according to the flesh. Against them an information was laid, as being of the family of David : and Evocatus brought them before the Emperor Domitian ; who, like Herod, dreaded the coming of Christ. He asked them if they were descendants of David, and they acknowledged that they were. Then he asked them what property they had, and how much money they could command ? They both replied that they possessed no more than nine thousand denarii, [equal to about 283*l.*] the half of which sum was the property of each : and they said that they had not this in money, but that it was the valuation of thirty-nine plethra of land, [one *plethron* is supposed to have been about the fourth part of an English acre ;] from the produce of which they paid their taxes, and gained their livelihood by their own labour. And then they showed their hands ; presenting, as a proof that they lived by their own labour, the hardness of their skin and the callous parts on their hands from continual toil. Being further questioned about Christ and his kingdom, of what description it was, and when and where it should be manifested, they gave this account ; that it is not worldly nor earthly, but heavenly and angelical, and that [ἐπὶ συντελείᾳ τοῦ αἰῶνος γενησομένη] it will take place at *the end of the world*, when he will come in glory and judge the living and the dead, and will render to every one according to his [ἐπιτηδεύματα] pursuits. Upon this Domitian did nothing against them ; and, though he carried the air of despising them, as beneath his notice, he set them at liberty, and issued a decree to put an end to the persecution against the church. After they were released, they were called to preside over churches, as being both witnesses for the Lord, and his relatives. A peaceful season was enjoyed, and they lived till the reign of Trajan." *Hegesippus* in *Euseb. Hist. Eccles.* lib. iii. cap. 20.

" There is nothing at all incredible," says Mosheim, " in this narrative, which has all the appearance of simplicity and ingenuousness. It is probable that some enemy of both Jews and Christians stated to the Emperor, that the Jews looked for a king of the posterity of David, who should become the sovereign of the whole earth; that the Christians likewise believed that Christ would return and set up an illustrious kingdom; and that therefore turbulence and dangers were to be apprehended from both these classes; and hence it is very likely that the tyrannical Domitian was so alarmed and enraged, that he ordered all the descendants of David to be sought out and put to death; and to prevent any attempt on the part of the Christians, directed that they also should be put under severe restraint, and some of them capitally punished." *De Rebus Christ. ante Constant.* p. 111. Helmstadt, 1753.

Capitule V.

THE PERPETUAL PRESENCE OF CHRIST.

The Name of Christ.—The regard here implied to that Name.—The phrase, *to the Name ;*—its defined and important use.—Being *gathered together to the name of Christ,* an expression implying religious worship to him.—In what sense Christ is present in religious assemblies.—Allegations of the Annotator in the Unitarian Version of the New Testament, and of the Calm Inquirer.—The promise not restricted to the apostolic age.—Jewish use of the phrases, *to bind* and *to loose.*—Hypothesis of an occasional presence of Christ with his apostles. —Examination of cases alleged.—None of them give evidence of a corporal presence.—Other declarations of the New Testament contradict it.—Further objections to the hypothesis.—The hypothesis of an ideal presence ;—inapplicable to the case.—The hypothesis of a virtual presence ;—replied to.—Intent of the phrase, *to be with* any one.—The fair meaning inferred to be a real and Divine Omnipresence.

" Where there are two or three gathered together unto my name, there I am in " the midst of them."   Matt. xviii. 20.

WE have before adverted to the distinguished regard which the New Testament represents as due to the NAME of Christ, a term by which, in the scriptural idiom, *supremacy* and *power* are denoted.   It is not, however, the mere ascription of supremacy and power, constituting authority, which will prove any thing in his nature and condition above the rank of a human being.   The question turns on the kind and degree of the qualities attributed : and this question has already met us, and will again meet us, in a variety of forms.   The text just cited presents two remarkable points to our attention.

1. The respect which it assumes as due *to the name of Christ.*   Critics and interpreters appear not to have

sufficiently observed the difference between the two scriptural forms of expression, (בְּשֵׁם ἐν τῷ ὀνόματι,) *in* or *by the name*, and (לְשֵׁם εἰς τὸ ὄνομα,) *to the name.* The former is of much the more frequent occurrence, and always denotes *the originating impulse* of a specified action, such as a binding authority, or a voluntary attachment : the latter occurs but seldom, and it serves to point out *the object* or *final cause* of the action.

Examples · of the former phrase are numerous. Two specimens may be sufficient. " In the name of " our God we will set up our banners.[1] I have come " in the name of my Father, and ye receive me not : " if another come in his own name, him ye will re- " ceive."[2]

To illustrate the other, I shall first adduce the only passages which I have met with, that do not designate the object of some direct act of religious homage. " It shall be to Jehovah *to a name*, to an everlasting " sign : it shall not be cut off.[3] It shall be to me *to* " *a name* of joy, to praise, and to honour."[4] It is manifest that, in these instances, the phrase expresses the ultimate design of those acts of the divine benignity. The other instance is in the New Testament, but it is still a pure Hebrew idiom. The uncouthness which it wears at first sight, has probably been the occasion that translators have generally assumed it to be merely a variation, and not at all differing in sense, from (ἐν τῷ ὀνόματι,) *in the name.* This easy and hasty mode of slurring over a difficulty, by arbitrarily saying that one mode of expression is put for another, is not agreeable to any just principles of

[1] Psalm xx. 5.
[2] John v. 43.
[3] Is. lv. 13.
[4] Jer. xxxiii. 9.

language, and cannot be satisfactory to those who desire evidence for their belief. If the reader will consider the clauses in the ensuing text as designating *the object* of the action, I think he will perceive a beauty and expressiveness in them, well suited to the scope of the passage : whereas the ordinary mode of making the translation gives scarcely an intelligible sense. " He that entertaineth a prophet, *to the name* " of a prophet," (*i. e.* making his character *the object* of this respect,) " shall receive the reward of a prophet: " and he that entertaineth a righteous man, *to the name* " of a righteous man," (making the fact of his being such *the object* to be thus honoured,) " shall receive " the reward of a righteous man : and whosoever shall " give to drink to one of these little ones a cup only " of cold water, *to the name* of a disciple," (making this his *object*,) " verily, I say unto you, he shall not " lose his reward." [5]

The following are at least the principal places besides, of the Old Testrment, in which this formula occurs. The reader will perceive that they all refer to some act of religious homage, of which the Deity, as revealed by his glorious and venerable name, is *the object* :—

" To thy name, and to the remembrance of thee, is " [our] soul's desire. In every place incense shall " be presented to my name, and a pure offering. To " give glory to my name. They built to thee there " a sanctuary, to thy name. Not unto us, O Jehovah, " not unto us, but to thy name, give glory. It is " good to give thanks to Jehovah, and to sing praises " to thy name, O thou Most High! To give thanks

[5] Matt. x. 41, 42.

" to the name of Jehovah.   Sing praises to his name,
" for it is delightful."[6]

The instances of the occurrence of the phrase, in the
New Testament, besides those lately quoted and the
passage under consideration, are these :—

" Go, make disciples of all nations, baptizing them
" to the name of the Father and of the Son and of
" the Holy Spirit.   He gave them a right to become
" children of God, even those who give credit to his
" name.   He is already condemned, because he hath
" not given credit to the name of the Only-begotten
" Son of God.   They were baptized to the name of
" the Lord Jesus.   Were ye baptized to the name of
" Paul?   Lest any one should say that I have bap-
" tized to my own name."[7]

The candid inquirer will now, I think, perceive
that, in the sacred use of the Old Testament, the
phrase under consideration was a formula, to express
the direction and object of a religious act; and that
all the acts with which it is combined, are such as
express mental or external adoration.   He will also
perceive the same idea strongly marked in the examples from the New Testament.

What, then, is it, to be "gathered together to the
" name of Christ?"—The connexion plainly shows,
that it is the union of Christians, for the preservation
of good order and purity among themselves, with
social PRAYER for the divine direction and blessing.—
" Again, verily I say unto you, that if two of you

---

[6] Is. xxvi. 8.   Mal. i. 11 ; ii. 2.   2 Chron. xx. 8.   Psa. cxv. 1;
xcii. 1 ; cxxii. 4 ; cxxxv. 3.

[7] Matt. xxviii. 19.   John i. 12 ; iii. 18.   Acts xix. 5.   1 Cor. i.
13, 15.

" consent upon earth, concerning any matter about
" which they may supplicate, it shall be done for them
" by my Father who is in heaven : for where are two
" or three gathered together UNTO MY NAME, there
" I am in the midst of them."

It appears, therefore, that *the name* of the Lord
Jesus Christ (his PERFECTIONS and GLORIES *manifested*
in his revealed truth,) is *the object*, to do honour to
which the social worship of Christians is to be conducted ; and that the language especially selected by
him, for conveying this declaration, is in exact conformity with that which in the Old Testament is
appropriated to the Eternal Deity. Is it imaginable,
that the wisest, meekest, and best of teachers would
have selected such language as this, language by no
means of frequent occurrence, if he were conscious to
himself of nothing, in nature and condition, above
the rank of a human prophet ! Upon the hypothesis
of denying any such superior and truly Divine nature,
would not this language be a most unwarrantable,
unnecessary, and dangerous deviation from plain
modes of speech ; seeming, at least, to intrench upon
the prerogatives of the Divine Majesty, and likely
to be an occasion of serious error and actual idolatry !

2. Christ promises a peculiar presence of himself :
" there I am in the midst of them."

To be in the midst, (בְּתוֹךְ and בְּקֶרֶב,) is a Jewish
phrase, frequent in the Old Testament, applied to
every variety of subject, and simply denoting *presence :*
sometimes with the accessory idea of *presiding,* as in
the prophecy of Zephaniah ; " The righteous Jehovah
" in the midst of her ;—the King of Israel, Jehovah,

" in the midst of thee;—Jehovah, thy God, in the
" midst of thee, mighty." [8]

The question is, In what sense is this presence
attributed to Christ?

1. Some may apprehend it to be in the sense of a
legal fiction, as the king of England is supposed to be
present in all his courts. It is sufficient to reply that
this is an idea unknown to the Scriptures, so far as
refers to any sovereignty inferior to the divine. Under
the Hebrew theocracy, Jehovah was regarded as
present in the courts of judicature. But this was not
by a fiction. [9]

2. The Unitarian Annotator writes, " This promise,
and those in the two preceding verses, are to be
understood as limited to the apostolic age, and, perhaps, to the apostles themselves. To be gathered
together in the name of Christ, is to assemble as his
disciples, and as acting under his authority. And he
was in the midst of them, either by his personal presence, agreeably to his promise, Matt. xxviii. 20; or
by a spiritual presence, similar to the gift occasionally
conferred upon the apostles, of knowing things which
passed in places where they were not actually present,
1 Cor. v. 3, 4; or lastly, by that authority which he
had delegated, and by the powers which he had communicated to them to perform miracles in his name." [10]
These allegations must be considered separately.

(1.) I do not see any evidence that "the context
limits the promise to the apostles only," [11] or to the

---

[8] Zeph. iii. 5, 15, 17.

[9] Deut. i. 17; xvii. 12; xix. 17. See also *Michaelis on the Laws
of Moses, transl. by Dr. Alex. Smith;* article 35; vol. i. p. 192.

[10] *Impr. Vers.* Annot. in loc.   [11] *Calm Inq.* p. 178.

apostolic age. The connexion refers to contingent offences or injuries which one member, not of the apostolic body, but of any christian community, may commit against another. Few will deny that the Christian interest originally subsisted in such separate associations, and that the primitive believers were in the habit of constantly meeting together for instruction, worship, and maintaining mutual harmony. The case put by our Lord is one which the sins and infirmities of mankind have rendered of too ordinary occurrence in every age. The declaration, in verse 18, refers to nothing miraculous, or peculiar to the age of the apostles. Its difficulty to modern readers arises from unacquaintedness with the established Hebrew phrases, *to bind* and *to loose ;* of which, says the profound Rabbinist, Dr. Lightfoot, "one might produce thousands of examples out of their writings."[12] The obvious meaning is, that the decisions of a Christian community, formed on a faithful adherence to the rules here prescribed, will be approved by the righteous authority of Christ himself, the Head of his church. Neither does the second promise, in verse 19, demand a restriction to the apostles, or to any miraculous circumstances. It coincides with other declarations in the New Testament, on the duty and benefit of prayer ; and these the reason of every particular case, and the whole analogy of religion, direct us to understand of spiritual blessings, and in a subordination to the wisdom and will of God, which every genuine Christian regards in all his prayers as higher and dearer than all other objects of his desire. Here the

[12] See his admirable Note, *Hor. Hebr. et Talm.* in Matt. xvi. 19. *Works,* vol. ii. pp. 205—207.

meaning appears to be, that the solemn prayers of any
christian society, even the smallest and least regarded
by men, in reference to such occasions as the text
treats of, and in conformity with the rule of conduct
laid down, shall be favourably and fully answered.

(2.) The Annotator's next sentence is irrelevant;
as it neglects the distinction of two different phrases,
affirming that of the one which belongs only to the
other.

(3.) The next resort is to the modern Unitarian
hypothesis, of a corporal presence of Christ, which
they conceive to have been occasionally afforded to
the apostles, in circumstances of emergency, through
the interval of time from his ascension "to the termination of the Jewish dispensation by the destruction
of Jerusalem and the temple."[13] To judge of the
validity of this hypothesis, we must review the cases
to account for which it has been assumed.

Stephen "being full of the Holy Spirit, looked sted-
" fastly to heaven, and saw a glory of God, and Jesus
" standing at the right hand of God." Acts vii. 55.

" Suddenly there shone around him a light from
" heaven: and he fell upon the ground, and heard a
" voice saying to him, Saul, Saul, why persecutest
" thou me? And he said, Who art thou, Lord?
" And the Lord said, I am Jesus whom thou perse-
" cutest."—Ib. ix. 3—5; xxii. 6, 7; xxvi. 13—15.

Christ spoke to Ananias "in a vision." Ib. ix.
10—16.

" The Lord said, by a vision in the night, to Paul,
" Fear not, but speak and be not silent; for I am
" with thee, and no one shall lay hands on thee to

[13] *Calm Inq.* p. 179.

" injure thee: for I have many people in this city."
Ib. xviii. 9, 10.

" Having returned to Jerusalem, and while I was
" praying in the temple, I was brought [ἐγενέτό μοι
" γενέσθαι] into a trance: and I saw him, saying to
" me, Hasten, and depart quickly out of Jerusalem."
Ib. xxii. 17, 18.

" In the following night, the Lord stood before him,
" and said, Take courage." Ib. xxiii. 11.

" On account of this I besought the Lord three
" times, that it might depart from me: and he said to
" me, Sufficient for thee is my grace, for my power
" is perfected in weakness." 2 Cor. xii. 8, 9.

" At my first defence no one appeared with me, but
" all deserted me. May it not be laid to their charge!
" But the Lord stood with me, and strengthened me."
2 Tim. iv. 16, 17.

After a careful examination of these cases, I can
discover no evidence of a visible or, in any way, material presence. In the case of Stephen, there was, in
all probability, a miraculous impression made on the
perceptive faculties: for had Jesus been corporally
present he must have been seen by the surrounding
crowd, or, at least, by some of the spectators, of whom
Saul of Tarsus was one; but the history plainly shows
that they perceived nothing preternatural. The miracle at the conversion of Paul, in which he " saw the
" Righteous One, and heard a voice from his mouth,"[14]
is expressly called by him " a heavenly vision;"[15]
and the four following instances are clearly expressed
to be of a similar nature. They were effected by
miraculous *visions*, described in terms the same as

[14] Acts xxii. 14.   [15] Ib. xxvi. 19.

those which designate the usual method in which
JEHOVAH communicated the messages of inspiration
to the Hebrew prophets. Of the nature of such
visions, trances, or ecstasies; or the manner of their
affecting the subjects of them; we are necessarily and
totally ignorant. But there is not the smallest reason
to suppose that there was, in the cases before us, or in
any of those related in the Old Testament, a *solid*
and *tangible* substance presented to the individual, as
the Unitarian hypothesis supposes. As for the last
two instances, not the least intimation is given of any
corporal presence, any visible form, or any miraculous
intervention whatever, except that of communication
to the mind of the apostle; which it is most reasonable
to think was in the accustomed way of inspiration.
His prayer and dependence in his seasons of distress,
and the promise and protection of the Lord Jesus
afforded to him, are expressed altogether in the style
of that religious confidence which can rightly be reposed only in God, and that gracious help which God
only can give.

Thus the notion of a human and corporal presence
of Christ on earth, after his ascension, with Paul or
other apostolic men, appears to be an assumption,
resting on no grounds of scripture evidence.

But it is contradicted by plain declarations of the
New Testament. Our Lord had said, in reference to
his final departure from his disciples; " It is advan-
" tageous for you that I go away : I leave the world,
" and go to the Father : I am no more in the world;
" but these are in the world, and I come to thee." [16]
These expressions plainly teach that Christ, as a

[16] John xvi. 7, 28 ; xvii. 11.

human being, was no longer to be an inhabitant of this our earthly state; and that, whatever scorn the Calm Inquirer presumes to cast on the idea of a local heaven, the man Jesus occupies some actual regions of perfect purity and joy, from whence he shall, at the appointed season, "be manifested in glory, and shall " come to judge the living and the dead, at his ap- " pearing and his kingdom."[17]   In the mean time, we are solemnly assured that "heaven must receive " him till the times of the restitution of all things."[18] Such bodily visits of Christ as the hypothesis supposes might, not irrationally, be included in that "knowing " Christ, according to the flesh," of which the apostle Paul says, "but now we know him no more."[19]

Mr. Belsham had, on a former occasion, affirmed that Jesus "was no doubt generally present with him [Paul], though invisibly, and we know that he occasionally appeared to him during the course of his ministry : and, surely, it must have been an exquisite gratification to the apostle to reflect that he lived, and laboured, and suffered *under his master's eye*, to whom he might at any time have recourse in a season of difficulty, and of whose protection he was secure."[20]   Upon this passage some questions were, some years ago, proposed; which, as they still appear to me to be relevant, I venture to insert :—

" If Jesus was '*generally* present with' Paul, as the hypothesis supposes, what was the situation of the other apostles?   When Paul thus prayed to Christ,

[17] Col. iii. 4.   2 Tim. iv. 1.   [18] Acts iii. 21.
[19] 2 Cor. v. 16.
[20] *Mr. Belsham's Discourse on the Death of Dr. Priestley,* pp. 11, 12.

he was in Macedonia; what then became of the church at Jerusalem? Had James, and the company of our Lord's first disciples, no ‘ seasons of difficulty, nor any need of their master's protection ?' Would it have been no ‘ exquisite gratification' to John, the disciple whom Jesus had honoured with the distinction of eminent personal friendship, ‘ to reflect that he lived, and laboured, and suffered under his master's eye ?' When Paul was at Rome, Peter was probably at Babylon; had Peter no weaknesses, no infirmities, no difficulties and sufferings? Had he no need of ‘ the power of Christ to rest upon him,' and ‘ His grace to be sufficient for him ?' "[21]

(4.) The Annotator calls in the notion of "a spiritual presence, similar to the gift occasionally conferred upon the apostles, of knowing things which passed in places where they were not actually present: 1 Cor. v. 3, 4."

But Christ does not speak of an occasional and extraordinary action. His words conveyed the idea of a constant benefit to his disciples: "Where," in any place or at any time whatever, "two or three are " gathered together unto my name, there I am.—I " am with you always," all the days of your mortal course.

In the example of the apostle Paul's being "present in " spirit" with the religious assembly of the Corinthians, I perceive no evidence of any thing more than that exercise of the imagination, in cases strongly interesting to us, which it is no uncommon form of speech in all languages to denote by an ideal presence.[22] So

---

[21] *Smith's Letters to Mr. Belsham*, in 1804, p. 92.
[22] So Plutarch says, that a sincere, judicious, and attentive friend

the apostle wrote to the Colossians: " Though I am " absent in the flesh, yet I am with you in the spirit, " rejoicing, and beholding your order, and the sted- " fastness of your faith on Christ."[23]

(5.) The Annotator finally has recourse to the authority and miraculous powers communicated by Christ to his apostles, as if the exercise of these were all that is intended in the promise of his presence. The Calm Inquiry seems to adopt this interpretation, in giving the following as a paraphrase of the passage : " Such requests dictated by my authority, and prompted by the spirit which I will communicate,

---

of his city, his nation, and mankind, though he be not an official statesman, will yet confer extensive benefits on his country, in various ways,——in which (κἂν μὴ παραγένηται τῷ σώματι, παρόντα τῇ γνώμῃ), even when not present in body, he is present in thought, giving his approbation to some, and his disapprobation to others, of the measures which he learns have been adopted. *Plutarchi Moral.* ed. Xyland. p. 797. Wyttenbach, 8vo. Oxon. 1797, vol. iv. p. 197. Livy describes the influence of Carvilius on the military operations of the other consul, by saying (" absentis collegæ consilia omnibus gerendis intererant rebus,") the counsels of the absent colleague were present in the management of every affair. *Liv.* lib. 10. sect. 39.

> Rupe sedens aliquâ specto tua littora tristis,
> Et quo non possum corpore, mente feror.
> *Ov. Ep. Leand. Her.* 29.

> I gaze upon that much-lov'd shore,
> Here, mournful on a rock reclin'd;
> And, though my body cannot soar,
> I fly in mind.

[23] Col. ii. 5. The case of Elisha, 2 Kings v. 26, was clearly different; for there a revelation was made to him of a fact which had been studiously concealed, but which the divine influence seems to have exhibited, as in a vivid picture, to his mind; a frequent mode of the prophetic inspiration.

will be as efficacious as if I myself were personally present."[24]

The reply is obvious; that this interpretation does not appear to be the fair construction of our Lord's words: but, if it be admitted that such a reference is included, it will carry the implication that he who is acknowleged to be the Author of the miracles, and whose power was immediately exercised on every such occasion, was actually present; and this presence could only be either by the occasional and corporal action which has been considered, or by the manifestation of attributes properly divine.

The writer urges the absence of " any marks of astonishment at so extraordinary a declaration," as appears from the immediate course of the conversation. But, as this important branch of the argument extends much farther than to the passage now under consideration, we shall reserve it for a separate discussion.[25]

3. Much attention is due to the fact mentioned before, that, in the scriptural style, the phrase *to be with* any one, put absolutely, is a usual phrase, peculiarly applied *to* GOD, and implying the exercise of Divine Perfections on the behalf of any whom he is pleased to favour. As a further proof that this was the ordinary acceptation of the phrase, there are Rabbinical passages cited by Lightfoot, Schöttgenius, and Wetstein : such as these : " If two or three sit in judgment, the Divine Majesty (*Shechinah*) is with them. When two sit together and study the law, the Divine Majesty is with them. When two sit at table and converse about the law, the Divinity rests upon

[24] Page 178.   [25] In Chap. V. of this Book.

them. If ten pray together, the Divine Majesty is
with them. Where ten children of men come together to a synagogue, the Divine Majesty is with them ;
or even three or two or one."[26]

The inference from our Lord's thus using the
expression is strengthened, by comparing this his
gracious promise with one of similar import in the
Old Testament, to which it is highly probable that he
might have a mental reference : " In every place
" where I record my name, I will come unto thee,
" and I will bless thee."[27]

It remains for me to express my conviction, founded
on the preceding reasons, that the only fair and just
interpretation of this important passage is that which
regards it as a declaration of such a spiritual and
efficient presence as implies Divine perfections : such
a special exercise of power and mercy as, in the use
of this phrase, the Scriptures habitually ascribe to the
Deity ; and such as involves the attribute of OMNI-
PRESENCE.

[26] See those authors *in loc.*   [27] Exod. xx. 24.

Capitule VI.

ON OUR LORD'S DECLARATIONS OF HIS PERSONAL AGENCY IN THE
RESURRECTION OF THE DEAD AND THE FINAL JUDGMENT.

The testimony of Christ concerning himself, as the Author of the future resurrection of the dead, and the universal Judge.—The conclusion from these facts, that he has a really Divine nature.—Considerations proposed by Mr. Belsham to escape that conclusion.—The human nature affirmed in Scripture to be necessary to the person of the Judge of mankind.—The wisdom and kindness of this appointment.—Its perfect consistency with the position, that the Divine nature is not less necessary.—This office ascribed to Christ in connexion with other Divine attributives, as necessary qualifications.—Reasons why our Lord did not use an impassioned style in expressing this fact.—Whether any astonishment was felt by his hearers.—No improvement of a finite intellect adequate to this work.—The case essentially different from the judgments attributed to saints and apostles.—The case incapable of being rationally solved by referring to the use of figurative language.

It is the unequivocal language of Scripture that " God, who raised up the Lord, will raise up us also by " his own power :"[1] and certainly a due consideration of this stupendous miracle, which we are assured will be wrought at the appointed season, must impress the complete conviction that OMNIPOTENCE alone can effect the RESURRECTION OF THE DEAD. But Jesus Christ, in the most deliberate and solemn manner, affirmed Himself to be the future Author of this work, and the Arbiter of those awful destinies which will immediately succeed it. " The hour is coming, in " which all who are in the tombs shall hear his voice, " and shall come forth ; they who have done good " actions, to the resurrection of life ; and they who

---

[1] 1 Cor. vi. 14.

" have done base actions, to the resurrection of con-
" demnation."[2]　We have before offered some considerations on the interpretation of this passage and its
connexion.[3]　To those we now add, that Jesus taught
the same doctrine on other occasions, and in various
other forms of expression.　With respect to every
sincere believer on himself, he uttered the gracious
assurance, " I will raise him up at the last day :" a
second and a third time he repeated the declaration,
evidently for the purpose of stronger impression : and
he comforted the mourners by saying, " I am the
" resurrection and the life ;"[4] the abstract effects
being put as the strongest expression of their Cause
and Author.　The same doctrine is a prominent
object in the several parables in which he represents
himself as the Lord of a household, the King of a
sovereignty, returning after a season of absence, at a
day and hour when he is not looked for, taking an
account of the commissions and conduct of his servants,
honouring the faithful, and condemning the wicked
and slothful to the " outer darkness where is wailing
" and gnashing of teeth."　It is, with inimitable
beauty and solemnity, brought forth in the parable,
which depicts THAT DAY, " when the Son of man
" shall come in his own glory, and all the angels with
" him :" when " he will sit upon his own throne of
" glory, and before him shall be gathered together all
" the nations."　There we learn, that it is HE that
will discriminate their moral state, amidst the compli-
cated varieties of human character ; it is HE that will
estimate their actions, by an infinitely penetrating and

---

[2] John v. 28, 29.　　　[3] Pages 72, 73, of this volume.
[4] John vi. 39, 40, 44 ; xi. 25.

accurate developement of their motives; HE it is that will infallibly, completely, and for ever separate them one from another; HE is announced in calm majesty as THE KING; and it is HE that will perform the very highest of judicial and regal acts, when " he will say " to those on his right hand, Come, ye blessed of " my Father, inherit the kingdom prepared for you " from the foundation of the world; —— and to " those on his left hand—Depart from me, accursed, " into the fire the everlasting, the [fire] prepared for " the devil and his angels." [5]

Such is the testimony of Christ concerning himself. If we believe that testimony, is it possible to resist the conclusion, that HE is Omniscient, the Just One of essential and infinite righteousness, the Sovereign Universal, Almighty, and Eternal; and, since these cannot be the properties of a human or of any other created being, that in his person ANOTHER nature must exist, even that which is " over all, blessed for " ever ?"

With a laudable candour, Mr. Belsham observes on this subject, " That this is a great difficulty, cannot be denied;" and therefore himself, and other labourers in the same field, have put forth their utmost strength to surmount it. " Possibly," he adds, in a tone of moderation which deserves respectful notice,— " Possibly it may be alleviated by attention to the following considerations." [6]—Alleviated!—Is it then become an object with these persons to diminish the weight of His doctrines, whom they still acknowledge as the wisest and best of Teachers, the great one commissioned by God; to strip his words of their awful

---

[5] Matt. xxv. 31—46.　　　　　　[6] Page 341.

import, to extinguish their majesty, and to lighten their pressure upon the human conscience?—With good reason was it said, by one of the most judicious as well as amiable of men, whose memory can never be dissociated, in the mind of the writer of these volumes, from the warmest feelings of love and veneration ; " How innumerable are the expressions, used by the writers of the New Testament, as well as in the ancient prophecies of the Messiah, which Socinian 'good sense' [alluding to an expression of Mr. Belsham's, attributing that quality preeminently, if not exclusively, to his own party,] would have carefully avoided !——On Socinian principles, it is a hard task indeed to expect enough from Christ, both now and at the last day, and yet not to make too much of him. Other idolatrous practices have been introduced in plain opposition to the Scriptures, but it is *by the strong expressions* of Scripture ; in which, as the Socinians themselves contend, the later writers of the New Testament were still bolder than those that wrote first, that we have been led to believe in the Divinity of our Lord." [7]

But, much as we must lament and condemn the spirit of these *alleviating considerations,* we will endeavour to pay to them the most serious and candid regard.

1. It should always be kept in mind that our sole object is to obtain, by careful induction from the Scriptures, the *entire* amount of their testimony on our interesting question. If different parts of that testimony should, in any respect, wear the appearance

[7] The late *Dr. Ryland's Letter to Mr. Rowe, on the Partiality and Unscriptural Direction of Socinian Zeal ;* 1801. pp. 52, 57.

of opposition, it is not for us, imperfect and limited as
our best efforts of intellect on such subjects must be, to
reject either of those portions of evidence ; or readily
to believe that there is in reality any discordance
between them.   Some intermediate links of the chain
of truth may be wanting, which, if we possessed them,
would produce a demonstrative agreement: and yet
these may be impossible to be attained in our present
state of knowledge and capacity.—Therefore the full
admission of all that the Inquirer has advanced as his
first consideration,[s] does not draw after it the least
necessity to relinquish our preceding conclusions from
the unequivocal declarations of the Lord Jesus himself.   We believe the humanity of Jesus, his "*proper*
humanity,*" (meaning by the epithet *real* or *true*,) as
well as the Unitarians : and we do not feel this article
of our belief to be any impediment to our holding,
with equal firmness, that, to constitute the person of
the Christ, Deity was necessary no less than humanity.
That such is the fact, we believe, because the Scriptures appear to us to affirm it ; and could we go
no farther, this would be enough for the satisfaction

---

[s] 1 " The Scriptures teach that Jesus Christ is appointed to judge
the world.   The same Scriptures, in connexion with this very
appointment, expressly represent Jesus as a MAN delegated to this
high office : Acts xvii. 31.   Whatever, therefore, our prejudices may
suggest to the contrary, it is in fact not inconsistent with divine wisdom, nor with the reason and order of things, that a human being
should be appointed to the office of universal judge.   It is even
implied, John v. 27, that the proper humanity of Christ is an essential qualification for the office.   And it is certain that wherever
Jesus is mentioned under the character of a judge, he is never in
that connexion represented as a being of an order different from, and
superior to, mankind.   Nor is this qualification ever hinted at as
necessary for executing this solemn office."   Page 341.

of reason and the acquiescence of faith. When we read, then, that the Christ is the Judge of the world, we understand the proposition of him *as the Christ,* that is, in his whole person; conceiving that the nature of the case, and the all-wise constitution of the Eternal Father, render the attributes of Deity and the properties of humanity, *both* to be necessary for this unspeakably momentous function.

Accordingly, it appears to us strictly proper in itself, and entirely in accordance with the full doctrine concerning our Lord's person, that, when the Scriptures speak of his relation in his human nature to the final judgment, they should use the mode of representation, that he is "the man whom God hath ordained"[9] for that purpose; and that "God will judge the hidden things of men, through Jesus Christ."[10] We also think that we can perceive a wise and gracious propriety in the *frequency* with which the New Testament brings into view this mode of representation; since the fact is pregnant with consolation to the sincere and upright, that our Judge is he who died for our sins, the partaker of our own flesh, and perfectly alive to all the tenderest sympathies of our nature; whilst on the other hand the rising of a presumptuous thought is solemnly forbidden by the knowledge, that our Saviour now and Judge hereafter is "HE that is HOLY, HE that is TRUE,—whose eyes are as a flame of fire,—who is over all, God blessed for ever."[11]

To the latter part of the Inquirer's First Consideration I demur:

[9] Acts x. 42; xvii. 31　　　[10] Rom. ii. 16.
[11] Rev. iii. 7; ii. 18.　Rom. ix. 5.

other, that the words are selected, evidently on purpose, from the sublime passage of the prophet in which Jehovah declares this knowledge to be his own unrivalled possession.

2. [17] It is assuming too much, that, on the position of our interpretation, it must follow that our Lord himself might be expected to have "felt difficulty" in the annunciation of his own doctrine. On the supposition of its truth, it could be no matter of surprise, either to Christ in his superior nature, or to Jesus as a man instructed and inspired with the unmeasured fulness of divine influence. It is one of the well-known characters of our Lord's teaching, that he treats upon the most sublime and heavenly things, without astonishment, without effort, without any of that sinking and prostration of mind, which sometimes befell the ancient prophets,[18] when they received the communications of the Most High. His discourses have a calmness, an ease, a sublime simplicity, a sententious dignity, which indicated a mind *habitually and perfectly familiar* with the most profound truths of God and eternity.

As to the apostles, it is to be considered, that in proportion to their faith in the Messiahship of Jesus, must have been their readiness to admit concerning

---

[17] " Jesus and his apostles do not appear to have felt any difficulty in the appointment of a human being to the office of universal judge. They simply state the fact in the clearest and most unequivocal manner, that God will judge the world by the MAN whom he hath ordained. They give no explanation; they make no comment; they obviate no objections. This is a strong presumption that, according to their ideas, the office required no qualifications which a man appointed and assisted by God might not possess." *Calm Inq.* p. 341.

[18] Moses, Exod. iii. 6. Habakkuk, ch. iii. 16. Isaiah, ch. vi. 5.

him all that they had previously conceived as charac-
terizing the Messiah ;[19]—that their minds evidently
laboured under extreme deficiencies of knowledge
and remarkable inconsistencies ; that the Evangelists,
who recite the discourses of Jesus to which these
observations refer, give no information whatever as
to the actual effect produced on any class of hearers,
whether disciples, strangers, or enemies, and that
consequently we are not entitled to assume that no
impressions of astonishment and awe were produced
on any of them ; and that we have information of the
utmost surprise and horror being felt or affected when
Jesus asserted this truth, though less pointedly, before
the most learned assembly in the Jewish nation :
" Hereafter ye shall see the Son of man sitting on the
" right hand of Power [*i. e.* the Deity, by a Hebraism]
" and coming in the clouds of heaven. Then the

---

[19] That the Jews, in their generally received doctrine of the Messiah, believed that he would be the Author of the future resurrection,
appears at least probable from Mary's answer to our Lord's declaration ;—" I am the Resurrection and the Life :——believest thou
" this?——She saith unto him, Yea, Lord, I am persuaded that thou
" art the Christ, the Son of God, that was to come into the world."
John xi. 27. Mary evidently considered this reply as an assent to
our Lord's assertion concerning himself. Bertholdt adduces passages from the Book Zohar, and others of the ancient Rabbinical
writings, fully proving that they held that the Messiah will be the
Author, both of *the first resurrection*, which they believed will
belong only to the Israelites ; and of *the second*, which their theology
extended to all the rest of mankind. *Christologia Judæorum, Jesu
Apostolorumque Ætate;* pp. 176—181, 203—206. I select two
passages. " —The servant of the Lord :——and who is he ? He
is the Metatron, as we have said, who will restore to beauty the
bodies that are in the tombs." *Zohar*, fol. 77, ed. Sulzbach. " The
Messiah —— will raise those that sleep in the dust." *Midrash
Mishle*, fol. 67.

" high-priest rent his garment, saying, He hath blas-
" phemed!"[20]

3. "That the faculties and enjoyments of the man
Jesus Christ, though raised to an unspeakable degree
at the moment of his glorification, have yet proceeded
from that moment along an indefinite range of the
most glorious and happy improvement, and will so
proceed to immortality, is by no means denied.   Such
a progression must be the necessary effect of circumstances the most advantageous that could possibly
exist, operating upon a perfectly holy and unclouded
intellect : for those circumstances comprehend not
only the results of observation and reflection, but the
stupendous advantage of the intimate, unique, and
mysterious UNION with the Divine Nature.   But we
conceive, that, *in no other way than by such a union*
could a man, an angel, or a created Logos on the
Arian hypothesis, be qualified for this immense work.
This conclusion we draw, from the obvious nature of
this "grand occasion," and the qualities of intellect
and power which common reason teaches that it cannot
but require; and which no conceivable improvement
of any finite mind, by experience · or any other
advantageous circumstances, could possibly reach;
and from the various and independent evidence that,

[20] Matt. xxvi. 64, 65.

[21] " 3. If to judge the world be an office which Jesus is to execute
in person, and if it requires powers and qualifications superior to
those which he possessed on earth, these may be attained either by
the regular and progressive improvement of his powers, in the long
interval between his ascension and the day of judgment, or they may
be imparted to him for the occasion by God himself, whose organ
and delegate he will be on that grand occasion : and who could as
easily qualify a man, as an angel, or a Logos, for this important
purpose."   Page 342.

by such a union, the Person of the Christ has been in fact constituted.

4. [22] That the distinction mentioned by the Inquirer is not "gratuitous and unauthorized," we apprehend is fairly deducible from this consideration; that the ascription of supreme and final judgment to Christ is made in the New Testament so copiously, expressly, and particularly, as to furnish a rational ground for conceiving an essential difference between the two cases. Not only by our Lord himself, but by his inspired apostles (in various passages which will fall under a subsequent head of our examination) is this right and power of "eternal judgment" claimed for him; and, according to our conceptions, it comports with every other part of the scripture testimony to his person, qualifications, and offices. This superiority in the clearness and abundance of the evidence prevents us from feeling our conclusion shaken by the two passages adduced by Mr. B., whether those passages refer to the triumphs of the gospel in the present state, or, as may perhaps appear the more satisfactory

[22] " 4. Whatever may be intended by the expression ' judging the world,' the apostles of Christ, and believers in general, are to share in that honour and office with their Master.—Matt. xix. 28, ' When the Son of Man shall sit on the throne of his glory, ye also shall sit on twelve thrones, judging the twelve tribes of Israel.' 1 Cor. vi. 2. ' Do ye not know that the saints shall judge the world ?' Ver. 3. ' Know ye not that we shall judge angels ?' It is indeed alleged that Christians are said to judge the world only in a figurative and improper sense; but that this office is attributed to Christ really, properly, and without a figure. But this distinction is quite gratuitous and unauthorized. For any thing that appears to the contrary, the apostles and other Christians will be constituted judges of the world in the very same sense with Christ, though probably in an inferior degree. For he, in this, as in all other things, must have the preeminence." Page 343.

interpretation, to some extraordinary dignity that will be conferred, in the day of judgment, on the holy apostles, and on other singularly eminent and active servants of Christ.

5. The Inquirer urges his final considerations[23] with great acuteness and ability, and they are certainly entitled to every serious attention.

It is true that writers on the biblical idioms have laid down the rule, that verbs denoting simple being or action are sometimes used, when only a *declaration* is intended, or even a mere *expectation* or *supposition*, that the act is done or will be done.[24] But, it is manifest that such a rule as this, if it be not held under a very clear and strong line of restriction, would go far towards destroying the use of language, and rendering any declaration of Scripture, or of any other book, absolutely uncertain. It therefore,

---

[23] Note [A], at the end of this Capitule.

[24] It may not be an unsuitable digression to annex some of the most important instances.—Gen. xxvii. 37. " Behold, I have fixed " him a sovereign to thee, and all his brethren I have given to him " for servants, and with corn and rich wine I have sustained him."— Levit. xiii. 3. " When the priest shall see him, he shall make him " unclean," *i. e.* pronounce him so : ver. 13, " he shall cleanse him," *i. e.* shall pronounce him clean.—Isa. vi. 10. " Make gross the " heart of this people, and make heavy their ears, and cover their " eyes," *i. e.* declare that they are so.—Job x. 2. " Do not make me " wicked," *i. e.* do not treat me as such.—Matt. x. 39. " He that " findeth his life," *i. e.* expects to secure himself.—John v. 31. " My " testimony is not true," *i. e.* would not be considered so.—Rom. iv. 15. " The law worketh wrath," *i. e.* denounces that wrath is wrought by disobedience : Chap. vii. 9. " I was alive," *i. e.* I deemed myself so.—2 Cor. iii. 6. " The letter killeth," *i. e.* declares death as the consequence of sin.—Rom. v. 20. " That the offence might " abound," *i. e.* might be shewn to abound.—Phil. iii. 7. " What " things were gain," *i. e.* had been so esteemed.

I submit with deference to the serious consideration of competent judges, can be reasonably and safely held in those passages only which palpably and undeniably require it, and which admit of no rational interpretation without it ; at least, if it be resorted to in any other cases, those cases must be proportionately liable to be doubted. Now the passages in which Jesus Christ is declared to be the future Judge of mankind and the Arbiter of their state in the eternal world, are so numerous, so plain, and expressed in such an impressive variety of manner as, in my apprehension, to place them immeasurably beyond the legitimate range of the rule adduced.

The strong language and awful scenery, by which our Lord represents the destruction of Jerusalem and the miseries of the people, certainly have a remarkable conformity with some parts of the descriptions of the universal judgment. But before we can accede to the conclusions to which the writer evidently inclined, there are some circumstances important to be considered.

(1.) Those who hold the proper Deity of Christ not only have no difficulty in believing that HE personally inflicted those judgments on the Jewish nation, but their system actually requires it. They believe that, in his essential and unalterable nature as the Son of God, he is the Lord of all providential government; that " all things which the Father doeth, the " same doeth the Son in like manner ;" that the " Father worketh hitherto, and HE worketh." They also believe that the peculiar, delegated, and official dominion which the Scriptures attribute to Christ in his Mediatorial capacity, extends to all things that have relation to the progress and various fortunes of his spiritual empire among men. Now the visible retributions of divine righteousness, upon the people whose summit of crime lay in their aggravated rejection of Christ and their utmost malignity of effort to crush his gospel, were WITH PECULIAR PROPRIETY to be expected, personally and immediately from Christ himself, the Lord of glory, and the Prince of the kings of the earth. "They murdered the Lord "Jesus and the prophets, and persecuted us," says the holy and injured apostle, "and were not pleasing to "God, and were contrary to all men, forbidding us "to preach to the nations that they might be saved : "unto the filling up constantly of their own sins : "and the wrath came upon them to the uttermost." [25] This is confirmed by the numerous passages which describe the Messiah as personally executing judgments on his impenitent enemies : [26] and by those which speak of the destruction of the Jewish polity as "the coming (παρουσία) of the Lord, and the day of "Christ, and the shaking of the heavens and the "earth" by Him "who speaketh from heaven, the "Lord Jesus Christ :"[27]

(2.) That there is a conformity in the descriptions of the two events, with regard to the circumstances of visible scenery, ought not to create difficulty : for there appears sufficient reason to regard those descriptions as figurative in reference to both the events. We know not what will be the *manner*, any more

---

[25] 1 Thess. ii. 15, 16.

[26] See Vol. I. pp. 275, 277, 285, 306, 332, 365, 419.—Matt. xxi. 41.

[27] James v. 8.   2 Thess. ii. 1, 2.   Heb. xii. 25.

than the day and hour, of that " coming of the Son of
" man," which will be "to judge the living and the
" dead." As, in regard to the judgments on the
Jewish nation, the circumstances of " the sun being
" darkened, and the moon not giving her light, the
" stars falling from heaven, the mighty sound of a
" trumpet, and the Son of man coming in the clouds,"
—were sensible images borrowed from the ideas current among the men of that age : so, I apprehend, we
may justly regard the introduction of similar imagery
in the descriptions of that infinitely more awful event
which is yet to come. The great circumstances of
that event,—the raising of the bodies of all human
beings to an imperishable state of existence—the
scrutiny and perfect developement of all minds, motives, and characters—the adjudication of rewards and
punishments—the presidency and action of our Lord
Jesus Christ—and the complete publicity of the whole
procedure,—will assuredly take place ; and in such
manner, and attended by such circumstances, as will
be worthy of Infinite Wisdom, Holiness, and Mercy,
and most consummately adapted to answer all the
purposes of a public and universal judgment : but
WHAT that *manner*, WHAT those *circumstances*, will
be ; and how far any physical convulsions of nature
may be employed as *the least and lowest* appendages to
the MAJESTY AND GLORY AND TERROR of that awful
day ;——I presume not to conjecture. Such circumstances, conceive of them as we may, will be beneath
notice in comparison with *our* great concern in the
awful transactions. That concern will be MORAL and
SPIRITUAL ; and it will be PERSONAL. May the Lord
our Saviour and Judge grant, that the writer and the

readers of this page may find mercy of the Lord, in THAT DAY!

(3.) In the passage cited by the Inquirer, (John xii. 47, 48,) our Lord is manifestly speaking of the design of his *then present* coming into the world, which was " not to judge, but to save." But, to draw from this declaration a conclusion clearly contradictory to so many other parts of the Saviour's doctrine; and, because he represents his " word," the gospel of grace and authority, as what will be the *rule* of judgment, to infer that therefore he will not personally preside in the acts of that judgment;—appears to me very inconclusive arguing.

(4.) The mode of interpreting which Mr. B. seems to have approved, would require, in consistency, to be followed into an application to the whole system of revealed truth: and then I question whether every position of Scripture, beyond the rules of natural ethics, would not be exterminated. By the dexterous use of *mythus*, and *figure*, and *analogy*, and *accommodation* to Jewish modes of thinking and phraseology, (which modes of thinking and expression, it must always be taken for granted, were merely the opinions of the time, and have no claim on our adoption,) the New Testament might, with little trouble and in a very plausible way, be stripped of every thing supernatural; and even the doctrine of a future state, under any conception of it, might be got rid of. All " the terrors of the Lord" might be resolved into the calamities of Judæa, and the ordinary consequences of vice in the present state: the benefits of the gospel might be reduced to the liberation of the human mind from enslaving superstitions, and from the tyranny of custom; the giving a new spring to our energies; the discoveries of science; the improvement of reason; and the possession of an admirable engine for managing the lower orders of the community: and the magnificent promise of eternal life, might be coldly affirmed to have originated in the benevolent policy, or the sublime opinion, or the sanguine expectation, or the noble enthusiasm[28] of Jesus and his followers. This is not a fanciful representation. The Unitarians of this country have not indeed proceeded to these lengths; and I sincerely pray that they may

[28] For the following extract I am indebted to Dr. *Augustus Hahn*, Prof. Theol. at Leipzig, in his *Offene Erklärung an die Evangelische Kirche, zunächst in Sachsen u. Preussen;* Leipzig, 1827, *i. e.* " An Appeal to the Lutheran Churches, particularly those of Saxony and Prussia." The book from which it is taken is *Briefe über den Rationalismus*, &c. *i. e.* " Letters on Rationalism, for the setting right of wavering and doubting Judgments upon the modern important Controversies respecting Theological Doctrines :—by John Fred. Röhr, D.D." Zeitz in Saxony, 1813. This author was made, in 1820, Superintendent-General of the Lutheran Churches of Weimar, and First Chaplain to the Court!! and he, Von Ammon, and Bretschneider, were the three German divines who attended the tricentenary celebration of the Reformation, at Geneva, in August, 1835; as a sort of assumed, or self-chosen, representatives of Protestant Germany.

" ' Great minds,' says Eberhard, ' who with the noblest enthusiasm pursue so holy an object as the intellectual and moral reformation of their age, cannot but be greatly inclined to ascribe the origin of those rapid coruscations, which out of the dark profound suddenly dart into their souls, to immediate operations of the Deity.' If therefore JESUS, *the sublimest, the noblest enthusiast* that ever was upon earth, conceived a personal conviction that he had been called by God to the holy work to which he had devoted his life, he by no means merited the base appellation of a *deceived* person; neither was he a *deceiver*, when he uttered this conviction to others. He spoke according to his own most inward conviction, of his heavenly mission and the divinity of his doctrine." *Röhr's Letters,* p. 304.

not : but that, notwithstanding individual instances of a propensity in this direction, they may return nearer to the truth, rather than recede farther from it. But these are the principles which have been for several years promulgated in the theses, dissertations, lectures, annotations, and still more elaborate works, of some of the men who hold forth themselves, and compliment each other, as the enlightened and liberal scripture critics of Germany.[29]

In the mean time, the caution administered by the early Christian writers may prove to be the wisest and best : let those who regard the Lord Jesus Christ as a figurative Saviour, a figurative Lawgiver, King, and Judge, beware lest, in the day of their extremity, they find *only a figurative salvation !*

[29] On this topic I may be permitted to request the reader's referring to some passages in the former volume of this work, to *Four Discourses on the Sacrifice and Priesthood of Christ*, pp. 165—172, 260—272 ; and to several articles on the *Neologism of Germany*, in the *Eclectic Review* for 1827 and 1828.

SUPPLEMENTARY NOTE TO CAPITULE VI.

Note [A], page 248.

" 5. The sense in which a prophecy is fulfilled is often very different from that which the literal interpretation would lead us to expect. It is therefore highly probable that the mode in which Christ will eventually execute the office of judging the world will bear little or no resemblance to that which the expressions naturally suggest ; and in their true sense they may mean nothing more than what a human being, exalted and endowed, as Jesus is, may be qualified to perform. God declares to the prophet Jeremiah, chap. i. 10, ' See, I have set thee this day over all nations, to

'root out, and to pull down, and to destroy, and to build, and to
'plant;' when nothing more was intended than to authorize the
prophet to declare the divine purpose. And the promise to Peter,
Matt. xvi. 19, that whatsoever he bound or loosed on earth, should
be bound or loosed in heaven, is usually understood in a similar
sense. The prophecy concerning the destruction of Jerusalem is
expressed in language as strong, and in figures as awful, as those
which relate to the last judgment : and the personal appearance of
Christ himself, with his angels, is as expressly asserted ; see Matt.
xxiv. 29. Luke xxi. 25, &c. ; yet, for any thing that appears, these
calamitous events were brought to pass by natural means, and probably without any personal, certainly without any visible, interference
of Christ. He was only so far concerned in it, as, in the symbolical
language of prophecy, to declare authoritatively that the event would
happen.

" 6. May we not then be permitted to conjecture, that when
Christ is represented as appointed by God to judge the world, nothing
more may be intended by this language, but that the final states of
all and every individual of mankind shall be awarded agreeably to
the declarations of the Gospel? This supposition is perfectly analogous to those cases which are cited under the preceding head,
especially to the strong expressions which are used concerning our
Lord's advent for the destruction of Jerusalem ; the accomplishment
of which in a figurative, and not a literal sense, seems intended to
direct our minds to the interpretation of those symbols which typify,
and of that language which announces, the personal agency of Christ
and his disciples in the awful solemnities of the final judgment. This
explanation affords a very easy solution of the language of Paul concerning the saints judging the world. The apostles and Christians in
general may fitly be represented as assessors with Christ on the
tribunal of judgment, as by the very profession of Christianity they
bear their solemn testimony, to the unbelieving world, of the divine
declaration by Jesus Christ, that there is a life to come, in which
men shall be rewarded according to their works.

" In perfect analogy to this interpretation, Christ is figuratively
represented as a lawgiver, because the precepts of his gospel are laws
to govern the conduct of his disciples.—He is figuratively a priest,
because he voluntarily delivered himself up as a victim ; and sacri-
ficed his life in the cause of truth, and in obedience to the will of
God.—He is figuratively a conqueror and a king, and universal
dominion is ascribed to him, because his gospel and religion will
gradually prevail through the world, and all nations will eventually

submit to its authority.—In like manner, Christ is figuratively a judge, because the final states of all mankind will be awarded in a future life, agreeably to the solemn, repeated, and explicit declarations of his gospel.

"Our Lord himself appears to give some countenance to this interpretation, by the language which he uses, John xii. 47, 48, ' If any man hear my words and believe not, I judge him not, for I ' came not to judge the world, but to save the world. He that re-' jecteth me, and receiveth not my words, hath one that judgeth him. ' THE WORD THAT I HAVE SPOKEN, THE SAME SHALL JUDGE HIM AT ' THE LAST DAY.'" *Calm Inq.* pp. 343—347.

—— Almighty God, in his infinite mercy, grant that this citation may produce its best effect upon every reader of this page ! That day is coming. It is, as to personal effect, as near to each of us as the speedily arriving hour of death. How soon, then, will the great disclosure be made, whether we have received or have rejected THE WORD OF CHRIST !

Capitule VII.

ON THE HOMAGE WHICH CHRIST PERMITTED TO BE PAID TO HIMSELF.

Cases enumerated and examined, of peculiar homage paid to our Lord during his ministry.—The words of Thomas, John xx. 28,—shown not to have been an exclamation of surprise;—nor an address to the Almighty Father:—but an address to Christ, and approved by him.—Evidence of this construction.—The term God not used in an inferior sense.—Objections from the apostle's probable state of knowledge;—and from the implied reasoning:—answered.—The other instances not all of the same character.—Christ would not accept civil honour. —Nor, on the hypothesis of his mere humanity, would he have accepted religious homage.—Dr. Carpenter's arguments stated, and answered.—Investigation of the sense of John xvii. 3,—and of passages in which Jesus calls the Father his God, and prays to him.

It is recorded that our blessed Lord, on several occasions, accepted with approbation from his disciples and others, expressions of homage which carry some appearance of religious adoration.

But the word generally made use of on these occasions does not necessarily signify the external act of religious worship. It properly denotes that bending down, or sometimes prostration, which was the mode, among the oriental nations, of expressing civil respect to persons of superior rank. The cases, therefore, in which it is to be understood of religious adoration, and those in which it denotes nothing but civil homage, can be discriminated only by attending to the circumstances of each.

This word ($\pi\rho o\sigma\kappa v v\epsilon\hat{i}v$) occurs sixty times in the New Testament. Of these there are two, which, without

VOL. II.   s

controversy, denote the customary act of civil homage,[1]
fifteen refer to idolatrous rites,[2] three are used of
mistaken and disapproved homage to creatures,[3] about
twenty-five clearly and undeniably respect the worship
due to the Most High God, and the remaining number relate to acts of homage paid to Jesus Christ.
The last class require to be individually examined.

1. Matt. ii. 2, 11. " We are come to worship him.
" —They fell down and worshipped him." As we
do not know the precise opinions and expectations of
these eastern philosophers, and as they sought Jesus
under the character of "the King of the Jews;" we
might attribute to them no farther intention than that
of treating him with the obeisance which they were
accustomed to pay to the sovereign of their own
country, probably Persia. But we must consider that
they were actually favoured with a divine and miraculous revelation (ver. 12); whence it is no unreasonable conjecture that, in a similar way, supernatural
knowledge had been before communicated to them, as
the consequence of which they paid to the infant Jesus
such homage of adoration as comported with their
views of a divine dignity. Upon the ground of such
a revelation, the learned and acute author of the
History of Philosophy considers it probable that their
intention was to pay divine honours to the true Star
of hope and happiness to the world, and especially of
the gentiles.[4]

[1] Matt. xviii. 26. Rev. iii. 9.
[2] John iv. 22. Acts vii. 43. Rev. ix. 20 ; xiii. 4, 8, 12, 15;
xiv. 9, 11 ; xvi. 2 ; xix. 20 ; xx. 4.
[3] Acts x. 25. Rev. xix. 10 ; xxii. 8.
[4] Brucker, in the Variorum Leipsig Bible, vol. xii. p. 131.

2. Matt. v. 8. " That I also may come and worship
him." This hypocritical profession of Herod is most
probably to be taken in a general sense, which the
tyrant did not very exactly define or even consider.
His object was to make his own ends of the foreign
inquirers, and, at all events, to prevent a rival from
rising up to rescue the throne of Israel from his
usurpation.

3. Ib. viii. 2.   " A leper cometh and worship-
" peth him, saying, Lord, if thou wilt, thou canst
" make me clean." In Mark, it is " kneeling to him :"
in Luke, " falling upon his face." This person had
undoubtedly formed high, though vague, conceptions
of the character and powers of Jesus. In this early
stage of our Lord's ministry, it might appear not probable that the man knew him to be the Messiah. But,
on the other hand, the variety of opinion and expectation concerning the Messiah, which we have before
shown to have existed among the Jews, throws weight
into the scale of supposing that to this sufferer the better
order of knowledge had been directed : and may we
not, on just reasons, believe that his mind was enlightened and guided by a divinely gracious influence?
How otherwise could he have attained the assurance
of the power of Jesus to deliver him from his terrible
disorder ? Imperfectly developed as his faith, thus
incipient, might be, it laid hold of something " sure
" and stedfast ;" and he applied to Christ with the
most impassioned desire of the physical benefit which
he needed : and Christ honoured his confidence and
received his homage.

4. Ib. ix. 18. " A ruler [of the synagogue] came
" and worshipped him." In the corresponding passages

of Mark and Luke, the expression is that " he fell at
" the feet" of Jesus: the attitude of reverence, submission, and earnest supplication.

5. Matt. xiv. 33. The disciples " came and wor-
" shipped him, saying, Truly thou art the Son of God !"
The miracles which excited this exclamation were
understood by our Lord's attendants as a demonstration of his Messiahship; but how far they at this
time comprehended the meaning and extent of the title
Son of God, is probably not in our power to ascertain.
We have before seen some evidence[5] that this
appellation was understood by the Jewish people
generally, to belong to the Messiah; and that it was
not a mere synonym of that word, but had a respect
rather to the person than to the office of the expected
Saviour. But it is very credible, and agreeable to the
usual course of opinion and feeling in large bodies of
men, that individuals would differ greatly from each other
in their notions and expectations on this head, and that
the views of even the most enlightened would be extremely vague and obscure. It seems impossible that,
in their circumstances, it should have been otherwise.
Indeed we have seen evidence that the fact was so.[6] It
would follow, therefore, that they would regard the
wondrous Person with whom they were conversant,
and whose command over the powers of nature filled
them with such overwhelming astonishment,[7] as an
object of unknown and mysterious greatness; and that

[5] Page 59, of this Volume.   [6] Vol. I. p. 597.
[7] In the parallel place of Mark vi. 51, 52, it is said that they
were " exceedingly beyond measure amazed," and that " their heart
[a Hebraism for the entire powers of the intellect] was stupified,"
or, as it were, petrified with astonishment.

the motive of their homage to him would partake of this indefinite and awful character. Such appears to have been the state of Peter's mind, when, on another disclosure of the miraculous power of Christ, " he " fell at the feet of Jesus, and said, Depart from me, for " I am a sinful man, O Lord !"[8]—A similar interpretation we have before given to John ix. 35.

6. Matt. xv. 25. The Syrophœnician woman " came " and worshipped him, saying, Lord, help me !" The relation in Mark says, " she fell at his feet—and " entreated him." This suppliant either was a proselyte to the Mosaic religion, or she had received some fragments of information from the neighbouring Jews upon their expectation of the Messiah: for she addressed Jesus as the " Son of David." But we have no evidence to authorize the belief that she had any extensive acquaintance with his proper character and office. We cannot, therefore, infer any thing with respect to her views and intention, beyond a most reverential and humble importunity, united with some perhaps indistinct, yet very exalted conceptions of greatness and dignity in Christ, and a just confidence in his power.

7. Ib. xx. 20. " The mother of the sons of " Zebedee came to him, with her sons, worshipping, " and asking something from him." As this was altogether an ambitious project of Salome and her sons, and referred to their expectation of Christ's setting up a worldly monarchy, to which they probably applied his promise recently made to them,[9] it is reasonable to understand her obeisance as in-

[8] Luke v. 8.   [9] See Chap. xix. 28.

tended to be the homage customarily paid to a
temporal sovereign.

8. Matt. xxviii. 9. The female disciples who had
visited the tomb of Jesus—" came to him, clung to
" his feet, and worshipped him." Here the prostrate
posture, which denoted the highest reverence and
respect, is manifestly described: but the expression
does not necessarily import more than the most exalted
kind of civil homage.

9. Ib. v. 17. The disciples, " when they beheld
" him, worshipped him ; but some doubted." The
kind of homage intended by the disciples on this
occasion, could only be determined by means of a
precise knowledge of their state of mind and sentiments at the time. That this state was one of great
agitation and confusion, is beyond a doubt ; and some
of them, it is added, (ἐδίστασαν) were held in such
perplexity as not to know whether what they saw was a
reality or a dream. They certainly knew and believed
that Jesus was the Messiah : but their acquaintance
with the real character, qualifications, and functions
implied in that term, could not but be extremely imperfect and obscure. It is reasonable to believe that
their views, as to the character and intention of
the homage which they paid, were in like manner
indistinct.

10. John xx. 28. " Thomas answered and said unto
" him, My Lord and my God !"

Of these remarkable words different interpretations
have been proposed.

(1.) That it was a sudden, and almost involuntary,
exclamation of conviction and astonishment.[10] To

[10] *Enjedin. Expl. Locorum*, p. 249. He adduces as similar in-

this it is replied, that to use the Divine name as an exclamation of surprise, however practised by the ancient heathens, and, to their shame, by many called Christians in later times, was not the custom among the Jews. Not the semblance of such a form of speaking appears in any part of the Old or New Testament. The outward reverence of the Jews for the names of Deity was maintained to extreme punctiliousness. And, if it were supposed that the language of Thomas had this character, it would be incredible that our Lord should instantly commend his faith, and not rebuke his bordering, at least, upon profaneness ; not to say, also, that the deliberate recording of an imprudent and irreligious outcry is little consonant with the judgment of an apostle, and still less with the wisdom of inspiration.

(2.) That it was an ejaculation of admiration and gratitude, addressed directly to God the Almighty Father. This opinion is said to have been first promulgated by Theodore of Mopsuestia, who flourished about the close of the fourth century.[11]

Samuel Crellius supposed that the first member of the sentence, " My Lord," was addressed to Jesus Christ ; and the next, " My God," to the Father : and he further conjectured that some interval of time passed between the two. But this is so artificial and unnatural a resort, so regardless of the very words, which are joined by the copulative, so evidently made to serve a purpose, and so destitute of any

stances, the heathen exclamations, *Hercules ! Jupiter ! Great gods ! Good gods !* and the modern ones (he says, " Christiano more,") *Jesu ! Maria ! Good God !*

[11] *Lardner's Cred.* vol. ix. p. 410.

rational evidence, that it does not call for further refutation.

Unitarians in general refer the whole address to the Father: "This is a sudden exclamation of astonishment and joy: *q. d.* My Lord! and my God! How great is thy power! Or, My Lord and my God has done this!"[12]

By a remarkable inattention, the Annotator on the Improved Version has subjoined, as a note, a posthumous passage of Whitby, taken at second hand from Archbishop Newcome;[13] of which the apparent design, and certainly the effect on the uninformed reader, is to represent Theodore Beza as patronizing this interpretation. The fact is, however, the reverse. As Beza's annotation is not long, it is here inserted: "From the pronoun *to him*, it appears that the words which follow are not merely the expression of the apostle's admiration, as the Nestorians used to evade this passage; but the words represent him addressing Jesus himself as the true God and his Lord. The Vulgate therefore is mistaken in translating the passage in the nominative case; and there is not a more express instance in the gospels, of the invocation of Christ as the true God. It is an exclamation, the nominative being put for the vocative, as in chap. xix. 3."[14]

[12] *Calm Inq.* p. 219.

[13] "These words are usually understood as a confession. Beza says that they are an exclamation: q. d. *My Lord and my God!* how great is thy power! Eph. i. 19, 20. Whitby's Last Thoughts, 2d ed. p. 78. *Newcome." Impr. Vers.*

[14] "*Ei, αὐτῷ.* Hæc igitur verba quæ sequuntur non sunt tantùm admirantis Thomæ, ut hunc locum eludebant Nestoriani, sed ipsum illum Jesum ut verum Deum ac Dominum suum compellantis. Malè igitur Vulgata interpretatur hunc locum recto casu, ' Dominus meus

To this interpretation, usually received among the Unitarians, two objections lie.

[1.] Had such been the intention of the words, it is very extraordinary that they should have been left in a state of defect so objectionable and dangerous. Two additional words would have filled up the sentence, and have precluded all mistake.

[2.] The connected clauses, "Thomas *answered*, and " said *to him*," do not agree with this interpretation; but, in their proper and manifest construction, limit the succeeding words as an address to Jesus Christ.

It has been, indeed, attempted to support this application by adducing a passage in the Old Testament as a parallel instance. " And Jonathan said unto David, " Jehovah, God of Israel (when I have sounded my " father—if there be good towards David, and I then " send not unto thee and show it thee,) Jehovah do " so and much more to Jonathan !" [15]   But this is an irrelevant case.   That the clause, "Jehovah, God of " Israel," is not the language of invocation, is manifest from the whole structure of the paragraph; especially from the immediate sequence of the particle כִּי *that, because, for, when,* and the verb in the future tense.   A verb may, therefore, either be understood by ellipsis, or may have been left out by the oversight of an early copyist.   In a manuscript, No. 560, of Dr. Kennicott's enumeration, and which he assigns to the thirteenth century, חַי *liveth* is found in the text immediately before יְהֹוָה *Jehovah ;* and the same word

et Deus meus.' Nec alius est locus in his libris expressior, de Christo ut vero Deo invocando. *Domine, ὁ Κύριος·* exclamatio est, rectis vocativi voce positis, ut supra, xix. 3." *Bezæ Annot.* in loc.

[15] 1 Sam. xx. 12, 13. *Monthly Repos.* Vol. xiv. p. 414. July, 1819.

is added in the margin of his No. 224, a still earlier
copy, which the learned Lilienthal considered of extraordinary value, and as a transcript from a manuscript of a very high antiquity, and free from the
Masoretic revision.[16]   Thus the construction is filled
up, and the sentence runs in the form of a solemn
oath : " Jehovah, the God of Israel, liveth !   For I
" will sound my father ;" or, as our translators have
usually rendered this idiom in other places, " As the
" Lord God of Israel liveth, I will sound my father."
This mode of supplying the passage is rendered probable, as the omission would thus appear to have
occurred from the similarity of contiguous letters ;
a very frequent cause of various readings.   That some
word is wanting is also evinced by the ancient versions, though they supply it differently.   The Septuagint fills the chasm thus, " The Lord the God of
Israel knoweth :" the Syriac, and the Arabic in Walton's Polyglott, " The Lord, the God of Israel, is
witness."   Le Clerc adopts the latter resolution of the
passage, and very properly supports it by observing
that the same supplement is requisite in verse 23d.
Michaelis understands the phraseology in verse 20th
as an adjuration ; in the 23d he follows the Septuagint
and Le Clerc.   But there is really no necessity for
any of these modes of obviating the difficulty.   The
first clause, " Jehovah God of Israel," may be fairly
understood as the nominative to the verb " shall do"
(יַעֲשֶׂה) in ver. 13th, where " Jehovah" is repeated, on
account of the words which have intervened, and which
may be read as a parenthesis.

[16] *Kennicott. Dissert. Gen.* pp. 105, 89.

The objections therefore to this Unitarian gloss are, I apprehend, left in full force, and are sufficient to prevent our acquiescence in this turn to the words.

[3.] The remaining interpretation is, that the apostle intended his words as an address directly to the Lord Jesus, and that they were so accepted by Jesus.

This is the just and regular meaning of the sentence, and any deviation from it is contrary to the ordinary use of language. Though harsh and unusual constructions must be sometimes admitted, every candid critic will allow that we should resort to them never but in cases of necessity, inextricable by other means.

No difficulty arises from the words not being in the vocative case; for the use of the nominative for the vocative is so common in the Greek writers, profane as well as sacred,[17] that it cannot be called a peculiarity of the scriptural style. In the Septuagint the frequent invocation, "O God," is almost invariably in the nominative form.[18] Indeed a distinguished scripture critic goes so far as to lay it down in the form of an aphorism, that, "in the New Testament, the

[17] See Luke xviii. 11, 13. Eph. vi. 1, 4, 5, 9. The ancient Greek grammarians, Johannes Grammaticus, and Gregory the author of a treatise on the Dialects, both adduce it as an Atticism. J. F. Fischer has brought many classical examples in his *Animadversiones in Welleri Gramm. Gr.* vol. i. pp. 352, 412 ; vol. iii. p. 320 ; and he remarks, " Græci vetere, atque adeo Attici, hoc quoque in genere sequuti esse videntur Hebræos." " In this kind of expression the ancient Greeks, and of course the Attics, seem to have imitated the Hebrews ;"—for the Hebrew and other languages of the same family have no declension by cases.

[18] See Vol. I. pp. 314, 319, 323.

nominative is put for the vocative in *addresses*, but
not in *exclamations* ;—for which latter purpose the
vocative is used, either alone or with the interjection Ω." [19]

This also the earliest writers extant that advert to
the passage, and whose native language was Greek,
evidently regarded as the just construction. So
Origen quotes it ; [20] and so it stands in Nonnus, whose
poetry is in this passage scarcely a paraphrase, but
rather a mere version. [21]

The Calm Inquirer feeling perhaps that the weight
of evidence lay in this scale, had prepared himself
with a paraphrase, framed to conciliate this view of
the passage with his own principles. [22]

The scripture instances of the inferior applications
of the term *God*, have been before collected, and some
observations offered upon them. [23]   I would intreat the

[19] *Chr. Stockii Interpres Græcus N. Test.* p. 31. Jena, 1726.

[20] *Excerpta Procopiana ex Origene,* apud *Opera, ed. Delarue,*
vol. iii. p. 98.

[21] Θωμᾶς δ' ὑστερόμητις ἀμοιβάδα ῥῆξατο φωνὴν,

Κοίρανος ἡμέτερος καὶ ἐμὸς Θεός.——

" Thomas, thus at last informed, uttered the reply, Our Sovereign
and my God !"

[22] " If, then, the words are not to be taken as a mere exclamation, but as an address to Christ, the apostle's meaning seems to be,
q. d. Convinced of the truth of thy resurrection, I acknowledge thee
as my master, and submit to thee as my god, as a prophet coming,
with divine credentials, and supported by divine authority. See
John x. 34, 35." *Calm Inq.* p. 220. Upon the same principle, and
referring to John x. 35, Dr. Carpenter paraphrases the address of
Thomas ; " I again own thee as my Master, I again acknowledge
that thou speakest the words of God, and under his authority."
Proof that the Father is the Only Proper Object of Religious Worship,
p. 17.

[23] See Vol. I. p. 503. It is deserving of observation that the
accomplished orientalist, Gesenius, admits the implication of a

reader to compare any of those instances with the passage before us; and to consider whether he does not perceive in each, and even the strongest of them, a very palpable line of demarcation, broad enough to remove the subject far from the possibility of misapprehension,—from the possibility, that any person possessed of ordinary faculties, and reading with honest intention, could, from this phraseology, impute to Moses, or to any of the parties figuratively called God, a *really divine* nature and perfections: while, in this address of the apostle, he finds a weighty brevity, an unhesitating comprehension, an unchecked emphasis, which he cannot, on any principle of rational interpretation or of common sense, identify with the Unitarian paraphrases above given, and which irresistibly direct his judgment to take the terms in their propriety and full measure of signification;——My Lord and my God!

plurality in those constructions of Elohim, which were noted in the former volume; though, unhappily, yet, as might be expected, he solves the question by acceding to Eichhorn's opinion, mentioned in the former volume of this work, p. 476. But it would not be just in me to withhold the following remark, which he adduces as corroborative of that opinion:—" The later writers of the Hebrew Scriptures did not allow this use of plural forms; and, therefore, in those places where they borrowed from the more ancient, they substituted the singular. For הָלְכוּ אֱלֹהִים, 2 Sam. vii. 23, the writer of the Chronicles (Book I. xvii. 21,) puts הָלַךְ אֱלֹהִים. For אֵלֶּה אֱלֹהֶיךָ in Exod. xxxii. 4, 8, we find זֶה אֱלֹהֶיךָ in Nehem. ix. 18. Probably those later Hebrews, from their strict attachment to monotheism, disapproved of that expression as seeming to savour of polytheism. At least the Rabbinical writers expressly did so. See *Onkelos* on Gen. xx. 13, and the *Jerusalem Gemara*, fol. 47. It is to be observed also that, in the preceding passages of the Pentateuch, the Samaritan text substitutes the singular form." *Lehrgebäude,* p. 710.

Let the serious inquirer further observe, that the combination of the two sacred names forms the strongest representation of Divine Majesty of which the language is capable. Let him also reflect on the word of appropriation, My Lord, My God; and duly ponder, whether it does not imply the acknowledgment of a divine appropriating right, and the consequent submission of soul and dedication of religious feeling which amount to a real homage of adoration.: Let him consider, whether he can think it probable, or rationally possible, that any Egyptian or Israelite could have been led, by the Scripture declarations adverted to, ever to accost Moses or one of the princes of the people, in any circumstances, with the solemn address, " My Lord and my God!"

On the other hand, it is very properly asked, Could this be the actual meaning of the apostle, however convinced and gratified? His doubts had been whether Jesus, the man of Galilee, was indeed returned to life from the state of the dead: those doubts had now been removed by the evidence of sight, hearing, and touch; and he was fully satisfied that the same man Jesus was standing alive before him. This sensible evidence proved the resurrection of the man who had been unquestionably dead: but could it prove any thing more? Could it be a demonstration of so very remote and stupendous a proposition, as that this man is a unique being, possessed of a superior and invisible nature, a nature no less than that of the Immortal Deity?—This objection Mr. Belsham has not failed to place in a strong light." Wishing to meet it, and

---

" " But who can believe that this sceptical apostle, who immediately before had been doubting whether his Master was a living

every other difficulty, with fairness, I submit the following observations to the serious judgment of the reader.

1. It is universally admitted that the discourses and conversations of Jesus Christ are not given by the evangelists at full length. Of his own sayings, and those of his interlocutors, *great points* are preserved, but very often the intermediate parts are withheld. Thus a want of connexion, among the sentences and paragraphs of such discourses and conversations, must occasionally appear. It is not for us to complain of this circumstance. For the facts and truths which are actually communicated by the Christian revelation, we are infinitely indebted : they are altogether a boon of undeserved kindness : and we may be assured that they are sufficient for all the purposes of devout obedience, though not for the allaying of all curiosity, or the extermination of all difficulties. With respect to the case before us, there might be something, either in the discourses held, or more probably in the mind and feelings of Thomas, which, if we knew it, would show that the confession of that apostle, understood as to us it appears necessary to understand it upon the fair principles of the interpretation of language, was not insulated or irrelevant. The little that is recorded concerning him, shows him to have been a man of an extremely cautious temperament, prompt to the apprehension of difficulties, and not easily yielding to considerations which might allay them.[25]

man, would, from the sensible and satisfactory evidence he had now obtained of his resurrection, directly infer that he was the living and eternal God ? What an infinite distance between the premises and the conclusion." *Calm Inq.* p. 219.

[25] John xiv. 5 ; xx. 25.

2. It cannot be deemed improbable, that Thomas
had been present on those occasions when the Jews
charged our Lord with making himself equal to God,
and claiming to be the Son of God, in a manner
which they understood, and which it appears to us
that he confirmed, to be representing himself as God.[26]
He had also heard the Saviour avow, in a manner the
most solemnly impressive, " He that hath seen me, hath
" seen the Father;—I am in the Father, and the Father
" in me."[27]   Those assertions and claims of his Lord,
though at the time very imperfectly understood, might
have been laid up by Thomas in his heart with
peculiar observation, and often reflected upon with
strong feelings of interest.   He was probably, also,
well acquainted with the charge of blasphemy upon
which Jesus had been condemned, and with the lofty
declaration by which he had met the accusation,
asserting his own dignity as the Son of the living
God, and predicting his exaltation to " the right hand
" of power," and his " coming in the clouds of hea-
" ven :" that is, his exercise of supreme dominion and
his administration of mercy and justice to mankind.
Our Lord's resurrection from the state of death was
the first step towards that glorified state, and was the
pledge of all that should follow.   When satisfied of
that fact, Thomas could look forward to the entire
assemblage of glorious things, which his imagination
had delighted to picture under the reign of the
Messiah : and, if his mind was tinctured with those
lofty sentiments upon the person and characters of the
Messiah which, we have before shown, were cherished,

[26] See of this Chapter, Capitule I. Sects. V. and VI.
[27] John xiv. 9, 10.

though shrouded with much obscurity and imperfection, by the most pious of the Jewish nation, his exclamation of acknowledgment and confidence was congruous with that very peculiar combination of sentiments, feelings, and expectations which now agitated his mind.

3. There is another cause, of still greater importance than these; a cause which we are entitled to assume as really existing, which is abundantly sufficient to produce the effect, and which furnishes a complete solution of the difficulty; the DIRECTION AND INSPIRATION OF THE HOLY SPIRIT. At the mention of this, I am aware that there are persons called Christians who will put on the affectation of contempt:—but on themselves the impiety and inconsistency must fearfully rest!—The smallest portion of true candour would have taught them, that not only our assuming this is perfectly logical, as being an independent fact according to our own views of Christian truth, but that the assumption is one to which no Unitarian ought, on his own principles, to object; for the occasional inspiration of the apostles is a doctrine, which none of their respectable writers in England have as yet followed the Antisupranaturalists of the continent in denying. It is true, that the time was not yet come, in which they were to be " invested " with power from on high, and led into all truth :"[28] but it by no means follows from this admission, that the suggestions of inspiration were given on no previous occasions; and no occasion can be conceived more suitable than that of bearing a solemn testimony for Christ. It was by the revelation of the Holy

[28] Luke xxiv. 49.   John xvi. 13.

Spirit, that Simeon acknowledged Jesus, when an
infant, to be " the Lord's Messiah," and foretold the
effects of his dispensation.[29]   It was in consequence of
a revelation from heaven, that Peter had confessed
Jesus to be " the Messiah the Son of God."[30]   It was
by a divine impulse that even Caiaphas " prophesied
" that Jesus should die—to gather together into one
" the scattered children of God."[31]   So " the Spirit
" of Christ" in the ancient prophets " testified before-
" hand of the sufferings of Christ, and the glories that
" should be after them."[32]   Can it, then, be thought
incredible, that a similar influence should, in the present instance, have enabled the apostle Thomas clearly
to declare a truth which, at the time, he could not
know in its full comprehension?

To the judicious reader it is now submitted, whether our examination of this important case has been
complete, our arguments just, and our interpretation
valid.[33]

We now return to the subject, of which the case of
Thomas was the concluding instance; the homage
paid to our Lord Jesus Christ in the days of his abode
among men.

Some of the instances appear plainly to have implied
nothing, in the intention of the parties presenting their
homage, beyond the recognition of superior rank as
a teacher, or a sovereign, or a miraculous benefactor.
In others it appears probable that there was an indefinite impression of such greatness in the object, as
imported a superiority of nature, and bore the

[29] Luke ii. 25, 26, 27, 34, 35.   [30] Matt. xvi. 17.
[31] John xi. 51, 52.   [32] 1 Pet. i. 11.
[33] See Note [A], at the end of this Capitule.

character of religious adoration. But the obscurity which lies upon the sentiments and intention of those who offered this homage to the Redeemer, may perhaps be diminished by attending to the manner in which he received it. A review of our Lord's conduct in this respect furnishes the following remarks.

It was a point which the Lord Jesus evidently held very important and sacred, never to countenance any claims of worldly sovereignty, either acknowledged to himself, or made by others on his behalf. He strongly disavowed the " receiving of honour from men."[34] He refused to interfere, when solicited, in the matter of a contested inheritance.[35] Attempts were made to invest him with the regal dignity ; but he constantly and inflexibly disclaimed them.[36] When an epithet was applied to him to which he had the clearest right, and which he might have accepted very inoffensively, he rebuked the person who gave it, because it was the language of compliment: " Why callest thou me " good ?"

It is, therefore, reasonable to expect that he would have equally refused those tokens of homage which were the known signs of regal dignity, or at least denoted some kind of secular honour. But he did not refuse them. He always accepted them with approbation. They must, therefore, have been regarded by him as the due acknowledgments of a *spiritual* and *sacred supremacy,* a supremacy which he openly claimed as the Lord and Master and King of his church.

Yet, it may be said that this was no more than the supremacy of a religious leader, the most illustrious of

[34] John v. 41.   [35] Luke xii. 14.   [36] John vi. 15.

the prophets of God;[37] and that, under such a character, every expression of homage was due by a right
far better than that which could result from worldly
empire.

Undoubtedly so : but it is also to be considered
that Jesus was the most lowly of mankind, the most
tender of his Father's honour, and endowed with the
most sagacious discernment of the tendencies and
effects of moral actions. Upon the hypothesis, then,
of this allegation, he must have regarded the homage
paid to him as what carried no implication, or hazard
of seeming implication, of accepting the honour which
belongeth to God only. We have, however, evidence
that the same action, when offered to other persons,
whose moral worth and divine commission entitled
them to every token of human respect, was apprehended to imply a more than created dignity, and was
therefore rejected with the strongest disapprobation.
When Peter, in his character of an inspired messenger,
entered the house of Cornelius, the pious but imperfectly instructed Roman " fell down at his feet and
" worshipped him."[38] If this act of homage, the very
same that had been accepted without scruple by Jesus
Christ, had implied nothing above respectful honour
to an inspired religious teacher, it was, though in a
less degree, due to Peter as well as to Jesus : and, if
his humility disposed him to decline it, the reason of
such declining would have been laid in that becoming

[37] " The homage paid to Jesus, and accepted by him, might be
paid to him as a most distinguished Messenger of the Most High, as
the beloved Son of God. The honour due to him whom God sent,
Jesus claimed; he of course accepted of *such* honour." *Dr.
Carpenter on the Only Proper Object of Religious Worship ;* p. 42.

[38] Acts x. 25, 26.

modesty, and not in any apprehension of committing an act of idolatry, of which (upon the hypothesis of the objection) there could be no danger. But the apostle assigned the latter, as the *express* and *sole reason* of his disclaiming the respect offered by the centurion : " Peter raised him up, saying, Arise, I " myself also am a man ;" thus undeniably implying not only that this act of homage was " prompted by feelings wrong in *kind* and in *degree*,"[39] but that the acceptance of it would have been an arrogating of a dignity superior to that of man.

A similar example occurs in the apostle John's description of his own feelings, when he saw the apocalyptic visions. Dazzled by the displays of· glory which he beheld, and not improbably mistaking the celestial attendant for his Lord, at whose feet he had before fallen as dead,[40] " he fell down to worship " before the feet of the angel who showed him those things."[41] But he was instantly prevented by the sudden and as it were alarmed admonition—" See " that thou do it not![42] I am thy fellow servant.". Here, likewise, is the manifest implication that this act of homage could not have been innocently performed to a fellow creature.

Thus tender and jealous have the inspired messengers of Jehovah shown themselves, to avoid, in action or in connivance, the smallest appearance of infringing upon those honours which are due to the Eternal Majesty alone.

[39] *Dr. Carpenter*, p. 43.   [40] Rev. i. 17.

[41] Rev. xix. 10 ; xxii. 9.

[42] Ὅρα μή· an exclamation which scarcely admits of being literally translated : but it conveys the idea of anxiety and alarm, and of the eager rapidity of an effort to prevent a great evil.

And could Jesus be deficient in this holy cir-
cumspection, this solicitude to preclude the occasion
and avoid the appearance of evil? Was this meek
and lowly prophet, the most circumspect of teachers,
the wisest and the best of men, less moved with
jealousy for his Father's honour, less careful to guard
his fellow-creatures against the crime of idolatry,
or less modest, less humble, less cautious, than his
servants were?—If he were not conscious of possessing a NATURE entitled to receive divine honours,
can he be acquitted of arrogance and presumption,
or even of flagrant impiety? To my best judgment
it appears that our Lord's conduct in this respect
can be accounted for, only on the supposition of his
having that consciousness.

The Unitarian objections to this conclusion have
been urged with great ability and earnestness, by an
amiable man and most respectable writer, Dr. Lant
Carpenter: and as I presume to think that a better
advocate on that side of the question cannot readily
be pointed out, I shall briefly state his argument, and
respectfully offer some observations in reply.

Dr. Carpenter lays down, what is universally admitted, that " the grand doctrine of the law and the
" prophets is, that JEHOVAH is the ONLY God, un-
" rivalled in all his great and glorious perfections;"
and that this one Jehovah is the God and Father
of our Lord Jesus Christ, whom he worshipped as
" the Only True God," and taught us to " worship
" and pay religious service (λατρεύειν) to HIM ONLY."
He assumes that the sentiment which he disapproves,
is the introduction of *another* BEING as an object
of religious worship. The conclusion, therefore, is

easily and promptly drawn, that religious worship paid to the Messiah is not the worship of the Only God, and is consequently idolatrous and impious.

That this objection presents a great and serious difficulty, it would be disingenuous not to admit. It is, in fact, the point of convergence of all the Unitarian arguments in this part of the controversy: and it presents, in the most concentrated form, the chief difficulty that lies on the Trinitarian doctrine. It is capable of being modified in different ways, but its essential principle is the same: namely, that to attribute the characters of divinity to the Messiah and to the Holy Spirit, is to set up *other beings* as Divine besides "the Living and True God." To this objection we have already paid distinct attention,[43] and probably shall again do so in future parts of this investigation. The following remarks are offered with reference to the present case.

1. Whatever our opponents may think of the credibility and rationality of our sentiments, they ought to do us the justice of recollecting that *we constantly and strenuously* DENY *the assumption*, by them made. Our doctrine is that, whatever may be the kind of distinction which we conceive to subsist in the Divine Nature, *that Nature is* ONE. The Deity of the Son, and the Deity of the Holy Spirit, we believe to be ONE and THE SAME with the Deity of the Father. Let this doctrine stand or fall, according to the evidence: but let it not be forgotten or overlooked that THIS *is* our doctrine. In honouring the Redeemer and the Sanctifier, we believe that we are honouring the Father and Fountain of all

[43] See Vol. I. pp. 12—15, 506.

being and blessedness, and that in each case, the OBJECT of our honour *is the One and Only* GOD. It is not, therefore, correct in argument to represent us as introducing other beings than the Father into the honours of Deity.

2. The formal ground of that religious homage which we conceive the Scriptures represent as due to the Lord Jesus Christ, is the Divine Nature which the same authority appears to us to attribute to him, and which we regard as essential to the value and efficacy of his mediatorial office.

3. Dr. Carpenter and other Unitarians lay great stress on this very important passage: " This is the " eternal life, that they may know Thee, [to be] the " Only True God; and him whom thou hast sent, " Jesus [to be], the Christ."" Certainly a most emphatical passage; but to the opinion that it asserts the sole Deity of the Father, to the exclusion of the Son, I think there are sound reasons of demur.

(1.) If this text contained all the information which the Scriptures, directly or indirectly, furnish on the subject, we should probably coincide in the Unitarian interpretation : but the case is widely different. To the reader of these volumes I trust I may, without arrogance, appeal, whether ample proofs have not been brought that the prophets, and apostles, and Jesus Christ himself taught his preexistence and deity, in no little variety of modes, both implied and express. Believing, therefore, in the consistency of inspired scripture, we cannot attribute a sense to one passage without listening to the voice of others; in other words, without collecting the general testi-

" John xvii. 3.

mony of the sacred books on the topic. We wish to hear *all* the evidence before we give the verdict.

(2.) It must be clear to every reader of our Lord's prayer, from which the present passage is detached, that it proceeds throughout upon the ground of his mediatorial state and office. Now, we have had repeated occasion to observe the language of entire subordination in which it was his practice to speak of himself under this character; referring his commission, doctrine, miracles, obedience, and sufferings, to the grace and sovereignty of the Father; and yet that he frequently united with it certain attributives, which appear incompatible with any other than the supreme nature. In this prayer itself, according to our best endeavour to ascertain the sense of the expressions, we have found some such attributives.[45]

(3.) According to our views of scriptural truth, it is peculiarly the official character of the Father to sustain the legislative and rectoral honours of the Deity, and to be the primary Author of all the acts of authority, power, and grace by which the Deity is made known to mankind. Now, with this sentiment, the terms of the passage under consideration, and of other passages in the New Testament, are strictly coincident. , The wise and gracious arrangement of the parts and methods of Jehovah's moral government and his covenant of salvation, is properly expressed thus: " There is one God, and One Mediator between " God and men, the man Christ Jesus. To us there " is One God, the Father, of whom are all things, " and we unto him: and One Lord, Jesus Christ,

---

[45] See Cap. II. Sect. V. of this Chapter.

" through whom are all things, and we through him."[46]
It is reasonable, that in this mediatorial prayer of our
Lord Jesus Christ, the same economy of the divine
operations should be intimated. The nature of the
occasion plainly requires, that he should speak of
himself in his official and delegated capacity.

(4.) In pursuance of these ideas, it appears strictly
proper, and most requisite to the occasion, that this
form of expression should be used, to declare *the sole
Deity* of the living and true God, in opposition to the
fictitious gods of the nations to whom the gospel was
soon to be promulgated; and *the Messiahship* of
Jesus, for the restoration and eternal salvation of the
human race, according to the Jewish scriptures. This
reference to the two classes of men, the Gentiles and
the Jews, accords with the immediately preceding
sentence ; " As thou hast given to him power over all
" flesh, that to whomsoever thou hast given him, he
" may give eternal life."

(5.) Exclusive, as well as universal, terms in Scripture are not to be regarded as necessarily and without
farther examination signifying absolutely; but they
must be understood frequently with a limitation suggested by the nature and circumstances of the case.[47]

---

[46] 1 Tim. ii. 5.   1 Cor. viii. 6.

[47] Instances of this use of μόνος· Mark vi. 47. John viii. 9.
1 Cor. ix. 6. " Cùm quidam observarent Deum Patrem, ubi etiam
à Filio distinguitur, vocari solum potentem, solum verum, solum
sapientem Deum, et hìc et Rom. xvi. 27. 1 Thess. i. 9, 10. 1 Tim.
vi. 15, 16, inde Christum nec Deum esse, nec verè Deum dici posse,
collegerunt. Quæ interpretatio et ipsius Johannis disertis verbis
(Joann. i. 1,) initio Evangelii positis contradicit, et usui loquendi.
Nam nec *verum* semper opponitur *falso ;* vid. Joann. i. 9 ; vi. 32;
xv. 1. Heb. viii. 2. 1 Joann. ii. 8, cùm et lux solis, et manna, et
vitis, et tabernaculum *vera* utique omnia fuerint : nec *solus, unicus,*

One instance will serve, both to the illustration of this remark, and to confirm the application of it to the passage under consideration. The Almighty Father is sublimely called, " The Blessed and ONLY Poten- " tate, the King of kings, and Lord of lords, who " ONLY hath immortality."[48] But of the Saviour it is also, with equal clearness, asserted that he is " King " of kings and Lord of lords ;"[49] that " all power " hath been given unto him in heaven and upon " earth ;" and that he is the " First and the Last, the " Living One, the Life, the Eternal Life,"[50] terms which, in scripture language, designate the possession of life in a superlative degree, and, when the nature of the subject admits of it, may justly be construed to express an absolute immortality.[51]

singularis, simpliciter et ex omni parte pluribus opponitur, sed pro *eximio, egregio*, et *excellenti* dicitur."—" Some, having observed that God the Father, even· when mentioned in distinction from the Son, is called the only powerful, the only true, the only wise God, both in this place and in Rom. xvi. 27. 1 Thess. i. 9, 10. 1 Tim. vi. 15, 16, have inferred that Christ neither is God, nor can with propriety be called God. But their interpretation is contrary, both to the express words of this apostle in the beginning of his Gospel, and to the use of language. For the adjective *true*, is not always put in opposition to *false*; see John i. 9; vi. 32; xv. 1. Heb. viii. 2. 1 John ii. 8, as, in reference to those passages, the ordinary light of the sun, the manna in the wilderness, the natural vine, and the ancient tabernacle, were all *true* ; nor are such terms as *sole, only, singular*, opposed to the idea of plurality in the most absolute and exclusive manner, but they frequently denote that which is *most eminent, distinguished*, and *excellent*." *Wetstein in loc.*

  [48] 1 Tim. vi. 15.

  [49] Rev. xix. 16; xvii. 14. The use of the participles can make no difference in the argument.

  [50] Matt. xxviii. 18. Rev. i. 17, 18. John xi. 25. 1 John i. 2.

  [51] " The abstract being put for the concrete, to denote a peculiar emphasis and energy in the quality." See *Glassii Philol. Sacra,*

(6.) It ought not to be passed by that the *knowing* of God and the Messiah, which this passage lays down as the necessary means of spiritual and immortal happiness, must refer principally to an acquaintance with all the essential parts of the revealed testimony on those points. The *eternal life* cannot be the effect of a mere persuasion, or rational certainty, that there is one God, the Creator and Ruler of all things, and that Jesus was his messenger to the human race : for many have this knowledge to the degree of entire conviction, without deriving any moral effect from it, or applying it at all to the great and holy purpose here specified. The knowledge which is intended must embrace the designs and the tendency of God's moral government and his revealed grace, so far as they refer to this practical purpose : or those particulars which our Lord in the very connexion expressly brings forward, the glory which he had with the Father before the world existed, his being sent into the world, his setting himself apart for the sake of his people, his being glorified in them, and his possessing all things which the Father hath.[52] No knowledge short of this could be connected with the unspeakable blessing of ever-lasting life. In scriptural use, the verb *to know* is sometimes taken for acknowledging, revering, highly regarding, and loving :[53] and this sense it is reasonable to apply to the present case.

Let the whole comprehension of this text, therefore,

lib. iii. tr. i. can. vii. *Tittmanni Meletemata Sacra*, pp. 37, 38. *Wetstein in Joh.* i. 4.

[52] Verses 5, 8, 18, 19, 20.

[53] *Schleusn. Lex.* " Sign. 4. Agnosco. 17. Magnifico, revereor, amo."

be considered, under the guidance of another inspired maxim: "Whosoever denieth the Son, hath not the "Father: he who acknowledgeth the Son, hath the "Father also."[54]

There is another passage, in which, according to the opinion of many critics and divines, Christ himself is styled, in express words, "The true God and the "eternal life:" but, as the examination of that passage will come more properly in another part of this inquiry, I decline to adduce it here.

4. Dr. Carpenter reminds us, that Jesus Christ called the Father "his God," and that the apostles frequently use the title "the God of our Lord Jesus "Christ;" that also he constantly prayed to the Father, and "it is obviously absurd to say that God prayed to God—for if really and truly God, he could not at any time be otherwise than God, even if in some incomprehensible way he were man at the same time."[55] To these remarks I submit the following reply.

(1.) If for the sake of the argument, this estimable author would for a moment admit the Trinitarian hypothesis, he would advert to this part of it: that though the Son be God, truly and properly so, yet he is not the Father, neither is the Father the Son: the unity of the Godhead being conceived to be not discrepant with an UNKNOWN but REAL and NECESSARY mode of difference.

(2.) The act of the Son of God, in becoming a Mediator and Saviour to mankind, is considered as

[54] 1 John ii. 23. For the genuineness of the latter clause, see any critical edition of the Greek Testament.

[55] *Dr. Carpenter*, p. 2.

that which involved a temporary cessation or diminution of the developements, or manifestations *ad extra*,
of the essential divine glories.   It is therefore, according to our apprehension of the meaning of those
phrases, described as coming forth from the Father,
coming down from heaven, being sent into the world,
becoming flesh and making his tabernacle among
men, being sent in the likeness of sinful flesh, divesting himself, taking the form of a servant, humbling
himself, bearing our sins and our sorrows, becoming a
curse for us.—It cannot but be immensely difficult,
and probably to human powers impossible, to form
perfect conceptions of all that is included in the fact
which these expressions designate : yet it seems undeniable that they contain the idea of degradation,
humiliation, and submission to a subordinate capacity.
Such a state we may, with reverence and humility,
conceive to be congruous with the supposition which
the gospel history sets before us,—that the habitual
consciousness and feelings of THE MAN Christ Jesus
were not those of unspeakable delight, in the enjoyment of intimate communications from the inexistent
Deity ; but that, on the contrary, they were the feelings of a mental depression which no words could
describe, no imagination represent.

SUPPLEMENTARY NOTE TO CAPITULE VII.

Note [A] page 274.

Upon this interesting passage, I subjoin the remarks of John
David Michaelis, written in his most cautious spirit, and of some
other distinguished critics ; and I submit to the reader whether the
very circumstances of difference do not corroborate the reasonings
and conclusions proposed above.

"*My Lord! and my God!* I do not understand this as an address to Jesus; but thus, *Yes; he it is indeed! He, my Lord and my God!* Yet, in giving this interpretation, I do not affirm that Thomas passed all at once from the extreme of doubt to the highest degree of faith, and acknowledged Christ to be the true God. This appears to me too much for the then existing knowledge of the disciples; and we have no intimation that they recognised the divine nature of Christ, before the outpouring of the Holy Spirit. I am therefore inclined to understand this expression, which broke out from Thomas in the height of his astonishment, in a figurative sense, denoting only, *Whom I shall ever reverence in the highest degree.* If he only recollected what he had heard from the mouth of Jesus, ten days before, (chap. xiv. 9, 10,) that recollection might have given occasion to an expression, which probably Thomas himself could not have perfectly explained; as is often the case with such words as escape us when we are under the most overpowering surprise. But yet the expression might be equivalent to saying, *He! My Lord! With whom God is most intimately united, and is in Him! In whom I behold God as it were present before me!* Or, a person raised from the dead might be regarded as a divinity; for the word *God* is not always used in the strict doctrinal sense." [Michaelis then shows the incongruity of explaining the words as an exclamation.] "Besides; the first compellation, *My Lord!* certainly is directed to Christ." *Michaelis Anmerk. in loc.*

. "*My Lord and my God* (thou art!) A mere exclamation, such as are used in common life, this could not have been, in the language of that time. The heathenish corrupt practice of deifying men or the meritorious dead, was abhorred by a conscientious Jew. Thomas had but a little time before given occasion to a question of Philip, which Jesus answered by the declaration, 'He who 'seeth me, seeth the Father.' Those words had he thus heard from the mouth of him who now, as risen from the state of the dead, demanded his entire faith: and this apostle had always shown himself to be a man who was in the habit of reflecting cautiously on what he did and said. Hence the conclusion is scarcely to be avoided, that he actually recognised in Jesus the Son of God, that Redeemer who is so often by the prophets called *the Lord, Jehovah.* Notwithstanding this, he might still be retaining some of his former prejudices, respecting an earthly kingdom to be set up by the Messiah. If he was, in any tolerable degree, acquainted with the prophets of his own nation, if he had attended to the doctrines which Jesus had delivered; then, he could scarcely have failed to acknowledge the important

truth of his Redeemer's Godhead.   If, moreover, we attend to the
especial design of John in his Gospel, at the very beginning of which
the doctrine of the Deity of Christ is made most prominent, and that
the discourses of Jesus, throughout the whole book, are selected with
an express view to the confirmation of that doctrine ; the probability
rises very high, that here, in drawing his writing to a close, and
having brought together the other proofs of the doctrine, the faithful
evangelist introduces this confession of his fellow-apostle, as a signal
confirmation of his grand point, the Deity of Christ.   Had there
been any lurking notion of a superstitious kind, in this abrupt expression, Jesus would not, on the very account of these words, have
commended the faith of him who uttered them, nor have given the
approving reply which he did."   *Seiler's Grössre Biblische Erbau-
ungsbuch ; N. T.* vol. iv. p. 37.

" The remarkable words of Thomas, ' My Lord and my God !'
are not the expression of one full of admiration, and breaking out
with an invocation of the Divine Majesty, as [profane] persons in
modern times often do, under the influence of wonder or sudden
surprise : but they are a solemn profession that Jesus Christ was his
Lord and God.   This is evident, first, because the verb *he answered*,
and the pronoun *to him*, do not accord with the idea of an exclamation : and next, because the Lord commends the faith of Thomas ;
which he would not have done, had the words been merely an exclamation of wonder.   It is further to be remarked, either that the
nominatives Κύριος and Θεός, are put for the vocative, as is frequently
done ; or that εἶ σύ must be understood, ' Thou art my Lord and
' my God.'   Thus then Thomas declared that the person whom he
beheld was no visionary appearance, but Jesus himself; and professed his most full persuasion that Jesus had returned from the
state of death and lived again, and was truly Lord and God.   But it
may indeed be doubted whether, at that time, Thomas had a full
conception of Jesus Christ as Lord and God ; since the other disciples received it afterwards by the communication of the Holy
Spirit."   *Tittmanni Meletemata Sacra,* p. 694.

" Now Thomas, overpowered with humility, repentance, and surprise, uttered the words, ὁ Κύριός μου καὶ ὁ Θεός μου, *my Lord, my
God!* The nominative is put for the vocative, as in Mark v. 41 ;
xv. 34.   Matt. i. 20.   John xix. 3.   Heb. i. 8, 9.——Therefore
Thomas addressed these words to Jesus, and therein declared him to
be at once his Lord and the Messiah ; for it is expressly stated, ' he
' said to him.'   From this address of Thomas, many suppose that
the Divine Nature of Christ may be established, and conceive that

the filling up of the sentence would be thus : *I am not faithless ; I doubt no more ; but thou art my Lord and my God.* But, on the other hand, critics justly observe that Thomas used the term *God* in the sense in which *Elohim* is applied to kings and judges, who were considered as exercising the functions of God upon earth, and pre-eminently to the Messiah ; see Ps. lxxxii. 6, 7 ; xlv. 7, 8 ; cx. 1. John x. 35. Some adopt the opinion of Theodore of Mopsuestia : considering the words as merely an exclamation of admiration, and referring them not to Christ but to God. But others properly remark, as objections to this interpretation, first, that there is no proof of the use of this expression, as an interjection of surprise, by the Jews in the time of Christ ; (see *Storr on the Design of the Gospel History of John,* p. 441,) further, that the introductory phrase is, ' he saith *to him,*' not ' he saith' merely ; and that in the next words Christ commends the *faith* of Thomas, which would not have appeared from an exclamation of admiration." *Kuinöl in loc.* With regard to this author's notion on the inferior application of the name *Elohim,* I request the reader's consideration of what was advanced in Vol. I. pp. 482—504.

Capitule VIII.

MISCELLANEOUS DECLARATIONS OF CHRIST, INTIMATING THE EXIST-
ENCE AND ACTION OF A SUPERIOR NATURE IN HIMSELF.

Jesus Christ exercises a legislative authority in matters of morality, and claims
  obedience in his own right.—His supremacy in the gospel œconomy ;—and the
  prerogatives, acts, and qualifications which it implies.—Christ the author of the
  forgiveness of sins, in a sovereign and efficient sense.— He attributes to
  himself the power of relinquishing and resuming his human life, at his own
  pleasure ; and that he was the author of the resurrection of his human body.—
  With characters of perfect subordination to the will and appointments of the
  Father, he unites various and remarkable declarations of absolute equality and
  union with the Father.

On various occasions, Jesus Christ attributes to
himself, usually in the way of implication, different
powers and *prerogatives* which deserve a close attention.

I. He recites several particulars of the divine law,
each of which he introduces with the formula, " Ye
" have heard that it was said to those of old time ;"[1]
and, to each he then subjoins his own commandment
in the full tone of legislative authority, prefixing the
words, " But I say unto you." Does he not, by this
style and expression, represent that his own authority

---

[1] Matt. v. 21, &c. *Impr. Vers.* Some translate " by those of old
time," and understand it of the Jewish teachers who corrupted the
original law. But it is manifest that the passages are all taken from
the Pentateuch, except that in two instances only, vers. 21 and 43, a
gloss from the traditionary teachers is introduced. The old Syriac
Version, which, in a verbal question of this kind, is our best authority, renders the words in the dative form.

is *equivalent* to that which gave the law to the Israelites under Moses; — which will involve, that the
authority of Jesus and the authority of Jehovah are
equal: that is, that they are *the same?* The remark
of the evangelist was not without reason, that Jesus
" taught as one having authority, and not as the
" scribes." Their best and highest appeal was to the
law and to the prophets: he claimed religious obedience in his own right. In this view, most observable is the expression with which the Lord Jesus
marks that property of his people's obedience which
will be the very basis and formal reason of the everlasting retributions; " ye did it UNTO ME; ye did it
" not UNTO ME."[2] Is this befitting language for any
mere creature?

It may be replied, that Jesus spoke in the name
and by the authority of the Father alone. I answer,
he does not say so; but, on the contrary, he uses the
language of his own personal authority, repeating it
constantly, and introducing no corrective or modifying
clause whatever. So did not Moses: so did not the
apostles. Moses uses the expression, " Keep all the
" commandments which I command you this day:"
but he anxiously subjoins, " Thou shalt obey the voice
" of the Lord thy God, and do HIS commandments
" which I command thee."[3] The apostles also gave
commandments; but they took care to state, so that
it could never be mistaken, that they were acting in
their delegated capacity as " the messengers of the
" Lord and Saviour."[4] " Ye know," says Paul,
" what commandments we gave you by the Lord

---

[2] Matt. xxv. 40, 45.   [3] Deut. xxvii. 1, 10.

[4] 2 Pet. iii. 2.

" Jesus: what I write unto you are the command-
" ments of the Lord."[5]   Thus they were not merely
careful to remove the appearance of assuming any
degree of a personal authority, but they clearly defined
the proper source of moral jurisdiction to be in the
Lord Jesus Christ.

II. " Pray ye the Lord of the harvest, that he may
" send forth labourers into his harvest."[6]   It is true
that, in this passage itself, nothing occurs to mark
definitively that Christ is designated under the appellation, *Lord of the harvest :* but, in other places of the
New Testament, he is so clearly exhibited in the same
character, as the Chief in the legislation and authority
of the Christian church, that a doubt can scarcely be
entertained of a reference to him here.   His " fan is
" in his hand, and he will thoroughly cleanse his corn-
" floor ; and he will gather his wheat into the granary.
" He that soweth the good seed is the Son of man.
" The Son of man will send forth his angels; and they
" will gather out of his kingdom all seducers and
" workers of iniquity.   Behold, I send unto you
" prophets, and wise men, and scripture-teachers."[7]
Accordingly, the whole dispensation of the gospel is
His kingdom, and all the agents and instruments in it
receive their appointment, guidance, and success from
him.   The miracles by which it was established were
likewise wrought " in his name ;" which all admit to
signify, by his authority.   Now an *authority* to control
the established constitution of nature implies a *power*
to do so, and such a power cannot be conceived as an
attribute of any other being than the ONE SUPREME.

---

[5] 1 Thess. iv. 2; 1 Cor. xiv. 37.   [6] Matt. ix. 38.
[7] Matt. iii. 12 ; xiii. 37, 41 ; xxiii. 34.

The body of revealed truth is called not only " the
" word of God," but " the word of the Lord, the
" word of Christ." To his messengers he said,
" As my Father sent me, even so send I you :" and
they constantly averred that all their offices, whether
those of " apostles, or prophets, or evangelists, or
" pastors and teachers," were " the GIFT of Christ :"
and that they " received it not of man, but by the
" revelation of Jesus Christ."[9] All their labours
were " the work of Christ," and were performed " for
" His name's sake."[10] He is clearly declared to be
" the Master of the house," of the whole gospel
economy; to whom it belongs to judge of the qualifications of its subjects, and to admit or reject them by
his own sovereign authority.[11] Its institutions and
services are *his*; its discipline is by *his* commandments; its day of ordinances is *his* day, as he was
Lord of the Jewish sabbath : its chief sacrament is *his*
supper; in all things HE hath the preeminence.[12] Its
privileges and all its happiness were bestowed in his
name.[13] To his effectual power and grace its success
is attributed.[14] As its agents derive their commission
from him, so they own their responsibility to him.[15]
And all those who receive its blessings form a universal body, which he claims as his own, especial property. In language analogous to that which is

[8] Acts xi. 1 ; xiii. 48. Col. iii. 16.
[9] John xx. 21. Eph. iv. 7—11. Gal. i. 11, 12.
[10] Phil. ii. 30. 3 John 7.   [11] Luke xix. 25—27.
[12] 1 Cor. xiv. 37. Matt. xii. 8. Rev. i. 10. 1 Cor. xi. 29.
Col. i. 18.
[13] See Acts iv. 7—12 ; x. 43.
[14] John xv. 1—6. Rom. xv. 18.
[15] Gal. i. 10. 1 Tim. vi. 14. 2 Tim. ii. 3, 4.

appropriated to the Deity in the Old Testament, they
are called *his* people, *his* sheep, *his* church, *his* elect.
In this view, very remarkable is his authoritative
declaration concerning the calling of his church
among the gentiles: " Other sheep I have, which
" are not of this fold; them also I MUST BRING, and
" they shall hear MY VOICE: and there shall be one
" fold, one Shepherd."[14] This is the unequivocal
language of Almighty and Efficient Power.

Thus, the entire constitution and administration of
the system of mercy revealed to the children of men,
proceeds upon the principle of a SUPREMACY in Christ.
Let the serious inquirer consider the extent and the
implications of this supremacy: what objects it respects, what powers it requires, and what qualifications
it implies in the person who exercises it. Let him
reflect on the myriads of true Christians, " the re-
" deemed from among men," in all the ages of time,
in all the states and varieties of nature, grace, and
glory, in all their mental principles and acts, their
constitutions, tempers, and characters, their outward
conduct, their relations to other beings, and to the
infinite diversity of events, the instruments of their
instruction and edification, their trials, their dangers,
their difficulties, their deliverances, and their preservation, so that " none of them shall perish, nor shall
" any pluck them out of His hand." Of all these,
the supremacy which the Scriptures thus attribute to
Christ implies a PERFECT INTUITION, a SYSTEMATICAL
DEPENDENCE upon him, and a PERPETUAL AGENCY in
their management. Can these exist, without the
properties of wisdom and power in a degree which

[14] John x. 16.

surpasses, all that our reason can possibly ascribe to
any creature? In the view of these relations to the
labours and success of the Christian ministry, our
Lord afterwards said, "All power is given unto me
" in heaven and upon earth : go, make disciples of all
" nations :—and behold, I am with you always, even
" to the end of the world." Of this passage a more
detailed consideration has already been given.

Upon the Unitarian hypothesis, our Lord, however
great and good, the wisest and most virtuous of men,
and however richly endowed with the supernatural
gift of inspiration, was still a *fellow-servant* with other
faithful and inspired persons. He must have had the
same wants, trials, and difficulties; and have both
needed and intensely desired the same supports which
were necessary for them. Yet we find a marked and
even astonishing difference in his own conduct and
that which he enjoined upon them. He never claimed
indulgence for weaknesses and oversights; he never
put himself upon a par with his disciples, in the circumstance that, though differing in rank, they were
servants in common of the one Supreme Lord; he
never sought their condolence and moral aid; never
did he, penetrated with a sense of the unutterable
weight which lay upon him, entreat his friends to
" strive together in their prayers to God for him,"
that his efforts might be successful, for the benefit of
the world; he did not put himself into a similarity of
position with them, by joining with them in common
supplications, to "his Father and their Father, his
" God and their God." His whole conduct manifested that he stood in a relation to God, essentially
different from that which belonged to them : and that

conduct appears incapable of being accounted for, if it could have been ever proper for him to say, with the ministering angel, " I am thy fellow-servant, and of " thy brethren the prophets." [17]

These thoughts have been suggested to me by an esteemed brother in the ministry, the Rev. John Medway, of Melbourn, in Cambridgeshire; and, as it would be unjust for me to appropriate his sentiments without acknowledgment, I think it no more than a plain duty to insert extracts from his own letters; trusting that he will not disapprove of my so doing without having asked his permission; for truth and reasoning are a common property for all men."

III. Reason and Scripture teach that *to pardon sin*, in the proper and complete sense, is an act to which no being is competent besides the Supreme Moral Governor of the universe. Forgiveness implies a change in the order and relations of some part of the accountable world, with respect to the Being to whom it is accountable; who alone can, and assuredly will, " judge the world in righteousness." This implied change is such as the criminal cannot make on his own account, and no other can make for him, except the Being who presides over the judicial arrangements of the moral universe; and this Being can be no other than " the God of judgment, by whom actions " are weighed, and to whom belongeth vengeance and " recompense." It implies a removal of the Divine displeasure itself, and of that tremendous sense and conviction of the Divine displeasure which justice requires to be produced in the consciousness of the offender; and it further implies a reinstatement in the

<hr />

[17] See Note [A], at the end of this Capitule.

approbation of "the righteous Lord, who loveth right-
"eousness." It is, therefore, an article in the inspired
enumeration of the peculiar prerogatives of JEHOVAH,
that " HE pardoneth iniquity, transgression, and sin."
But it is recorded, that Jesus " said to the paralytic
" man, Son, take courage, thy sins are forgiven
" thee; and, behold, some of the scribes said in them-
" selves, Why doth he thus speak blasphemies? Who
" can forgive sins but God alone? But Jesus, know-
" ing their thoughts, said, Why do ye think evil in
" your hearts? For which is the easier, to say, Thy
" sins are forgiven; or to say, Arise and walk? But,
" that ye may know that the Son of man, upon earth,
" hath a right to forgive sins, (he saith to the para-
" lytic) Arise, take up thy couch, and go to thy
" house." [18]

Three different interpretations have been put upon
this conduct and words of our Lord on this occasion.

1. It is maintained that he did not assume to himself the actual right to give a judicial forgiveness of
sin, but intended only to declare to the person whom
he saw to be penitent, that his sins were forgiven by
God, in the same manner as Christ gave to his apostles
authority to " remit sins." [19] To this interpretation it
may justly be objected:

(1.) That this sense of the expression would have
furnished no colour for the charge of blasphemy,

[18] Matt. ix. 2—7. Mark ii. 3—12. See another instance in
Luke vii. 47, 48.

[19] Matt. xviii. 18. John xx. 23. " He seemed to intimate
that God had invested him with a power of discerning the real characters of men, and consequently of pronouncing whether they were
entitled to the Divine forgiveness or not." *Dr. Priestley's Notes on
Scripture*, vol. iii. page 149.

which the Jews so promptly advanced. That charge
unquestionably supposed that Jesus was invading the
Divine prerogative: and his own reply accepted the
sense of a proper forgiveness of sin, thus admitting
the construction of his adversaries to be the fair and
just meaning of his words.

(2.) Whether we take the remitting of sins predicated of the apostles, in a declarative or a metaphorical
sense, it is manifest that it was understood by themselves in a manner essentially different from that in
which they attributed to Jesus Christ the blessing of
forgiveness. In no part of their discourses or writings
do they profess to forgive sins. They never employed
language approaching to that of our Lord on this
occasion. They always taught that, " by faith in HIM,
" we receive the remission of sins," that " in him we
" have redemption through his blood, even the for-
" giveness of sins," and that " by the grace of our
" Lord Jesus Christ we are saved." [20]   But, with
respect to themselves and their office, they advanced
no higher claims than that they were messengers and
ambassadors of Christ, announcing the pardon of
human guilt and all the blessings of eternal life, as *his
gift*. A very observable instance occurs of the declarative remission of offences, upon the proofs of peni-
tence in the offender ; as a branch of the ecclesiastical
discipline enjoined in the New Testament. The
apostle Paul directs the church at Corinth " to grant
" forgiveness, and restore to consolation ;" and he
adds his own approval and ratification of their act, on
the ground of his apostolic commission : but he is
especially careful to mark that he does this with an

[20] Acts xxvi. 18 ; xv. 11. Eph. i. 7.

explicit reference to CHRIST as the Possessor of the
authority and efficiency to forgive. " To whom ye
" grant this forgiveness, I also : for whatever forgive-
" ness I grant, I grant it for your sake, in the pre-
" sence of Christ." [21]   In another passage, the apostle
enjoins the mutual forgiveness of Christians towards
each other, from this express motive, " even as CHRIST
" HATH GRANTED FORGIVENESS to you." [22]

2. It is affirmed by Unitarian writers, that our
Lord's words were framed to conform with a Jewish
opinion, that not only was sin the immediate cause of
bodily disorders and human sufferings in general, but
that each disease and calamity was the specific punishment of some particular crime ; and that, therefore,
Jesus meant no more than if he had said, " May thy
disorder be removed !" [23]   Upon this opinion I remark :

[21] 2 Cor. ii. 7, 10. Though the word here is χαρίσασθαι and not
ἀφιέναι, the sense is the same, but with an emphatical reference to
the *free and gracious* bestowment of the blessing. See Col. ii. 13.

'Εν προσώπῳ Χριστοῦ, " *in the presence* of Christ, *before* Christ ;
or Christ being the inspector and approver of the transaction, as
Theodoret understands the expression. Luther and others translate
it, *in the person*, i. e. *in the place and stead* of Christ. The sense is
nearly the same, in either version." *Semler in loc.* " With a religious regard to Christ, having the mind directed to him, as the ever
present and observant Lord of the church, and seriously considering
what will be agreeable to his will." *Rosenmüller*, and so De Wette,
and Nähbe, a very judicious interpreter. Wetstein, Michaelis, Seiler,
Van Ess, and Scholz, accord with the common interpretation; *in the
name and place* of Christ. Schleusner considers it as a solemn
attestation, of the nature of an oath, calling Christ to witness :
" Christum testor, per Christum juro." Billroth (who died in the
prime of life, March, 1836,) urges the same view as that of Theodoret,
as what best suits the connexion.

[22] Col. iii. 13.

[23] *Dr. Priestley*, ubi supra. *Calm Inq.* p. 329.

(1.) The general principle, that all the afflictions and sorrows of men are the effect of the sinful state into which we have fallen, is by no means to be represented as a Jewish prejudice, or to be spoken of with contempt. Nothing can be more certain, on every ground of rational consideration, than that physical evil could not have taken place, under the government of Infinite Righteousness, unless as the judicial effect of sin against God.

(2.) Admitting our Lord to have alluded to this principle, which is not improbable though we cannot regard it as proved, it by no means follows that the expression, "Thy sins are forgiven thee," was synonymous with the other, "May thy disease be removed." On the contrary, it is much more consonant with reason and probability, to suppose that Jesus designed a reference to moral offence, as the actual cause, under the Divine administration, of this individual's distressing malady. It may be reasonably conceived that our Lord, who " knew what was in man," saw the mind of this afflicted person to be overwhelmed with compunction and penitential sorrow, on account of his own sinful condition; and that he intended, therefore, first to speak the words of healing mercy to the wounded spirit, and then, as the inferior blessing, to restore soundness to the helpless body.

(3.) There is no evidence, excluding the passages under dispute, that the expression used by our Lord, or its cognate term, " the forgiveness of sins," was ever employed by a New Testament writer to denote any other than a proper remission of the pains and penalties due to moral transgression. On the contrary, all the passages in which it occurs, appear to require this as their necessary construction.[1] Even in one of the very places under dispute, the connexion most clearly proves that a moral forgiveness is the only thing intended: for Jesus said, "Her sins, "which are many, are forgiven, for she loveth much; "but he, to whom little is forgiven, loveth little."[25]

(4.) If such was the meaning of our Lord's words, and if it thus coincided with current opinion, the design must have been sufficiently intelligible, and there would have existed still less ground than upon the former interpretation, for the accusation of blasphemy.

These appear decisive reasons for the rejection of each of the interpretations proposed. There remains only another.

3. That Jesus Christ spake under the consciousness, and by the authority, of a superior nature: which, from the clear tenor of Scripture as to the right and power of bestowing this particular blessing, could be no other than that of " Jehovah, Jehovah! God, merci-"ful and gracious, who forgiveth iniquity and trans-"gression and sin."

This conclusion is strengthened by the designating expression, " the Son of man upon earth :" which is the fair position of the clauses, and seems intended to point out our Lord's humbled condition, as distin-guished from his preexistent state, and from his subse-

---

[24] See Matt. vi. 12, 14 ; xii. 31, 32. Mark iii. 28 ; iv. 12 ; xi. 25, 26. Luke xii. 10. James v. 15 ; where the disease and the sin are clearly distinguished. 1 John i. 9 ; ii. 12. And, for (ἡ ἄφεσις τῶν ἁμαρτιῶν) " the forgiveness of the sins ;" Matt. xxvi. 28. Luke i. 77. Acts ii. 38 ; v. 31 ; x. 43 ; xiii. 38 ; xxvi. 18, Eph. i. 7. Heb. ix. 22 ; x. 18.

[25] Luke vii. 47.

quent glory. "The Son of man, upon earth," that is,
the Messiah in his assumed state and his veiled glory,
is not less Divine in the exercises of his power and
grace, than under the brightest manifestation of his
eternal attributes.

In the sequel of the narrative we read, " The mul-
" titudes, beholding [this,] were amazed, and gave
" glory to God, who had given such power [or
" authority] to men." This fact does not, I humbly
think, preclude our reasonings upon the whole circumstance. It expresses the feeling of the bystanders.
It cannot be supposed that they knew any thing of
Jesus, beyond the visible appearance; or that they at
all recognised him as the Messiah. Their astonishment, therefore, was well-grounded; and, in the more
matured state of the gospel dispensation, it would
have been met by the declaration, that peace was
made between the righteous government of God and
the sinful race of man, by the Messiah, as Lord of all,
and through the blood of his cross; that the eternal
life, which he had power and authority to give, included
deliverance from sin and the remission of its penalties;
and that, while this prerogative was, by the wise
decree and covenant of the Divine Father, conferred
upon the Mediator, his capacity to receive and his
competency to exercise it arose from his being the
Son of the Father in truth and love, to whom the
ascription would rightfully be made, " Unto Him who
" hath loved us and washed us from our sins in his
" own blood, be the glory and the power."[26]

IV. It is the constant declaration of the Christian
Scriptures, that the resurrection of the Lord Jesus

[26] Acts x. 36. John x. 28. Col. i. 20, 21. 2 John iv. Rev. i. 5.

from the dead was effected by "the glory of the
"Father," by "the exceeding greatness of his mighty
"power:—God raised him from the dead." But we
find Christ attributing this same work to HIMSELF.
"Destroy this temple, and in three days I will raise
"it again.—He spake concerning the temple of his
"body."[27] The Calm Inquirer contends that, because
"the resurrection of Jesus is uniformly ascribed in
the sacred writings to God—*therefore* our Lord's
expression is to be understood figuratively; *not that
he would* raise himself, but that he would be raised by
God."[28] To this remark we reply, first, that it gives
the contradiction direct to our Lord's own words,
which affirm that *he would* raise himself: and next,
that we do not admit any force in the argument
employed; for the belief, that the Divine Nature of
the Son raised from the state of death the human body
which he had assumed, is not in any opposition with
the truth that God did so raise him. Those who hold
the former hold also the latter, and they regard them
as two modes of expression of the same fact. They
conceive, that all acts of the Divine perfections, considered in themselves and as distinguished from the
economical arrangement of the method of redemption, are properly predicable of the Divine Nature
absolutely; or respectively and equally of the Father,
or the Son, or the Holy Spirit. Thus, from the same
premises as the Inquirer's, they draw the contrary
conclusion, and believe that "what things the Father
"doeth, the same doeth the Son in like manner;" and
that HE "and the Father are ONE" in nature, perfections, and divine operations.

[27] John ii. 19, 21.   [28] Page 173.

· " On this account the Father loveth me, that I lay
" down my life, yet so that I may take it again.   No
" one forceth it from me, but I lay it down of myself;
" I have power to lay it down, and I have power to
" take it again.   This commission I have received
" from my Father."[29]

· It is immaterial whether ἐξουσία here be rendered
power or *authority :* for the authority to do an act
implies a sufficient ability, either inherent or communicated, in the agent, for the performance of it.[30]
It is also obvious that the commission or commandment of the Father refers, not only to the resuming of
life, but to *the whole* transaction, the laying down and
the receiving again : and this is a repetition of the
fundamental doctrine of Christianity, that " all things
" are OF the Father, and THROUGH" the Son ;—that
" God so loved the world, that *he gave* his Only-
" begotten Son—and *sent* him into the world, that
" the world through him might be saved."[31]

---

[29] John x. 17, 18.   The reason for adhering to the Common Version, in rendering λαβεῖν differently in the two parts of the paragraph, will appear from the remarks.—" Hoc ἵνα non est τελικὸν
sed, ut sæpe, ἐκβατικόν."   Grotius.——'Εντολὴ, *commission*, as the
word sometimes signifies ; answering, says Rosenmüller, to the
German *Auftrag.*   Michaelis renders it *Vorschrift*, prescription or ·
rule of conduct.   Seiler, Stolz, Van Ess, and Scholz have *Auftrag*,
commission.

[30] See p. 211 of this volume.   Schleusner puts this passage under
his second signification of the word : " *Libertas agendi*, quæ et
Latinis *potestas* dicitur."   Grotius gives the preference to *potentia*.
Michaelis, Seiler, Stolz, Van Ess, and De Wette, have *Macht*, power,
inherent might.   Scholz has *Vollmacht*, authorization.   Seiler observes, that " Jesus here describes the dignity of his person—that he
is Lord of his own life :——the Lord over life and death!" *Gr. Bibl.
Erb. Buch ; N. T.* vol. iii. 225.

[31] 1 Cor. viii. 6.   John iii. 16, 17.

The manifest point of our Lord's argument is the spontaneity of the act which he performs in obedience to the Father's will, and for which the Father loves him. This spontaneity cannot but imply *ability*; and both are applied, by the terms of the passage, equally to the two parts of the entire transaction. If our Lord's laying down his human life was *his own* act; it is impossible, without the most unfair and arbitrary resistance to the meaning of words and the scope of argument, not to admit that the resumption of that life was *his own* act likewise.

Mr. B. supposed that a different construction is made out from the use of the verb, (ἵνα λάβω, ἐξουσίαν λαβεῖν,) which he considered as signifying a merely passive *reception*; as if our Lord had said, ' I have authority to lay down my life, and I have the same authority to receive it, when it shall be again given to me by my Heavenly Father.'

But was not this sacrificing sense to system; and one part of a system to the exigencies of another part?—Mr. B. held that consciousness, and even intellectual existence, ceases with animal life. What idea then can we form of *authority*, in a passive and unconscious mass of matter, to receive an act of Omnipotence? Authority can reside only where there is intelligence and volition. If his principles of interpretation were just, we might say that the universe had authority to be created; and that the bodies of all mankind, after the processes of dissolution and decomposition have gone on for ages, will have authority to be raised from the dead!

He also says, " The word is by no means necessarily taken in an active sense;" and he quotes

Schleusner most partially, omitting much that would
have discountenanced his interpretation. The truth
is, and Schleusner's whole article is in perfect accordance with it, that the word properly signifies such
taking or *laying hold of*, as implies active power in
the subject : and that instances in which it denotes a
merely passive reception belong to the remoter and
less proper applications.[31] Such expressions as the
following are exemplifications of the native meaning
of the word : " We have taken nothing : he took the
" seed : she took the leaven : he took the loaves : to
" take thy coat : they who take the sword : he who
" taketh not his cross : that no one take thy crown :
" receive him not into your house :"[33] and many such
phrases, familiar to every one who is but moderately
skilled in the language, either generally or according
to the Hellenistic usage.

The Inquirer appears, however, to incline most
to a wayward notion of Grotius, that the passage does
not refer at all to the death and resurrection of Jesus
Christ, but to his frequently exposing his life to danger from the fury of his enemies, and his miraculously
preserving himself. Of this gloss it seems quite sufficient to say, that it is plainly confuted by the scope
and design of the passage ; which so evidently is the
salvation of mankind, both Jews and Gentiles, by
Christ's " laying down his life FOR them." That
Grotius proposed such an interpretation, is one out of
many proofs of that learned, but sometimes light and

---

[31] E. g. Λαμβάνειν or λαβεῖν ἀρχὴν,—λήθην,—ὑπόμνησιν,—αἰδὼ,
to begin, to forget, to be reminded, to be ashamed.

[33] Luke v. 5. Matt. xiii. 31, 33 ; xiv. 19 ; v. 40 ; xxvi. 52 ;
x. 38. Rev. iii. 11. 2 John 10.

inconsiderate, writer's injudicious propensity to desert
an old path for some novelty of his own, especially if
that novelty appeared in an anti-evangelical garb.
The cruel usage which he received from the dominant
party in his native country, and his unmeasured
hatred of Calvinism, together with a politic suppleness
which seems to have deeply infected his character,
betrayed him into the semblance of homage to almost
every thing, whether Popish or Socinian, which
opposed the great principles of the Reformation. But
on his dying bed, we have reason to believe that his
best feelings revived and he fled to the glorious hope
of the gospel.[34]

[34] This great man, when suffering under feeble health and great
anxiety of mind, was shipwrecked on the coast of Pomerania; then
travelled, in most rainy weather, and in a wretched open car, nearly
200 English miles, to Rostock. There he betook himself to a poor
public-house, and sent for a physician, who conceived some hope
from rest and restoratives; but the next day he saw the tide of his
patient's life fast ebbing. In the evening the Lutheran pastor, John
Quistorp, was sent for; who, on hearing the name, exclaimed,
What! Are you the great Grotius? "I found him" (writes
Quistorp,) "almost at the last agony. Upon my saying, how it
would delight me to see him restored to health, and to enjoy the
pleasure of his conversation: he replied, *If God so please.*—I
exhorted to a suitable preparation for death, the confession of sin,
and the necessity of repentance; and alluded to the publican's
prayer for divine mercy. He rejoined, *I am that publican.* I proceeded to speak of Christ as the Only Saviour: he uttered, *In Christ
alone is all my hope.* I solemnly recited the German prayer beginning" [&c. see below.] " He joined his hands, and followed me in
a low voice. Afterwards I asked if he understood me; he replied,
Yes, well. I went on to recite passages of Scripture usually deemed
suitable for the dying. He said, *I hear your voice, but I can
scarcely understand the words.* He never spoke again; and in a
short time breathed his last, at midnight:"—Aug. 18, 1645;
62 years old. *Præstantium Viror. Epistolæ;* p. 828. Amst. Henr.
Wetstein, 1684.

For the reasons which have been proposed, the only fair and just interpretation of this passage appears to me, to be that which attributes to the Lord the Messiah, an inherent power of relinquishing and resuming at pleasure his human life; a power which, of plain necessity, includes the existence in him of a superior nature, and that nature not less than DIVINE.

V. " If ye loved me, ye would rejoice that I go to " the Father; for my Father is greater than I." [35] This reason for joy seems to be a kind of truism, upon the supposition that the speaker was merely a frail and peccable mortal.   That any human being should, in any circumstances, gravely allege that the Deity is his superior, would be difficult to reconcile with the ideas of wisdom, or modesty, or any becoming sentiment: still less could we suppose such an assertion to come from the best and wisest of teachers, and the

The German clergyman appears to have wanted judgment, and to have talked too much: but the mere facts are deeply affecting. How many of Hugo Grotius's persecutors died in all outward comfort!—But—

The Prayer, or rather Hymn, to which Quistorp refers, is one of Paul Eber's Hymns, (the friend of Luther, and who died in 1569,) and in some of the old Hymn Books in which Germany is happily rich, it is entitled, *Composed for his Children*. It may be found in many of the recent as well as the ancient Collections used in the different Protestant States.   It begins,

> *Herr Jesu Christ, wahr Mensch und Gott!*
> *Der du littst Marter, Angst, und Spott;*

and it proceeds to implore blessings in the last conflict, from him whom it acknowledges as God-man, the Redeemer from sin, the Saviour, and the Judge.   The sentiments are very impressive, and the manner mellifluous and simple; the character of many of those Hymns of the 16th century, as it is of much of our English poetry of the age of Elizabeth.   I cannot attempt any imitation of it in verse, and a prose rendering would be an affront.

[35] John xiv. 28.

most exemplary of all mankind for meekness of temper
and propriety of judgment. This expression of our
Lord evidently has its ground of propriety in the fact,
that to him belonged some properties or attributes of so
eminent a kind, and which placed him in such a relation
to the Deity, that it was no superfluous thing for him
to say, " My Father is greater than I." Now he had
just before said, " He that hath seen me hath seen the
" Father :—believest thou not that I am in the Father
" and the Father in me ?"[36] Yes, he who had made
such an astonishing claim, stood before his disciples in
circumstances which they had soon to perceive were
of the most humiliating and distressing character ; and
how could these extremes be reconciled ? — What
could be so properly the reconciling sentiment as the
grand fact, the basis of all the hope and happiness of
man, that he stood in the middle place between a
guilty world and the Majesty of heaven ; " the one
" Mediator between God and men, a man, Christ
" Jesus." [37] The disciples were about to see him
thrown into the deepest agonies of suffering. Yet
those sufferings were the necessary path to his exaltation ; he was, in his capacity of " Captain," Leader,
Obtainer and Author, " of salvation, to be made
" perfect through sufferings." The termination of
those sufferings was to be in his exaltation " above all
" heavens, that he might fill all things." Had his
disciples rightly understood these things, had they
" loved" their Master with more of a spiritual and
elevated affection, they would have exulted in the

[36] John xiv. 9, 10.
[37] The absence of the article appears to justify this rendering,
according to Lachmann's punctuation.

prospect of his departure to a state in which he could
never be again assailed by pain, sorrow, and death :
in this happy issue all the followers of Christ have an
interest : their salvation is bound up in his triumphant
mediatorship : and the guarantee of this result lies in
the supremacy of the Divine Father as the Head of
the mediatorial covenant.   The sentiment is the same
that was afterwards expressed, when our Lord said,
" I ascend to my Father and your Father, my God
" and your God."   The mediatorial exaltation of
Jesus Christ is every where in the New Testament
attributed to the Father ; as, for example, when it is
said, after a description of his humiliation, " Where-
" fore God hath highly exalted him, and hath given
" him a name which is above every name." [18]

VI. The Lord Jesus uniformly represented himself
as performing all his acts for the instruction and salvation of men, in the most perfect subserviency to the
will of his Father and dependence upon him : and
this fact he stated, in a variety of expression and on
different occasions, so as to manifest an anxiety to
impress it deeply on his followers.   " I have not
" spoken of myself: but the Father who sent me, he
" gave me commission, what I should speak, and what
" I should teach.—The word which ye hear is not
" mine, but the Father's who sent me.—My doctrine
" is not mine, but his who sent me.—I do nothing
" from myself, but as my Father hath instructed me,
" I say these things.—That which I have seen with
" my Father, I say.—I can do nothing from myself :
" as I am instructed I judge.—The words which I say
" to you, I say not from myself : and the Father who

[18] Phil. ii. 10.

" abideth in me, he doeth the works."[39]   In these and
similar passages, our Lord declares that, in his plans,
his will, his pursuits, in the whole of his conduct as
the Messiah, there was nothing in any kind or respect
separate, independent, or insulated from the authority
and purpose of the Father ; but that every thing, of
doctrine or action, already performed or hereafter to
be done, has been and will ever be in the most exact
conformity to the commission which he had received
from God : so that his own words and acts were,
in a sense, absorbed in the will and authority of
Him concerning whom he says, " My Father is greater
" than I."[40]

Yet these declarations of functionary subordination
are combined with others which bring to light such
characters as appear inconsistent with any idea of a
total and essential disparity.   This association of characters of supremacy with characters of subordination,
has been before considered.[41]   We add a passage
which connects both :—

" I am the way, and the truth, and the life. No one
" cometh to the Father, but through me. If ye had
" known me, ye would also have known my Father :
" and from this time ye know him, and have beheld
" him. Philip saith to him, Lord, show us the Father;
" and that will complete our wishes. Jesus saith to
" him, So long a time am I among you, and dost thou
" not understand me, O Philip! He who beholdeth

---

[39] John xii. 49. Λαλεῖν is used in the sense of *teaching orally*,
(see *Schleusneri Lex.* signif. 8,) and this rendering is peculiarly proper
when it is joined with another verb of speaking.——xiv. 24 ; vii. 16 ;
viii. 28, 38 ; v. 30 ; xiv. 10.

[40] John xiv. 28.   [41] See pp. 69—81, of this volume.

" me, beholdeth .the Father: how then sayest thou,
" Show us the Father? Believest thou not that I am
" in the Father, and the Father is in me? The words
" which I say to you, I say not from myself; and the
" Father who abideth in me, he doeth the works.
" Believe me, that I am in the Father, and the Father
" in me: but if not, believe me on account of the
" works themselves. Verily, verily, I say to you, he
" who believeth on me, .the works which I do, he
" also shall do; and greater than these shall he do;
" because I go to my Father: and whatsoever ye shall
" ask in my name, that I will do; that the Father
" may be glorified in the Son."[42]—" He [the Spirit of
" truth] will glorify me; for he will take of that
" which is mine and will declare it to you. All
" things which the Father hath are mine: for this
" reason I said, He will take of that which is mine,
" and will declare it to you."[43]

. In these words of our Lord, several important particulars are to be observed.

. 1. He lays it down, or assumes it as known, that
the highest dignity and happiness of man consists in a
holy communion with God. This he represents by
the sensible ideas of approaching to the Father, having
with him a social intimacy, and seeing him. Such
were established expressions in the Hebraized idiom,
to denote *clear* and *convincing knowledge*, especially
when united with *high intellectual enjoyment*.

2. Of such intercourse with the source of all goodness and happiness, Jesus represents HIMSELF to be
the *only medium:* yet not a passive and merely
instrumental medium, but a living, designing, efficient

---

[42] John xiv. 6—14.   [43] John xvi. 14, 15.

Agent; "the Way, the Truth, and the Life;" not only the medium, but the Mediator; not only the path, but the Guide; not only the announcer of holy and immortal life, but the Giver of that blessing by bringing men to reconciliation and moral union with its Heavenly Fountain.

3. He proceeds to represent that *the knowledge of* HIMSELF, which had already been in part communicated to his disciples, and should shortly be so more fully, was in effect *the very knowledge* of the Father of which he had been speaking: "He who hath seen me, " hath seen the Father." Our Lord could not intend natural vision: for, in that sense, "no man hath seen " or can see the King eternal, immortal, invisible ;" and many had enjoyed an ocular, frequent, and intimate sight of Jesus Christ, who remained totally insensible to his glory and the glory of God in him. He must, therefore, have meant such a mental perception of his moral excellency and worth as would lead to correspondent affections towards him : and his words imply that those affections exercised towards himself were, *as really and by the very act*, exercised towards God. Thus our Lord bears testimony to the same truth which was afterwards expressed by his inspired servant, as "the enlightening of the know- " ledge of the glory of God in the person of Jesus " Christ," who is "the refulgence of his glory, and " the exact impression of his manner of existence." "

4. He then asserts the same fact in another form, a form which he had used on preceding occasions, and which was peculiarly striking and sublime—*a mutual*

" 2 Cor. iv. 6. Heb. i. 3. See the remarks on these passages in the ensuing volume.

inhabitation of the FATHER and the SON: "I am in
"the Father, and the Father is in me." The reader
is requested to turn to the observations made in a
former Section on the meaning and application of this
phrase." The reference, in the present instance, evidently is to THAT *in Christ* which was an exhibition of
the Father, and an exhibition *so perfect,* that "he who
"had seen him, had seen the Father." But our Lord
does not stop at this point: he goes on to apply the
idea to his works of power, and appeals to those
works as a demonstration of this union and mutual
inhabitation. Thus the *oneness* assumed is shown to
be both that of moral excellencies and that of efficient
operation: in each respect, whosoever had seen or
known the Son had so seen or known the Father;
the doctrine taught, the miracles performed, the spiritual excellence and glory displayed, by the Son, are
identically those of the Father: they are the doctrines,
the works, the glory, of GOD. In a word; the PER-
FECTIONS of the Father are the perfections of the
Son.

5. Hence light is cast upon our Lord's expressions
before adduced: "I speak not from myself; my doc-
"trine is not mine; I do nothing from myself:" as
if he had said, "I do not proceed upon any authority
or power distinct from that of my Father: my plans
and actions are inseparable from his: my doctrine
and works and glory are his, and his are mine: the
union between the Father and the Son is intimate,
perfect, and incapable of dissolution: I and the Father
are ONE, in mind and counsel, and in efficiency of
operation."—It seems a reasonable inference, from

" Pages 89—97 of this volume.

such a singular and perfect oneness of *attributes*, that there is a oneness also of NATURE in the Father and the Son.

6. With these declarations the Saviour connects language which seems to put himself on a level with his disciples, or even on an inferior degree; but a closer examination will correct this surmise. "He "who believeth on me shall do the works which I do "—and greater." It cannot be questioned that the designation, "he who believeth on me," must be taken in a very limited sense; as referring only to that confidence in the power of Christ with which his apostles, and some others of his immediate followers, were endowed, and by which they wrought miracles in his name. The equality, or superiority, of the miracles wrought by the apostles and their coadjutors, cannot refer to their number or to their kind; for, probably in the former respect, and beyond all doubt in the latter, the miracles of the Lord Jesus were far transcendent. The reference must have been to the *effects* produced by the ministry and miracles of the inspired teachers of Christianity, in the extensive conversion of men to truth and holiness ; effects which far exceeded the actual and present success of our Lord's own ministry. Now be it observed what our Lord assigns as *the cause*, which would insure those wondrous effects. It is HIS OWN POWER, exercised in his glorified state: "Because I go to my Father ; and " whatsoever ye shall ask in my name, that I WILL " DO : that the Father may be glorified in the Son." Thus it proves, in the issue, that HE who had withheld, and as it were confined, the manifestations of his power and glory, with regard to the success of his

own labours, was the Cause and Author of those more splendid effects which followed the gospel in the hands of powerless and sinful men. At the same time, all this honour and majesty is laid at the feet of the Eternal Father, " OF WHOM and TO WHOM are all things." The Father is glorified in the Son.

7. In reference to THIS *glory*, Jesus further declares the *equal possession and honour* of both the Father and the Son. " The Spirit of truth shall glorify ME ; " He shall take of that which is mine and shall declare " it unto you ; ALL THINGS that the Father hath are " MINE." Universal terms must be understood according to the nature of the things spoken of. The " all things," therefore, here mentioned, must be those objects which, on being made known to intelligent and virtuous minds, will excite the emotions which the Scriptures imply in the frequent phrase, *giving glory* to God. The Holy Spirit glorifies Christ by the manifestation of *that* in the person, character, and work of Christ which is, in a moral sense, lovely and worthy of being honoured by holy beings. What is THAT in the All-perfect God, which is thus excellent and honourable ?—It is his WHOLE MORAL GREATNESS, the sum of his wise and holy, righteous and benignant attributes, what the Scriptures call HIS GREAT NAME. This it is which makes him the infinitely worthy Object of admiration, love, and all possible homage : —and of this, our Blessed Lord says, " ALL THINGS " which the Father hath are mine."

SUPPLEMENTARY NOTE TO CAPITULE VIII.

Note [A], page 296.

" THE manner in which the Saviour *called* his disciples is altogether peculiar : it was not done by persuasion ; not by unfolding to them his plans ; not by making them parties to his designs ; all this is evident, not only from their mistakes, but also from the frankness with which their mistakes are made known.

" The disciples were called in a manner the most sudden and unexpected ; and their instant and unhesitating compliance with the call, is one of the singularities of the New Dispensation. That they should obey such a call, and obey so promptly, is a wonder of wonders, if their Master possessed only human power and influence.

" The manner in which the Saviour *employed* his disciples is equally singular. They were never used as helps ; were never even consulted, as though their advice was likely to be of service ; never afforded the least aid in what might be termed cases of emergency and difficulty. They moved and acted solely as directed and empowered by their Master. On a few occasions, indeed, as when two of their number wished to call down fire from heaven, and when Peter smote the servant of the high priest, we see the exertion of an authority independent of their Master : yet here it is most evident, that when they acted without Him, they acted wrong. In the developement, the progress, and the completion of the great plan, Christ was the sole mover. His disciples were witnesses, learners, agents ; but not designers, not even coadjutors. They were never treated, never spoken *to* or *of*, as though they had any thing approaching to a parity of power and of influence with their Master. Yet they were in every case as fully disposed, as completely qualified to obey Christ subsequent to their being called by him, as they were prompt in yielding to his call in the first instance.

" When the former Dispensation was introduced, Moses alone was not competent to the work : nay, he avowed reluctance as well as incompetency. Aaron was appointed to assist him ; but Jehovah himself, not Moses, made the appointment : see Exod. iv. 10—16 ; vii. 19, 20. And it is equally interesting to notice, that when Joshua was to take the place of Moses, the appointment was from the Lord; an appointment preceded, as in the former case, by a confession of incompetency on the part of Moses: see Numb. xxvii. 15—23.

" I will not intrude upon your time by any remarks on the contrast between the modes adopted in introducing the two Dispensations. Yet, I may be allowed to say, that as God's accredited messengers held office immediately from himself under the Jewish economy; we may fairly conclude that his accredited messengers under the New Testament, held their office from God ' manifest in the flesh.' "

" Some time ago, in a conversation with a gentleman on the subject of social prayer, my arguments in favour of the duty were met by a declaration to this effect, that Christ, who is our example, always appears to have prayed alone. As my friend has a leaning to Socinianism, I at once felt and urged the fact which he mentioned, as an incidental evidence, of no feeble kind, of the divinity of the Saviour. Finding that he was not prepared to oppose the inference, I have been induced to examine the four gospels with a particular reference to the subject; and the result of that examination is satisfactory in the highest degree.

" There are two classes of texts to be noticed :—the first, includes those in which Christ gives directions to his disciples on the duty of prayer; the second, those which relate to his own practice. Under the first, we may place Matt. vi. 5—15 ; vii. 7—12 ; ix. 38 ; xviii. 19, 20. Mark xi. 24—26 ; xiii. 33. Luke xviii. 1—14. Now, in all these instances the phraseology confines in the strictest manner the directions to the disciples: there is not the least approach to language which would in this duty place the servant on an equality with the Master. The petitions which he commanded them to use are in several cases utterly inappropriate to himself. Indeed, if we attempt to include him, in either the confessions or the supplications which the holiest of men are often constrained to utter, we shall do the greatest violence to the language of Scripture, as well as to our general impressions of his character.

" The second class of passages includes those which relate to the way in which the Lord Jesus was himself accustomed to discharge the duty of prayer. Of these there are many; as Mark i. 35. Matt. xiv. 22, 23 ; and see the whole account of the agony in the garden, Matt. xxvi. 36—46. In all the passages of this class, it will appear strikingly evident that Christ prayed alone ; the disciples were not suffered to unite with him in the exercise. Indeed, this fact could not have been more fully brought out, had the evangelists written with a special reference to it.

"There are three texts—Luke iii. 21 ; ix. 29. John xii. 28 ;—in which Christ offered up short petitions in the presence of other persons; but in each case he was answered by a voice from heaven : as though, for an important purpose, he had made a distinct appeal to heaven, which was followed by the appropriate response. The only passages which seem to oppose the principle stated in this letter are Luke ix.18, and xi. 1. The latter can scarcely be called an exception to the rule : and when, in the former, it is said, ' his disciples were with ' him,' it may admit of question, whether they were with him in a sense which would invalidate the assertion, that ' he was alone ' praying.' It was not unusual for the Master to withdraw to a little distance from his disciples, in order that he might pray alone. It is further worthy of serious attention, that not a single instance is to be found in which Christ either commanded or entreated his disciples to pray *for* him. He never threw himself in the least degree upon their sympathy.[1]

"But the principle stated here is rendered much more prominent, if we examine such passages as these : Rom. xv. 30. 2 Cor. i. 11. Eph. vi. 18, 19. Col. iv. 2, 3. 1 Thess. v. 25. 2 Thess. iii. 1. Heb. xiii. 18. Nor can the difference between Christ and his apostles in this respect be accounted for by asserting his inspiration, since this is predicable of Paul as well as of his Master. The difficulty rests exclusively on that system which maintains the mere humanity of the Son of God. And until it can be proved that we are on an equality with Christ, his refraining from social prayer cannot be a pattern for us."

[1] " Matt. xxvi. 38—40, cannot be said to contradict this position. The watching might either be to prevent surprise, or that the three disciples might be witnesses of the scene which then took place. And whatever was its object, it is evident that the disciples did not accomplish it."

CAPITULE IX.

IN the survey which we have taken of the doctrines which Jesus, in his personal ministry, taught concerning himself, either directly or in a remote and implied manner; or which, though proceeding from others, he admitted and acquiesced in; we have found the following particulars.

He was described by the voice of inspiration as being the Son of God, the Son of the Most High; in reference to his miraculous birth, and to his royal dignity and power, as the Sovereign of a new, spiritual, heavenly, and everlasting dispensation.[1] He admitted, on the charge of his enemies, that he was the Son of God, in a sense which the highest judicial authorities of his country considered to be a blasphemous arrogating of attributes which were not compatible with the rank of a human being.[2] He declared that a perfect knowledge of his person was possessed by God his Father only, that he himself had the same perfect and exclusive knowledge of the Father, that this knowledge was reciprocal and equal, and that it was above the powers of human comprehension.[3] He affirmed himself to be the Son of God in such a sense as included an equality, or rather an identity, of power with that of the Father; the same dominion

---

[1] Capit. I. Sect. I. II.   [2] Sect. III.   [3] Sect. IV.

in the arrangements of providence ; the same superiority to the laws which were given to regulate the
seasons of human labour ; and the same right of religious homage and obedience.[4] In like manner he
asserted that he was the Son of God so as to be One
with the Father, by a unity of power ; which he
justified and confirmed by declaring a unity of
essence, or of nature and distinguishing properties.[5]

Our Lord, with a remarkable frequency, styled
himself the Son of man ; an appellation equivalent
to that of Messiah, but the least capable of any
injurious construction. This designation he often
combined with the assertion of a preexistent and
heavenly nature : the condescension of which, in
forming a new and interesting relation with mankind,
is represented by the same expression that is used in
the Old Testament to denote peculiar acts or manifestations of the Divine personal interposition. To
this superior nature Jesus appears to refer as a
Witness to the truth of his doctrines, in accession to
the testimony of the Almighty Father.[6]

Our Lord further adverted to the pristine condition
of his superior nature, as a glory which he had with
the Father before the existence of the created universe ; and which was to be displayed to the contemplation of holy intelligences, in the most exalted
manner, when the purposes of his humiliation to
sufferings and death should be accomplished, and
that assumed state of humiliation should cease. He
showed that this glory consisted in the manifestation
of those moral excellencies which form the unrivalled
perfection of the Divine Nature ; and this mani-

[4] Sect. V.   [5] Sect. VI.   [6] Capit. II. Sect. I.—IV.

festation he affirmed of the Father and of himself, reciprocally.[7] He solemnly averred that he had existed ages before his human birth, and before the birth of Abraham.[8]

Christ affirmed that a POWER was given to him, in his mediatorial capacity, which involves the absolute control of the minds, passions, and actions of mankind, and the management of providential agency; qualities clearly incongruous with any nature or capacities merely created: and he declared the exercise of this power to be coeval with the duration of the present dispensation of the divine government.[9]

He spoke of the holding of religious assemblies, as a usage which would be characteristic of his followers, and as an act of religious homage to himself: and he assured his disciples that, on all such occasions, which must of course include all times and places, he would be with them, in such a manner as allows of no rational interpretation except on the admission of his possessing the attributes of omnipresence and the exercise of special grace.[10]

He described himself, with remarkable strength and particularity of expression, as the Being who will effect the stupendous miracle of the universal resurrection, and will determine the everlasting retributions of all human beings; works for which infinite power, knowledge, wisdom, and righteousness are indubitably necessary.[11]

During the period of his debasement and humiliation, he accepted of religious homage, and that of such a kind, and under such circumstances, as cannot

---

[7] Sect. V.   [8] Capit. III.   [9] Capit. IV.
[10] Capit. V.   [11] Capit. VI.

be reconciled with the integrity, humility, and piety of his character, upon the hypothesis of his simple humanity.[12]

He also assumed an absolute jurisdiction in matters of moral obedience; thus claiming that authority over the hearts and consciences of mankind which can belong only to the Supreme Lord, and which involves both a right and power of taking cognizance of the secret sentiments, principles, and feelings of men's souls. He represented himself as the Sovereign Head of the gospel-dispensation, and was uniformly so considered by his apostles; in relation to whom, he conducted himself as one possessed of an immeasurable superiority, and as exercising the most gracious condescension. The miraculous establishment of the gospel-dispensation is attributed to his personal and peculiar power, a power to modify and control the laws of nature: and, in all its arrangements, offices, ordinances, diffusion, and success, he is constantly declared to be the real and ever-present Agent. The exercise of this power manifestly implies a universal dominion over the whole course of natural and moral events; the causes and occasions of human action; the understandings, passions, and motives of men, in every state and of every character; and an efficient determination of what shall be the issue to all the purposes and actions of all mankind. In a perfect analogy with these high prerogatives and powers, the Lord Jesus ascribed to himself a spontaneous power to relinquish his own human life, and to resume it; and the resurrection of his body from the state of death, is expressly imputed to his own will and agency.[13]

[12] Capit. VII.   [13] Capit. VIII.

With all this, Jesus uniformly maintained his entire subordination to the will of God his Father; that all which he performed and suffered, taught and commanded, in the great work of his mission to mankind, he did, for no private or separate purpose, but solely in pursuance of the appointment, and for the accomplishment of the gracious designs, of Him who sent him. Not only did he reject the idea of having any detached interests or objects, but he even affirmed that he had not a detached existence from the existence of the Father. The will and work and glory of the Father, are repeatedly stated to have been identically the will and work and glory of the Son. It is declared that the Father is in the Son, and the Son in the Father; and that He and the Father are ONE.[14]

Such is the purport of the testimony which our Lord Jesus Christ bore concerning himself. Whether these particulars have been fairly deduced from their premises, by legitimate criticism and honest interpretation, has, throughout the preceding disquisitions, been carefully submitted to the judgment of the learned and intelligent reader: and he is again requested to exercise that judgment upon this recapitulation of the results. It has been, also, my honest endeavour to present the grounds of the evidence, at every step, in a manner so detailed and perspicuous, that, I flatter myself, any attentive and serious reader, though not possessed of the assistances to be derived from an acquaintance with the original languages of Scripture, will find it no difficult task to follow each argument, with a clear perception of every thing on which its validity can depend.

[14] Capit. II. III. VI. VIII.

Let me intreat him, then, to meditate anew upon the character, both mental and moral, of the Person by whom all these attributives have been avowed as his own, or plainly assumed, or more or less indirectly implied, or permitted to be ascribed to him by others: and let him consider whether it is possible to believe the soundness and sobriety of mind of that Person, and still more his perfect holiness, humility, and piety, on the supposition of his knowing himself to be nothing more than a mere human creature, however singularly wise and virtuous; a fallible and peccable man: and whether, on the other hand, it is not *necessary*, in order to support the integrity of his character and the truth of his teachings, to believe that he possessed, not the nature of man only, but *another* Nature, superior and preexistent, celestial and really DIVINE.

CHAP. IV.

SECTION I.

THE HUMAN NATURE, WITH ALL ITS INNOCENT PROPERTIES,
AFFIRMED OF JESUS CHRIST.

Jesus Christ really and properly a man.—The progress of his intellectual and
moral excellence.—His passions and susceptibilities.—His conduct under sufferings.—His moral qualities.—The causes, means, and extent of his intellectual
acquirements.—The limitation of his knowledge.—Inquiry into the meaning
of Mark xiii. 32.—The perfection of our Lord's moral character vindicated,
against insinuations.—Investigation of the causes and peculiar nature of the
Redeemer's sufferings.—I. Designs of those sufferings.—1. To succour the
human race.—2. To deliver from the terror of death;—not physical dissolution,—but spiritual and eternal ruin.—3. To propitiate for sin.—4. Sympathy
with suffering Christians. — 5. The efficiency of salvation.—II. Reasons of
those sufferings. — III. Their unparalleled kind. — Our Lord's agonies and
prayers consistent with his moral perfection and his union with the Divine
Nature.

A BEING who acts and speaks and is addressed as a
man, and who exhibits all the properties which distinguish man from other beings, must be a *real* MAN.
To such a being, possessing the nature and the essential attributes of a man, it is correct to ascribe a
proper humanity; even if it should be the fact that, by
the possession of a different class of properties which
are known to be the attributes of another nature, this
other nature should appear to be preternaturally conjoined with that being.

Therefore, a believer in the proper Deity of the Messiah, has no obstruction, on that account, to an equal assurance of the Messiah's proper humanity. He regards it as a case absolutely of its own kind, having no known analogy to any other fact or existence in the universe, and which is to be judged of solely from its own evidence, *competent testimony*.

By himself, by his friends and disciples, by his enemies and persecutors, Jesus Christ was spoken of as a proper human being.

His childhood was adorned with filial affections and the discharge of filial duty. " He went down with " his parents, and was subject to them."[1] And on his cross he showed the same dutiful tenderness.

His intellectual powers, like those of other children, were progressive: and so was the developement of his moral excellencies. " The child grew and was " strengthened in spirit, being filled with wisdom; " and the favour of God was upon him :—he advanced " in wisdom, and in stature, and in favour with God " and men."[2]

In his earliest years, he embraced with eagerness the means of improvement. " They found him in " the temple, sitting in the midst of the teachers, both " listening to them and inquiring of them: and all " who heard him were astonished at his understanding " and his replies."[3] It cannot, with reason, be doubted that he availed himself of whatever opportunities besides were placed within his reach, in his obscure and lowly station.

He had large experience of human suffering: and he was, in the strongest manner, both by insidious art

[1] Luke ii. 51.   [2] Luke ii. 40, 52.   [3] Luke ii. 46, 47.

and by violence, solicited to moral evil: but he was
tempted in vain. His lot was one of severe labour,
poverty, weariness, hunger and thirst. He affected
no austerity of manners, nor did he enjoin it upon his
followers. While he mingled in the common sociability
and the innocent festivities of life, he sustained
a weight of inward anguish which no mortal could
know: he was a man of sorrows, and acquainted with
grief. He experienced disappointment of expectation,
the pain of ungrateful and injurious requital, the
attachments and the griefs of friendship, sorrow for
the miseries and still more for the sins of men, a virtuous
indignation at unprincipled and hardened
impiety, and the most generous pity towards his
malignant enemies.[4]

He looked forwards to the accumulation of sufferings
which he knew would attend his last hours, with
feelings on the rack of agony, with a heart "exceed-
" ingly sorrowful even unto death;" but with a meek
and resigned resolution, a tender and trembling constancy,
unspeakably superior in moral grandeur to the
stern bravery of the proudest hero. "I have a bap-
" tism to be baptized with: and how am I held in
" anguish till it be accomplished!—Now is my soul
" distressed: and what shall I say?—Father, save me
" from this hour!—But for this cause came I to this
" hour.—Father, glorify thy name!"[5] Through his
whole life he was devoted to prayer: and when his

---

[4] John iv. 6. Matt. iv. 6; xi. 19. John ii. 1—10. Isaiah
liii. 3. Matt. xxi. 18, 19; xi. 20. John xi. 35, 36. Mark iii. 5.
Matt. xxiii. 37. Luke xix. 41; xxiii. 34.

[5] Luke xii. 50. Συνέχομαι, "vehementer angor;" Schleusn.
John xii. 27.

awful hour was come, " he was in an agony and
" prayed more earnestly, and his sweat was as drops
" of blood falling upon the ground."⁶   He was
" sorrowful, and overwhelmed with anguish, and dis-
" tressed to the utmost."⁷   " He fell upon his face,
" and prayed, and said, My Father, if it be possible,
" let this cup pass from me !   Nevertheless, not as I
" will but as thou willest."⁸   In his last hours, with a
bitterness of soul more excruciating than any bodily
sufferings, he felt as if deserted by his God and
Father ; while yet he promised heaven to a penitent
fellow-sufferer, and died in an act of devotional confidence, triumphing that his work was FINISHED.
Thus he died: but he rose again, that he might be
Lord of both the dead and the living ; and he ascended to his Father and our Father, his God and
our God.

This was " the man Christ Jesus ; a man demon-
" strated from God by miracles and prodigies and
" signs which God did by him :—a man ordained by
" God to be the Judge of the living and the dead."⁹

It is delightful to dwell on the character of this
unrivalled MAN: not only because in no other, since
the foundation of the world, has the intellectual and
moral perfection of our nature been exhibited, but
because the contemplation of such excellence refreshes
and elevates the mind, and encourages to the beneficial effort of imitation.

⁶ Luke xxii. 44.
⁷ — λυπεῖσθαι — ἐκθαμβεῖσθαι, — ἀδημονεῖν.   Matt. xxvi. 37.
Mark xiv. 33.
⁸ Matt. xxvi. 39.
⁹ "Ανθρωπος, 1 Tim. ii. 5.   'Ανὴρ, Acts ii. 22 ; xvii. 31 ; xiii. 38.

He "always did the things which pleased" his
heavenly Father. Love, zeal, purity, a perfect acquiescence in the divine will on every occasion, and
the most exalted habits of devotion, had their full
place and exercise in his mind. The most refined
generosity, but without affectation or display; mild-
ness, lowliness, tenderness, fidelity, candour, a delicate
respect for the feelings as well as the rights and
interests of others, prudence, discriminating sagacity,
the soundest wisdom, and the noblest fortitude, shone
from this Sun of righteousness with a lustre that
never was impaired.

His intellectual attainments were partly acquired,
as we have before remarked, by diligence in the use
of proper means; but principally by that transcendent
communication of spiritual influences which the Father
conferred upon him: for "God gave the Spirit, not
" by measure," unto him. " On him rested the Spirit
" of the Lord, the Spirit of wisdom and understand-
" ing, the Spirit of counsel and might, the Spirit of
" knowledge and of the fear of the Lord; and made
" him of quick understanding in the fear of the
" Lord." [10]

But, however extensive, profound, and exact his
knowledge was, we cannot regard it as unlimited: for
no *infinite* attribute can be possessed by a finite
nature. The union of the Divine nature and the
human, in the person of the Messiah, does not involve
the communication of omniscience to his human mind,
any more than of omnipresence, unchangeableness, or
eternity. [11]   All the knowledge which his offices re-

---

[10] John iii. 34.   Isaiah xi. 2, 3.
[11] "This union, the ancient church affirmed to be made ἀτρέπτως,

quired, or to the use of which his commission extended, he unquestionably enjoyed : but, beyond this sphere, there is an indefinite field for the acquisition of new knowledge, as well as of higher felicity, even in his glorified state. It seems to me a most reasonable opinion, that the communication of supernatural knowledge to the human mind of Jesus Christ, was made as circumstances and occasions were seen by Divine wisdom to require. Upon this principle, I cannot

without any change in the person of the Son of God, which the Divine Nature is not subject unto; *ἀδιαιρέτως*, with a distinction of natures, but *without any division* of them by separate subsistence ; *ἀσυγχύτως*, *without mixture* or confusion ; *ἀχωρίστως, without separation* or distance ; and *οὐσιωδῶς, substantially*, because it was of two substances or essences in the same person, in opposition to all accidental union, as ‘ the fulness of the Godhead dwelt in him bodily.’—Each nature doth preserve its own natural, essential properties, entirely unto and in itself; without mixture, without composition or confusion, without such a real communication of the one unto the other as that the one should become the subject of the properties of the other. The Deity in the abstract is not made the humanity ; nor, on the contrary [is the humanity made the Deity.] The Divine Nature is not made temporary, finite, limited, subject to passion [*i. e.* suffering] or alteration, by this union ; nor is the human nature rendered immense, infinite, omnipotent. Unless this be granted, there will not be two natures in Christ, a divine and a human ; nor indeed either of them ; but somewhat else, composed of both." *Owen on the Glorious Mystery of the Person of Christ*, chap. xviii. 1, 3. " This nature of the man Christ Jesus is filled with all the divine graces and perfections whereof a limited created nature is capable. It is not deified ; it is not made a god ; it doth not in heaven coalesce into one nature with the divine, by a composition of them ; it hath not any essential property of the Deity communicated unto it, so as subjectively to reside in it ; it is not made omniscient, omnipresent, omnipotent. But it is exalted in a fulness of all divine perfection, ineffably above the glory of angels and men. It is incomprehensibly nearer to God than they all : it hath communications from God, in glorious light, love, and power, ineffably above them all. But it is still a creature." Id. *On the Glory of Christ*, Part I. ch. vii. p. 3.

but regard as rational and satisfactory the common
interpretation of our Lord's declaration, that *he did
not know* the precise time when his prediction of the
final ruin of the Jewish polity would be fulfilled.
" Concerning that day, or hour, no one knoweth;
" neither the angels who are in heaven, NOR THE SON:
" but only the Father."[12]   As, in various passages
which have been before considered, we have found
predicates affirmed of the Messiah under the title of
the Son of man, which can belong only to his superior
nature : can it be deemed extraordinary, if here we
find that asserted of him as "the Son," whether we
understand the appellation to be Son of man or Son
of God, which can attach only to his dependent and
limited capacity?

This interpretation, however, has been often treated
by Unitarians with high scorn, as paltry and evasive;
and as imputing to the Blessed Jesus a "gross and
criminal equivocation."[13]   Against such a charge we
can reply only by declaring that we do not perceive
it to be applicable, and by appealing to the good sense
and argumentative justice of the considerate reader.

Mr. Emlyn has been lauded for his invention of a
case, which those who have adopted or gone beyond
his sentiments have thought a happy contrivance for
the exposure of this disliked interpretation.[14]   But it

---

[12] Mark xiii. 32.   [13] *Calm Inq.* p. 201.

[14] " With much good sense Mr. Emlyn remarks ' that to suppose
Christ knows the day of judgment with his divine nature while he is
ignorant of it in his human nature, is charging him with an equivocation similar to that of a person who, conversing with another with
one eye shut and the other open, and being asked whether he saw
him, should answer, that he saw him not; meaning, with the eye
that was shut; though he still saw him well enough with the eye

seems a little surprising that so many penetrating men
and acute reasoners should have been pleased with
this piece of flippancy, and should not have stopped to
inquire whether there is any justice in the representation. To my apprehension, I must confess,
there appears an entire want of such analogy as
would justify the argument. To make it hold, it
must be supposed that the doctrine of the Deity of
the Messiah involves a belief that the properties of
the Divine Nature are necessarily and of course communicated to the human nature; a belief which,
though it has been contended for in the Roman
Catholic and the Lutheran communions, few in the
Reformed Churches will, I apprehend, feel themselves
at all disposed to vindicate. We readily avow that
we pretend not to know in what manner the Divine
and human natures, which we attribute to the Messiah,
are united in his sacred person. We believe that, in
this respect especially, "his name is WONDERFUL ;"
and that "no one knoweth the Son, except the
" Father." The Scriptures appear to us, on the one
hand, to teach the existence of such a union as pro-
duces a personal oneness ; and, on the other, to
exclude the notion of transmutation, or confusion, or
any kind of metamorphosis, of the essential properties
of either nature with respect to the other. It follows
that, whatever communication of supernatural qualities, powers, or enjoyments, was made by the indwelling Divinity[15] to "the man Christ Jesus," it was
made in various degrees and on successive occasions,

that was open. A miserable evasion, which would not save him from
the reproach of being a liar and a deceiver.' *Emlyn's Tracts*, p. 18."
Calm Inq. p. 201.   [15] Col. ii. 9.

as the Divine wisdom judged fit: and this necessary
limitation would apply to "times or seasons which the
" Father has put in his own power,"[16] as much as to
any other conceivable class of objects.

Where, then, is the analogy between this representation, and Mr. Emlyn's case of a man denying the
impression of his own senses and the use of his voluntary powers?

Another important particular in the human character of our Lord is his MORAL PERFECTION.   To this
fact the Scriptures bear an unequivocal testimony.
" The HOLY offspring shall be called the Son of God.
" I do always the things which please him.   The
" prince of the world cometh, and in me he hath
" nothing.   He was manifested that he might take
" away our sins, and sin is not in him.   He did no
" sin, neither was guile found in his mouth.   He was
" holy, harmless, undefiled, separated from sinners;
" the Holy and Righteous."[17]

Yet, in defiance of these declarations, Dr. Priestley
ventured to call into question, if not plainly to deny,
the absolute moral perfection of Jesus; and he lets
us into the secret of his motive for this daring, a
motive worthy of being seriously pondered.   It was
no other than that, if this were admitted, the simple
humanity of Christ could not be maintained.[18]

---

[16] Acts i. 7.

[17] Luke i. 35. John viii. 29 ; xiv. 30. 1 John iii. 5. 1 Pet. ii. 22.
Heb. vii. 26.   Acts iii. 14.

[18] Dr. Priestley contends that Christ could not have been exempted from all the moral infirmities of human nature ; and on the
contrary supposition, that is, that Christ was actually sinless, or
possessed of " absolute perfection," he goes on to say ; " If he was
so perfect, it is *impossible not to conclude* that, notwithstanding his

Mr. Belsham also has remarked that "the moral character of Christ, through the whole course of his public ministry, as recorded by the evangelists, is pure and unimpeachable in every particular;" and that our Lord's conduct was distinguished by "uniform and consummate wisdom, propriety, and rectitude." But with these encomiums he thought proper to connect a most extraordinary and offensive passage.[19]—Alas! What could move him to so gratuitous a display of irreligious scepticism? On what ground of probability and justice did he rest his insinuation? Did he wish us to surmise that the private life of Jesus was "less pure and unimpeachable" than his *public* conduct? Or did he choose to show how cheap he held the testimony of prophets and apostles? Or was this an affectation of virtue, so jealous that it was apprehensive, forsooth, of finding "errors and failings" in Him who is "the Wisdom and the Power of God?"—Or was it only the wantonness of unbelief, "blaspheming "with regard to things of which it is ignorant,—sport-"ing itself with its own deceivings?"[20]—

From whatever perversion of mind or feeling this unhappy paragraph flowed, I will borrow the martyr's petition, "LORD, LAY NOT THIS SIN TO HIS CHARGE!"[21]

appearance 'in the fashion of a man,' he was, in reality, something more than man." *Theol. Repository*, vol. iv. p. 449.

[19] "Whether this perfection of character in public life, combined with the general declarations of his freedom from sin, establish, or were intended to establish, the fact, that Jesus through the whole course of his private life was completely exempt from all the errors and failings of human nature, is a question of no great intrinsic moment, and concerning which we have no sufficient data to lead to a satisfactory conclusion." *Calm Inq.* p. 190.

[20] See 2 Pet. ii. 1, 2, 12, (ἐν οἷς ἀγνοοῦσι βλασφημοῦντες,) 13.

[21] I do not suppress this record of past feeling and prayer, as it was twice published before the death of Mr. Belsham.

An anonymous Unitarian writer has advanced
farther, and has endeavoured to fix on the Blessed
Jesus the charge of, at least, *moral feebleness*, in relation to the two remarkable seasons of his extreme
suffering.[22]

In this daring attempt, our Lord is not only represented as making a mistaken assumption, and uttering
words without any definite meaning, but is taxed with
inconsistency and impatience, which is undoubtedly
a sinful state of mind; for, though the accuser is

[22] "' My God, my God! Why hast thou forsaken me?' Matt.
xxvii. 46.—Was it quite consistent——in the mouth of Jesus? He
possessed a knowledge of his impending fate, and even declared that
to the fulfilment of his mission such a consummation was indispensable; which therefore could be no indication that his God and
Father had forsaken him. Whatever inconsistency, however, may
be imputed to this invocation, it is a slight, and if the expression be
allowable, a venial one, upon the hypothesis of the simple humanity
of the sufferer. That he was not unappalled by the sufferings he
contemplated, is evident from his prayer that, if possible, the cup
might pass from him. Though prepared to suffer and to die, it is no
violent presumption that his actual sufferings might be more acute
than he had anticipated : and, in a paroxysm of agony, this perhaps
convulsive expostulation might break from him without any definite
meaning.——He had submitted to all that it behoved him to endure,
but did not sustain the extremity of suffering without the expression
of such a sense of it as was natural to a simply human being; and,
in words neither weighed nor resembling any language that he had
ever used, or was capable of using, in a state of mental composure.
There is nothing, therefore, staggering in the inconsistency which
has been suggested. But another far more important consideration
is behind :—what will the orthodox say to it? Will they contend it
to be possible that 'God made man,' or that a man in any pro-
foundly mystical identity with God, could have ejaculated such a
sentence? That Jesus, in his blended character, could thus have
expostulated with himself? That such a preposterous interrogation
could have passed the lips of a being conscious of the Divinity within
him, and that God had neither forsaken, nor could forsake him?"
Monthly Repos. August, 1819, p. 475.

pleased to allow that it was a slight and *venial* inconsistency, it must, from the very term, have needed
forgiveness from God.

Fain would I hope that those persons would have
refrained from taking upon their souls the awful
responsibility of these charges, had they considered, or
been disposed to admit, the scripture testimony concerning the CAUSES and the NATURE of the Redeemer's
sufferings.

" Even the Son of God," says Mr. Locke, " whilst
clothed in flesh, was subject to all the frailties and inconveniences of human nature, sin excepted."[23]   The
chief passages of the New Testament which refer to
this subject, are the following :—" God, having sent
" his own Son in the likeness of sinful flesh," that is,
of the nature which has fallen into sin.[24]—" Since,

[23] *Ess. Hum. Und.* Book III. ch. ix. sect. 23.

[24] Rom. viii. 3. This paraphrase of the concluding words appears
to me to be no more than the meaning of the Hebraized and
elliptical expression, ἐν ὁμοιώματι σαρκὸς ἀμαρτίας.   Grotius's annotation on the clause is, " That is, that he might be treated as sinners
[*nocentes*] are : Isaiah liii. 12.   Mark xv. 28.   Phil. ii. 8."   Koppe
considers it as an abbreviated form for what would run thus at length :
ἐν σώματι ὁμοίῳ τῷ τῶν λοίπων ἀνθρώπων ἀμαρτώλων σώματι, " in
a body like to the body of the rest of men who are sinners."   Rosenmüller adopts the same in substance.   Morus, to whom the German
critics deservedly pay the highest honour for his erudition, sagacity,
and judgment, makes this remark :—" This expression is, I confess,
somewhat difficult [*paullò durius*]; and we should not have understood it, did we not possess the history of Jesus Christ and other
passages of the New Testament, which informs us that the Son of
God was sent, clothed in a human body, and therefore so far like
the rest of men, having a body such as ours, and which we make
the instrument of sin."   *Prælect. in Ep. ad Rom.* p. 28. Leipz. 1794.

Among the figurative acceptations of the term *flesh* in the New
Testament, and particularly in the use of the apostle Paul, these
are the principal :—*Human nature with an especial reference to its
material constitution*, e. g. 1 Tim. iii. 16. 1 John iv. 2. (Rom. viii.

" then, infants are partakers in common [κεκοινώνηκε]
" of flesh and blood, he himself also in like manner
" partook of the same, that through means of death
" he might depose him who holdeth the dominion of
" death, that is the devil: and might deliver those
" who in fear of death were, through the whole of
" life, subjects of bondage. For truly it is not the
" angels whom he succoureth, but he succoureth the
" posterity of Abraham. Whence it was necessary
" that he should be made like to his brethren in
" all respects, that he might become a merciful and
" faithful high-priest, in the things which relate to God,
" in order to propitiate for the sins of the people.
" For in that he hath suffered being himself tempted,
" he is able to relieve those who are tempted."[25]
" For we have not a high-priest who is incapable of
" sympathizing with our weaknesses, but one who
" has been tempted, in such a manner as we are, in
" all respects except sin."[26]   " Who, in the days of
" his own flesh," *i. e.* his mortal and suffering nature,
" having offered prayers and supplications, with vehe-
" ment crying and tears, to Him who was able to
" save him from death, and being delivered from his
" anguish (for indeed though he was the Son, he
" learned, from the sufferings that he endured, what
" was the obedience)" which he had undertaken,
" and being completed," *i. e.* having finished his immense undertaking for the redemption of sinners,

3. ἐν τῇ σαρκὶ, *an einer menschennatur :* Koppe.)—*Human nature
as frail and mortal ;* Col. i. 22. 1 Cor. xv. 50——and, which is
almost peculiar to St. Paul, *Human nature as depraved and sinful ;*
Rom. vii. 18, &c. Vid. *Koppe, Excursus de Sensu vocis Σαρκὸς
in N. T.* ad calcem *Ep. ad Gal.* Götting. 1791.

        [25] Heb. ii. 14—18.   [26] Heb. iv. 15.

" he became to all who obey him the Author of
" eternal salvation."[27]

These passages supply most important information,
concerning the Objects or Ends of the Redeemer's
sufferings; an attention to which may perhaps enable
us to deduce some precise conclusions concerning
their Reasons, their peculiar Character, and, as apparent in the whole train of considerations, their *Consistency* with the doctrine of a superior, impassible,
and divine Nature in the constitution of his Person.

I. The following appear to be clearly stated as the
designed ENDS of the Redeemer's sufferings.

i. To *succour*, or to bring help and deliverance,[28]
to the human race expressly, as distinguished from
any superior order of creatures. The reason of the
apostle's specifying only " the posterity of Abraham,"
was, in all probability, because he was addressing
Hebrews, to whom the promises and advent of the
Messiah primarily belonged ; but the argument plainly
intends mankind generally.

ii. To *deliver* his faithful followers from a state
which is described as a most painful and terrific
bondage. It is necessary to ascertain what the sacred
writer means by the *death* to which this subjection
refers. For this purpose, the following considerations
are proposed to the reader's serious attention.

1. The most pure and holy Christians are, no more
than the rest of mankind, exempted from subjection

[27] Heb. v. 7—9. " Εἰσακούειν is used to signify σώζειν in 2 Chron.
xviii. 31. Ps. xxii. 24. LXX. 'Από for ἐκ."   *Rosenm. in loc.* See
also Schleusner on Εὐλάβεια and Εἰσακούω. *To hear* is frequently in
the Old Testament used to denote the granting of deliverance in
answer to prayer.

[28] See Note [A], at the end of this Section.

to corporal death; nor from any of the distressing and often excruciating circumstances, which frequently precede and accompany the awful article of dying. Neither does the existence and even the powerful influence of genuine piety, always, and as a matter of necessary consequence, free its possessors from the natural and innocent dread of death which is common to all animated nature. The different degrees in which this principle operates in particular persons is found to depend upon the various susceptibility of the nervous system, upon education and habits, and upon other constitutional and accessory causes; more than on the presence or the absence, the strength or the weakness, of the religious principle. The dread of dying has been sometimes very conspicuous in persons who were conscious, on the most just grounds, of no distressful apprehensions of what would come after death: and many very wicked men have shown, through their whole lives, and down to the last moment, an astonishing fearlessness and even a strong contempt of death.

2. The death which the apostle speaks of, is by him affirmed to be a state which lies under the *dominion*, force, or power (κράτος) of the fallen spirit, the seducer of men, and the cruel exulter over their moral ruin. To this wicked and wretched creature I can see no grounds for attributing any dominion, power, or agency in the causation of natural death; but, on the contrary, every ground of reason and Scripture supports the belief, that the cessation of animal life takes place, under the sovereign appointment of the Most High, as the immediate and necessary consequence of certain changes in the mechanism

of the body, which cannot but be produced sooner or later. It is true that this law of dissolution "entered "into the world by sin," and that "the serpent who ".beguiled Eve through his subtlety," was the successful tempter to the first human sin : but it by no means follows in the reason of the case, nor is the idea supported by any doctrine of revelation, that the worst enemy of God should thenceforth be invested with "the dominion of death," a prerogative of the most mighty interference with the whole natural and moral government of Him who is the Blessed and Only Potentate, and who "has the keys of death, and of "the unseen world."[29]

For these reasons, and confirmed also by the scope and connexion of the passage, I am induced to think that the apostle here applies the term *death* to the *state of misery* in the world to come; the privation of *life* in its best sense, a sense often occurring in Scripture, that of *a holy and happy existence ;* a condition to which the awful term may well be applied in 'its most aggravated and terrible capacity of signification. This acceptation of the word was in use among the ancient Jews,[30] and it is exemplified in the New Testament.[31] On the admission of this interpretation, it is easy to perceive the propriety of the expression which attributes to the apostate and malignant spirit a dominion over the state of final perdition. It plainly imports his insatiable desire of the ruin of souls; his hunting for victims "as a roaring lion "seeking whom he may devour," tempting to sin in

[29] Rev. i. 18.   [30] See *Wetstein*, on Rev. ii. 11.
[31] John viii. 51 ; xi. 26. Rom. vi. 23. Rev. ii. 11 ; xx. 6, 14; xxi. 8.

order to drag them down to the eternal death; his
preeminence in guilt, and in the misery which grows
from guilt; his superior title to that unutterable and
everlasting punishment which is "prepared for the
"devil and his angels." This view also gives a rational conception of the *fear* and *bondage*, which
cannot but press upon the minds of those who entertain serious reflections on the evil and demerit of sin,
but who have no adequate knowledge of the way of
pardon and deliverance; and it furnishes an intelligible and most consolatory understanding of this
great end of the All-gracious Redeemer's sufferings
and death; namely, to depose the usurper and deliver
his despairing captives.

It may be objected that, in the former part of the
sentence, our Lord is said to effect this deliverance
"by means of death," his own proper dying for the
redemption of men; and that, therefore, it is requisite
to preserve the same sense of the term in the subsequent clauses. To this I reply:—

(1.) That it is not unusual in composition, for the
same word, after it has been introduced in a proper or
ordinary signification, to be resumed in a more
extended sense, or in a sense entirely figurative.[32]

But, (2.) that the figurative acceptation is more
suitable and applicable to this instance of the word

---

[32] See these instances in our Lord's own discourses, Matt. viii. 22;
x. 39; xxvi. 29. John iv. 13, 14; vi. 27. "Vixit, dum vixit,
bene." *Ter. Hecyra*, III. v. "Dum vivimus vivamus." *Adag.*
"Ista culpa Brutorum? Minimè illorum quidem, sed aliorum brutorum, qui se cautos ac sapientes putant; quibus satis fuit lætari,
nonnullis etiam gratulari, nullis permanere." *Ciceron. Ep. ad Att.*
Lib. xiv. ep. 14. This figure was called by the technical rhetoricians, *Antanaclasis.*

also. The manifest design of the passage appears to
me to require, that *the death*, which is here stated to
have been the means of accomplishing the stupendous
purposes of eternal mercy, should be understood, not
of the mere physical death of the Lord Jesus, but of
the whole comprehension of his sufferings for the redemption of the world. The fact of natural death,
the mere ceasing to live, was the smallest part of
those sufferings: it was their termination and relief.
The sorrow which he endured, ineffably transcended
all corporal agony.   It was DEATH IN THE SOUL.
Our moral feelings sin has made slow and torpid : so
that we can form none but very faint conceptions of
the load of distress and horror which pressed on that
soul, whose unsullied innocence and perfection of sensibility were without an equal in all human nature.
He suffered all that a perfectly holy man could suffer:
but the highest intensity of his anguish lay in that
which was mental.   As "the Prince of salvation, he
"was made perfect through sufferings :" and the TOTAL
of those sufferings it seems proper to comprehend in
THE DEATH, by which he spoiled the destroyer, and
delivered the captives.

3. I would reverentially submit, that the death of
Christ, considered merely as an instance of dying,
seems not calculated to answer the purpose here attributed to it ; that of delivering our minds from the
fear of death.   Many of the children of men, sincere,
though weak and sinful servants of Jesus, have met
death, in outward forms more appalling than the
death of the cross, with triumphant joy.   Such deaths
might be appealed to as examples to take away the
fear of dying.   But the death of our Lord Jesus

Christ was not of this kind. It was an example, not of a happy state of mind in the approaches of dissolution, but of one mysteriously and awfully the reverse. It was, therefore, much more calculated to inspire the hearts of guilty mortals with dismay, than, considered as an example, to emancipate them from the terrors of death. Our Lord's own reasoning would bear a most alarming application, to aggravate our fears: " If they do these things in the green tree, what shall " take place in the dry ?" [33]

For these reasons, I conceive that this part of the design laid down in the passages under consideration, is evinced to have been a deliverance, not from the apprehension of physical death, but from the sad forebodings of conscience, the condemnation of God's righteous tribunal, the inevitable retribution of sin, " the second death."

iii. The next of the great Ends stated in these passages, is the offering of a sacrifice *to propitiate for the sins of men*. On this momentous object of the mission of Christ, I shall only recite a very few other testimonies of the divine word, as a specimen of its general doctrine. " Christ hath redeemed us from " the curse of the law, being made a curse for us. " Who himself bore our sins in his own body on the " cross. He hath suffered for us, the just for the " unjust. Him hath God set forth, a propitiation, " through faith by his blood. He, through the Eternal " Spirit, offered himself without spot to God."[34] Thus is it declared, that this great propitiation was to be effected *by suffering*. This was " the obedience "

[33] Luke xxiii. 31.
[34] Gal. iii. 13. 1 Pet. ii. 24 ; iii. 18. Rom. iii. 25. Heb. ix. 14.

which Christ learned by the bitter experience of such sorrows: and thus was he "completed" as the All-sufficient Saviour.

iv. That he might possess a capacity of *sympathizing* with his servants in their afflictions, trials, and difficulties; especially in those mental distresses which are peculiar to tenderness of conscience and fidelity of obedience, under the innumerable oppositions and temptations of the present state. In the eye of Infinite Wisdom, it was needful that the Saviour of men should be one who has the FELLOW-FEELING which no being but a fellow-creature could possibly have: and therefore it was necessary that he should have an actual experience of all the *effects* of sin that could be separated from its actual guilt. " God sent " his own Son in the likeness of sinful flesh."

v. That, as the merited reward of his humiliation and agonies, his expiatory sacrifice, and his gracious sympathies, he might be the *Author* (Αἴτιος,) Cause, or Efficient Producer, of *eternal salvation* to all who obey him. This immensely comprehensive blessing is, in another place, by the same writer, called THE GREAT SALVATION.—Let the serious mind reflect on the nature, malignity, and inveteracy of the evils from which it is a deliverance, and on the unutterable felicity to which it is the introduction; and then let him say what must be the greatness of HIM who is its Cause and Bestower!

" Thus it is written, and thus IT WAS NECESSARY " that the Christ should SUFFER." [35]

II. The review of these designs supplies a corresponding series of moral REASONS why the Saviour of

[35] Luke xxiv. 46.

the world should be, and could not but be, " the man
" of sorrows and acquainted with grief; *stricken*,
" *smitten of God*, and afflicted :" and as the result of
the whole, it appears to the closest attention and the
best judgment that I am able to exercise, that a proposition is brought out to this effect :

That, for the purposes of the Saviour's great work,
it was NECESSARY, and by the wise and holy decree of
the Almighty, it was DETERMINED, that he should have
NO RELIEF or CONSOLATION from the fact of his proxi-
mity to God, or from his consciousness of that fact ;
and that, in so far as that consideration had place, it
should not prevent the full tide of misery from overwhelming his soul, nor be the means of any alleviation
of suffering, or any sense of support under it.

III. From this scripture evidence it is further in-
ferrible, that the sufferings of our Blessed Lord were
strictly *unparalleled* and *peculiar*, not in their degree
only, but in their very *nature* or *kind*.   He felt the
horrors of guilt, though without the slightest tinge of
its criminality.   He sustained the punishment of sin,
though not the shadow of its defilement had ever
touched his spotless mind.   The most vivid and piercing sense of our apostasy, in all its enormity, malignity, and contrariety to God, was omnipotently pressed
into the very heart of a sensibility incomparable, and
a holiness the most exalted· that ever dignified a
dependent nature.   " The Lord laid upon him the
" iniquities of us all." [36]

[36] " He suffered in such a manner as a being perfectly holy could
suffer.   Though, animated by the joy that was set before him, he
endured the cross and despised the shame ; yet there appear to have
been seasons in the hour of his deepest extremity, in which he

I am well aware that these statements will by many be disposed of in a summary manner, with the easy answer of indifference or derision ; but I confidently look for a different attention to them, from those who reverence, and " tremble at, the words of God." To such the appeal is now made, whether, in his exclamations in the garden and on the cross, the Lord Jesus was guilty of an " inconsistency," any dereliction of character, any moral impropriety, however " venial ;" —whether those bitter outcries were not the innocent and holy indications of the reality of his human feelings, and the extremity of his sufferings ;—whether the agitation and agony from which they evidently flowed, was the smallest deviation from the purity and perfection of his character ?

endured the entire absence of divine joy and every kind of comfort or sensible support. What, but a total eclipse of the sun of consolation, could have wrung from him that exceedingly bitter and piercing cry, ' My God ! my God ! why hast thou forsaken me ?'—The fire of heaven consumed the sacrifice. The tremendous effects of God's manifested displeasure against sin he endured, though in him was no sin : and these he endured in a manner of which even those unhappy spirits who shall drink the fierceness of the wrath of Almighty God, will never be able to form an adequate idea ! They know not the HOLY and EXQUISITE SENSIBILITY which belonged to this immaculate sacrifice. That clear sight of the transgressions of his people in all their heinousness and atrocity ; and that acute sense of the infinite vileness of sin, its baseness, ingratitude, and evil, in every respect, which he possessed ;—must have produced, *in him*, a feeling of extreme distress, of a kind and to a degree which no creature, whose moral sense is impaired by personal sin, can justly conceive. As such a feeling would accrue from the purity and ardour of his love to God and holiness, acting in his *perfectly peculiar* circumstances ; so it would be increased by the pity and tenderness which he ever felt towards the objects of his redeeming love." *Disc. on the Sacrifice of Christ*, 1813. pp. 34, 35 : or in *Four Discourses on Sacrifice, Atonement*, &c. 1827. pp. 46, 47.

It was as a man that he suffered: and as a man he felt his sufferings, and prayed for their alleviation or for deliverance from them. "Save me from this "hour! If it be possible, let this cup pass from me!" The desire of relief sprang from the very necessity of human feelings; feelings which proved him to be not an enthusiast, nor a deranged person: and the prayer for relief implied that limitation of knowledge which is inseparable from the condition of a created nature, and which, as has been observed above, belonged necessarily to the man Christ Jesus. Yet that this natural desire of deliverance from unutterable pain made no infringement on the perfection of his creature-holiness, is manifest from its being combined with the most absolute deference to the will of God. The exclamation on the cross requires in fairness to be understood, as connected with the sequel and the general design of the Psalm of which it is the commencement, and which could not but be familiar to our Lord's involuntary and instantaneous recollection; a Psalm prophetic of the Messiah's sufferings, and of his glory likewise. It is therefore, I conceive, not warranted by any just reason, to consider this exclamation as implying "that God had forsaken him, or could forsake him," in such a sense as the anonymous writer insinuates, as implying an actual abandonment, or as inconsistent with the peculiar fact of our Lord's personal union with the Deity. The only just construction, as it appears to me, is that it expresses the extinction of all *present* and *sensible* comfort, and yet a confidence that light would succeed to the dreadful darkness.

SUPPLEMENTARY NOTE TO SECT. I.

Note [A], page 339.

" When some more recent translators first introduced this version of ἐπιλαμβάνεται, an outcry of novelty and even of a disposition to heterodoxy was raised against them. Yet it is indubitably clear, on an examination of the Greek fathers who have written comments on this passage," [viz. Chrysostom, to whose homilies on the Epistles of Paul, this exquisite scholar, J. Aug. Ernesti, affirms that *all antiquity has nothing equal ;* Theodoret, Theophylact and Œcumenius :] " that in this sense alone the expression was understood by the whole Greek church ; and that the mode of translating which has been generally adopted by our commentators and common-place writers, is a modern innovation derived from the Latins, who finding in the Vulgate this schoolboy rendering of the Greek verb, blindly formed by imitating its composition, *assumit,* of course applied it to the incarnation ; and indeed could do no otherwise, while they depended on their own Latin version. And this is only one instance out of many, in which the same source of error has infected our modern versions : it therefore demands the particular observation of every one who desires to be a faithful interpreter." *Ernesti Inst. Interp. N. T.* Part II. Cap. ix. Sect. 46. See also *Schleusner,* in ἐπιλαμβάνομαι.—But it is very remarkable that both these distinguished authors are mistaken in imputing *assumit* to the Vulgate, which has *apprehendit :* and though the Latin fathers, and Roman Catholic writers in general, regard the latter word as synonymous with the former, I cannot discover that the reading *assumit* ever belonged to that venerable version. Ernesti probably wrote from memory, and attributed to the Vulgate what was the impression of some modern Latin version ; for Calvin, Beza, and Castellio each adopted *assumere :* and Schleusner, without suspicion, followed Ernesti.

· The first divine since the Reformation who pointed out the true meaning of ἐπιλαμβάνεσθαι, in this passage, appears to have been John Cameron, a native of Scotland, but chiefly known by his intimate and honourable connexion with the Protestants of France, among whom he was successively Professor of Greek, (which language he wrote and spoke as if it were his native tongue,) Philosophy, and Divinity. He died at Montauban, in 1625, at the age of 46 ; in consequence of a personal assault cruelly made upon him by some Popish fanatics. His Annotations on the N. T., entitled *Myrothecium Evangelicum,* are peculiarly valuable, and they often anticipate the remarks of later and more celebrated writers.

Section II.

SCRIPTURAL DESCRIPTIONS OF THE MESSIAH'S HUMANITY, INVOLVING
THE RECOGNITION OF A SUPERIOR NATURE.

I. Examination of John i. 14.   The meaning of γίνομαι.—Error of Mr. Cappe
and Mr. Belsham.—True sense of the passage.—II. On Heb. v. 7.—III. On
Rom. viii. 3.—IV. On Gal. iv. 4.—V. On 2 Cor. viii. 9.—The Calm Inquirer's
Interpretation considered.—Signification of πτωχεύω.—Its use by the LXX.—
Construction of the clause.—Mr. Pickbourn's canon on the construction of the
aorist;—examined.—Fischer and Hermann.—Antithesis with πλουτεῖν.—Authority of Greek writers.—Opinions of eminent scholars.—VI. On Philip. ii.
6—8.—Question on the structure of the sentence.—Meaning of ἁρπαγμός—
Deficiency of critical materials.—Best to be deduced from the context.—Citations of early Christian writers.—The phrase ἴσα Θεῷ investigated.—In what
respect it is applied to Christ.—Opinions of Enjedin, Mr. Cappe, and Mr.
Belsham;—examined.—" Form of God."—" Form of a servant."—General
inference from the comparison of the phrases.—Evidence of the Ancient Versions, and of early Christian writers.—The "self-emptying" of Christ.—Unitarian interpretation;—examined.—Investigation of the true sense.—The
" servitude " referred to the penal effects of sin.—The "likeness" and " condition of man," and " obedience unto death."—Recapitulation.

It is now proper to direct attention to a class of
passages which speak of the human condition and circumstances of the Saviour, in such terms as involve a
recognition of another nature; and that superior,
preexistent, and Divine.

I. " The Word became flesh."[1]   The late ingenious Mr. Cappe, of York, and Mr. Belsham, translate ἐγένετο as if it were the simple substantive verb,
" The Word was flesh :" and they affirm that the
most common and usual meaning of γίνομαι is " to be,"

---

[1] John i. 14.

referring to ver. 6, and Luke xxiv. 19.[1]   To this assertion I reply :—

1. That the proper sense of γίνομαι, (or its other forms, γίγνομαι, γένομαι, γείνομαι,) is *to be brought into existence,* or *into a new state or mode of existence.* It is the passive of the ancient verb γένω and γείνω, *to beget, bring forth, produce.* This radical idea runs through all its derivative applications : whatever form or mode of existence they refer to, it is always with the idea, sometimes remotely, but in general obviously, of an *extraneous cause* producing the effect.[2]

2. That not only were these gentlemen mistaken, when they asserted that "the most usual meaning of γίνομαι is *to be ;*" but that, correctly speaking, this is *never* the meaning of that word, except when modified, as above stated, by the accessory idea of passiveness to a previous cause. The instances which they allege appear to me insufficient for their purpose :—

(1.) Verse 6. Ἐγένετο ἄνθρωπος, ἀπεσταλμένος παρὰ Θεοῦ· "a man *was* sent, not was *made* sent, or *became* sent," says Mr. B.   But however burlesque may appear the renderings which he adduces to reject, it is very clear that the leading idea of γίνομαι, as distinct from εἰμὶ, has place here : "a man *was produced, was brought forwards, was raised up,* as a messenger from God."   This use of ἐγένετο is similar to the formula

[1] *Critical Remarks and Dissertations, by the late Rev. Newcome Cappe;* vol. i. p. 86.   *Impr. Vers. in loc.   Calm. Inq.* p. 38.
[2] See *Dammii Lex. Hom. et Pind.* in γάω, γέω, γείνω, p. 319. Berl. ed.   *Fischeri Animadv. ad Gramm. Græc.* pars i. spec. iii. p. 58.   *Lennepii Etym. Ling. Græc.* tom. i. p. 209.   *Godofr. Hermann. de Emendanda Ratione Græcæ Gramm.* p. 273.   *Passow's Gr. Wörterb.* i. 443.

which sometimes occurs, καὶ ἐγένετο, *and it came to pass.*

(2.) Luke xxiv. 19. " Jesus of Nazareth (ὃς ἐγένετο ἀνὴρ προφήτης) who *was*, not who *became* a prophet." But why should not the proper idea of the verb be admitted here also :—" who *was made* a prophet ?"

It may be difficult to find a neat phrase in modern idiom, which will accurately convey the original force of the word; and perhaps the simple verb *to be* may sometimes answer better than any other, to avoid running into periphrasis : but safe argument can be built only on the strict signification of terms.   In both these instances, the common rendering, *was,* is probably the most eligible; yet it is unquestionably the intention of the writers to express that the subjects of the propositions *were brought into* the state expressed by the respective predicates.

Schleusner, in his large and excellent article upon this word (which furnishes abundant confirmation of the remarks above advanced,) has indeed given for his eighteenth signification, "*I am*, the same as εἰμὶ, for in different passages the Septuagint uses it for the Hebrew חיה, as Nehem. vi. 6."   But a reference to those passages will prove that they without exception fall under the observations which we have made.[4]

On these grounds, it appears to me that the translation, " The Word was flesh," is erroneous by being defective ; and that any fair translation must express

---

· 4 There are only three instances of חָיָה, viz. Josh. ix. 12 ; Ruth i. 12 ; Dan. ii. 1.   Four have הָיָה, Gen. xxvii. 29 ; Nehem. vi. 6; Job xxxvii. 6 ; Eccl. ii. 22.   And there are two passages in which the LXX. have read חָיָה, where the present Hebrew text has the interjection הוֹי, Jer. xxx. 7 ; Micah ii. 1.

this idea, that the word *was brought into that state or mode of existence* which is known by the term *flesh*, that is, the human nature. Our language perfectly expresses it by the plain form, " The word BECAME flesh."[5]

I conceive, therefore, that we may regard as sufficiently proved, that the just construction of this passage indubitably represents the human existence of our Lord as *assumed* by a preexistent intelligence.

II. " The days of his flesh."[6] This phraseology plainly implies that he had *other days*, another manner or state of existence, which might be contrasted with his debased and afflicted state on earth.

III. " God sent his own Son in the likeness of " sinful flesh :"[7] thus paraphrased by Semler ; " That which the law could not effect, God hath accomplished in the best manner, by sending his own Son ; who, besides his invisible nature, had flesh resembling this flesh of ours, which is often overcome by sin."[8]

IV. "God sent forth his own Son made [γενόμενον, " brought into the state of being] from a woman."[9] On this passage, the celebrated critic just quoted has this annotation : " God sent forth, that is *from him-*

---

[5] " Λόγος *ille factus est homo,* pertinet eò ut indicet Λόγον illum ad humilem conditionem se demisisse." *Mori Recitationes in Joann.* p. 9.

[6] Heb. v. 7. " Die tage seines mühevollen lebens auf erden." ' The days of his life full of sufferings upon earth.' *Mori Comm. Exeg. Hist. in Theol. Christ.* vol. ii. p. 7.

[7] Rom. viii. 3. See the Note in page 337 of this volume.

[8] " Eam rem Deus feliciter ipse procuravit, misso suo Filio, qui, præter istam invisibilem naturam, simillimam carnem nostræ, cui peccatum solebat dominari, habuit." *Paraphr. et Notæ in Ep. ad Rom.* 1769, p. 91.

[9] Gal. iv. 4.

self, the Son who was before described as being *with the Father*, and *in the bosom of the Father ;* and who himself therefore frequently said that he should *return* to the Father *from whom* he came forth.   This does not involve any necessary idea of a local change ; though we know. not what precise conceptions the men of that age might form.   The fact itself is abundantly plain, that such expressions as this are irreconcilable with the opinion that Christ had no existence before he was, as here stated, born of a woman."[10]

V. " Ye know the grace of our Lord Jesus Christ, " that on account of you he became poor, though he " was rich : in order that ye, by his poverty, might be " enriched."[11]

Mr. B. expresses contempt for those who infer the preexistence of Christ from this text ; while he admits that " if the fact were antecedently established, this passage might indeed be admitted as a graceful allu- sion to it."[12] If, however, his interpretation of the terms be just, it would scarcely be warrantable, admit- ting the concession, to suppose such allusion ; but, if a fair examination should show that the interpreta- tion is erroneous, the passage will remain, not as an allusion merely, but as a positive and strong implica-

---

[10] " 'Εξαπέστειλεν, emisit Deus, scilicit *à se,* illum Filium qui antea dicebatur esse *apud Patrem, in sinu Patris ;* qui ideo sæpius ipse dicit *redeundum* jam ipsi esse ad Patrem *à quo* exiit : John viii. 42. Non opus est ut loci quasi mutationem cogitemus, licet ignoremus ecquid homines ejus temporis cogitarint. Res ipsa sufficit: talibus sententiis reprimi omnes illos qui exsistendi initium repetunt ab hac nativitate, ἐκ γυναικὸς, quæ hic commemoratur." *Paraphr. et Notæ in Ep. ad Gal.* 1779, p. 337.

[11] 2 Cor. viii. 9.   [12] Page 122.

tion. The sense according to him is, "that Christ was rich, and, at the same time, that he lived in poverty;—rich in miraculous powers, which it was at his option to employ for his own benefit;"—but he submitted to the severest privations; "he made no use of his miraculous powers for his own advantage." Undoubtedly this, so far as it goes, is true; and is capable of being applied to the design of the connexion, as a motive to compassion and liberality: but that *it is not the entire sense*, nor that which was *specially intended* by the apostle, may, I submit, be maintained on solid grounds. The reasons produced for this interpretation are two.

1. " The verb πτωχεύω does not properly signify *to become poor*, but *to be poor :*" and Stephens's Thesaurus and Constantine's Lexicon are quoted in support of the assertion. But the significations given by those eminent scholars express the *classical* use of the word. It is unnecessary to say that Homer, Theognis, and Aristotle, are not the sources from which to derive authority, for the sense of words and phrases in the Greek of the New Testament. Stephens has, indeed, introduced this text as falling under the general signification which he assigns,[13] and which is unquestionably correct in reference to the pure Greek usage. He has closely followed Constantine. But they both appear to have overlooked the proper authority for understanding the diction of the New Testament; namely, the Septuagint and the Apocrypha, compared with the Hebrew text. In them this oversight was

[13] " Mendicus sum, mendicus vivo, mendicando vivo, mendico : —— egeo, indigeo : —— mendicus oberro, mendicans peto." *Hen Steph.*

excusable; as the fact of the Hebraized diction of the apostles and evangelists was, in their day, scarcely recognised.

The word is not very common in Greek authors after Homer, and in the New Testament it occurs only in this place: but we find it several times in the Septuagint; and, in each instance, if I am not greatly mistaken, the signification is, not simply *to be poor*, nor, as in the classical use, *to lead the life of a beggar*; but it is TO BECOME POOR from a previous better condition. The passages will speak for themselves.

" When the children of Israel sowed corn, the " Midianites —— came upon them, and destroyed " their produce, —— and left no sustenance for life " in the land of Israel, nor ox nor ass in the folds: " —— and Israel (ἐπτώχευσε σφόδρα) *became* exceed- " ingly *poor*." Judges vi. 6.

" Have you invited us with a view (πτωχεῦσαι) *to* " *reduce us to poverty?*" Ib. xiv. 15. *Ed. Alexandr.*

" The rich have *become poor*: (πλούσιοι ἐπτώ- " χευσαν)." Psalm xxxiii. (xxxiv.) 10.

" We are exceedingly *impoverished*: (ἐπτωχεύσαμεν " σφόδρα)." Psalm lxxviii. (lxxix.) 8.

" Every drunkard and whoremonger (πτωχεύσει) " shall *come to poverty*." Prov. xxiii. 21.

" Fear not, my son, because (ἐπτωχεύσαμεν) we " have *become poor*." Tobit iv. 21.[14]

These are the authorities which ought to direct our

---

[14] Symmachus, who made another Greek version of the O. T. about the end of the second century, used the word in Prov. xiii. 7. " There are who *affect to be poor* (πτωχευόμενοι) but have abundant riches." *Drusii Fragm. Vet. Interp. Gr.* p. 1132.

interpretation of the word in question; unless some very weighty reason could be shown for taking it out of the proper range.   But certainly there is no such reason.

The reader ·will observe the resemblance of the language of the text under consideration, (ἐπτώχευσε πλούσιος ὤν,) to the third of the passages above enumerated.   It is not impossible that the passage might have suggested the phrase to the apostle's mind.

Thus the whole evidence that applies to the case, appears to me most clearly to entitle us to reverse Mr. B.'s proposition, and to say that, in the Hellenistic and scriptural Greek, this verb INVARIABLY denotes *to become poor* from a previous condition of competency or opulence.   In this sense, therefore, unless we would disregard one of the most certain rules of honest interpretation, we are bound to understand it in the passage before us: " our Lord Jesus Christ *became,* or *was made,* poor."

2. " The construction requires that the two states should be simultaneous.   The aorist expresses a perfect action, in past definite time; which time is ascertained by the connexion.   *Christ* ἐπτώχευσε *was poor.*   When? Πλούσιος ὤν, at the time *when he was rich.*" [15]

To a considerable extent, this rule is true; but we cannot make it a universal canon.   Let us try it by two or three examples in the writings of the same apostle. Συνεζωοποίησε, *he hath made us alive with Christ.*

---

[15] *Calm. Inq.* p. 124.   For this grammatical observation Mr. B. acknowledged himself indebted to " a learned and ingenious friend ;" the late Mr. James Pickbourn.

When? At the time *when, ὄντας ἡμᾶς, we were dead in trespasses and sins.*[16]   The two states must be simultaneous : the Christian converts were dead in sin, and alive through Christ at the same time.   So likewise must we reason on the recurrence of similar phraseology in the Epistle to the Colossians.[17]——Κατηλλάγημεν, *we have been reconciled to God*.   When? At the time *when, ἐχθροὶ ὄντες, we were enemies.*[18]   The two states are simultaneous : we are enemies to God and in a state of reconciliation with him at the same time.——Such would be the theology, such the sense, of this rule, applied after the manner recommended.

If the aorist "expresses a perfect action in past definite time," it follows that the translation of ἐπτώχευσε is not so properly *he lived a life of poverty*, which expresses a continued action, and would require the imperfect tense ; but that, according to the common Greek signification of the word, it is, *he begged* ; or, according to the scriptural acceptation, *he became poor*.

The same conclusion is supported also by a doctrine of the aorists, which is maintained by Fischer and Hermann, critics whom all will acknowledge to be among the few who have occupied the first rank in this department of literature ; whether we consider the extent and accuracy of their acquaintance with Greek authors, or their surprising acuteness in penetrating, and sagacity in explaining, the rationale of the language.   The former of these authors says, that " the second aorist denotes a perfect action, in a past and continued time, but uncertain and undefined ; and the first aorist expresses the same affections of

---

[16] Eph. ii. 1, 5.   [17] Col. ii. 13.   [18] Rom. v. 10.

time, but *without the idea of continuity.*[19] The latter makes three cases of the aorist : the first, the notation of an action completed within some portion of time which is not only *now* past, but *has been* past a certain space of time ago, which space of elapsed time is left undefined : the second, the intimating of repetition, frequency, or habit : the third, the idea of possible or probable action.[20] It is only the first of these that can apply to the text under consideration ; and according to it, ἐπτώχευσε, will admit of being rendered, either *he became poor,* or *he lived a life of poverty :* but it gives no evidence of the assumed community of time with πλούσιος ὤν.

The Inquirer appears to think that, when the participle ὤν is used in reference to past time, some adverb is requisite to mark the transition to another time : as in John ix. 25. " Being (that is, having been) " blind, *now* I see : τυφλὸς ὤν, ἄρτι βλέπω." But any scholar, in his ordinary Greek reading, may observe

---

[19] *Fischeri Animadv. in Gramm. Græc.* Specim. ii. p. 260.

[20] *Hermann. de Emend. Ratione Græc. Gramm.* pp. 186—189. It is remarkable, and it surely is a corroboration of the truth of our interpretation, that the same result is given by another and very different doctrine on the force of the aorists, promulgated by the sharp-sighted and philosophical grammarian, Prof. Buttmann. " The 1st and 2d aorist —— different forms of the same tenses, and differ not in signification.——The aorist differs from all [the other past tenses] in expressing simply a past action, without any connexion in idea with present, or any other past, time ; *I saw it.* The past tense *in English* [i. e. the English and German imperfect] is an aorist : *in Latin,* the perfect is used to express the Greek aorist. Ex. Πύῤῥος —ὁδεύων ἐνέτυχε κυνί·—By substituting *has met, had met,* or *was meeting,* for *met,* the difference between the aorist and the other past tenses will be felt.—" *Gr. Gramm.* p. 236. The very same doctrine, though less amply unfolded, is laid down in *Matthiæ's Grammar,* Mr. Blomfield's Translation ; vol. ii. p. 723, ed. 1829.

the frequent instances of this participle occurring in the sense of past time without any adverbial intimation :[21] and every schoolboy knows that the present participle is also the participle of the imperfect tense.

A sentence closely resembling that under consideration, occurs in the former Epistle to the same church: " Though I was free from all, I subjected myself as a " servant to all." [22] Will it be pretended that these two states were simultaneous? The meaning evidently is, that the apostle abdicated his liberty, and entered into a new and opposite state.

Some light is also gained to the sense of ἐπτώχευσε from its position with πλουτήσητε ; for, if the latter express a change of state, *a becoming rich* from the previous condition of spiritual poverty, it is reasonable to regard the former as correspondent. It is worthy of observation that this is the construction of those whose native language was Greek, and who of course would have an instantaneous perception of their own idioms. Gregory of Nazianzum, evidently alluding to this passage, and to Philippians ii. 7, says : " The author of riches becomes poor ; for he becomes poor [with regard to] my flesh, that I may be enriched [with regard to] his Deity. He who is full is emptied ; for he is emptied of his own glory for a little time, that I may partake of his fulness." [23]

In the expository collections of Photius we find the

---

[21] As in Luke xxiii. 12.   Acts ix. 39; xxiv. 10.   John i. 49. 2 Pet. i. 18.

[22] 1 Cor. ix. 19, ἐλεύθερος ὢν —ἐδούλωσα.

[23] Ὁ πλουτίζων πτωχεύει· πτωχεύει γὰρ τὴν ἐμὴν σάρκα, ἵν' ἐγὼ πλουτήσω τὴν αὐτοῦ Θεότητα· Καὶ ὁ πλήρης κενοῦται· κενοῦται γὰρ τῆς ἑαυτοῦ δόξης ἐπὶ μικρὸν, ἵνα ἐγὼ τῆς ἐκείνου μεταλάβω πληρώσεως. *Opera, ed. Bill. Par.* 1630. vol. i. p. 620.

following annotation : " He became poor [by taking]
our flesh :—we are made rich [by receiving] forgiveness of sins, holiness, adoption, and the kingdom of
heaven." [24] The comments of Chrysostom show that
he understood the terms in the same sense. " He
emptied himself of his glory, that ye, not by his riches,
but by his poverty, might be made rich. If he had
not been made poor, thou wouldst not have been
made rich. All these blessings have come to us
through his poverty ; and what kind of poverty ? His

[24] The candid scholar will admit that, as the chasms in this quotation, and in that from Gregory, occasioned by the common ellipsis
of κατὰ, must be supplied in any translation, the modes of supplying
them here adopted are fair and consonant with the design of the
writers. I copy the entire passage, that it may be read in its connexion.—Ἐπτώχευσε γὰρ τὴν ἡμετέραν σάρκα. Εἶτα κατεδικάσθη καὶ
ἐσταυρώθη, καὶ τοῦτο δι' ἡμᾶς τοὺς ἀναξίους· ὅτι δι' ἡμᾶς ἐπτώχευσεν.
Εἰ οὖν ἐκεῖνος, φησὶν, ἐπτώχευσε διὰ σὲ, σὺ οὐδὲ χρήματα δίδως δι'
αὐτόν; Πλούσιος ὤν· Καθό ἐστι καὶ νοεῖται Θεὸς, οἷον ἀνέκφραστος,
ἀπερινόητος, ἀόρατος, ἀκατάληπτος, δόξαν ἔχων ἀπόῤῥητον, φῶς ἀνεκ-
λάλητον, μεγαλωσύνην ἀνείκαστον. Ἵνα ὑμεῖς τῇ ἐκείνου πτωχείᾳ
πλουτήσητε· Εἰ γὰρ μὴ ἐκεῖνος, φησὶν, ἐπτώχευσεν, οὐκ ἂν ἡμεῖς ἐπλουτήσαμεν. Ἐπλουτήσαμεν δὲ ἄφεσιν ἁμαρτιῶν, ἁγιωσύνην, υἱοθεσίαν,
αὐτὴν τὴν βασιλείαν τῶν οὐρανῶν. "He became poor [by taking]
our flesh. He was moreover condemned and crucified, and that for
us unworthy; since for our sake he became poor. If then, says the
apostle, he became poor for thy sake, wilt not thou give alms for his
sake ?——Being rich : inasmuch as he is, and is proved to be, God,
namely the unutterable, whom no created mind can grasp, invisible,
incomprehensible, possessing the glory which cannot be declared,
the unspeakable light, the incomparable majesty.——That ye, by his
poverty, may be made rich : for, says the apostle, unless he had become poor we should not have become rich. But we are made rich
{by receiving] forgiveness of sins, holiness, adoption, and the kingdom of heaven itself." Œcumen. in Act. et Epist. Verona, 1532,
p. 542. " Fix your eyes on the Creator and Sovereign of the universe, the Only-begotten Son of God, who, for your salvation, went
into the condition of extreme poverty, (τὴν ἐσχάτην μετελήλυθε
πενίαν.)" Theodoret. in loc.

taking flesh, and becoming a man, and suffering what he did suffer." [25]

Thus then, I humbly conceive, there is a preponderance of reason for taking πλούσιος ὢν in reference to an antecedent state : " being rich, for your sake he " became poor."

The Inquirer adduces, as a corroboration of his views, that " the most accurate critics and commentators translate and expound the words as expressing simultaneous and not successive states :" [26] and he refers to Grotius, Schlictingius, and Brennius, as these authorities. But the latter two are party writers, and Grotius can scarcely be considered as free from a similar bias. If, however, authority is to be called in, (and undoubtedly, on questions of philological difficulty, much respect is due to competent authority,) I conceive that the appeal should be made to those critics who are distinguished for their purely grammatical investigations, and who treat the text of the New Testament precisely as they have done, or would do, any Greek classic whom they had undertaken to edite and illustrate. Of this description are the following.

Semler, than whom no man more prided himself upon his latitude of thinking, or more heartily spurned the being a follower of venerable names or popular doctrines, thus paraphrases and comments upon the clause. "Our Lord Jesus Christ, though possessed

---

[25] Ἐκεῖνος δόξαν ἐκένωσεν, οὐχ ἵνα ὑμεῖς τῷ πλούτῳ αὐτοῦ, ἀλλὰ τῇ πτωχείᾳ, πλουτήσητε.——Εἰ μὴ ἐκεῖνος ἐγένετο πτωχὸς, οὐκ ἂν ἐγένου σὺ πλούσιος.——Ταῦτα ἅπαντα διὰ τῆς πτωχείας γέγονεν ἡμῖν· ποίας ; Διὰ τοῦ σάρκα ἀναλαβεῖν, καὶ γενέσθαι ἄνθρωπον, καὶ παθεῖν ἅπερ ἔπαθε· Homil. xvii. in 2 Epist. ad Cor.

[26] Page 124.

of supreme riches as Lord of all things, yet for you
Gentiles submitted to that poverty.—The concise
phrase, *being rich*, respects the doctrines concerning
the state of Christ before his human existence, and
with the Father, which the apostle had more largely
delivered in his personal teachings ; and which he
thus recalls to the recollection of those whom he
addresses. The participle ὤν has the same signification
as ὑπάρχων in Phil. ii. 6, and can by no means be applied only to the human life of Christ, the relation of
both fact and time being different. The expression
he became poor, likewise answers to that in the passage
just referred to, *he emptied himself;* and it denotes
another condition and state of the person of whom this
new condition of humanity is affirmed." [27]

Morus, a liberal but not extravagant theologian,
the editor of Xenophon's historical works and of other
Greek classics, and on whom as an exquisite scholar
the encomium of Wyttenbach was pronounced; [28] explains the words thus : "Christ being rich, that is,

---

[27] " Cognoscitis illam beneficentiam Domini nostri Jesu Christi,
quòd cùm esset rerum omnium dominus ditissimus, tamen propter
vos gentes illam paupertatem subiit.—Res eadem describitur ac
Phil. ii. etiam simillimè : idem participium, ἐν μορφῇ Θεοῦ ὑπάρχων.
Ideas de statu Christi ante vitam humanam, apud Patrem—plures
quas Paulus sermonibus suis exposuerat, eas hic in animum revocat :
γινώσκετε, scil. me vobis exposuisse.   Illud (ὤν, Phil. ii. ὑπάρχων)
minimè potest, alio rei et temporis ordine, rejici tantùm in vitam
humanam.——'Επτώχευσε, ἐκένωσεν ἑαυτὸν, occupat jam alium ordi-
nem et statum hujus subjecti, ad quem hic novus ordo humanus
refertur. *Paraphr. et Not. in Ep. ad Cor.* Hal. Magd. 1776, vol. ii.
p. 222.
[28] " Haud minoris in judicando diligentiæ ac doctrinæ, quàm
modestiæ." *Wyttenbachii Adnot. ad Xenoph. locos illustres*, p. 391.
Saxii Onomast. Liter. vol. viii. p. 200.

possessed of the highest happiness, was made poor, that men might be enriched with blessings." [29]

Rosenmüller, the father, after copying at length from Morus, but without acknowledgment, adds : " Christ was possessed of the highest happiness before his advent and appearance on earth." [30]

Schleusner refers the expression, *being rich*, to a previous state of perfect happiness ; and he adds, " The reference is to the glory which Christ is explicitly declared in the New Testament to have had from eternity with God." [31]

Dr. Gustavus Billroth (who died early in this year, 1836,) a critic of distinguished learning and sagacity, regardless of all theories and parties, and especially devoting his talents to the eliciting of the meaning of the apostle Paul by a thorough logical sifting of his intellectual character and his peculiarities of thought and style, gives this paraphrase : " Our Lord Jesus Christ—who, for the sake of men, entered into the low state of humanity, though he as the Son of God possessed the [divine] glory with God, that men, through his depriving himself, might become rich in heavenly blessings." [32]

From all that has been adduced, it appears to me

---

[29] " Christum divitem factum esse pauperem, ut homines locupletarentur.—Non potest simpliciter ita verti, sed cum additamento, *beatitate abundantissimus; bonis locupletati sumus.*" *Dissert. de Discrimine Sensûs et Significationis in Interpretando*, p. 30.

[30] " Fuit autem beatitate abundantissimus priusquam in has terras adspectabilis venit." *In loc.* The passage which he has copied from Morus is not that cited above.

[31] " Intelligitur autem ibi δόξα illa quam Christus ab æterno habuisse apud Deum disertè in N. T. traditur." *In voce πλούσιος.*

[32] *Commentar zu d. Br. an d. Corinth.* Leipzig, 1833.

no more than a reasonable and necessary conclusion, that, in this passage, there is a definite recognition of a preexistent and glorious state of the Messiah.[33]

VI. "Let this disposition be in you which was even in Christ Jesus, who [though] existing in the form of God, did not esteem it an object to be caught at to be on a parity with God: but emptied himself, taking the form of a servant, becoming in the likeness of men: and being found in condition as a man, he humbled himself, becoming obedient unto death, even the death of the cross." [34]

It has not been without long, careful, and anxious consideration, that I have given the preceding version of this important passage. That, in the particulars in which it differs from the commonly received version,

[33] Michaelis takes a different view of the passage, but which includes the principle of the interpretation supported above.

"*Ye know well the favour which our Lord, Jesus Christ, hath conferred upon us; that, though he was rich, he became poor for your sake, that ye, through his poverty, might become rich.* The eternal Divine nature is not here the subject of discourse, but Jesus as a man. Even in that respect he had the greatest right to be rich, to live in the greatest abundance, and to enjoy every comfort. As Son of David, he had to expect, pursuant to the promise of God, a splendid kingdom, the sovereignty of a noble country, which was at that time certainly in its most flourishing and populous condition. Besides, something more and loftier was his due, as being not merely a Son of David, but *the* Son of David, the divinely promised Messiah. Adding to this, that his human nature was united with the Divine, it results that all the treasures and property in the world belonged to him. Of all this he divested himself, came poor into the world, and lived poor in it; not indeed actually in the very lowest condition, that of a beggar, for in his whole life we find the indications of a station not otherwise than honourable; but yet poor and without possessions, sometimes even in peculiar want and necessity. Thus was he to obtain for us true and everlasting riches." *Ammerkung in loc.*

[34] Philippians ii. 5—8.

and which many excellent writers have preferred, it does no more than truly and faithfully represent the sense of the original, appears to me established by the following considerations.

i. The first question is, How far, in the construction of the sentence, does that part extend which was called by the ancient rhetoricians the *protasis ;* that is, the proposal of the terms or considerations, which prepare the way for the rest of the sentence, called the *apodosis,* and from which it is to flow, as a deduction, or application to the matter in hand?[35] The common version supposes this point to be at the close of the third member, which, therefore, would run thus: " who, existing in the form of God and esteeming it no usurpation to be as God:" and then the apodosis would follow, " yet emptied himself," &c. But this so far as I can perceive, would have required a difference in the words.[36]

On the other hand, I must own that the most exact and impartial study of the passage which I can exercise, leads me to regard the just construc-

[35] An apology may seem due for using these technical forms of expression ; but they appeared necessary to help the perspicuousness of the explication. Perhaps these distinctions, and the denominations of them, are too much neglected now, as formerly they were too severely observed. A judicious attention to them would greatly aid the study of the sacred and other books. The reader who is conversant with Baxter's and Gesner's Notes on Horace, must have observed the excellent use which they make of these distinctions. A similar benefit may be obtained by the same mode of studying the Epistles of the apostle Paul: he often leaves the *apodosis* to be supplied by the intelligence of his reader. See *Vossii Rhet.* lib. iii. cap. iv. *Theoph. Ernesti Lex. Technol. Græc. Rhet.* Leipzig, 1795, pp. 36, 297.

[36] *Viz.* to have stood thus, Ὃς, ἐν μορφῇ Θεοῦ ὑπάρχων, καὶ οὐχ ἁρπαγμὸν ἡγησάμενος τὸ εἶναι Ἴσα Θεῷ, ἑαυτὸν ἐκένωσε, &c.

tion as terminating the protasis with the clause, " existing in the form of God ;" and that the subsequent members all belong to the apodosis and point to one object, the declaration of our Lord's unspeakable condescension.[37]

ii. Another important consideration is the meaning of ἁρπαγμός. Every one knows that the verb from which it is immediately derived, signifies, *to seize, to catch at, suddenly to lay hold of, to take by force;* and it is used with respect to the prey of a wild animal, the booty captured by a warrior, the instantaneous snatching of a weapon out of the hand of another, the prompt imitation of the manners of others, and many objects of a similar kind. With regard to the noun, the question is, whether it denotes *the act of seizing,* or *the thing seized.* According to the strict rule of derivation, it might be pleaded that it must be the former :[38] but we are prevented from resting in this conclusion by the abundant evidence

[37] A *spicilegium* of eminent interpreters, who have regarded this as the distribution of thought and turn of argument intended by the apostle, will be in the Supplementary Note [A], at the end of this Section. At the same time, it must be confessed that the common construction is still maintained by respectable scholars, among whom are my excellent friend Dr. Wardlaw, and the late Mr. Cappe. The former has devoted an elaborate Note, or rather Disquisition, to this question, which well deserves the attention of the serious inquirer. *Discourses on the Socinian Controversy,* pp. 547—555, fourth ed. 1828. The latter, a zealous Unitarian, and one who pushed his views to a wider extreme than many of his class, has an elaborate Dissertation, written with his usual ability, which was not small, in vindication of that construction, and to maintain its consistency with Unitarian views. *Critical Remarks on Scripture, &c.* Vol. i. pp. 232, 269—313.

[38] That verbal nouns derived from the perfect passive, in μός denote *actively,* in μα *passively.* Thus ἁρπάζω, ἥρπαγμαι, would give ἁρπαγμὸς, *the act of seizing,* ἅρπαγμα, *the object seized.*

that the best Greek authors either did not know, or
practically disregarded, this rule of the grammarians.[39]
The word occurs nowhere besides, in the New
Testament, the Septuagint, or the Apocrypha; nor,
it is believed, in any Greek classic, except once in
Plutarch,[40] who uses it *actively*, to signify a peculiar kind
of *forcible abduction*, an infamous action which Strabo,
in largely describing it as one of the customs of the
licentious Cretans, calls ἁρπαγὴ, *rapine*.[41] Another instance, also, the laborious industry of Wetstein has
discovered among the volumes of the Greek fathers,
in one of the works of Cyril of Alexandria, who
flourished in the fifth century; where it is manifestly
taken in the *passive* sense, to denote *that which occurs
unexpectedly and is gladly caught at*.[42] Thus the

---

[39] Ὡς δὲ ξεσμὸς, ξέσμα. οὕτω δεσμὸς, δέσμα.—Ῥωχμὸς δὲ καὶ
ῥῆγμα, ταῦτα ἐστὶν· ὡς καὶ βρεχμὸς καὶ βρέχμα, καὶ πλεχμὸς καὶ
πλέχμα. *Eustathius in Hom.* pp. 1386, 1425 : apud *Wakefield
Silv. Critic.* P. iii. p. 112.

[40] *De Liberorum Instit.* sect. 15. *Opera Mor.* ed. *Wyttenbachii*,
vol. i. p. 41. *in ed. Tho. Edwards*, Cant. 1791, p. 49. The immensely laborious and voluminous Wyttenbach has only a brief
annotation on the passage, and does not indulge us with a single
remark on ἁρπαγμός. See his *Animadv. in Plutarchi Mor.* vol. i.
P. i. p. 134.

[41] *Strabo ;* lib. x. *ed. Falconer*, pp. 704, 705, tom. ii.

[42] This author is discoursing on the modest declining of the divine
messengers (Gen. xix. 2,) to accept of Lot's invitation; which he
considers as a trial of the patriarch's sincerity, and as a motive for
more strongly urging the invitation. He then says, Ὁ δὴ καὶ συνεὶς
ὁ δίκαιος μειζόνως κατεβιάζετο, καὶ οὐχ ἁρπαγμὸν τὴν παραίτησιν ὡς
ἐξ ἀδρανοῦς καὶ ὑδαρεστέρας ἐποιεῖτο φρενός. " Which the righteous
man understanding, pressed them the more ; and did not, like a man
acting from a versatile and insincere mind, make their declining his
invitation *a thing to be caught at*." *Cyrilli Alex. Opera*, vol. i.
pars ii. p. 25. Par. 1638.

only actual authorities that exist are opposed to each other : and it would appear impossible for any man now to determine, whether the writer who was born fifteen years before the apostle died, but who was a heathen ; or the other who was a Christian, but lived almost four centuries after ; were the more likely to employ the rare word in the exact sense in which the apostle himself had used it.[43] We seem, therefore, obliged to acquiesce in the doctrine of Eustathius, which might also be confirmed by many other examples from Greek authors ; and to regard the connexion of the passage as our only criterion.

The construction here adopted is that in which the Greek fathers, from the earliest example of a quotation of this passage to the fourth century and downwards, have generally understood it. Without attributing to those authors any *authority* in the decision of theological doctrines, or *deferring* to their opinions and arguments in the general interpretation of scripture ; it is reasonable to consider them as entitled to great regard in mere verbal questions, which refer to the signification of the terms and idioms of their native language; provided that due judgment be exercised, in applying our conclusions to the interpretation of the New Testament, not to confound the genuine Greek with the Hebraized diction of the sacred writers. But the phrase before us does not fall under the head of that Hebraized diction : nothing like it is to be found in the Old Testament or the Apocrypha.[44]

[43] See Note [B], at the end of this Section.
[44] Grotius, indeed, affirms that " it is a Syriac expression :"

To adduce numerous instances of the manner in which the text is cited and applied by the fathers, would be tedious. The reader may find many in Wetstein and Lardner, and he may increase the number by the help of the Tables of Texts, in good editions of the authors themselves. Two or three passages, however, I shall copy; and they shall be the earliest.

The first occurs in the Epistle of the persecuted churches at Vienne and Lyons, to the Christians in Asia and Phrygia, written about the year 177: which all admit to be one of the most interesting monuments of Christian antiquity. " To such a degree were they the zealous followers and imitators of Christ, *who, being in the form of God, did not esteem it a thing to be caught at to be as God ;* that, though being in such glory, and having not once or twice, but many times, borne the testimony of martyrdom, and been taken back again from the wild beasts, and having the marks of the fire, and stripes, and wounds, on almost every part of their bodies, they did not represent themselves as martyrs, nor would on any account permit us to address them by that appellation."[45]

(*Annot. in loc.*) but he has no ground for the assertion, except the occurrence of a similar phrase in a Syriac liturgy, which can scarcely be placed higher than the fourth or fifth century, and in which the phrase is, at all events, much more reasonably to be deduced from the passage of the apostle.

[45] Οἱ καὶ ἐπὶ τοσοῦτον ζηλωταὶ καὶ μιμηταὶ Χριστοῦ ἐγένοντο, ὃς ἐν μορφῇ Θεοῦ ὑπάρχων, οὐχ ἁρπαγμὸν ἡγήσατο τὸ εἶναί Ἶσα Θεῷ· ὥστε ἐν τοιαύτῃ δόξῃ ὑπάρχοντες, καὶ οὐχ ἅπαξ οὐδὲ δὶς, ἀλλὰ πολλάκις μαρτυρήσαντες, καὶ ἐκ θηρίων αὖθις ἀναληφθέντες, καὶ τὰ καυτήρια καὶ τοὺς

Clemens of Alexandria, who flourished at the close of the second and the beginning of the third century, cites the text thus : " To thee the Lord himself will speak, *who being in the form of God, esteemed it not a thing to be caught at to be as God ;* but the compassionate God *emptied himself,* longing for the salvation of man." [46]

Origen, the pupil of Clemens, has this observable passage : " I might even venture to say that the goodness of Christ appeared more abundant, and more divine, and truly after the image of the Father, when *he humbled himself, becoming obedient unto death, even the death of the cross,* than if he had *esteemed it an object to be caught at to be as God,* and had not chosen

μώλωπας καὶ τὰ τραύματα ἔχοντες περικείμενα, οὔτ' αὐτοὶ μάρτυρας ἑαυτοὺς ἀνεκήρυττον, οὔτε μὴν ἡμῖν ἐπέτρεπον τούτῳ τῷ ὀνόματι προσαγορεύειν αὐτούς. *Eusebii. Hist. Eccl.* lib. v. cap. 2. On this passage the learned Dr. Routh, the venerable President of Magdalen College, Oxford, (who adorns his extensive learning by a spirit as eminently candid and amiable,) observes, that the writer or writers of this Epistle certainly understood the clause which we are considering as referring to the *humiliation* of Christ ; and that this was also the interpretation of many of the Christian fathers. "Quomodocunque interpretanda verba sint, οὐχ ἁρπαγμὸν ἡγήσατο τὸ εἶναι ἴσα Θεῷ, hoc quidem constat, Lugdunenses ex illis argumentum duxisse τῆς ταπεινοφροσύνης Christi. Neque verò hi soli id fecerunt, sed et alii multi veteres scriptores ; imò verò id suscipere velim, nullum ecclesiasticum auctorem ad Nicænorum usque tempus adduci posse, qui significari τὸ *non alienum à se esse arbitratus est* verbis οὐχ ἁρπαγμὸν ἡγήσατο, clarè atque apertè indicaverit. Haudquaquam tamen id fraudi est firmissimo argumento contra Humanistas quos vocant, ex istis verbis apostoli sumendo." *Reliq. Sacr.* vol. i. p. 328.

[46] Αὐτός σοι λαλήσει ὁ Κύριος, ὃς, ἐν μορφῇ Θεοῦ ὑπάρχων, οὐχ ἁρπαγμὸν ἡγήσατο τὸ εἶναι ἴσα Θεῷ· ἐκένωσε δὲ ἑαυτὸν ὁ φιλοικτίρμων Θεὸς, σῶσαι τὸν ἄνθρωπον γλιχόμενος· *Admon. ad Gentes ;* inter *Opera,* ed. Par. 1629, p. 7.

to become a servant for the salvation of the world." [47]
The other instances in which this father cites the passage before us, are indeed very numerous; but, while some of them concur in the sense and application of the preceding, in the larger number no light is afforded to the manner in which he understood the difficult clause. A remarkable fact, however, presents itself in the examination of these passages, and which seems to show that perplexity in the interpretation of the clause was felt even then. This is, that, in two instances, so far as I have discovered, Origen has taken ἁρπαγμὸς actively, and has understood the clause in the sense of our common version and many modern interpreters. [48]

The difficulty of the case must be admitted to be considerable: and perhaps neither of the constructions can be adopted without some remaining hesitation. The preponderance, however, appears to me to be in favour of that which has been already stated, and which I believe to have been approved by many, at

[47] Τολμητέον γὰρ εἰπεῖν πλείονα καὶ θειοτέραν καὶ ἀληθῶς κατ' εἰκόνα τοῦ Πατρὸς, τὴν ἀγαθότητα φαίνεσθαι τοῦ Χριστοῦ, ὅτε ἑαυτὸν ἐταπείνωσε, γενόμενος ὑπήκοος μέχρι θανάτου, θανάτου δὲ σταυροῦ, ἢ εἰ ἁρπαγμὸν ἡγήσατο τὸ εἶναι Ἴσα Θεῷ, καὶ μὴ βουληθεὶς ἐπὶ τῇ τοῦ κόσμου σωτηρίᾳ γενέσθαι δοῦλος. Origenis Opera, de la Rue; tom. iv. p. 37. This passage is referred to by the Calm Inquirer, p. 137.

[48] Καὶ γὰρ αὐτὸς, ἐν μορφῇ Θεοῦ ὑπάρχων, οὐχ ἁρπαγμὸν ἡγησάμενος τὸ εἶναι Ἴσα Θεῷ, γέγονε παιδίον. "Even he himself, being in the form of God, not esteeming it an act of usurpation to be as God, became a child." Vol. iii. p. 661. Ἐχρῆν—ἐξαίρετα παρὰ τὰ λελαλημένα πώποτε ἐν τῷ κόσμῳ ἢ γεγραμμένα, ἀποκαλυφθῆναι ἀπὸ τοῦ οὐχ ἁρπαγμὸν ἡγησαμένου τὸ εἶναι Ἴσα Θεῷ, ἀλλ' ἑαυτὸν κενώσαντος καὶ μορφὴν δούλου εἰληφότος. "Things excellent, beyond all that had ever been spoken or written in the world, were to be revealed from him who esteemed it not an act of usurpation to be as God, but emptied himself and took the form of a servant." Vol. iv. p. 260.

least, of the most learned, judicious, and moderate
interpreters.   Cameron, who was well intitled to this
character, conceived that " the phrase was derived
from a custom of that age, that conquerors erected
trophies of the spoils stripped or taken from their
enemies ; and that the clause might with strict propriety be translated, *He made not a triumph*, or
trophy, of his being equal with God ; that is, he did
not ostentatiously show it, he did not seem to glory
and boast of it." [49]   Grotius, Meric Casaubon, Calo-
vius, Michaelis, and others, have embraced this interpretation.   But whether this allusion be admitted or
not, is of little importance : as, in any case, the idea
is plainly indicated that the object intended would not
have been, to Jesus Christ, an act of seizure, a usurpation, a thing to which he had no right ; but, on the
contrary, that to which he had a just claim, a claim to
waive which is laid down by the terms of the passage,
as an act of the most gracious condescension and
humiliation.[50]

[49] " Optimè sic Gallicè vertas, *Il ne fit point de triomphe*, ou
trophée, de ce qu'il était égal à Dieu ; h. e. non jactavit, non visus
est gloriari et insolescere." *Myrothec. Evang.* p. 214.   " Etsi Dei
similis erat, tamen non rapiendam judicavit similitudinem cum Deo."
Morus, in Append. ad Prœl. in Ep. Rom. p. 243.   " Quamvis esset
conditionis divinæ et Deo æqualis ratione naturæ et attributorum,
tamen *non raptum ivit*, non cupide et ubivis usurpavit, hanc cum Deo
æqualitatem ; immo verô ab eâ re abstinuit.——" *Tittmanni Meletemata Sacra.* p. 542.   See also the different versions and illustrations in Note [A], at the end of this Section.

[50] So Chrysostom, whose ability to construe his native language
none will dispute, understood the implication ; and he argues dif-
fusely upon it, in his Seventh Homily on this Epistle.   Τοῦτο τὸ
εἶναι ἴσα Θεῷ οὐχ ὡς ἁρπαγμὸν εἶχεν, ἀλλὰ φυσικόν· διὸ ἐκένωσεν
ἑαυτόν.   " This *being equal to God*, he did not hold as *a thing to be
caught at*, but his own natural right ; wherefore he emptied himself."

iii. "On a parity with God." It has not been without long thought, and some hesitation, that I have at length adopted this, as the most just rendering that I can devise of ἴσα Θεῷ. The expressions, *like God,* and *as God,* appear most evidently to be below the proper signification : and the mode used in the common version and many others, *equal with God,* has the objection of not preserving the adverbial form of the phrase, and therefore of assuming a more defined sense than it can be at once said that the peculiar form justifies. Schleusner explains the phrase as denoting "to sustain the person of God, or to be equal to God in nature and majesty :" and he maintains that ἴσα is not put adverbially, but that, by a kind of enallage, it stands for the singular masculine adjective.[51] He assigns no reason for this opinion ; and I must own that I can discover none. Such an enallage seems unsupported by any principle or authority of the language ; while the use of adjectives in the neuter plural as adverbs, though to be supplied as ellipses,[52] is extremely common.[53] A very eminent scholar, and who was familiarly acquainted with the

---

Homil. vii. in Ep. Philipp. apud *Op. ed Francof.* 1698, vol. vi. p. 64. See also another important passage from Chrysostom, in the valuable article on Ἁρπαγμὸς, in *Mr. Ewing's Greek Lexicon,* the edition of 1828.

[51] *Lex. in voce.*

[52] Schleusner follows Bos in supposing that the full phrase would be κατ' ἴσα μέρη· but a most distinguished Græcian, Schæfer, maintains, "ἴσα, additâve præpositione ἐπὶ ἴσα, κατὰ ἴσα, adverbialiter dicuntur, nihilque subaudiendum est." *Adnot. in Bosii Ellips. Gr.* p. 171.

[53] As ῥᾷστα *most easily,* λῷστα *excellently,* ἐξάπινα *suddenly,* ἀέλπτα *unexpectedly,* ἀβρὰ *elegantly,* πάντα *wholly,* πολλὰ *abundantly,* νήποινα *with impunity :* &c. &c.

niceties of the Greek idiom, Erasmus Schmidt, observes that the verbs γίνομαι and εἰμὶ give to their
conjoined adverb the force of a noun; and that the
grammatical construction of this clause is precisely the
same as if the adjective had been put in the accusative
singular: "to be equal with God." [54]

The interpretation of this phrase is of so great importance, that I trust to the indulgence of the reader
for subjoining a considerable number of instances;
which will, I think, enable even those who have not
studied Greek literature, to form a satisfactory opinion
on the propriety of the mode of translation which I
have adopted. [55]

The proper signification of ἴσος has respect to *quan-
tity*, as that of ὁμοῖος has to *quality*. [56]   The former

---

[54] "Esse æqualiter Deo, *i. e.* esse æqualem Deo. Lutherus, *Gotte gleich
seyn.*   Nam verba substantiva, γίνομαι et ἐμὶ, cum adverbio idoneo,
sæpe adverbii significationem faciunt nominalem: ut, Odyss. B. 82.
Πάντες ἀκὴν ἔσαν· omnes erant tacitè, *i. e.* taciti.   Iliad. Γ. 95.
ἀκὴν ἐγένοντο· fiebant tacitè, *i. e.* taciti.   Sic hoc loco, τὸ εἶναι ἴσα
Θεῷ, pro τὸ εἶναι ἴσον Θεῷ." *Adnot. in N. T.* Nuremb. 1658,
p. 1189.

The late eminent C. G. Heyne, in his remarks on Erasmus
Schmidt's edition of Pindar, while he blames him for want of taste,
and for his invention of an erroneous metrical system, speaks in
rather strong terms of his learning and sagacity as to what regarded
the mere language.   "Saltem doctus et æquus quisque judex fate-
bitur, Schmidii acumine et diligentiâ infinitis locis emendatiorem nos
habere poetam; tum in iis quoque in quibus hallucinatur, ingeniosè
tamen et sagaciter hariolari virum doctissimum.——Ejus—doctrina
præclara.——Magnâ Græcarum literarum copiâ instructus. ——"
Præf. ad. Pind. vol. i. pp. 29, 30, ed. Oxon. 1807.

[55] See Note [C], at the end of this Section.

[56] *Dammii Lex. Hom. et Pind.* pp. 561, 1703.   Euripides, in a
single verse, has marked the distinction.   Νῦν δ' οὔθ' ὅμοιον οὐδὲν,
οὔτ' ἴσον βροτοῖς·   "But nothing now is *fair*, nothing *equal*, among
men."   *Phœnissæ*, ver. 511, ed. Porson.

word was applied, in the propriety of·Greek usage, to cases of equivalence in number, lines and figures, motion, time, distance, weight, community of shares, equality of political rights, and other objects in which the leading idea is that of *commensurate quantities ;*[57] and the latter term was used to designate *resemblance in qualities.* The former attributive was the answer to πόσος, *how much?* the latter to ποιὸς, *of what kind?*[58]

From the whole, it appears to me a just conclusion, that the word under consideration denotes, in every instance of its occurrence, an *equality* or *parity* between two subjects, in such respect as is pointed out in each case by the nature of the subjects, and the connexion of the passage.

Applying this rule to the instance before us, we have first to inquire, if there is any thing ascertained in the nature of the case, which will define *the respect* in which Christ is " on a parity with God." Here we must appeal to the reader's serious and impartial judgment, whether abundant and weighty evidence has not been adduced, in establishment of the fact, that the Saviour of mankind possesses a superior

---

[57] This is exemplified by the use of ἴσος in the works of the Greek mathematicians. Let the reader also consider such words as ἰσοχρονέω, ἰσοδρομέω, ἰσόῤῥοπέω, ἰσομοιρέω· and ἰσοβαρὴς, ἰσοζυγὴς, ἰσοστάσιος, ἰσοκλινὴς, ἰσοταχὴς, ἰσοσθενὴς, ἰσότιμος, ἰσοτελὴς, and the phrase ἴσον ἴσῳ. See *Budæi Comment. Ling. Gr.* Bas. 1557, col. 1221 —1223. *Athenæus,* lib. x. cap. 8, vol. iv. p. 79, ed. *Schweighæus,* et *Casauboni Animadv.* col. 726, Lugd. 1621.

[58] Hesychius does, indeed, say ἴσον, ὅμοιον· and Suidas, ἴσα, τὰ ὅμοια· but that writers of a lower age should have occasionally fallen into a lax use of terms, and have become inattentive to the propriety of the language, is no argument against the use of better times. Besides, many of the verbal explications given by the Greek lexicographers are not synonyms, but only approximations.

nature and mode of existence, which are truly and properly DIVINE. If this be admitted, we have, in the known kind and properties of the subject, a principle enabling us safely and with intelligence to apply the declaration, THE MESSIAH IS ON A PARITY WITH GOD. This remark is not a begging the question, but a fair reference, to what, in the best exercise of my reason, I am conscientiously persuaded is a body of impregnable proof.

We are next, therefore, to inquire whether the terms of the connexion will furnish any assistance to the interpretation of this particular clause.

The circumstance of declining the object stated, is laid down by the inspired writer, as one of the articles of the Saviour's humiliation. That object was something which he did not catch up, take hold of, or with eagerness and promptitude avail himself of the opportunity to seize : it therefore lay before him, and was at his option. His waiving the presented enjoyment is assigned as a part, and a proof, of his condescending and gracious abasement : it was therefore something which was his own by right, which he might justly have claimed, and which, had he been so pleased, he had both the power and the authority to have taken. Also, as the " existing in the form of God" stands, in the antithesis, opposed to the " assuming the form of a servant ;" so this member of the enumeration appears to have its contrast in the "becoming in the likeness of men." These are the attributes of the state, or manner of being, here predicated of the Lord Jesus Christ, and which is denominated τὸ εἶναι ἴσα Θεῷ, "the being on a parity with God."—WHAT, then, was that state, or manner of being?

1. It was the assumption of the regal power and
dignity, say Enjedin[59] and some others, over the
Jewish nation, to which Christ had an unquestionable
right, by his royal descent and by divine appointment,
and which he had both the opportunity and the power
to have seized and secured. So the Hebrew magistrates were styled gods; and so the father of classic
poetry frequently denominates his heroes θεοείκελοι,
godlike, and ισόθεοι, *equal to the gods*.

We reply, that, on the case of the Hebrew magistrates, we beg to refer the reader to a former
passage of this work;[60] that the epithets from Homer
are founded on the mythology which, having made
gods like the vilest of men, easily elevated men to the
rank of gods; that such language is totally abhorrent
from the style and sentiments of the New Testament;
and that, to suppose ἴσα Θεῷ to signify nothing more
than royal state and power, is quite incongruous with
all sobriety of interpretation.

2. An eminent modern Unitarian answers the
question thus: " In the authority with which he
spake to his apostles; in the appellation of Lord and
Master, which he assumed; in his requisition that
they should keep his commandments, and be faithful
in that which he committed to them and enjoined
upon them; in the terms in which he spake of himself, (according to the ideas of the Jews) when he
called himself the Son of God; in the terms in which
he spake of his doctrine, as being the word of God."[61]

That this is a part of the truth, none will be disposed to question; but whether a just interpretation

[59] *Explic. Locorum*, p. 324.   [60] Vol. I. p. 504.
[61] *Cappe's Crit. Rem.* vol. i. pp. 240, 241.

of the particular passages referred to; and of other language which our Lord used of himself, or permitted to be addressed to him, is compatible with any rational notions of the state and condition of a mere human being, is a great part of the question at issue, and upon which it has been attempted, in the preceding pages, to submit the scriptural evidence to the reader's serious and candid judgment. If the writer's endeavours have not been very unsuccessful, a considerable body of evidence has been presented, that our Lord gave frequent intimations of his possessing a preexistent and celestial nature, that he permitted and even claimed honours unsuitable to any but the Divine Being, that he allowed himself to be addressed as Lord and God, that he maintained himself to be One with the Father, and that he admitted and confirmed the imputation of " making himself EQUAL " to God."

3. Mr. Belsham's opinion is, that the expression designates our Lord's possession of a divine commission, and a voluntary power of working miracles, which it was at his option to employ for his own benefit.[62]

The " possession of a divine commission," certainly furnishes some ground for appropriating the expression; as, on that account, Moses is called " God " and " for God " to Pharaoh.[63] But it is manifest that this idea is totally inapplicable to the present case; for the very obvious reason, that our Lord's divine commission was, at no time and in no sense, an object which he laid aside, or declined to use. On the

---

[62] *Calm Inq.* pp. 144, 326, 126.
[63] Exod. vii. 1 ; iv. 16.

contrary, he always professed it, and was constantly acting upon it.

The supposition that Christ, viewed merely as a man and a prophet, had an inherent and optional power of working miracles, does not appear tenable. We know that, on one occasion, he referred to express prayer as having preceded the miracle :[64] and he ascribed, in the most direct terms, his miraculous works, equally with his heavenly doctrine, to the indwelling energy of the Father.[65] It is true that, on most occasions of this kind, our Blessed Lord spake and acted in the style of absolute authority and independence :[66] but this the advocates of the doctrine of his Deity look upon as an intimation, not very obscure, of his possessing a nature with which alone that style of dignity could comport; even the Eternal and Almighty Nature which could " speak and it was

---

[64] John xi. 41.   [65] John v. 19; xiv. 10.

[66] For example : " He rebuked the wind, and said unto the sea, " Peace ! Be still !" Mark iv. 39. " Go thy way ; thy son liveth." John iv. 50. " I will : be thou clean." Matt. viii. 3. " Damsel, " I say unto thee, Arise." Mark v. 41 ; and a similar instance, Luke vii. 14. " Lazarus, come forth." John xi. 43.

Such language, associated with no modification or corrective, seems little becoming to a man of even common piety. How can we imagine it to have belonged to the most perfect of human characters ? The doctrine of the Divine Nature of Christ affords a satisfactory solution of the difficulty : but it seems to me to press insupportably on the opposite hypothesis. Mr. Cappe, in the quotation given above, expressly excludes our Lord's *will* from having any concern in the business : his office was, accurately speaking, nothing more than to *predict the operation.* Upon this statement, was not Jesus very criminal,.when he received, with evident complacency, the address which, according to Mr. Cappe, was absolutely false ; " Lord, if thou WILT, thou canst make me clean !" and confirmed it by his reply, " I WILL : be thou clean !"

" done," which could " command and it stood fast."
Upon the opinion which Mr. B. supported, Mr. Cappe
has these animadversions.   The possession of miraculous powers by Jesus Christ " could neither be
laid down, nor declined, nor suspended.   It could not
be *laid down ;* because it was not an inherent quality
that depended upon his will : it could not be *declined ;* because it was not offered to his acceptance
or refusal, neither originally nor occasionally : it
could not be *suspended ;* because whenever the power
of God was present with him to perform a miracle, it
was accompanied with an impulse on his mind to employ it, or rather to predict its operation." [67]

4. It appears evident that the most probable
method, for ascertaining the intention of the phrase,
is to determine the meaning of that which is laid as
the ground and reason of our Lord's right to what the
clause assumes.   This ground is the " being [68] in the
form of God."

The word used by the apostle, and very properly
translated *form*, signifies the external shape or figure
of a material object.   Of course it can be understood
of the Divine Being, only in the way of an imperfect
analogy.   As the visible and tangible figure of a
sensible object is, in ordinary cases, the chief property
and very frequently the only one, by which we know
that object and distinguish it from others ; so, THAT
part of " what may be known of God" [69] which to
our rational conceptions DISTINGUISHES HIM from all
other objects of apprehension, may thus allusively

[67] *Critical Remarks*, vol. ii. p. 274.
[68] See Note [D], at the end of the Section.
[69] Τὸ γνωστὸν τοῦ Θεοῦ· *cognoscibile* Dei. Rom. i. 19.

be called *the form* of God. Therefore, dropping the figure, the notion is evidently that of *specific difference,* or *essential and distinguishing properties.* It might, I conceive, be unexceptionably expressed by the phrase, *the characteristics of God.*[70] Schleusner, accordingly, gives this as the secondary sense of the word : " the very nature and essence of any subject, the same as φύσις and ουσία." [71]

[70] Μορφὴ occurs once besides in the N. T. Mark xvi. 12, and several times in the Septuagint, e. g. Job iv. 16. Dan. v. 6, 9, 10. Wisd. Sol. xviii. 1 ; every where in the proper sense. The Greeks often applied it to their carnal conceptions of Divinities. But Wetstein and Schleusner have referred to examples of the metonymic application, in Josephus and Plato. Ὁ Θεὸς ἔργοις μὲν καὶ χάρισιν ἐναργὴς, καὶ ὁντινοσοῦν φανερώτερος, μορφήν τε καὶ μέγεθος ἡμῖν ἀφάνεστατος. " God is displayed in his works and his gracious bestowments, and [thus] is more clearly manifested than any other being ; but, as to his *nature* [literally *form,*] and majesty, he is to us invisible." *Joseph. contra Apion,* lib. ii. sect. 22. The connexion of this passage shows that Josephus uses the term to express a spiritual perfection, and not any sensible quality. The following passage from Plato is less clear, as his conceptions were probably influenced by heathen prepossessions. Ἀδύνατον ἄρα, ἔφην, καὶ θεῷ ἐθέλειν αὑτὸν ἀλλοιοῦν· ἀλλ', ὡς ἔοικε, κάλλιστος καὶ ἄριστος ὢν εἰς τὸ δυνατὸν ἕκαστος αὐτῶν, μένει ἀεὶ ἁπλῶς ἐν τῇ αὑτοῦ μορφῇ. " It is then impossible, I replied, for even a god to be willing to undergo any change : but, as seems probable, each of them [the gods] being in the highest possible degree of beauty and moral excellence, always remains simply in the same form." *De Republ.* lib. ii. *Opera,* p. 606, ed. Francof. 1602.

The Greek Fathers understood μορφὴ in the sense of οὐσία· but whether this is to be regarded as a fair grammatical interpretation, or as a theological explication, may be difficult to determine.— E. g. Ἡ μορφὴ τοῦ Θεοῦ ταὐτὸν τῇ οὐσίᾳ πάντως ἐστίν· " The *form of God* is the very same as his *essence,*" *Gregor. Nyss.* apud *Suiceri Thesaur. Eccl.* vol. ii. p. 377. Ἡ μορφὴ τοῦ Θεοῦ φύσις νοεῖται Θεοῦ. " The *form of God* signifies the same as the *nature* of God." *Theodoreti* (if he was the author) *Dialog.* i. apud *Suicer.* ib.

[71] *In vocem.* See the same remark in *Suicerus, ubi supra.*

We may receive further assistance by considering
the antithesis of the sentence. This appears to be
stated, not strictly with any one particular, but generally with all in the enumeration; " the form of a
servant, the likeness of men, the condition as a man." [72]
Christ had the *form*, the *characteristics*, of the debased
and oppressed situation of a bond-servant; the subjection of the human race to pain and sorrow, " the
bondage of corruption," the universal curse, the consequence of our common depravity : he *resembled*
the rest of men, in every thing requisite to a proper
humanity ; and be it remembered that this *resemblance* was in fact an *identity* : his *condition* was
that of a man, in all the accidents and attendant
circumstances of our common nature ; such as growth
from infancy to manhood, developement of physical
and of mental powers, liableness and acute sensibility
to all the kinds of natural suffering, and every other
external circumstance which was proper to demon-
strate him a child of man.

Now let the terms of the contrast be weighed
against each other. If the characteristics of human
nature, as subjected to the penal sorrows of its fallen
state ; if the reality of the same nature appearing in
its properties and adjuncts; if all the appropriate
circumstances of external condition ;—if these marked
the Saviour to be incontrovertibly a real and proper
man, what are we required, in equitable construction,
to understand by his " existing in the form," the
distinguishing characteristics, " of God," and his " being
on a parity with God?"   Are we not clearly *obliged*

[72] Μορφὴ δούλου, compared with Rom. vii. 25 ; viii. 21 ; Gal. iv.
24.——ὁμοίωμα ἀνθρώπου·——σχῆμα ὡς ἄνθρωπος.

to understand these predicates as denoting THAT
which is *peculiar* and *distinctive* to the Divine Being ;
the very nature and essential attributes of God ?

Thus guided by the context and the argument
we find the sense of the passage to be to this effect :
" Although he possessed the essential characteristics
of the Divine Nature, he declined the display of himself as on a parity with God : but, quite otherwise
than that,[73] he deprived himself of the manifestation to
men of those glories and enjoyments of which he had
the rightful possession ; and he assumed the servile,
degraded, distressful state of fallen humanity, submitting to the deepest sorrows in life, and to the extremity of suffering in death. For it is obvious that,
in order thus to suffer, he must have a nature capable
of pain and grief ; he therefore was, ' made in the
likeness of men, and evinced[74] to be in his outward
condition really[75] a man.' In this nature he suffered

---

[73] The proper meaning of ἀλλά. See *Dr. John Jones's Greek
Grammar*, 3d ed. p. 280, and his *Greek and English Lexicon* on the
word.

[74] Εὑρεθείς· See Schleusner in εὑρίσκω, signif. 3. " *experio, com-
perior, cognosco, intelligo, sentio.*" Tertullian confirms this interpretation. " Nam et *inventum* ratione posuit, id est *certissimè*
hominem : quod enim invenitur, constat esse." *Adv. Marcion.*
lib. v. ed. Par. 1664. p. 486.

[75] See Schleusner in ὡς, signif. 15. " *reverâ, verè utpote,* et
respondet Hebraico כ veritatis :—— et אך *utique profectò.*" 'Ως—
ἀληθῶς. *Hesych. ed. Alberti,* col. 1597. " 'Ως et ὡσεί, quomodo
כ veritatis, uti vocant Hebræi, ad quam respondent, non semper
designant nudam similitudinem, sed et θετικαὶ sæpe fiunt, veritatis
notæ βεβαιωτικαί." *Sir Richard Ellys, Fortuita Sacra,* p. 227.
Gesenius regards this *Caph veritatis,* or *confirmationis,* or *iden-
titatis,* as a peculiar idiom, expressing the *usual* way and manner of
a class of subjects ; and he gives as examples, Nehem. vii. 2, Job
xxiv. 14. Hos. iv. 4 ; v. 10. Is. i. 7—9 ; x. 13 ; xiii. 6 ; l. 4,

and in this nature he received his reward. On this meritorious account, God his father, whose gracious purposes of mercy to mankind he hath so divinely accomplished, has conferred upon him, in this same assumed and official capacity, the highest honour and happiness; by the diffusion of holiness and its attendant blessedness, by the homage of all human and celestial intelligences, and by his universal dominion as the Messiah, to the everlasting and most glorious manifestation of the holiness, the righteous government, the free benevolence, and the wisdom of God the Father."

It appears therefore to my own apprehension, to be clearly established, by the signification of the words and by the sense of the connexion, that "being in the form of God," was designed to denote the *possession* of the Divine Nature and Perfections; and that, " being (ἴσα Θεῷ) as God, or on a parity with God," expresses the *manifestation* of those perfections.

The only remaining kind of evidence is what may be derived from the Ancient Versions and the citations of early Christian writers.

The translator of the Peshito Syriac has evidently laboured to maintain an anxious closeness to the Greek; and, where he could not find a term in his own language strictly equipollent, he has preserved the Greek word itself. " Who, though he was in the likeness[76] of God, did not esteem this a usurpa-

Numb. xi. 1. Lam. i. 20. *Lehrgeb.* p. 846. *Wörterb.* p. 338. Another illustrative example is in Is. lviii. 5.

[76] The same word is used in the three places. It denotes *an image, a likeness, a model, a resemblance.* It is put for εἰκὼν in 1 Cor. xi. 7; xv. 49, twice. 2 Cor. iii. 18; iv. 4. Col. i. 15; iii. 10. μορφὴ, Mark xvi. 12. σύμμορφος, Phil. iii. 21. Rom. viii. 29.

tion,[77] that he was on a parity[78] with God ; but he emptied himself and took the likeness of a servant, and was in the likeness of the children of men, and in condition[79] was found as a child of man."

The Vulgate: "Who, being in the form of God, esteemed it not a rapine that himself should be equal to God ; but emptied himself, taking the form of a servant, made into the likeness of men, and found in condition as a man."[80]

Of the earliest Latin versions we can have no better information than the citations of Tertullian, the most ancient of the Latin Fathers: "Being constituted in

ὁμοίωμα, Rom. i. 23 ; v. 14 ; vi. 5 ; viii. 3. ὁμοίωσις, James iii. 9. ὅμοιος, Rev. iv. 3 ; ix. 7. ἀφωμοιωμένος, Heb. vii. 3. ὁμοίως, Rev. ii. 15 ; viii. 12. κατὰ τὸν ὅμοιον τρόπον, Jude 7. ὑπόδειγμα, Heb. iv. 11 ; viii. 5 ; ix. 23. James v. 10. παραπλησίως, Heb. ii. 14. τύπος, Acts vii. 43, 44. Rom. v. 14 ; vi. 17. Phil. iii. 17. 1 Thess. i. 7. 1 Tim. iv. 12. Tit. ii. 7. 1 Pet. v. 3. ἀντίτυπος, Heb. ix. 24. The case deserves the reader's studious attention to all these passages : they will furnish the best comment on the venerable Syrian's understanding of μορφή.

[77] *Plundering, rapine.* See the Hebrew original of the Syriac word in Judges xxi. 21. Ps. x. 9. Prov. xxiii. 28. It is used for ἁρπαγὴ in the three places in which that word occurs. Matt. xxiii. 25. Luke xi. 39. Heb. x. 34.

[78] The word occurs only this once. Its proper idea is *balancing or comparing together.* See its verb in Ps. lxxxix. 6. Luke ii. 19. 1 Cor. ii. 13. 2 Cor. x. 12, 13.

[79] The very word σχῆμα is preserved, as in the only place besides of its occurrence, 1 Cor. vii. 31. The word was adopted into the Syriac language. We find it for μόρφωσις, 2 Tim. iii. 5. τιμὴ, 1 Cor. xii. 23. καταστολή, 1 Tim. ii. 9. κατάστημα, Tit. ii. 3. With the prefix, for εὐσχημόνως, Rom. xiii. 13. 1 Cor. xiv. 40. 1 Thess. iv. 12.

[80] " Qui, cùm in formâ Dei esset, non rapinam arbitratus est esse se æqualem Deo ; sed semetipsum exinanivit, formam servi accipiens, in similitudinem hominum factus, et habitu inventus ut homo."

the likeness of God, he esteemed it not a rapine to be on a parity with God; but emptied himself, taking the likeness of a servant, and made in the likeness of man, and found in figure a man."[81]

The Arabic of Walton's Polyglott: "Who ceased not to be in the likeness of God, [yet] did not embrace his being equal with God, as an allurement to be caught at for himself; but depressed himself, then took the likeness of a servant, was made in the likeness of men, and was found in conformation as a man."

The Æthiopic Version I can cite only as represented in the Latin translation of Loftus and Castell: "Who though he was the likeness [countenance] of God, usurped not from him who was God; subjecting himself, and transformed so as to become a servant, as a man becoming obedient."

In the same manner I borrow from Wilkins's translation of the Coptic: "Who, existing in the form of God, believed it not to be a prey that he should become equal to God; but debased himself, assumed the form of a servant, being made in the likeness of man, found in condition as a man."

To the earlier Christian writers, as was before said, we refer only as aids and evidences, to afford light to the grammatical construction, and by no means as doctrinal authorities. The passages which have already been adduced, sufficiently prove that the best and earliest of the Greek Fathers understood our

[81] " Qui in effigie Dei constitutus, non rapinam existimavit pariari [*in other places*, esse se æqualem] Deo; sed exhausit semetipsum, acceptâ effigie servi, et in similitudine hominis factus, et figurâ inventus homo." *Tertull. Op.* pp. 328, 486, 504, &c.

Lord's " being in the form of God," to signify his *existing in the characteristic properties of the Divine Nature.;* and his " being as God," to express the *manifesting of that glory and dignity which was rightfully his own.* The learned reader can, if he pleases, add to the number; particularly from the works of Basil and the two Gregorys. I shall, therefore, quote only two passages more; which though they do not belong to a very early period, are interesting and little known.

In an Epistle of Six Bishops to Paul of Samosata, written about A. D. 269, we read : " Jesus Christ, himself God and man, was prophesied of in the law and the prophets; and throughout the whole church under heaven, he has been believed to be both God, *who emptied himself* from being *on a parity with God,* and man, *being of the seed of David according to the flesh.*"[82]

Peter of Alexandria, the few fragments of whose writings indicate great simplicity and piety, and every where an unequivocal deference to scripture authority, and who suffered martyrdom at the beginning of the fourth century, has the passage : " Since most certainly *grace and truth came by Jesus Christ,* therefore *we are saved by grace,* according to the apostolic declaration ; *and this,* he says, *not of ourselves; it is the gift of God, not of works, lest any one should boast.* By the will of God *the Word becoming flesh,* and *being*

---

[82] Ὁ αὐτὸς Θεὸς καὶ ἄνθρωπος Ἰησοῦς Χριστὸς προεφητεύετο ἐν νόμῳ καὶ προφήταις, καὶ ἐν τῇ ἐκκλησίᾳ τῇ ὑπὸ τὸν οὐρανὸν πάσῃ πεπίστευται Θεὸς μὲν, κενώσας ἑαυτὸν ἀπὸ τοῦ εἶναι ἴσα Θεῷ· ἄνθρωπος δὲ, καὶ ἐκ σπέρματος Δαβὶδ τὸ κατὰ σάρκα. *Routh, Reliq. Sacr.* vol. ii. p. 475. έ *Concil. Labb. et Cossart.* tom. i. p. 843.

found in condition as a man, did not relinquish his Deity. Neither when he, *being rich, became poor,* was it so done that he might desert his power or perfect glory; but that he might undergo death for us sinners, *the just for the unjust that he might bring us to God, being put to death in the flesh, but restored to life by the Spirit.*[83]

The correct philology and sound judgment of Theodoret entitle him to be adduced, though he lived in the latter part of the fifth century. He thus interprets verses 6 and 7;—" For, being God and by nature God, and thus possessing equality with the Father, he did not take this up as a great thing. For so to act is a characteristic of persons who have happened to get some honour beyond their desert. But he, hiding his own dignity, took the condition of extreme humiliation, and clothed himself in the human form."[84]

Thus the evidence of the Ancient Versions, and the early citations, is clearly in accordance with that which we have before deduced from the meaning of the words and from the connexion and scope of the passage.

iv. The next clause is ἑαυτὸν ἐκένωσε, " he emptied himself." This is the literal signification of the verb:

[83] Ἐπειδὴ καὶ ἀληθῶς ἡ χάρις καὶ ἡ ἀλήθεια διὰ Ἰησοῦ Χριστοῦ ἐγένετο· ὅθεν καὶ χάριτι ἐσμὲν σεσωσμένοι, κατὰ τὸ ἀποστόλικον ῥητόν· καὶ τοῦτο, φησὶν, οὐκ ἐξ ἡμῶν, Θεοῦ τὸ δῶρον, οὐκ ἐξ ἔργων ἵνα μή τις καυχήσηται. Θελήματι Θεοῦ ὁ Λόγος σάρξ γενόμενος, καὶ σχήματι εὑρεθεὶς ὡς ἄνθρωπος, οὐκ ἀπελείφθη τῆς θεότητος. Οὐδὲ γὰρ ἵνα τῆς δυνάμεως αὐτοῦ ἢ δόξης τελείας ἀποστῇ, πτωχεύσας πλούσιος ὤν, τοῦτο ἐγένετο· ἀλλ' ἵνα καὶ τὸν θάνατον ὑπὲρ ἡμῶν τῶν ἁμάρτωλῶν ἀναδέξηται, δίκαιος ὑπὲρ ἀδίκων, ὅπως ἡμᾶς προσαγάγῃ τῷ Θεῷ, θανατωθεὶς μὲν σαρκὶ, ζωοποιηθεὶς δὲ Πνεύματι. *Routh,* vol. iii. p. 334. *Labb. et Cossart,* tom. iii. p. 508.

[84] —— οὐ μέγα τοῦτο ὑπέλαβε, ——*Interp. in loc.*

and, in all its applications, it carries the idea of *reduction* from a previous state of fulness, in respect of
strength, efficiency, or some other mode of possession
or excellency.   Where it occurs in other places of
the New Testament,[85] it has reference not to persons
but to things, as the predicate; and the signification
just given will be found to suit them all.   The idea,
when applied to persons, is metaphorical, and plainly
imports a privation of external possessions or internal
qualities, and a consequent diminution of condition
or enjoyment.   In the Septuagint it occurs twice,[86]
and serves to describe the extreme distress of national calamities.   The same is the meaning of the
word by which it is represented in the Old Syriac
Version.[87]   The forms in which the other Ancient
Versions have conveyed the expression, have just been
detailed.   Few modern translators have preserved
the original expression; but, perhaps, from conceiving
the metaphor to be somewhat harsh, they have generally given what they conceived to be its intention
in another way.[88]   But it would be wasting words to

[85] *Viz.* Rom. iv. 14.   1 Cor. i. 17; ix. 15.   2 Cor. ix. 3.

[86] For the conj. *pual*, or, according to the more accurate grammatical system of Schultens and Gesenius, *pylal*, of אָמַל, Jer. xiv. 2;
xv. 9.

[87] See *Schaafii Lexicon*, p. 396.

[88] He made himself of no reputation : *the Common Version*, which,
in this rendering, has followed *Cranmer's, or rather Tyndale's*, 1539 :
the Geneva English by Coverdale, Knox, &c. 1560 (which adds this
explanation, " He brought himself from all things, as it were, to
nothing :") and *Parker's or the Bishops' Bible*, 1568.   Made himself
of none account : *Abp. Newcome.*   Divested himself : *Impr. Vers.*
Semetipsum inanivit : *Leo Judæ, Calvin, Beza, Piscator.*   Seipsum
eousque ad nihilum redegit : *Castellio.*   Seipsum ad statum tenuem
depressit : *Döderlein.*   Voluit tenuis esse ; se vacuum, se inanem,

show, that all the forms, in which the expression may be varied or explained, unavoidably carry with them the same principal idea, that of descending from a state of dignity to one of inferiority.

This, indeed, is universally admitted. But the Unitarians maintain that the state of dignity from which Christ descended, is to be referred wholly to certain circumstances in his condition as the messenger of God among men. In his acceptableness and celebrity among his countrymen, the authority with which he spake in the name of God, and his miracles, they place this superior state: and the *self-emptying* they apply to his submitting to the meanest rank in life, to poverty and want, to indignity, cruel treatment, and a violent and unjust death.[89]

It appears to me a solid objection to this interpretation, that it is extremely remote from the just signification of the terms; that it is evidently forced to help the exigency of a system; and that it scarcely comports with fact. Let the studious and candid reader examine what has been advanced on the meaning of the terms, and the scope and sense of the connexion; and impartially consider whether this inter-

reddidit : *Morus.* Extenuavit, depressit se ad humilitatem : *Rosenmüller.* Aeusserte sich selbst; (*i. e.* divested himself, or etymologically, put himself to the last extremity :) *Luther, and other German translators. See the Supplementary Note* [A]. Heeft hem selven vernietight; (*i. e.* reduced himself to nothing :) *Dutch authorized Version.* Agotóse à si mismo ; (*i. e.* exhausted himself to the very utmost :) *Cassiodoro del Reyna.* Annichilò se stesso ; (*i. e.* reduced himself to nothing :) *Diodati.* Il s'est anéanti lui-même : *De Sacy, and the French Protestant Versions, from those of Olivetan and Calvin down to that of Geneva,* 1805.

[89] *Enjedin. Expl. Loc.* p. 326. *Cappe's Crit. Rem.* vol. i. pp. 230—235. *Impr. Vers. note. Calm Inq.* p. 139.

pretation is at all in congruity with them.   As to the
facts of the case, there does not appear to have been
any such contrast between the prior and the latter
parts of our Lord's public life, as the interpretation
supposes.   The history shows that he was always
" a man of sorrows and acquainted with grief."   It is
recorded of a very early period of his ministry, that he
" had not where to lay his head." [90]   Reproach and
calumny were heaped upon him through its general
course : [91] and his stupendous miracles, his engaging
address, his admired wisdom, his occasional and fugi-
tive popularity, only gave a keener edge to the blasphemies of his adversaries, and to the pangs of his
own soul, while " he beheld the transgressors and was
" grieved, and reproach broke his heart."   With respect, also, to the closing scenes of his life, which these
writers conceive to have constituted this humiliation
and emptying himself ; it is proper to observe, that
the evidences of power and majesty were really not
suppressed during that period, in the manner that
their hypothesis supposes.   On the contrary, his peculiar glory was displayed in various ways, and those
more calculated to impress the beholders with awe and
terror, as well as with admiration and gratitude, than
any previous demonstration of our Lord's superiority
had been.   Such were his striking to the ground the
band of armed men with a glance of his eye, his healing the high-priest's servant, his showing mercy and
promising heaven to the penitent robber, the preternatural darkness, the rending of the veil of the temple,
the terrific earthquake, and the still more astonishing
miracle, that " the tombs were opened, and many

[90] Matt. viii. 20.   Luke viii. 3.   [91] Matt. x. 25.

" bodies of holy persons were raised."[92] These events possessed a grandeur till then unequalled: and they turn the argument of the writers referred to, completely back upon themselves. According to their own manner of interpretation, these circumstances, more than any that can be adduced in the previous life of Jesus, amounted to a being *in the form of God* ("teaching and working miracles in God's name, exercising authority, judging mankind,"[93]) and a being *like God*. Thus is their interpretation inconsistent and self-destructive.

Some good writers have advanced that κενόω is to be considered as representing the Hebrew verb הֵרִיק, and that the signification is to be sought from that of רֵיק and רֵיקָם, in the Septuagint κενὸς, and applied to persons in poverty and destitution. So that the meaning is, he brought himself into a state of extreme want, destitute of the ordinary necessaries of life. This makes no difference in the ultimate sense of the whole passage; for it leaves untouched the question of the state out of which his descent to poverty took place. On this criticism, however, the following remarks are submitted :—

(1.) The Septuagint never translates the Hebrew verb by this Greek one; and, if it did, the proper meaning of the Hebrew word is also *to empty*. It is true that the adjectives are sometimes rendered by κενὸs, in the acceptation above stated: but this does not seem to be a sufficient ground for the criticism, in a case when the word in question requires no departure from its established meaning.

(2.) The only place in the Old Testament in which

[92] Matt. xxvii. 52.   [93] *Cappe*, vol. i. p. 232.

either of the adjectives is used, and which carries a
sense at all approaching to that of the apostolic passage, is Nehemiah v. 13, " Thus will God shake out
" every man who shall not confirm this declaration,
" from his house and from his property : even thus
" shall he be shaken out and *empty* (רֵק *κενός*)." Here
the word manifestly denotes the privation of former
possessions.

(3.) For reasons before intimated,[94] considering the
circumstances in which the apostle wrote and the
people to whom he was writing, inhabitants of a
Macedonian town, it is more probable that he would
use the verb in its ordinary sense, the sense which
would be obvious to native Greeks, rather than in an
acceptation deduced somewhat circuitously from the
Hebrew idiom. The Jewish sense of words and
phrases would be more ready to occur in those expressions which were of frequent and habitual occurrence ;
while, in such as were very rarely employed, the
common usage would naturally be taken.

(4.) The sense pleaded for is unexampled in the
New Testament. In the other instances of its occurrence in the writings of the apostle Paul, the word
always signifies the *taking away* of some properties or
circumstances which the subject before possessed, or
was supposed to possess.[95]

(5.) This interpretation makes the clause altogether
redundant and tautological : for a following clause,
" he humbled himself," contains the meaning which is
thus unnecessarily anticipated.

[94] See page 407 of this Volume.
[95] Rom. iv. 14. 1 Cor. i. 17 ; ix. 15. 2 Cor. ix. 3. Except in
the passage under consideration, the word occurs nowhere else in
the New Testament.

It appears, therefore, that a faithful adherence to the rules of fair construction and interpretation obliges us to understand this clause as referring to a PREEXISTENT STATE of dignity and glory, and declaring that the Messiah divested himself of the attributes belonging to that state.

It is objected that, upon the admission that the superior and preexistent nature of the Messiah was properly DIVINE, this self-emptying, divestment, or reduction to a lower point in the scale of existence, was *plainly* IMPOSSIBLE; for the necessary unchangeableness of the Divine Nature forbids any idea of degradation from its glory or laying aside of its attributes.

To this objection we have replied before, in considering those passages which represent the Messiah to have come down from heaven. It is scarcely necessary to repeat that we understand such declarations in all the different forms in which they occur, as implying nothing inconsistent with the essential and immutable perfections of the Divine Nature; but as referring to MANIFESTATIONS and outward EXERCISES of the Divine perfections. Such language is derived from comparison with human actions, and is abundantly exemplified in the Old Testament. Indeed, without such analogical language, it would be impossible for human beings to reason and discourse on subjects purely spiritual. Applying this principle to the expression before us, its intention is easily perceived to be, that the assumption of human nature, by HIM who is the True and Unchangeable God, into a close and ineffable union with himself, was an act of infinite *condescension;* —— that this condescension extended, not only to the assumption of the human nature, but to all the particular and minute circumstances of extreme *debasement* and *suffering*, which, in the scheme of Divine Wisdom, were requisite ;—— and that a material part of that debasement and suffering consisted in a *suspension* of those inward joys which the union with the Divine Nature must otherwise have produced to the human mind of Jesus, and in a *withholding* of external acts which would have manifested the peculiar presence and perfections of God : a suspension and withholding, the aggregate of which has been very fitly called by divines, an *occultation of the Divine Glory.* This, we conceive, is with the greatest propriety called an *emptying of himself;* a veiling, a suspending, a ceasing from manifestation, of the uncreated and unchangeable Majesty of Him who has the characteristics of God, and is on a parity with God.

The remaining clauses of the passage will require only a shorter consideration.

v. "Taking the form of a servant." Though in him was no sin, yet he came "in the likeness of *sinful flesh.*" He wore the marks and manacles of the curse entailed by the apostasy of man ; the *characteristics* (as we have before shown that the word is justly to be interpreted) of that *servitude* and dishonour which sin has inflicted upon our nature, and upon all our circumstances in the present state ; that which is called in Scripture (ἡ ΔΟΥΛΕΙΑ τῆς φθορᾶς) "the *bondage,* " servitude, or slavery, of corruption.[96]

vi. "Becoming," or being made, "in the likeness of men." This likeness, as all admit, was the reality

[96] Rom. viii. 21.

of human nature. In all respects, except such as would have involved what was sinful, he was like the rest of the human race. " Since infants are partakers in common of flesh and blood, he himself also *in like manner* partook of the same.[97]

vii. " And, being found in condition as a man :"——in mental powers and susceptibilities, in natural wants, appetites, and passions, in the necessity of labour, care, and anxiety, in the relationships and connexions of life, and in all outward state and circumstances, he was really a man, and like other men.[98]

viii. " —— he humbled himself, becoming obedient " unto death, even the death 'of the cross." The clause "he humbled himself," is most probably to be understood in the sense of an expression repeatedly occurring in the Old Testament, and rendered in our common version by the phrase *to afflict the soul.*[99] That expression was applied to persons who underwent *voluntary* sufferings from religious motives. It well expresses the Saviour's generous self-devotion for the highest benefit of the world, his " bearing our griefs " and carrying our sorrows." This he did, in the most perfect compliance with the will of his Divine Father, through all the varieties and degrees of pain and woe, with deepest and unmitigated anguish of soul, down to his last and most excruciating agonies : " obedient unto death, even the death of the cross."

Endeavouring now to bring together all the parts of this remarkable portion of apostolic scripture, I

---

[97] Heb. ii. 14.

[98] See page 384 of this Volume.

[99] עִנּוֹת נֶפֶשׁ rendered in the LXX. by ταπεινοῦν τὴν ψυχήν. The Hebrew verb signifies both *to afflict* and *to humble*. See Lev. xvi. 29, 31. Isaiah lviii. 3, 5, and other instances.

must confess that, under every variety of fair interpretation, none appears tenable which does not recog-
nise a nature in the Messiah distinct from the human,
preexistent, superior to all that is glorious and excellent in dependent existence, and really DIVINE. Every
explication of the terms and clauses, that wears the
aspect of grammatical integrity, seems to render this
conclusion unavoidable.

The importance and difficulty of the passage will,
I trust, appear a sufficient reason for the discussion
which has been employed upon it: and it may be a
further apology for the length to which the inquiry
has been carried, that other points of the controversy
have thus presented themselves to examination, and
that principles of interpretation have been elucidated
which will, I trust, be of more general use.

It will be recollected that this passage was brought
under consideration, in addition to others from the
New Testament, for the purpose of showing that the
human nature of Jesus Christ is described by such
terms, and in such connexion of argument, as *imply*
a superior, preexistent, and Divine Nature; equally
belonging to him in fact, and equally necessary to the
constitution of his PERSON as a competent SAVIOUR to
the human race.

SUPPLEMENTARY NOTES TO SECT. II.

Note [A], page 339.

" Let every one be disposed as Jesus Christ also was ; who, though
he was in a divine form, held it not for a [*raub*] seizure to be [*Gotte
gleich*] equal to God ; but divested himself and assumed a servant's
form, became [*gleich wie*] like any other man, and was found in

demeanour as a man: he humbled himself, and became obedient unto death, yea even the death of the cross." *Luther's Version.*
" Have ye those dispositions which Jesus Christ also had, who, though he was [*Gotte ähnlich*] like God, and was his image,[a] yet carried it not as a [*raub schau*] forced display that he should be [*Gotte gleich*] equal to God,[b] but renounced his preeminence, assumed the form of a servant,[c] equal to other men, and in conduct and every thing external was as a man, demeaned himself, and became obedient unto death, yea even the death of the cross." *Michaelis's Version,* 1790.

Selection from *Michaelis's Annotations* (published after his death) on the preceding Version. " [a] I have thus endeavoured to illustrate and make intelligible the expression which in Luther's translation is indeed given literally, but is somewhat obscure.—Jesus saith, ' He that hath seen me, hath seen the Father.' John xiv. 9.—Yet I must confess that I cannot satisfy myself, and that the expression, about which so much doctrinal and polemical matter has been uttered—has to my apprehension an obscurity which I am not able to remove.——[b] The imagery and the expression are derived from the public exhibition, in triumph, of spoils taken in war. A man who had taken his enemy's armour, wore it, to exhibit himself publicly as the conqueror. Stripped of the metaphor, the meaning is, Christ did not seek to make an ostentation of his high rank by appearing in the world as a King, or as one who was still more than that, even equal to God. ——[c] He did not show himself as a King and a Ruler, but merely as a servant of God, perfectly on a par with other men. It probably belonged to this ' form of a servant,' that Jesus, so far from appearing as a king, was himself a subject, acknowledged the right of magistracy, paid his poll-tax like other men to a foreign power which had reduced the Jews to subjection ; and, further, that his entire life was in a low condition. In his sufferings, since he was ' obedient unto the death of the cross,' this *servant's form* was displayed in the strongest manner."

" The design of the apostle was to persuade the Philippians to concord, the principle of which he showed to consist in humility and endeavours to promote the good of others. With this view, he makes use of the example of Jesus Christ, whose disposition and feelings he wished them to imitate : for he was ' in the form of God,' that is *a divine condition;* and yet he abased himself to the condition of a slave, for the salvation of men. I apprehend that this is the best mode of translating ἐν μορφῇ Θεοῦ, which very many understand of the Divinity itself, and the possession or use of the Divine Majesty. And it is undeniable that he who is in the form of God must possess a Divine Nature ; for it is immediately subjoined, as an equivalent expression, (τὸ εἶναι ἴσα Θεῷ) that he was ' equal to God.' But immediately after he is said to be ' in the form of a slave ;'—the last and lowest condition of human nature, as Cicero observes, as *De Off.* i. 13. Since therefore Jesus Christ was in a divine condition, and possessed the divine power and majesty, ' he did not esteem' that

condition to be (ἁρπαγμὸς) 'an object of seizure.' In the explication of this word, interpreters greatly differ. I should prefer translating it (*non raptum ivit*) 'he did not grasp at' that majesty so great,
the being 'equal to God:' that is, he did not eagerly hurry to the
use of such greatness. So persons are said (*rapere hæreditatem*)
'to seize the inheritance,' when they rush with indecent haste to
take possession of their bequests : and so the Emperor Tacitus, at
his accession, is described by Vopiscus as (*non raptum ivisse impe-
rium*) 'not having grasped at the empire,' as he began to reign with
urbanity and moderation, without haughtiness and pride." *J. A. Ernesti Opuscula Theologica*, p. 602.

"Be ye of the same disposition as Christ Jesus was ; who, though
he had it in his power to be in the lofty station of God, grasped not
at the splendour of the divine majesty, but divested himself, taking
the place of a servant, when he was made like to men. Moreover,
being found, in his whole condition, on a par with the rest of mankind, he submitted himself by yielding obedience to the last sufferings, even the sufferings of the cross." *Storrii Opuscula Acad.* vol. i.
p. 322. Tübingen, 1796.

"Let each one be disposed as Christ Jesus ; who, though he was
the visible image of God, yet did not stretch forth to it as to an
object of seizure, to be equal to God : but himself relinquished his
preeminence, assumed a servant's form, became like other men, had
the usual form of a man, abased himself, became obedient unto
death, yea, even the death of the cross." *Seiler, Erbauungsb.*

"In these few words is described the whole great work of the
humiliation of Jesus Christ. To the more accurate acquaintance
with this subject, we must consider Christ not merely as a man, but
also as the Son of God. As Son of God, he was the invisible image
of the Father ; he had the same properties and perfections as the
Father ; he acted in the work of creation with divine power, wisdom,
and goodness : for through him the Father created all things,
through him he governs the universe. The Son of God might now
indeed have appeared on earth in glorious splendour, in divine
majesty and form ; but, from love to us men, he did not so. He
united himself to a human nature, and appeared on earth in Jesus,
to accomplish the great work of the redemption of our race. Jesus
well knew who he was, the Saviour of men united to the Son of
God. It was also known to him that, after the suffering of death,
he should be exalted to the throne of God, and be manifested in
divine glory to angels and blessed spirits. Yet he did not stretch
out after this divine glory, as to an object of seizure ; but he waited

for the time when the Father would glorify him. Once indeed he appeared to Peter, James, and John, upon a mountain in splendid brightness : but he did not make a show of this before the whole people, as a conqueror might of a thing seized upon :[1] he deprived himself of this high distinction ; he retained the form of an ordinary man ; he lived as other men live ; like them, he supported himself with sleep, food, and drink ; like them, he was wearied with labour ; he had the experience of grief and pain, as feeble men are wont to experience them. From all this, he could easily have freed himself, by the might which dwelt in him ; by his miraculous power, he could have created for himself riches to the full : but for our sakes he became poor, that, through his poverty, we might become spiritually rich and truly blessed. He might well have enjoyed plentiful pleasures upon earth : but he denied himself the comforts of this life ; he would not once perform a miracle to assuage his own hunger, though he could have turned the stones into bread ; for he was to endure great trials in all kinds of suffering, that he might be merciful and sympathizing, that—as our High Priest—he might for us offer up himself. This was the command which he had received from his Father ; he was to lay down his life for his sheep, and he was obedient to his Father, to the death of the cross. That mode of death, crucifixion, was with the Romans the punishment of slaves. How low had the Son of God abased himself ! He took ' the form of a slave' in his life, and washed his disciples' feet. He was made like a slave in his death, yea, he was numbered with the transgressors." *Id.*

" For ye should be disposed as Jesus Christ was. He, though [*der Gottheit ähnlich*] like to the Deity, did not carry this likeness to God as a [*beute zur schau*] thing to be grasped at for ostentation; but set himself below his rank, conducted himself as a servant, [*ward menschen gleich*] became on an equality with mankind; did not in his external appearance distinguish himself from other men, abased himself, and proved obedient unto death, yea even the death of the

---

[1] " The words ' he held it not an object of seizure, are capable of two meanings. They may signify, *Christ did not grasp at that glory as a booty to be seized; he did not too eagerly long for it* : in this case, the expression applies to the human nature of Jesus ; it patiently waited the time for its exaltation. But the words may also be translated, *He did not make a display of it, as a thing seized*, as I have expressed the sentiment above ; and then they will refer to the Divine Nature of Christ, which was not disclosed before the world in its brightness and glory. It is difficult to determine which of these two was the apostle's intention ; but they both come to the same point, namely, that Christ did not reveal himself before the world in his Divine Majesty."

cross." *Stolz's* (Dr. and Prof. Theol. at Bremen, and afterwards at Zurich) *Uebersetzung des N. T.* Hanover, 1804.

" For such a disposition should be in you as that which was even in Christ Jesus ; who, though he came forth in [*Gottesgestalt*] a form of God, regarded it not as a thing to be grasped at, to be [*Gott gleich*] equal to God ; but set himself below his rank, in that he assumed a servant's form, became equal to men, was found in appearance as a man, abased himself, and proved obedient unto death, yea even the death of the cross." *Another new Version, by the same Dr. Stolz.* Hanover, 1820. This gentleman, who died in 1821, was not indeed an Antisupernaturalist, but in general respects he carried his Neological views very far, and was a warm admirer and imitator of Dr. Paulus. In his [*Erläuterungen zum N. T.*] " Illustrations of the New Testament," (6 volumes in 8vo. 1808— 1812) he gives several interpretations of this very difficult passage, and acknowledges himself unable or unwilling to decide among them. A similar remark may be made upon Heinrich's ample *Excursus*, at the end of his Koppian Commentary upon this Epistle ; though he manifestly inclines to the Unitarian explication.

" For ye should be so disposed as Jesus Christ was ; who, though he was of divine nature, held it not [*raub*] an object of seizure to be equal to God ; but divested himself, assumed a servant's form, became like to men, and in appearance was found as a man. He abased himself, and became obedient unto death, yea, even the death of the cross." *Leander van Ess's Version.* De *Wette's* is substantially the same.

" Ayez les mêmes dispositions d'esprit que Jésus-Christ a eues ; lequel, étant l'image de Dieu, n'a point regardé comme une proie à ravir de s'égaler à Dieu ; mais il s'est anéanti lui-même, en prenant la forme de serviteur, et se rendant semblable aux hommes. Il a paru comme un simple homme, et il s'est abaissé lui-même, s'étant rendu obéissant jusqu'à la mort, et même jusqu'à la mort de la croix." *Geneva Version of* 1805.

" Qui quamvis ipse Deus erat, tamen divina hac majestate non cupide ad vanam gloriam abusus est, sed sua sponte humilem conditionem amplexus servi forma humanam naturam induit, neque externo habitu ab aliis se hominibus distinxit, sed summa cum modestia obedientem se [Deo patri] ad vitæ usque finem, hoc est crucis supplicium, præbuit." *Reichard, N. T. Libri Latinitate donati;* Leipz. 1799.

" Is enim sensus [sentiendi ratio] insit in vobis qui etiam fuit in Christo qui, quamquam imaginem Dei referebat, parem esse Deo non rapinam [rem cupide arripiendam] esse duxit, sed semetipsum humilem gessit, forma [conditione] ministri sumpta, similis factus hominibus et habitu deprehensus ut homo [universa conditione externa hominibus par] se ipse demisit obediens usque ad mortem, ad mortem autem crucis [al. ita obediens ut adeo mortem subiret, supplicium crucis.]" *N. T. Er. Lat. Nähbe;* Leipz. 1831.

" Let there be among you the disposition, the very one that was in Christ Jesus, who, being of Divine Nature, held it not for a robbery to be [*Gott gleich*] equal to God ; but he divested himself thereof, became like to man, and outwardly was found as a man ; he humbled hinself and was obedient to death, death on the cross.—— *Sense :* Be ye so affected in mind as Christ was in his whole earthly life. He is of the Divine nature, and like essence with the Father ; (Col. i. 15. Heb. i. 3 ;) he regarded Deity not as something bestowed upon him, and the acceptance of divine adoration displayed from heaven not as an assumption, but as that which properly belonged to him : he divested himself of this infinite greatness, insomuch as he united himself to the human nature in Jesus, so intimately that he with it constitutes only one person." *Dr. Scholz* (the indefatigable editor of the Greek Testament, in 2 quarto volumes, Leipz. 1830 and 1836,) in the *Version and Notes* completing *Brentano and Dereser's Bible ;* Frankf. 1830.

Note [B], p. 369.

Heliodorus, who wrote at the close of the fourth century, but who was well acquainted with the proprieties and elegances of his language, has often been referred to for exemplifying the sense of ἅρπαγμα. We find the word several times in his romance of Theagenes and Chariclea, and in one instance connected with the same verb that is used by the apostle. Τί δὲ τὸ ;—οὕτω—ἀπωθεῖται ; καὶ οὐχ ἅρπαγμα, οὐδὲ ἕρμαιον, ἡγεῖται τὸ πρᾶγμα; "How is this?— Does he thus reject such a tempting opportunity ? and not *esteem* the occurrence *a thing to be caught at,* or a capital piece of luck ?" Lib. vii. sect. 20, vol. i. *ed. Coräy, Par.* 1804, p. 290. Ἡ δὲ Κυβέλη τὴν ξυντυχίαν ἅρπαγμα, καὶ ὥσπερ ἄγρας ἀρχὴν, ποιησαμένη ἔφη—· "Cybele, making the fortunate circumstance·*a thing to be caught at,* and as it were the beginning of her game, said,"—&c. ib. sect. 11, p. 274. Οὐχ ἅρπαγμα τὸ πρᾶγμα, οὐδὲ εὔωνον, καὶ τῶν ἐν μέσῳ τῷ βουλομένῳ προκειμένων· " This matter is not *a thing to be caught at :* it is not a cheap affair, or what any body that likes may take up." Lib. iv. sect. 6, p. 143. Ἅρπαγμα τὸ ῥηθὲν ἐποιησάτο ἡ Ἀρσάκη. ·" Arsace took advantage of this saying, as *a thing to be caught at.*" Lib. viii. sect. 7, p. 321.

This distinguished editor, M. Coräy, is a native Greek, who has devoted his life to promote among his countrymen the revival of their ancient literature. It may be presumed that no scholar trained in our schools and colleges, not even such men as Porson, Parr, and Burney, or Heyne, Hermann, and Wyttenbach, could rival M. Coräy in the accurate perceptions of the idioms which are, in fact, vernacular to him. To the following note, therefore, written in his own language, and annexed to the first of the preceding passages, the highest deference must be due :—" It is probable that Heliodorus, who in every other place says ἅρπαγμα ποιεῖσθαι, here has ἡγεῖσθαι, either for the sake of varying the expression, or, which is the more likely supposition, from an involuntary association with the Christian idea in Philippians ii. 6." Vol. ii. p. 244. Thus it appears that, in the correct Greek usage, the two forms of expression are equivalent.

Note [C], page 375.

Τὸ δὲ μεσημβρινὸν ψηλαφήσαισαν ἴσα νυκτί· " Let them grope at " noon-day *equally as* in the night." Job v. 14. Ἐτύρωσάς με ἴσα τυρῷ· " Thou hast coagulated me *like* cheese." Ib. ix. 10. Πίνων ἀδικίας ἴσα ποτῷ· " Drinking iniquity *as* his beverage." Ib. xv. 16. Ὁ παλαιοῦται ἴσα ἀσκῷ· " Which grows old *like* a skin-bottle." Ib. xiii. 28. Συντριβείη πᾶς ἄδικος ἴσα ξύλῳ ἀνιάτῳ. " Let every " unjust man be *like* a tree irrecoverably withered." Ib. xxiv. 20. Χόρτον ἴσα βουσὶν ἐσθίουσιν· " They eat grass *like* oxen." Ib. xl. 15. In all these instances, ἴσα is put for the Hebrew prefix כְּ. Ἀποβήσεται δὲ ὑμῶν τὸ γαυρίαμα ἴσα σποδῷ· " Your glorying shall " turn out *like* dust." Ib. xiii. 12. Here it is put for מָשָׁל *resemblances, proverbial examples.* Βροτὸς γεννητὸς γυναικὸς ἴσα ὄνῳ ἐρημίτῃ· " Mortal man, born of woman, is *like* the wild ass of " the desert." Ib. xi. 12. In this instance, there is nothing in the Hebrew to correspond with ἴσα. Πρώτην φωνὴν τὴν ὁμοίαν πᾶσιν ἴσα κλαίων· " Crying *equally* as the first sound that I uttered like all " other infants." Wisd. Sol. vii. 3. These are, I suppose, (for Trommius and Biel do not give complete satisfaction,) the principal instances in the LXX.—The dying exclamation of Antiochus furnishes an example, not exactly similar, but highly illustrative of the passage under consideration ; Δίκαιον ὑποτάσσεσθαι τῷ Θεῷ, καὶ μὴ θνητὸν ὄντα ἰσόθεα φρονεῖν ὑπερηφάνως· " It is just to be subject to " God, and that a mortal should not proudly imagine himself *equal* " *to God.*" 2 Macc. ix. 12.

This is one of the cases in which classical usage may with propriety be resorted to for the explication of N. T. language : for, in this phrase, there is no shadow of any Hebraism ; and the apostle, writing this Epistle at the close of a two years' residence in Rome, might have adopted, from the habits of daily conversation, more pure Greek expressions than he had before been in the practice of using.

Ἔτρεφε δῖα Θεανὼ Ἶσα φίλοισι τέκεσσι· " The princess Theano brought him up *on an equality* with her own children." *Iliad,* E, 70. Ἶσα φίλοισι τοκεῦσιν ἐτίομεν· " We honoured him *equally* with our own parents." O, 439. Τιμὴν δὲ λελόγχασ' Ἶσα θεοῖσι· " They have obtained honour *equal* to the gods." *Odyss.* Λ, 303. Σε ζωὸν ἐτίομεν Ἶσα θεοῖσιν· " We honoured thee during thy life, *equally* with the gods." Ib. 483. Τὸν νῦν Ἶσα θεῷ Ἰθακήσιοι εἰσορόωσι· " To him now the Ithacans look up, *the same as* to a god." O, 519.

Ἰὼ γενεαὶ βροτῶν, ὡς ὑμᾶς Ἶσα καὶ τὸ μηδὲν ζώσας ἐναριθμῶ· " Alas, generations of mortals, how justly may I reckon you *on a level* with the dead !" *Sophocl. Œdip. Tyr.* v. 1210.

Ἶσα καὶ ἱκέται ἐσμέν· · " We are here *in the same situation* as supplicants." *Thucyd.* lib. iii. sect. 14. Πυθαγόρας—Ἶσα θεοῖς παρὰ τοῖς Κροτωνιάταις ἐτιμᾶτο· " Pythagoras was honoured by the people of Crotona *equally with* the gods." *Diod. Sic.* frag. lib. x. Ποιοῦσι μὲν Ἶσα τοῖς ἀγαπητῶν τέκνων στερουμένοις. " They act *like* those who are bereaved of their dearest children :" *i. e.* the Egyptians perform *the same* funeral ceremonies for their sacred bull Apis. Ib. lib. i. sect. 84. Ἡ Πυθία χρᾷ σφισιν, ἀνευρόντας τὸ δένδρον ἐκεῖνο, Ἶσα τῷ θεῷ σέβειν· " The Delphic priestess delivered to them this oracle, that, when they had found that tree, they should honour it *as on an equality* with the god." *Pausanias, ed. Sylburgii,* Hanov. 1613. p. 89.

Note [D], page 381.

I do not press any argument from the use of ὑπάρχων rather than ὢν, because I do not conceive that it would be capable of being placed beyond exception. At the same time it is proper to remark, what every one conversant with the Greek language must have observed, that ὑπάρχειν, where it is used as a verb of existence (and not in its proper and classical sense, *to begin, to excite, to be the first mover in a course of action,*) cannot be regarded as absolutely synonymous with εἶναι, but as generally if not always carrying the additional idea of something peculiar, or emphatical, in the mode of the existence in any particular case. If the reader will examine all the passages, about fifty, in which the word occurs in the New Testament, he will find this to hold with regard to almost every one. I think also that he will perceive the accessory idea, in nearly half the instances, to be a mode of existence already established, conspicuous, and dating from a *prior* point of time. This signification of an antecedent existence is expressly recognised by Suidas, or some ancient author or scholiast, from whom he may have copied the passage. He says, ΥΠΑΡΧΩΝ, προκατάρχων· Ὡς οὐχ ὑπάρχων, ἀλλα τιμωρούμενος. Καὶ τὸ ὑπάρχειν οὐχ ἁπλῶς τὸ εἶναι σημαίνει, ἀλλὰ τὸ πάλαι εἶναι καὶ προεῖναι, φθάνειν· Μένανδρος.—" Ὑπάρχων, *taking the lead;* as used by the tragic poet Aristarchus, [see *Athenæus,* lib. xiii. *ad finem ; in ed. Schweighæuseri,* vol. v. p. 219.] ' I am not the beginner, but I will resent the affront.' Also ὑπάρχειν does not signify simply εἶναι *to be,* but *to be previously, to preexist, to get beforehand :* so it is used by Menander.—" He then introduces the citation, but it is in so mutilated and corrupted a state as to be, in Kuster's opinion, unintelligible. See *Suidas, ed. Kust.* vol. iii. p. 532. Mr. Toup thought that he could restore the passage in part. He observes, " The former portion of this fragment I give up as hopeless : the other may be easily restored ; thus, Δεῖ γὰρ ὑμῖν οὐ νῦν εὐνοεῖν, (or, Δεῖ γὰρ ὑμῖν οὐ νῦν εἶναι,) ἀλλὰ ὑπάρχειν τοῦτο· which latter appears the truest, and perfectly answers to the meaning of Suidas : [*i. e.* This must relate to you, not by being so now, but by being before.]" *Emend. in Suidam, Hesych.* &c. vol. ii. p. 298, ed. Oxon. 1790.

REVIEW

OF THE EVIDENCE COLLECTED IN THE PRECEDING CHAPTER.

THE scriptural testimonies which we have examined in this Chapter, have shown us that Jesus the Messiah was a MAN, truly and properly; born in humiliation and sorrow, and making the usual progress of human nature from infancy to youth and mature age; that his intellectual and moral excellencies were gradually unfolded, and were shown by constant and beneficent exercise; that he was the subject of divine influences, conferring gifts and qualifications for all good, in degrees altogether surpassing every other instance; that, not only was he exposed to the general difficulties and trials of humanity, but he was actually subjected to pain of body, sorrow, and anguish of mind, and a course of the severest sufferings, in a manner most extraordinary and anomalous to reason and the equity of the divine government; but that, in his extreme sufferings and temptations, he was never betrayed into a sinful feeling, act, or emotion; that, as a mortal man, he died and entered into the hidden state of the dead; that he was raised from death, to the condition of immortal perfection, considering him merely as a creature, and of a dignity peculiar, without a parallel in the creation, and wholly his own, arising out of the especial and unique circumstances in which he had stood.

We have further seen that the revealed designs of this series of unexampled dispensations were, to establish a method of deliverance for mankind from a situation of guilt, degradation, and misery, the most melancholy and otherwise absolutely hopeless; to effect this, by laying, on the surest foundations and for ever, a ground in reason and equity, upon which it should be a dignified and glorious proceeding in the righteousness of the divine government, to reverse that ruined state on the behalf of all among men who should sincerely concur in this system of heavenly mercy; that, further, Christ might console his faithful subjects by the assurance not only of his aid, but of his never-failing and most generous sympathy in their distresses and difficulties; and that, in this admirable way of power, goodness, and wisdom, he might be the Deliverer from the greatest evils, and be the Author of the greatest benefits of which a rational nature is capable through the whole of its immortal existence.

From the same sources, we have learned that the human constitution of Jesus, intellectual and corporal, was a vehicle or instrument, formed, taken, and used by another nature, superior and really divine; since the determined objects could not have been otherwise attained. We have found that the phraseology of inspiration is, in a variety of ways, most explicitly formed upon the position of this union of the human and divine natures; that this union does not merge the properties of the superior nature, nor overwhelm those of the inferior, nor commute the essence and attributes of either; that this fact is represented as the most consummate act of divine condescension; that, in this act and the entire series of acts requisite for its completion, the Messiah declined the display of his rightful possessions, and subjected his original and unextinguishable glory to a suppression of its proper manifestations; but that those possessions and that glory are the essential rights and properties of the Deity, as truly the characteristics of God as the necessary accidents of human nature prove the reality of that nature.

It now lies upon the reader's serious judgment, after comparing the details of investigation with this summary, to form his conviction whether the scripture evidence, and the reasonings founded upon it, afford satisfactory proof that these are the just deductions from the facts of the case.

CHAP. V.

The alleged ignorance of the apostles concerning a superior nature in the person
of their Lord.—Statements of the Calm Inquirer, not equitable.—The claims
of Jesus constantly referred to the Old Testament descriptions of the Messiah.
—Evangelical instruction communicated gradually to the apostles themselves.
—The whole Christian revelation constructed upon this principle of an advancing process.—How the reception of revealed truth is necessary to salvation.—
Our Lord's mode of instruction directed to excite the intelligence and direct
the ulterior conclusions of his disciples.—Peculiar state of belief and feeling in
the Jewish nation.—The most surprising facts related by the Evangelists without any impassioned expressions.—Instances of extraordinary impressions upon
the minds of our Lord's disciples.

DR. PRIESTLEY has introduced an argument in bar
of all our interpretations and deductions, which it
would be unjust not to acknowledge to be of very
serious weight. It is grounded upon the alleged
silence of Jesus himself, and of the majority of the
writers of the New Testament, and especially of the
first three evangelists, concerning the doctrine of a
superior nature in the person of Christ; upon the
apparent ignorance of our Lord's own disciples and
constant attendants, of any such extraordinary and
stupendous fact; and upon our inability to assign the
time when this fact, supposing its reality, was made
known to them.

Evidence has, I think, been adduced in the preceding pages, abundantly sufficient to refute Dr. Priestley's oft-repeated assertion, that "Christ did not teach his own divinity." The other parts of this argument are stated by the Calm Inquirer in his usual strength of assertion. From his work I subjoin some extracts, which will do ample justice to his views :[1] and upon them I submit the following observations to the reader's serious and impartial judgment.

i. The Inquirer overstates the case, and takes more than is equitable to his own side of the argument. We do not admit that the evidence in favour of the preexistence and deity of Christ "depends wholly upon the testimony of John and Paul." We have already adduced passages from the writings of Matthew and Luke, which, though few, cannot with justice be deemed "faint and obscure," in favour of the doctrine in question : and it will, perhaps, be seen in the following parts of this Volume, that the apostles Peter and Jude furnish also important materials, both incidentally and in a direct reference to this subject.

The same want of argumentative justice appears in the representation, that the evidence, adduced from the writings of Paul, in favour of the controverted sentiments, is derived principally or wholly from only two of his epistles, besides that to the Hebrews : and those such as the Inquirer is pleased to denominate the most figurative and obscure. We shall see, in the following parts of this work, how far this is from being a correct representation.

ii. It is necessary to a just representation of the

---

[1] See Note [A], at the end of this Chapter.

case, to recollect that the claims of Jesus, as advanced by himself, and as first urged by the apostles and the three earlier evangelists, were addressed to Jews, who admitted the authority of the Old Testament, and looked for *such a Messiah as it described*.   Their ignorance, indeed, and their prejudices were very great. It appears from the Gospels that both the higher orders of the Jews and the mass of the nation had very obscure, and probably inconsistent, notions concerning the Messiah, who was the object of their eager, but generally carnal and worldly, expectation. Yet this expectation rested upon the holy Scriptures; and it was proper to remit them to those Scriptures for the rectifying of their errors.   It is plain that the immediate object, in the writings of Matthew, Mark, and Luke, was to produce a conviction that Jesus of Nazareth was THE Messiah announced and described in the prophetic writings : and they evidently left the scrutinizing and application of details, to the duty and diligence of their readers.   A similar course was followed by the apostles and their fellow-labourers, in preaching Christianity ; as they regularly communicated to the Jews, in the first instance, the word of life.   The converts were directed to " search the " scriptures daily ;" they were assured that those scriptures testified of Christ; and it would follow of course, that all which they could discover in the inspired writings, concerning the characters, office, and dignity of the Messiah, would be transferred to the person of Jesus of Nazareth.   But this would not be a rapid process: and, in proportion as they made progress in this study, would their knowledge of the truth, in this respect and in all its other branches and relations, become extensive and accurate.

This method of proceeding was analogous to the whole system of means, which God has appointed for the information and improvement of the human mind; and we find it continually applied, by Jesus and his apostles, as an instrument for leading teachable and sincere persons into a "knowledge of the " divine will, in all wisdom and spiritual understand- " ing." It appears, therefore, congruous and probable that this method of institution should have had place here, and that men should have been stimulated to the exercise of their proper faculties, with the interesting materials which they had before them, in order to their making constantly higher attainments in the knowledge of true Christianity. Every attentive reader must have observed how frequently and strongly this "going on unto perfection" is urged in the epistolary parts of the New Testament; and that, in some places, this course of duty is expressly directed to the very subject of the characters and dignity of our Lord Jesus Christ.[2]

We have here also a right to avail ourselves of the positive evidence, detailed and scrutinized in the former parts of this work, concerning the opinions

---

[2] For instance: " That the God of our Lord Jesus Christ, the " Father of glory, may give unto you the Spirit of wisdom and reve- " lation, in the acknowledgment of him." Eph. i. 17. " Grow in " the grace and knowledge of our Lord and Saviour Jesus Christ." 2 Pet. iii. 18. " Till we all come into the unity of the faith, and " of the acknowledgment of the Son of God." Eph. iv. 13. " That " ye may be strengthened to comprehend——and to know the love " of Christ which surpasseth knowledge, that ye may be filled unto " all the fulness of God." ch. iii. 18, 19.

and expectations of the Jews relative to the Messiah. It has been shown that the state of current knowledge among them, in the period about the birth of Jesus, was indeed obscure and incoherent; but that it involved many particulars which were irreconcilable with the belief of the mere humanity of the Messiah, and which, in fact, plainly recognised his Divine dignity.[3] The most learned of the Antisupernaturalists, while they deny that this or any other doctrine, expectation, promise, prophecy, or precept, was at any time derived by an actual and positive revelation from God, have not been backward to admit, and have abundantly supplied evidence to prove, that the expectation of the Jews, in and long before the time of Jesus, was directed to a Messiah whom many among them conceived to be a Being possessed of attributes which may be justly called Divine, existing and operating before the created world, and, in an especial manner, the King and Protector of the Hebrew nation. We have likewise good reason to believe, that the sects which, in the earliest ages of the Christian history, denied any superior nature in Christ, and maintained his mere humanity, were derived from those among the Jews who had entertained the lowest opinions concerning the Messiah when he was the object of expectation; who transferred those ideas to Jesus of Nazareth, under the influence of an imperfect acquaintance with his personal ministry; and who refused to be carried forwards along the course of revealed doctrine, as it was successively unfolded, according to the promise of Christ to his

---

[3] See Vol. I. pp. 596, 599 ; and of this Volume, p. 59, 260, 262.

apostles, and by that unerring ministration of the Spirit which was to lead them into ALL truth.

To me it appears a very unavailing subterfuge of the Antisupernaturalists, that, among the ancient Persians and Chaldæans, they discover traces of a doctrine resembling the Hebrew expectation of a Divine Messiah. Of the different individuals to whom the name of Zoroaster or Zerdusht has been applied, there is not one of whom any certain knowledge has come down to us. Some not inconsiderable orientalists have thought that the most credible vestiges of a person bearing that name, are no other than narratives and traditions of the Jewish Ezra. The genuineness, and even the high antiquity, of the Zendavesta, have been contested by no mean authorities. But, admitting both, as the weight of evidence seems sufficiently to warrant, I appeal to those gentlemen themselves (if they be ambitious of meriting their assumed denomination of *Rationalists*) whether the most reasonable solution of the problem, concerning the true origination of the widely spread and dearly cherished HOPE of the human race, be not the ascription to *a common source ;* from which the streams of descent have flowed to all the great nations of antiquity, while the Hebrews alone had the advantage of its pure conservation and gradual increase.[4]

iii. This principle of progression in the œconomy of revelation appears, also, to have been acted upon by Divine Wisdom in relation to the apostles themselves. They manifestly laboured, during the whole period of our Lord's personal ministry, under the prejudices and obscurity of conception which prevailed

---

[4] See Note [B], at the end of this Chapter.

in the Jewish nation at large on all religious subjects; and particularly on such as respected the character and office of the Messiah. These erroneous opinions Jesus did not think fit to correct, till after his resurrection and ascension; and then he did it by the ministration of the Spirit, which he had before promised. Now it is evident that their inspiration, which was the result of this ministration of the Spirit, did not supersede the exercise of their ordinary faculties, but rather acted in the way of directing the operations and confirming the issue of those faculties, so far as their competency could extend. Thus, for example, they employed their own memories for the recollection and recital of.their Master's actions and discourses; and the Spirit of truth corroborated their recollection and gave it certainty, by" bringing to their " remembrance all things, whatsoever he had said unto " them." In like manner, they, like other men, lived under a conscious obligation to employ meditation, prayer, and all the discursive means in their power, for the attainment of divine knowledge; and they were animated to this duty, by the assurance, that "the Holy Spirit would lead them into all truth." Among these means, the study of the Jewish sacred books, which so largely contained " the testimony of " Jesus," must have held a principal rank. Hence, the whole revelation of the Christian system was given by an advancing process. It cannot, therefore, be a matter of surprise, that the doctrine concerning the person of the Messiah was developed gradually, and that its clearest manifestation is to be found in the latest written books of the New Testament.

. This plan of gradual revelation, and of gradual

preparation of the mind to understand and receive it, *with an especial regard to the application of scripture prophecy*, appears to me to furnish a rational solution, from causes real and sufficient, of a great part of the difficulty on which the argument of Dr. Priestley and Mr. Belsham rests.

iv. I submit to such of my readers as may be competent and inclined to the minute examination of the question, whether this plan of a gradual developement, connected with the study and application of the Old Testament, was not, though imperfectly understood and ill expressed, the object really intended by those Christian Fathers who maintained that the apostles, in their earlier ministry, refrained from divulging the preexistence and divinity of Christ, and that John was the first who advanced this doctrine. Though some of the citations made by Dr. Priestley are by him misconstrued, and others by being detached from their connexion appear stronger than they really are, it is undeniable that this opinion was held by Origen, Athanasius, Chrysostom, and others. But, when we consider the little judgment which those writers manifested in both the materials and the conduct of their arguments, and the extravagant kind of rhetoric in which they frequently indulged, the solution here proposed may appear not unreasonable. This single sentence of Chrysostom appears to me to supply the key to his meaning in other passages on this subject: " Neither John, though elevating himself to his more lofty subject, has neglected the assumption of humanity; nor have they [the three earlier evangelists,] so applied to the narrative of that assumption, as to have been wholly silent concerning his eternal preexistence."[5]

v. Mr. B. represents the doctrine which he so strongly disapproved, as implying that the evangelists had " their minds fraught with the idea——that the belief of this great mystery was necessary to the salvation of their readers." No exercise of candour can prevent our perceiving, that this is designed to keep up the strain of broad contempt, which characterises the whole paragraph. It is not, however, deserving of notice on this account; but because it manifestly tends to convey to the unwary reader an injurious impression of the doctrine itself. I conceive it therefore proper to remark, that no intelligent believer in that doctrine holds the reception of it to be essential to salvation, where it has not been sufficiently made known; and that the reception neither of this nor of any other truth is necessary to salvation *in itself*, or as a matter of theoretical belief, or in any other way than by its practical influence on the affections and the whole moral character as they are seen by the Unerring Judge. The victims of their own delusions are represented in the oracles of God as condemned, not for their want of an intellectual and professional belief in any doctrine, even the most vital and important; but " because they received not " the LOVE of the truth, that they might be saved."[6]

[5] Οὔτε οὗτος, πρὸς τὸν ὑψηλότερον ἑαυτὸν λόγον ἀφιεὶς, τῆς οἰκονομίας ἡμέλησεν· οὔτε ἐκεῖνοι τὴν περὶ ταύτης ἐσπουδακότες δήγησιν, τὴν προαιώνιον ἐσίγησαν ὑπαρξιν. *Chrysost. in Evang. Johann. Hom.* iii. ed. Franefort. 1697, vol. viii. par. ii. p. 34.

[6] 2 Thess. ii. 10.

vi. It was one of the characteristics of our Lord's teaching, that he very seldom made direct claims, or formally laid down express doctrines concerning himself. His more usual manner was, to propose questions; to introduce acknowledged principles, which would be the seeds of other most important thoughts; and to utter deep and comprehensive assertions, which carried with them the implication of remoter truths. These he delivered, so as to fix them strongly in the minds, both of his general hearers and of his more constant and intimate attendants; and then he left these impressions to produce their proper effect, by the exercise of thought and meditation in drawing the just inferences, and by the elucidations that might accrue from subsequent communications on his part.

That this was actually the case will, I conceive, appear to any person who will attentively study our Lord's dialogues and discourses. It may be difficult, it may even be impossible, for us to discover the reasons of this peculiar method: but, if it appear to have been really practised by the wisest and most perfect of teachers, we are bound to acquiesce in the ascertained fact, and to make the best use of it that we can. One use unquestionably is, that we should study the doctrines and discourses of Jesus Christ, by the aid of a constant comparison with the apostolic writings: which were intended to be " the ministration " of the Spirit" in the full and final developement of the Christian system.[7]

vii. A very considerable attention is due to the state of mind, and the habits of feeling, which must have belonged to the Jewish people in general, at the

[7] See pp. 44, 45, of this Volume.

time of Christ's personal ministry: and it is not a
ready and easy thing for us, to form a sufficient estimate of the nature and influence of circumstances so
greatly different from our own.   Their national history, the visions and writings of their prophets, their
persuasion of their own exalted station in the divine
favour, and their glowing expectancy of the grandeur
which they believed to be destined for them above the
whole human race besides; could not but produce in
them a body of opinions and feelings such as would in
a great measure preclude that awful and overwhelming
surprise, which Mr. B. assumes as inevitable on the
annunciation of a Divine Nature in the Person of the
Messiah.   They also believed in the frequent intervention of superior intelligences, and of the Deity
himself; and this belief gave a colour to their ideas
and their language on every occasion that had a relation to it.[a]   Hence, it appears probable, or even
necessary, that, as to the kind and degree of surprise,
with relation to the doctrine of a Divine Nature in
the Messiah, their impressions would be very different
from those which, with our widely dissimilar habits of
thought and feeling, we should entertain upon the
supposition of similar circumstances.

viii. Occurrences of the most surprising kind, and
which could not have been witnessed by men of any
intelligence without great astonishment, are very
often related by the evangelists, without the smallest

---

[a] As exemplifications of this, see Matt. xii. 24; xiv. 2. . Luke
i. 22; xxiv. 23, 37. Acts xxiii. 9.   The Jewish belief concerning
the dæmoniacs is, also, a striking proof; whether we adhere to the
common sentiment on that subject, or adopt the hypothesis of
Lardner, Farmer, Semler, &c.

expression of admiration on their own part, or the statement of such feeling in those who were spectators of the events.   Such, for instance, is the recital, that, immediately after our Lord's baptism, "the "heavens were opened, and John saw the Spirit of "God descending, as a dove, and coming upon Jesus: "and behold, a voice from the heavens saying, This "is my beloved Son, in whom I am well pleased!"⁹ Such is the case in the two several instances of his

---

⁹ Matt. iii. 16.   To exterminate, if possible, any ideas of miracle from this passage, some of the German critics affirm that, our Lord having prayed on coming up from the water, his countenance was, as it were, brightened with resolution and dignity, cheerfulness and pleasure ; that at this moment a cloud discharged a flash of lightning, or several flashes in succession ; that of course it thundered ; and that John and the bystanders put their own interpretation upon these natural phænomena.   In a similar way they interpret the narrative of the transfiguration.

It can scarcely be necessary to observe, that such interpretations as these cannot be sustained, unless we give up, not merely the inspiration, but either the intelligence or the veracity, of the evangelists ; and unless we admit that Jesus himself was chargeable with a want of integrity, since he availed himself of these as divine attestations.

Such was the spirit of absurd and impious licentiousness which has prevailed, within the last forty years, among the clergy, and in the universities, of Saxony, Hanover, and Prussia, that, not only has all supernatural revelation been by some publicly denied, but even Atheism is said to have been preached from the pulpit, with hardly the affectation of disguise.   "It was maintained, that GOD was nothing else than the moral order of the universe." (*Supplem. to the Encyclop. Britann.* 1819, vol. iv. p. 246.)   Happily this extravagance of mental wickedness has produced a revulsion ; and the voice of reason and piety begins to regain the ascendency.   The elder Tittman has some excellent observations on the unreasonableness and falsehood of these principles of interpretation, or rather of misinterpretation, and perversion, in the Preface to his *Meletemata Sacra,* Leipzig, 1816.

So stood this note in the first edition.   Since that time, much has

driving the buyers and sellers out of the temple; an action which, if we reflect on its very remarkable circumstances, cannot but appear among the most astonishing. These commercial transactions in the courts of the temple were sanctioned by long-established custom; they were connected with most extensive advantages, to numerous and powerful bodies of people; the priests, in particular, enjoyed a large profit for their connivance at this abuse; and there was a body of soldiers always at hand to watch, and quell any tumult, on the great annual festival; whose officers would undoubtedly have taken the part of supporting the allowed authorities, and defending the established usages. It would, therefore, appear incredible, on the ordinary principles of human conduct, that all the interested parties should have submitted, without resistance, to their ejection by an individual; a man unarmed, destitute of secular authority, poor, persecuted and hated by the generality of the great and powerful. Yet these transactions are related in the most brief and simple manner, without any comment, and without any expressions of amazement. A similar remark may be made on the relation, by the evangelists, of many of our Lord's most stupendous miracles.

been published in Germany, France, and England, relative to those remarkable examples of the wanderings of the human mind; and, upon various points in this branch of theology, the present edition contains additional facts and observations. See, in the Index, *Neologists*. *Sec. ed.*—Six years more have elapsed, and have shown that extensive learning, accurate research, and practical piety have acquired a preponderance, increasing every day, among our continental neighbours, on the side of Christianity in its scriptural and really " evangelical " form, disenthralled from the trammels of human systems.

ix. We have before observed that it was one of the characters of our Lord's manner of teaching, not so much to make direct avowals, especially on the doctrine of his own Person, as to furnish data from which weighty conclusions might afterwards be drawn. In consonance with this fact, and with the artless and unimpassioned method of narration, by which, as we have just remarked, the first three evangelists are distinguished, it might be expected that they would state the incidents as they appeared; acting in the quality of simple relators of that only which met the eye and ear, and leaving the further elucidations and the interior doctrines of the Christian institution to their proper mode and season of developement.

x. It is, however, observable that there were occasions in the life of Jesus Christ, when some peculiar manifestation of his power and glory is recorded to have produced very solemn, and even overwhelming, impressions, on the minds of his disciples and others. Of this nature were the two instances, lately adverted to, in which our Lord exercised an irresistible and triumphant authority in the temple, under circumstances which would have rendered such an act plainly impossible to be achieved by any man. Such appears to have been the impression on the mind of Peter, when, after witnessing a signal display of Christ's miraculous power, " he fell down at the knees of " Jesus, saying, Depart from me, for I am a sinful " man, O Lord!" [10] Such also, when, at the word of Christ, a storm was turned into a calm; and " they " that were in the ship came, and did homage to him,

[10] Luke v. 8.

" saying, Truly thou art the Son of God!" [11] And
such we cannot but conceive to have been the case
with the apostle Thomas, when " he said unto Jesus,
" My Lord, and my God!" Other such instances
may have existed, which are not recorded in the history. As a reason that they were not more frequent,
I would submit to the candid and judicious, the supposition, that there might be a special and divine
influence exercised upon the minds of the disciples;
so as to counteract the tendencies of human feeling,
and to administer a præternatural support in their
intercourse with the Saviour. That this is not a gratuitous supposition, may be argued from the reasonable
presumption that some such influence must have been
exercised on the minds of Abraham, Moses, and
others, under the Old Testament; sustaining their
faculties and their self-possession, in their miraculous
and awful communion with God.

I now request the serious reader to review the preceding considerations, and to subject them to the most
careful scrutiny. Let him then say, whether they
do not so far account for the facts, on which the
Unitarian advocates rest their preliminary objection,
as to reduce them within the limit of those difficulties
which are not only admissible, but which experience
teaches us to expect, in almost every department of
natural and moral science; difficulties which are not,
in the scale of reason, of sufficient weight to counter-
balance a well-ascertained body of affirmative evidence.
The objection is hypothetical; the evidence which it
opposes is positive and strong. The objection is of

[11] Matt. xiv. 33. See pages 261, 262, 272, of this Volume.

the class of difficulties, or apparent impossibilities, which would have antecedently occurred against many public facts in even the recent history of men, to have conjectured which, would have subjected any person to general ridicule, but which, when their time came, have made sure of existence. Or this kind of objections may be compared to that complacent sense of incredulity which, before instruction or experience, has a thousand times been entertained against the possible effectuation of new processes in art, or the actual being of astounding natural phænomena.

It would also become us to recollect, that we are immeasurably less furnished with a capacity to form precluding determinations upon details, in the method by which the Infinite Supreme is accomplishing the moral restoration of a world, than a child of the lowest vulgar ignorance would be to prejudge the truths brought to light by the sublimest mathematics. Would we but think with mental integrity, we could not avoid the conviction that a divine plan of salvation is a subject in comparison with which, the grandeur of creation and the mysteries of providence, with respect to the present state, become almost insignificant. At least, before we allow ourselves to speculate and prescribe upon the mode and shape of the constituent parts, we should put forth an effort, bearing some proportion to the occasion, for raising our understandings, I say not to the comprehension, but to a serious, devout, meditative sense of this vast amount of agencies, in which "now is made known, to the princi-" palities and powers in the heavenly places, the MANI-" FOLD WISDOM of God;" and "in which are hidden " ALL THE TREASURES OF WISDOM AND KNOWLEDGE."

SUPPLEMENTARY NOTES TO CHAP. V.

Note [A], page 411.

" The writers of the New Testament are commonly reckoned eight :—Matthew, Mark, Luke, John, Paul, James, Peter, and Jude. Of these writers, six, *viz.* Matthew, Mark, Luke, James, Peter, and Jude, are generally allowed to have advanced nothing upon the subjects of the preexistence, and superior nature and dignity of Jesus Christ. At least it will be admitted that, if there be any allusions in these writers, to this extraordinary fact, they are so faint and obscure that independently of the rest of the New Testament, they would not of themselves have proved, perhaps not even suggested the idea of the preexistence and divinity of Christ. The credit of these facts depends wholly upon the testimony of John and Paul.

" Of the six writers who make no mention of the preexistence and divinity of Jesus Christ, three are professed historians of the life, the miracles, and the doctrine of Christ ; and one continues his history to upwards of thirty years after our Lord's ascension ; and relates many interesting particulars of the lives, the sufferings, and the doctrines of the apostles, the subjects of their preaching, the miracles which they performed, and the success of their mission. But neither the history nor the discourses of Christ, nor those of his apostles for thirty years after his ascension, contain the least hint of his preexistent state and dignity.

" But how can this total silence be explained and accounted for, if the popular doctrine concerning the preexistence and divinity of Christ is true ? Is it credible, or even possible, that three persons, in different places and at different times, should undertake to write the history of Christ, each meaning to communicate all that was necessary to be known, with their minds fraught with the overwhelming idea that the person whose history they were about to write was a superior Being, a great angel, the Creator of the world, or the Almighty God himself in human shape, and that the belief of this great mystery was necessary to the salvation of their readers ; and yet through the whole of their narrative should abstain from mentioning or even glancing at this stupendous fact ? How would a modern Arian or Trinitarian have acted in similar circumstances ? Would he have left his readers under the impression which necessarily results from the perusal of the three first evangelical histories and that of the Acts, *viz.* that the founder of the Christian faith was a man like to his brethren, and only distinguished from them as the greatest of the prophets of God, who had been raised from the dead, and exalted to the right-hand of the Most High?—That six of the writers of the New Testament should have observed such a profound silence upon a subject of which their hearts must have been so full, and with which their imagination must have been so overpowered, may well induce a considerate mind to pause, and to reflect whether this could have happened if Jesus of Nazareth were in truth a being of high, perhaps the highest, order in the universe?

" Athanasius, Chrysostom, and others accounted for this extraordinary silence from the great prudence of the evangelists, and their unwillingness to give offence to the new converts; but this is a supposition which will not now satisfy an inquisitive mind.——

" The style of these two writers [John and Paul] is in many instances highly figurative. In the gospel of John our Lord sometimes uses metaphors of the most obscure and offensive kind, such as ' eating his flesh ' and ' drinking his blood,' to express the reception of his doctrine. Chap. vi. 56. And Paul in his epistles introduces many harsh and uncommon figures, *viz.* ' We are members of his body, of his flesh, and of his bones,' to express the union of true believers under Christ as their head, Eph. v. 30. It is therefore reasonable to expect that such writers will use figurative language concerning Christ; and it is peculiarly necessary, in reading their writings, to distinguish carefully between what is literal and what is figurative.

" With regard to the apostle Paul, it is worthy of remark that little or no evidence is pretended to be produced from his larger epistles, in favour of the popular doctrine concerning the person of Christ. Few proofs are alleged from the epistle to the Romans, the two to the Corinthians, that to the Galatians, the two to the Thessalonians, or those to Timothy, Titus, or Philemon. The principal appeal is to the epistles to the Philippians and Colossians, which are figurative throughout beyond all others; and to the epistle to the Hebrews, the author of which is doubtful, and in which the writer indulged himself in an ingenious, but forced and fanciful analogy between the Mosaic institute and the Christian dispensation.

" Is it possible to believe that this stupendous doctrine, if it were true, would be found clearly expressed in no other part of the sacred writings, but in the mystical discourses of the evangelist John: in two of the obscurest epistles of Paul; and in the epistle of another unknown writer? Surely, if it were fact that Jesus of Nazareth was truly God, or the Maker of the world in a human shape, it is a fact that would have blazed in every page of the New Testament; and would never have been mentioned by the sacred writers but with the most evident marks of astonishment and awe." *Calm Inquiry*, pp. 15—20.

Note [B], page 415.

The late Dr. Bertholdt was one of those (unhappy persons I must call them,) who regard all the religious and moral declarations of the Scriptures, Patriarchal, Mosaic, and Christian, without exception, as the productions of mere reason and reflection, the discoveries of wise and good men, without any miraculous revelation, or any other kind of communication from God than that which is included in his necessary, universal, and all-pervading providential agency. As a part of this deplorable system of error, he maintains that the whole doctrine of the Old and New Testament concerning a Saviour of mankind, the Messiah, was nothing more than a temporary accommodation to national traditions and prejudices, wisely employed by God's beneficent providence, as an instrument for the first introduction and acceptance of Christianity in the minds of the Jews, but, when that end was obtained, of no further use in religion.[1] The same notion pervades the admirable volumes of Gesenius, his *Commentar über den Jesaia*, so rich in philological and historical elucidation, and generally so faithful in giving the genuine sense of the *words*, however adverse they may be to his own theory of the prophetic character. That theory, alas! stands insolently independent of the words or belief of Moses or Isaiah, JESUS, John, or Paul. To them it imputes that, being among the wisest and best of men, and being the instruments of God's most beneficent plan for promoting virtue and piety, and enhancing the present and eternal happiness of the human race, either they were mistaken, though " noble enthusiasts," in conscientiously believing that the Supreme Being had actually communicated to them, in a supernatural manner, discoveries of religious truth and duty ; or, knowing that this was not the fact, they deliberately, consistently, harmoniously, and with perseverance to the end of their lives, said so to the world, and were, what one of them expresses horror at the bare supposition of, " false witnesses of God!" And this latter side of the alternative is

---

[1] " Omnes rerum sacrarum bene gnari probè norunt, omnia, quæ in doctrinâ Christianâ Christologiam Judaicam seu *Messianismum* sapiunt, merè esse σχηματισμὸν, quo Numen Supremum ceu fulcro seu vehiculo usum est, ut *nova doctrina divinitus patefacta* animis Judæorum insinuaretur, atque eo ceu fundamento, haud verò perenni sed tamen opportuno, superstruatur. Igitur non teneamus substratum facile interiturum, sed τὴν οἰκοδομὴν eo nixam, τὸν λόγον τῆς ἀληθείας οὐ μὴ παρερχόμενον." *Christologia Judæorum, Proœm.* p. xv.

put with the utmost coolness, and without any apparent, or at least, adequate, perception of its moral turpitude!

The following passages, translated from Bertholdt's *Christologia Judæorum, Jesu Apostolorumque Ætate,* will evince that I have not without reason made the observations to which this Note is appended; and will also be a confirmation, most unexceptionable as being that of an able and learned adversary, of the conclusions maintained in the First Volume, concerning the ancient faith of the Jewish nation.

" How was it possible, that the Jews, among whom Jesus, according to God's eternal decree, spent his life upon earth, could ever persuade themselves that, in his own spiritual nature, he was a being far superior to men and angels, equal to God, and most intimately united to God; unless some part of the Jewish nation had been imbued, from a remote antiquity, with the same doctrines concerning the future Messiah; doctrines which it was so easy to connect with the Christian system?" *Proœm.* p. xiv.

" The later prophets, expatiating as well as the more ancient ones upon the dignity of the Messiah, were accustomed to assign him a very eminent place (Jer. xxiii. 6. Mal. iii. 1); in which they merely exhibited the effect of a common principle in human nature, that, whatever men have for a considerable length of time made an object of their thoughts, admiration, and expectations, becomes by degrees in their estimation more and more lofty and magnificent. Besides this, the more reflecting part of those who returned from the captivity, very rationally judged that the restoration of their former flourishing condition was a thing far too great for any merely human power. They had also got their minds strongly tinctured with the doctrines of the Chaldæans and the Persians concerning spiritual existences. Thus they were the more readily led into the notion that a very exalted celestial being, assuming the outward person of the Messiah, would undertake the functions of the coming Saviour. Hence, in the book of Daniel (vii. 13,) the founder of the new theocracy is represented as coming in the clouds of heaven, with the honour and magnificent attendance of a celestial being far superior to men, yet clothed with a human body. Now, since this opinion, at the very time when Jesus arose, had taken a strong hold on the minds of many among the Jews, especially those whose studies had elevated them to the sublimer views in theology ; it is a matter of no surprise that, when Jesus declared himself to be *the Son of God,* the Messiah, those who did not believe in him charged him with blasphemy; (John x. 36 ; v. 18.) For they supposed the

Messiah to be possessed of such exalted dignity as far exceeded all other things, and approached in the closest way possible to the Divine Majesty. Their object was to have a Messiah superior to any of mankind, even more excellent and exalted than their own ancient patriarchs (Rom. ix. 5,) who had been most celebrated for their piety and their intimate communion with God, greater than the angels, even those who possess the highest dignity and power (Heb. i. 4), their Prince and Leader, and, in a word, above the whole universe : (Eph. iv. 10. Heb. vii. 26.) They therefore conceived the Messiah to be a spiritual Intelligence, in greatness and perfection next to God himself, who, before he assumed the human form and made himself visible upon earth, dwelt in the world of spirits, surrounded by the hosts of ministering angels (Matt. xvi. 27 ; xiii. 41 ; xxv. 31. Mark viii. 38. Luke ix. 26. 1 Thess. iii. 13. 2 Thess. i. 7. Jude 14) ; and was known by even the wicked spirits themselves. (Mark i. 24, 34 ; iii. 11, 12 ; v. 6, 7.)" Besides these scripture authorities, Bertholdt adduces corroboratory citations from the Rabbinical books Zohar, Jalkut Shimuni, Bereshith Rabba, and Netzach Jisrael.

After a discussion upon the application of the term *Memra, Logos,* or *Word,* to the Messiah, (of which we shall avail ourselves in a subsequent part of this work,) Dr. Bertholdt proceeds as follows.

" I cannot accede to the opinion of those who think, that the adapting of these speculations" [of the Persian and other oriental theology, adopted also in part by the Greek Platonists,] " to the doctrine of a superior nature in the Messiah, was foreign to the habits of thinking possessed by the Jews" [of Palestine] " in the time of Jesus and the apostles. All doubt on this matter is dispelled by the authority of the apostle Paul ; since he clearly attributes the same things to the Messiah (1 Cor. x. 4, 9,) which other Jewish writers had declared to belong to the Wisdom and the Word of God. (*Wisd. Solomon,* x. 15—19 ; xi. 1—4 ; xviii. 15.) Nor are other arguments wanting, equally plain and clear, to the same effect. It is impossible to be denied that the Targumists, in several places, treat of the Messiah as the *Memra of the Lord ;* plainly showing it to have been their belief that the Shechinah or Word, as some of them indeed expressly say, would employ the future Messiah, when he should be born, as the instrument of his gracious designs, and would be joined to him in a personal union." *Christol.* pp. 97— 104, 128—133.

The Rabbinical passages which he adduces, as authorities for these statements, are the following.

" The Memra of Jah helpeth them, and the Shekinah of their King is among them. *Targ. Onkelos*, on Num. xxiii. 21. The Memra of Jah is with them, and a shout from the majesty of their King protecteth them. *Jerus. Targ.* The Memra of Jah their God is their support, and the shout of the King Messiah shouteth among them. *Targ. attrib. to Jonath.* These three interpretations respect the opinion that the Messiah invisibly accompanied the Israelites in their wanderings through the Arabian deserts.——On Ps. cx. 1, the Targumist applies the name *Adonai* to the Messiah, as, with regard to his superior nature, indissolubly united to God.——Our father Jacob said, My soul waiteth not for the redemption of Gideon, which is but for a little time; nor for the redemption of Samson, which is a transitory redemption : but for the redemption which thou hast said, by thy Memra, shall come to thy people the sons of Israel; for this thy redemption my soul waiteth. *Jerus. Targ.* on Gen. xlix. 18.——This Son is a faithful shepherd. Of thee it is said, Kiss the Son. He is the Prince of the Israelites—the Shekinah of grace.——This is the Shekinah—and the Messiah is with it.—— This is written *Shiloh*, to mark the exalted name, that of the She-kinah.——The Shekinah is the Matrona.——When it is said, *His servant*, (Gen. xxiv. 2,) the servant is that of Him who is *Makom* " [i. e. who has the incommunicable name] " the elder of his house brought near for his service : and who is he ? He is the Metatron. [*From different parts of*] *the Zohar.* This is my servant the Messiah ; I draw near to him ; my chosen ; I delight in him ; my Memra. *Targ. Jonath.* on Is. xlii. 1."

If the reader will compare these passages with the former Volume of this work, pp. 517—524, 588—594, he will perceive that the Antisupranaturalist critic, whose investigations are purely philolo-gical and historical, has thought the evidence much stronger, for the application of the Targumic *Memra* to the Messiah, than I had ventured to regard it.

"—Yet this doctrine" [of a superior nature in the Messiah] " was entertained by only a few persons of superior intelligence and more cultivated minds. But the general mass of the people—— long adhered to the sentiment of their ancestors. This may be evinced from the doctrine of the Ebionites and Nazarenes ; who denied any divine dignity to Jesus, and considered him as a mere man. History informs us that those sects arose from the class of inferior Jews who believed in Jesus, but who could attach to him no other ideas of the Messiah than those which they had previously formed.——The chief object of the first preachers of the gospel was to induce belief in the proposition, *Jesus is the Messiah*. Some there were who studied this subject with extreme care and diligence : but those who received Jesus as the Christ, depending solely on the first annunciation of the gospel, could not enjoy the written instructions and explications afterwards given by the apostles; and therefore might easily relapse into their former persuasions concerning the person of the Messiah." *Bertholdt*, pp. 94—96.

These statements and admissions appear to me to afford very important grounds of moral evidence, that the most intelligent and pious part of the Jewish nation, in the period immediately preceding the birth of Jesus, had their faith and expectation fixed upon a Messiah preexistent, heavenly and divine : the position which, in the first Volume, I have endeavoured to show, was the just deduction from the fountain of inspired prophecy.

Another of the most learned and able of the Antisupranaturalists, Dr. Wegscheider (one of the Theological Professors in the University of Halle!!) says : "The Jews of Palestine had annexed the idea of a person to the phrase, *the Memra of Jah*, and transferred it to the Messiah. See a similar mythical representation derived from the sacred books of the Hindoos, concerning the universe being created by the Word; in *Anquetil du Perron's Upnekhat*, ii. 56 ; and some remarkable declarations of Zoroaster on the same subject ; *Kleuker's Zendavesta*, ii. 4." *Instit. Theol.* p. 254, Halle, 1824. That the originally revealed promise of a Deliverer from guilt and ruin, should have given rise to many streams of tradition, adulterated by commixture with the mythologies of apostates and idolaters, is in the highest degree probable, both on historical grounds and upon the known principles of human nature. But such corrupted traditions, impartial reason will say, are evidences of the primary fact ; and cannot, without absurdity, be all confounded in one mass, a mere object of curiosity, and all to be rejected as early national stories, the baseless fictions of uncultivated and credulous antiquity. I solicit the reader to compare these hints with pages 204—212 of the former Volume.

With respect to the doctrines attributed to Zoroaster, I derive the following epitome from Kleuker, through the medium of a very useful work, of which only the first volume has been published.

"Oromasdes creates, operates, and upholds the universe, by *speaking*. Hence this heavenly *Word*, so far as it is applied to him, designates his creative power. This pure, holy, instantaneously mighty Word was before the heavens and the sea, the earth and the animals—before pure human nature, before the Devs——before the whole actual world. Oromasdes spake this Word, and all pure existences that are, or have been, or shall be, were thence produced, and came into the world of Oromasdes. He still continues to speak this Word in its whole extent, and rich blessing is diffused. All pure existences in the world of light, each in its own mode, speak this Word; even by their own actuosity. All good is an expression, a sound and echo, of this heavenly Word.——It is the foundation and centre of all existences; it is all possible power, pure heavenly nature; the origin and bestower of all purity and goodness, understanding, wisdom, science; it is excellency, and what makes excellent; the king, which seeks for men happiness, averts evil, is unwearied in beneficence, directing men's works, all-seeing, fountain of health, judge of righteousness.—I meditate upon the great Word, the heavenly Word. How heavenly pure, how mighty, is this Word! How ancient and of wide extent; incalculably ancient, of unbounded extent! Conquering; all-conquering! Word of the highest happiness! Health for the pure! Healing the wounds of the reaper, the wounds of poisonous juice from plants! Repelling the words of the sorcerer! Let me thereby beat down envy, murderous desire, and all the powers of the wicked one!——Zoroaster's *law of light* is an expression, echo, or imitation of this heavenly Word; and it is also called a Word. The persons who are persevering speakers, that is doers, of this pure word—their souls shall soar free into heavenly habitations, become heavenly themselves, and acquire brightness like the heavens." *Bretschneider's Darstellung der Dogm. Apocryph.* pp. 271—273. Other similar passages occur in the Zendavesta.

For the following passage I am indebted to Dr. Brenner, Prof. Theol. in the Roman Catholic University of Bamberg; in his *Katholische Dogmatik*, vol. i. p. 196; Frankf. 1828. It is a summary of the doctrine of the ancient Egyptians, collected from various sources by Görres, in his *History of the Mythi of the Asiatic Nations.*

" God created the world, not with hands, but through his Word. —This word of the Creator is eternal, self-moved, incapable of increase, diminution, or corruption, or any alteration; always self-equal, self-like, self-filled, invariable, concentrated, the eternal existing according to [the model of] the first God. Proceeding from God, it is, after him, the first power, unbegotten, unbounded, perfect; the existing, fertile, and forming Demiurgus, ruling over all that he has formed; he is the first-born, purely true Son of the supremely Perfect. The first God, the Creator of all, hath brought forth this second, visible and sensible [person] as the first and only one; and since he already éxisted, and was rich in all possessions, therefore he hath consecrated him, and loved him as a part of himself, as his own Son. This therefore is the God whom the first Godhead continuing in its unity brought forth, into whom it flamed forth from its own all-sufficiency; he, his own Father, sufficient for himself; he the Emeph, the leader of the heavenly gods, that self-reflecting intelligent being, who turns all intelligences to himself, the creative [demiurgic] spirit, Lord of truth, and Wisdom itself."

These doctrines are evidently of the same family as the Persian theosophic system, derived undoubtedly from the same source, but more corrupted. The point to which these oriental relics lead, is to evince the early existence, among the nations which lay the nearest to the primeval revelations, of notions, obscure indeed and inconsistent from their having been perverted and mingled with incipient polytheistic tendencies, but implying that in the one Deity there is a second subsistence subordinate yet uncreated and having existed from eternity.

END OF VOL. II.

R. CLAY, PRINTER, BREAD-STREET-HILL.

CPSIA information can be obtained
at www.ICGtesting.com
Printed in the USA
BVHW040734260621
610556BV00026B/3